FAST MONEY

Caroline Reid and Christian Sylt have been writing about the Formula One industry for a combined total of nearly five decades and have contributed to many of the world's leading publications, including the *Daily Mail*, the *Daily Telegraph*, the *Financial Times*, *Forbes*, the *Guardian*, the *Wall Street Journal* and many more.

Outside journalism, in 2007 they founded Formula Money – the only business information service dedicated to F1. It manages the world's largest search engine of F1 sponsorship values and has produced economic impact reports for around a third of the F1 race organisers.

FAST MONEY

The Backroom Deals, Corporate Espionage,
and Legendary Power Struggles
that Drive Formula One

CAROLINE REID & CHRISTIAN SYLT

HODDER &
STOUGHTON

First published in Great Britain in 2025 by Hodder & Stoughton Limited
An Hachette UK company

The authorised representative in the EEA is Hachette Ireland, 8 Castlecourt
Centre, Dublin 15, D15 XTP3, Ireland (email: info@hbgi.ie)

1

A CIP catalogue record for this title is available from the British Library

Hardback ISBN 9781399723480
Trade Paperback ISBN 9781399723497
ebook ISBN 9781399723503

Typeset in Bembo by Hewer Text UK Ltd, Edinburgh
Printed and bound in Great Britain by Clays Ltd, Elcograf S.p.A.

Hodder & Stoughton policy is to use papers that are natural, renewable
and recyclable products and made from wood grown in sustainable forests.
The logging and manufacturing processes are expected to conform
to the environmental regulations of the country of origin.

Hodder & Stoughton Limited
Carmelite House
50 Victoria Embankment
London EC4Y 0DZ

www.hodder.co.uk

To the attendees of the Heathrow Excelsior meeting.
We couldn't have written this book without you.

Contents

CONTENTS

Preface

The Monaco Grand Prix. Sunday, 29 May 2016. As the cars lined up on the grid for Formula One's flagship race it was hard to find anyone who wasn't beaming. Every year the storied streets of the tiny Mediterranean principality are transformed into a race track for the social event of the sporting season.

Actors Patrick Dempsey and Rosamund Pike swanned down the grid trying to get a glimpse of pole-sitter Daniel Ricciardo, who was giving his trademark toothy grin to the gaggle of photographers. Over in the teams' compound, known as the paddock, the attention was on singing sensation Justin Bieber, who was decked out in a Day-Glo T-shirt as he cheered on his buddy Lewis Hamilton from the Mercedes control centre.

However, by far the most smug spectator was sitting on a yacht wearing a smart suit and sporting a prodigious handlebar moustache. His name was Chase Carey and he had good reason to be satisfied with himself.

A seasoned media executive, Carey was the linchpin in an audacious takeover bid for F1 by American investment firm Liberty Media. The deal was revving up, so Carey had been dispatched to Monaco to meet F1's 85-year-old chief executive Bernie Ecclestone. It was his first ever visit to an F1 race and he was captivated. 'You can't help but be awed,' he later said.

Carey suspected he would have to seize control from F1's eccentric billionaire boss to steer the sport into the social media sphere where it had been spluttering. Liberty was in pole position to buy F1 as, although the sport came with an $8bn price tag, Liberty had worked out a way to buy it using only $301m of its own money.

Surprisingly, the glitz and glamour weren't what drew Liberty to F1. One of its biggest attractions was that it hardly paid any tax on the high-octane profits it generated.

A powerful business engine beats under F1's bonnet. Unlike most other sports rights holders, F1 retains the lion's share of the revenues, including fees from broadcasters, trackside advertisers and race hosts along with corporate hospitality ticket sales. The ten teams receive just over 60 per cent of the profits made by F1's rights holder – in 2024 that equated to almost $1.3bn.

Money from the sale of race tickets is the only major revenue stream that F1 doesn't usually receive. This goes directly to the race organisers and usually covers the running costs so that the events just about break even. They have a bigger-picture benefit than profit.

The race organisers tend to be independent local companies or government-backed businesses in order to afford the hosting fees, which average at around $33.5m every year. Governments justify this spending on the grounds that the races drive tourism through exposure to F1's television audience, which came to 1.6 billion in 2024. They also recoup the hosting fees through the tax on the money spent in local businesses by spectators, with a total of 6.5 million attending F1 races in 2024.

It took more than 70 years to build and fine-tune F1's business model in a series of deals that cover everything from handshakes in bars and purchase prices written on scraps of paper to contracts drafted by armies of lawyers. There are usually so many twists and turns between the catalyst and the end result that it can be hard to connect them under the heading of a deal. In some cases, no money changed hands, even though the effect of the transaction added billions of dollars of value to the industry. This is how F1 has manoeuvred its way to becoming one of the world's richest sports.

Importantly, it is also one of the few global sports that is run by a privately owned company rather than a not-for-profit sports federation like its rivals the Olympics and the Football World Cup. There is no doubt that profit is F1's yardstick of success.

The scale of the money in Formula One is hard to comprehend. Over the 40 years to 2022, F1's rights holder made $7.2bn of operating profits on a staggering $27.3bn of revenue. F1 also has a halo effect that gives a glow to the finances of all of its participants from the 10 teams, 24 tracks and 20 drivers right down to the truckies who haul equipment around the world. They are all paid turbocharged sums.

World champion Max Verstappen receives an annual salary of around $60m, while his Red Bull Racing team receives an estimated $120m annually from US tech giant Oracle, which along with Mercedes' title partner Petronas is F1's biggest-spending sponsor. Their payments help to keep the teams' wheels turning, which is no mean feat.

According to Mercedes' latest accounts, in 2023 alone the team spent £432.7m, enough to buy a fleet of four Eurofighter Typhoons – one of the world's most advanced military jets.

Over the five years to 2023, the eight teams that file publicly available accounts had total costs of £9.1bn and every last penny of it was spent on a bid to win on track. There is a saying in F1 that the quickest way to become a millionaire from the sport is to start as a billionaire and buy a team. There is good reason for this, as the teams made combined net losses of £40.3m over the five years to 2023 with the deficit covered by a mixture of loans and investment from their owners.

The theory is that it is better to win on track and make a loss rather than make money and finish low down the standings. Victory on track increases the value of the team, which gives its owners a payout when they come to sell it. It also increases the team's ability to bring in more money from sponsorship since brands are prepared to pay more to be associated with a winner. While team owners can get a financial return from selling their squads in the long run, they have to resort to more abstract ways of justifying their investment when things are running at a loss in the meantime.

If the owner is a private individual who runs the team they can take an annual salary. This comes out as a cost to the team, just like salaries paid to staff. However, if the owner of a team is a company that sells products, such as Mercedes, Ferrari or Red Bull, the benefit they get while the team runs at a loss comes from the exposure their logos on the cars get on television.

This is quantified as Advertising Value Equivalent (AVE), the price a brand would have to pay for a similar amount of advertising time on television compared to the exposure it gets through the F1 cars.

According to filings from Mercedes, when its team last won the F1 drivers' title in 2020 it generated $5.8bn of AVE for its sponsors. The filings reveal that the value of the Mercedes-Benz brand itself accelerated from $31.9bn in 2013 to $49.3bn in 2020, according to Interbrand. It adds that F1 made an important contribution to the status of Mercedes-Benz as the eighth most valuable brand in the world.

There is a crucial difference that separates F1 sponsors from those in any other sport. A shirt sponsor of a football team can't increase the players' chances of scoring a goal but if an F1 sponsor supplies cutting-edge products to a squad it can be the winning formula. Oil, engine and tyre sponsors all have a direct impact on a team's performance, but the difference that many of the others make is much more subtle.

F1 cars are packed with technology. Hidden under their sleek shells is 1.5km of wiring and more than 300 sensors generating 3Gb of data and 1.1 million telemetry data points every second during a race. The faster the readings reach the team's pit crew, the more time they have to alter the car's settings and boost its performance. It can make the difference between winning and losing, as the cars are often just thousandths of seconds apart despite travelling at more than 220 miles per hour.

Tech companies, software suppliers, parts manufacturers and more showcase their products in action through their F1 sponsorships. It makes for a high-powered marketing message as the brands can quite rightly say that they helped to drive the team's success. And it doesn't stop there.

By supplying products which haven't hit the market yet, sponsors can give teams an edge over their rivals. It also allows brands to stress-test their products on the toughest stage in sport before they reach consumers. This benefit reaches beyond tech and automotive brands. High-end watch manufacturers even give F1 drivers their latest models to wear during races to see if they can withstand the rumbles and vibrations in the cockpit.

The teams each spend around $50m annually on developing their cars, with the material costs of each one coming to approximately $2.4m. Unlike the teams in rival race series, every F1 squad has to be a constructor, which means it must design and build its own chassis. That alone costs around $1.4m, followed by the floor at around $400,000. Even a single suspension strut can cost upwards of $13,500. The components aren't just expensive because they are made from high-tech carbon fibre, but also due to the tight window for manufacturing them.

Although the majority of each F1 car is designed the year before it hits the track, teams also rely on what are known as rapid prototype machines during the season. They use lasers to cut pieces of carbon fibre so that teams can manufacture new parts over the few days between each race in a bid to boost performance.

Even the seats in the cars are specially designed and anatomically crafted to suit the contours of the drivers' bodies. Several seat fittings can be required just to make them.

Since F1's technical regulations state that the driver must be able to get out of the car within seven seconds, removing nothing except the steering wheel, rapid release is essential. Hence, one of the most technically complicated parts of an F1 car is the snap-on connector that joins the steering wheel to the steering column. It has to be tough enough to withstand huge forces, but also has to provide the electrical connections between the controls and the car itself. The cost of this all adds up and the price tag of the steering wheel is a cool $75,000.

It's perhaps no surprise that the drivers in charge of these money machines are so well paid and that no expense is spared when it comes to the tools of their trade.

Drivers have to wear high-tech gloves featuring sensors stitched into the fabric to monitor their pulse rate and the oxygen levels in their blood. The gloves also transmit that potentially life-saving data back to the medical team at the track, before, during and after a crash. The drivers' principal form of protection is a fireproof suit, costing around $1,500, and a helmet. They start at approximately $7,000 each but can cost thousands more if they have an intricate paint scheme.

Very little is off-the-shelf in F1 and it even uses a special type of tarmac to withstand the pressure produced by cars racing at more than 200 miles per hour. Building a circuit isn't for the faint-hearted and can cost up to $400m in addition to the annual hosting fee. Although that averages at $33.5m, the sting in its tail is the escalator clause in the contracts. This can increase the fee by as much as 10 per cent every year over the duration of the deal, which is typically five years with a five-year extension. It brings the total fee to a staggering $534m and there is no way to short-cut it.

Hosting a race on city streets doesn't involve the high-octane upfront expense of buying and developing the land but the annual running costs of around $90m are more than double their counterparts at permanent circuits as they include the expense of transforming public pathways into a top-flight race track. The staff numbers alone are eye-watering.

Every year the Automobile Club de Monaco (ACM) recruits more than 600 marshals, 500 security personnel, 400 voluntary workers and 40 doctors to transform Monaco into F1's most famous circuit. According to the ACM, the race involves more than 3,000 people covering every state service from the police, fire and emergency services to civil engineering, town planning and cleaning.

It takes even more people to keep the teams' wheels turning. Seven of them are based in the UK, with the majority located in the so-called Motorsport Valley cluster around Oxfordshire and the Midlands. The teams have fuelled the development of a local industry that is home to around 4,300 motorsport businesses with an annual sales turnover of an estimated £10bn according to the Motorsport Industry Association (MIA). Together they employ more than 40,000 people, but the most significant person in F1's history isn't one of them.

The story of the business of Formula One is inextricably tied up with the fortunes of one man who essentially built the sport into what it is today. Bernie Ecclestone had a humble upbringing in the bleak inter-war Britain of the 1930s but used his street smarts to parlay a career selling used cars into one running F1. He steered it from an amateur pastime to becoming the world's most-watched annual sports series and at its heart is still the same company that he set up to run it more than 40 years ago. This enables the twists and turns to be traced back to the start in order to piece together a roadmap of the key deals that built the F1 industry into one that generated revenue of $3.4bn in 2024 and is valued at more than $20bn. It isn't just thanks to the foundations built by Ecclestone.

In 1981, Ecclestone, the teams and their lawyer Max Mosley decided among themselves that the rights to F1 were owned by motor racing's governing body, the Fédération Internationale de l'Automobile (FIA) – an organisation based in Paris made up of motoring and motorsport clubs across the world. Mosley was Ecclestone's closest confidant and became his greatest ally when he seized the role of FIA president in 1993 following a dramatic coup. It enabled him to hand Ecclestone the keys to the billionaires' club by steering the F1 rights to his company through a secret contract in 1995.

F1 has been engineered since then to ensure that as little tax as possible is paid on the billions of dollars of profits generated by the business; F1 may seem like it's purely a sport but actually it's a high-octane tax-avoidance vehicle for its owners and it is all entirely legal. The manoeuvres that enabled it have never been revealed. Until now.

The late team boss Sir Frank Williams once said that F1 is a sport for around 20 weekends every year but at all other times it is a business. As this book reveals, that is no exaggeration.

PART 1
THE EARLY DAYS

I

GOLDEN BEGINNINGS

Saturday, 13 May 1950. There's not a cloud in the sky over Silverstone, the former airfield in Northamptonshire where Wellington bombers were stationed during World War Two. The Royal Standard flutters in the wind; the drivers are greeted on the grid by King George VI. Hay bales separate the cars from a crowd of more than 100,000 fans – many of them have poured off coaches; plenty have snuck in through the hedge at Copse Corner.

Newsreel footage reveals Alfa Romeos and Maseratis resplendent in *rosso corsa*, the British automobiles in deep racing green; all national liveries unadorned bar for the bright white numbers and car manufacturer badges. Thai Prince Bira and Swiss Baron de Graffenried are on the grid in their Maseratis, vestiges of a time when motor racing wasn't seen as a sport but rather a hobby for wealthy aristocrats.

From the ashes of the war a new spirit of adventure has emerged and motor racing is at its vanguard. In the pits, a group of elderly French officials wearing blue blazers check the cars against the regulations they have written. The competitors must comply with this new formula in order to be allowed to compete in the event, which has been designated the opening round of the number-one racing series in the world. The officials are from motor racing's governing body, the Fédération Internationale de l'Automobile (FIA), and the category they have created is fittingly named Formula One.

But aside from the new name, there is little that day that is significantly different from the informal Grand Prix events that have gone before. Nino Farina, Luigi Fagioli and Brit Reg Parnell make a clean sweep of the podium for Alfa Romeo. There is no paddock as such and everyone piles into the beer tent for warm pints of Flowers Ale after the race. F1 still has a long way to travel to become the corporate money-making behemoth it is today . . .

★   ★   ★

There were just seven races in the first season of the 'world' champion-ship and only one of them was held outside Europe, the Indianapolis 500, which was included on the calendar due to its fame even though none of the regular F1 teams or drivers competed in it. The early years were dominated by glamorous Italian manufacturers such as Ferrari, Alfa Romeo and Maserati, but the teams were far from the big-budget corpo-rations that compete today.

Stirling Moss told us in 2005 that, 'In 1961, I was the highest-paid driver in the world. I grossed £34,750 which in today's money is about half a million. I had to pay all my expenses and I paid tax on £8,000, which in today's money is probably £100,000. You had to be a bloody good doctor to make much more than I was. I once said to one of the recent drivers from Mercedes that when I won a Grand Prix with the manufacturer we got a rather nice gold pin in the shape of a Mercedes star with sapphires in the centre of it. And they said to me, "We get the same thing today but we get a million dollars as well!"'

Racing was horrendously dangerous. Drivers did not wear seatbelts because their fear of being trapped in a car during a fire was greater than their fear of being thrown from it. In the 11-race 1958 season, drivers died at four of the events.

The season was also notable for other reasons. Prior to 1958, all races except for the Indy 500 were won by manufacturer teams such as Ferrari, Mercedes and Alfa Romeo. However, at the season-opening Argentine Grand Prix, Moss's Cooper Climax was victorious. The victory was remarkable in a number of ways. It was not only the first victory by a rear-engined F1 car, but also the first for a privateer team that had manu-factured neither its chassis nor its engine itself.

Moss's car had been entered by the Rob Walker Racing Team, owned by the Johnnie Walker whisky heir who had bought the car from John Cooper, the eponymous F1 team boss who would become famous for engineering the Mini Cooper. It paved the way for a new era of the sport. In 1959 and 1960, Cooper won both championships with Australia's Jack Brabham at the wheel. Lotus joined the winners' circle in 1961 and Brabham's own team in 1964. Within just a few years F1 had become dominated by teams that built only their chassis themselves and bought their engines from elsewhere.

Soon Ferrari was the only one of the original manufacturers left in the sport. Team founder Enzo Ferrari looked down on the teams that ran customer engines, believing that a constructor should build the entire car itself. He scornfully labelled these privateers *garagiste* teams, from the Italian for mechanic.

Life as a *garagiste* was tough. Unlike squads such as Ferrari, that had the backing of their car company parents, the *garagistes* had to fund their operations almost entirely through racing-based sources of revenue.

The FIA had extremely tight restrictions on branding that effectively banned most team sponsorships. Although trackside advertising at the circuits was rampant, the competitors were expected to be above commercialisation. Very small logos on the drivers' overalls were permitted for technical suppliers who had directly contributed to the cars, such as oil companies, tyre makers and components manufacturers. Although these regulations could in theory be overruled by local race promoters for local competitors, they rarely were, meaning that the branding opportunities were extremely limited and the cash contributions were therefore small, giving a distinct advantage to teams that had their own source of funding – the likes of Ferrari and Mercedes.

Race organisers paid the teams prize money and so-called 'start money', which was designed to offset their travel costs – but the sums involved were barely adequate to fully fund an outfit. Many teams also made money from selling their chassis to other squads and the customers weren't just full-time competitors like Rob Walker. At almost every race, local drivers tried their luck at Grand Prix racing, taking on the star names at the wheel of off-the-shelf cars bought from the bigger teams. The practice fuelled a tradition of non-championship Grands Prix running outside the formal world championship calendar. If anyone could buy and race an F1 car, then it followed that anyone could host an F1 race and have a ready pool of competitors to take part.

While some non-championship races saw grids that were almost identical to championship events, others had almost none of the big-name teams and drivers present. They often took place in far-flung or unexpected locations such as Mozambique, Brussels' Heysel Park, the island of Jersey, Scotland's Turnberry golf estate and the ominously named German forest circuit, Solitude.

The informal structure also meant that the main teams didn't commit to turn up for every race in a season. Ferrari in particular was famous for missing races at Enzo's whim. It even missed the first round of the world championship at Silverstone in 1950 because of a disagreement over start money. This continued as late as 1968 when it missed the Monaco Grand Prix in a dispute over safety standards.

Early F1 was precarious, riven with safety issues, and the series might easily have folded on a number of occasions. The 1952 season was run with Formula Two cars after Alfa Romeo pulled out, meaning that there were not enough F1 entrants to make up a full grid. In 1955, at least 84 people were killed at the 24 Hours of Le Mans sportscar race when Pierre Levegh's Mercedes crashed, catapulting pieces of burning car into a spectator area. It led to Mercedes quitting motorsport, including F1, while several countries temporarily banned motor races, including France, West Germany and Spain. Switzerland, which had hosted a Grand Prix every year since 1950, brought in a ban on racing that was only dropped in 2022 after it let electric cars compete against each other.

The 1967 oil embargo posed a new threat to F1. A group of Middle Eastern nations decided to stop selling oil to Western countries that showed support to Israel, including the United Kingdom and the United States. Although the dispute was settled by September, it dented the bottom line of many oil companies and they started to look for ways to cut costs.

Esso and BP withdrew from F1 at the same time as Firestone decided it would start charging teams for tyres. It left the *garagistes* in crisis. Facing a mass exodus of competitors, the FIA took a radical step in December 1967 when its sporting division, the Commission Sportive Internationale (CSI), voted to allow sponsorship in its series from the following year.

To assuage the concerns of the traditionalist FIA members who were horrified at the potential commercialisation of the sport, heavy restrictions were put in place in a bid to preserve the pure, heroic, untrammelled glory of racing. The rules permitted logos no larger than 55 square inches. Esteemed journalist Denis Jenkinson commented in *Motor Sport* magazine that 'at least this shows an appreciation of the fact that we are now living in the mid-twentieth century'.

It is unclear what the FIA expected would happen. The members presumably thought that it would go no further than the discreet oil company logos that adorned the noses of many of the cars when the F1 season got underway. But they had reckoned without one man who was famous for thinking outside the box.

Colin Chapman founded Lotus in 1952 and focused his energy on it after finding that his skills as an engineer far surpassed his ability as a racing driver. He attempted to enter the 1956 French Grand Prix in a beautifully sleek, minimal cigar-shaped green Vanwall and although he failed to qualify, the team asked for his help with engineering their cars. The resulting design won the first ever F1 constructors' championship in 1958.

Chapman was famous for putting speed and success before everything else. 'We stretch everything to the limit on our race cars,' he said. 'We find out just what a part will do and how much it will stand and we then know what sort of safety limit we can incorporate.'

Dan Gurney, who drove for Lotus in the Indy 500, said, 'Did I think the Lotus way of doing things was good? No. We had several structural failures in those cars. But at the time, I felt it was the price you paid for getting something significantly better.' Such was drivers' fear of the cars that upon receiving a Lotus 34 ahead of the 1965 Indy 500, the legendary A.J. Foyt requested that his mechanics rebuild the entire car and replace numerous parts.

After success in multiple series, Team Lotus entered F1 as a constructor in mid-1958, inspired by the independent success of Rob Walker. It won its first race at the 1961 United States Grand Prix and then took both championships in 1963 and 1965 with Jim Clark at the wheel. What the team lacked in power due to its customer Climax engines, it made up for in design. 'Adding power makes you faster on the straights, subtracting weight makes you faster everywhere,' Chapman said.

Chapman was an innovator. He designed a new type of rear suspension, developed four-wheel drive and introduced the monocoque (single-shell) chassis to F1. The fibreglass Lotus Elite was one of the first road cars to be made from a composite material.

When F1's engine regulations changed in 1966, catching Climax on the back foot and bringing an abrupt end to Lotus's success, Chapman didn't give up. He approached former Lotus employee Keith Duckworth, who with Mike Costin had just set up an engineering company called Cosworth. They were convinced they could build a winning F1 engine, but they needed £100,000 ($280,000) to do it, almost $2.5m in today's money. Chapman managed to convince Walter Hayes, Ford's UK head of public relations, and, in turn, Henry Ford II, that a hook-up with Cosworth would 'very likely' result in the engine winning a world championship.

Chapman's persistence in securing Ford's support was a skill he would later use to great effect to turn Lotus into one of the world's most iconic supercar brands. In 1975, upon hearing that the latest James Bond film,

The Spy Who Loved Me, was in production at Pinewood Studios, Chapman dispatched his head of PR to the facility where he bribed a doorman to let him park the prototype Lotus Esprit outside the main doors. It was not long before it was spotted by Bond producer Cubby Broccoli, who insisted that it must be used in the film. Lotus provided various cars for the production, one of which was converted into the famous submersible version that Bond uses to escape the clutches of pursuing villains. The result was a three-year waiting list for the car after the film was released.

The Ford relationship would also be marketing gold for Lotus. The Ford Cosworth DFV debuted at the 1967 Dutch Grand Prix and, although it was initially unreliable, it was described as 'not a bad old tool' by one of the men behind the wheel, Graham Hill. Lotus retired from 13 out of its 22 starts that season. However, it won on four of the other occasions, including the last two races of the season. But while its success on a technical front was mixed, on a PR front it was a winner.

Throughout the season, Ford's PR department followed the team around the world, resulting in the short film *9 Days in Summer* – lusciously shot with spectacular camera angles, aerial footage and a jazzy soundtrack – a very early forerunner to Netflix's *Drive To Survive*. The film was anchored not only on Lotus's quest for victory and its triumph over unreliability, but also the personalities of the key players involved.

Suave, cosmopolitan Hill was the star of the show. He was already well known in the UK from his frequent talk-show appearances. Famed for his Dick Dastardly moustache and sharp wit, he was often seen hanging out with celebrities such as The Beatles' George Harrison. (He even had a bit part as a villainous henchman in the 1974 spy thriller *Caravan to Vaccarès*. The film crew had wanted to borrow his helicopter for a key scene but he didn't trust anyone else to fly it.)

His team-mate in 1967 couldn't have been more different. Introverted Scottish sheep-farmer Jim Clark was far more famous for his on-track prowess than any off-track antics. However, unlike other dynamic driver pairings in F1 history such as Prost and Senna or Hamilton and Alonso, they were the best of friends. *9 Days in Summer* showed them relaxing between races, including at a pool party with Hill's son, the seven-year-old future world champion, Damon.

Such was the Cosworth DFV's potential that Ford decided to also supply McLaren and Matra in 1968. The *garagistes* now had access to quality engines for the reasonable price of £7,500 ($18,000) per unit, dramatically increasing the competitiveness of the F1 grid.

Matra reportedly had a budget of £80,000 ($192,000) in 1968, which comes to around $1.7m today when adjusted for inflation. Around £20,000 of this went on a retainer for Jackie Stewart, who at that stage had won two championship Grands Prix but not the title. As the top team of the era, Lotus's annual budget was likely higher, almost certainly above £100,000.

Rob Walker revealed in *Road & Track* magazine that start money ranged from around $500 to $3,000 per car at European races, depending on the event and the calibre of the entrant. Not every venue awarded prize money, but the United States Grand Prix at Watkins Glen was the big one, with a $20,000 reward for the winner. It paled in significance to the Indy 500, which at that time offered $100,000 for victory.

The leading technical suppliers generally paid between £5,000 ($12,000) and £10,000 a season, which was why the loss of the oil companies was a major hit for the *garagistes*. The new rules on sponsorship should have made a big difference. However, when the ban was officially lifted on 1 January 1968, coincidentally the same date as F1's season-opening South African Grand Prix, there were very few logos to be seen.

The new sponsorship regulations helped the teams in theory, but in practice they did not yet have the infrastructure to make it work. The teams had no marketing departments, no sponsorship agents and no contact with big brands, except for the technical suppliers that were fleeing from the sport in the wake of the oil crisis.

Even Lotus had only scraped together a smattering of small logos, and the team had more sponsorship experience than most. At the 1965 Italian Grand Prix Lotus had been permitted by the promoter to run sponsored cars for a local driver for which it was literally paid in sausages. A local meat producer, Salumi Rondanini, presented Chapman with two cases of salami and supposedly a pocketful of lire according to Denis Jenkinson. He clarified that 'the Italians have a national rule that permits their drivers to have advertising on their cars, in spite of an FIA rule that forbids it'.

Chapman, as always, was already thinking bigger, although in this instance the breakthrough came not from hard work but by random coincidence. Lotus's former chief mechanic, Dave Lazenby, had left in order to set up a team in the Formula Ford junior series and one of his mechanics had a girlfriend who worked for the PR firm that handled Imperial Tobacco. Following a UK ban on television advertising of cigarettes in 1965, the company had started sponsoring sports events and expressed an interest in motorsport. However, Lazenby's cars wouldn't be ready to race for another year, so in the wake of the recent FIA sponsorship ruling he connected Imperial with Chapman.

With only a 55-square-inch logo on the table, the initial contact, while promising, was not a priority for either Chapman or Imperial. Nothing was arranged by the time the Christmas holidays arrived and Lotus jetted out to Johannesburg for the season opener.

South Africa was an incongruous and controversial stop on the mostly European and North American calendar. The race had joined the world championship in 1962, one year after South Africa had been forced out of the Commonwealth due to apartheid. Although the International Olympic Committee had barred South Africa from competing at the 1964 Olympic Games in Tokyo, F1 persisted and four years into Nelson Mandela's prison sentence it was still a popular event.

There were practical reasons for its inclusion too. Many of the F1 teams also raced in the Tasman Series, a completely separate championship that took place in January and February in Australia and New Zealand using F1-spec cars. Stopping off in South Africa made sense from a logistical perspective and gave the teams another opportunity to earn start money. However, the early start created an odd gap on the calendar as the second round was not scheduled to take place for more than four months.

Clark won the 1968 South African Grand Prix, with Hill in second, giving the Scotsman a record 25 F1 victories. But it was at the other end of the running order where events were taking place that would determine the future of Lotus and the whole of F1. Unnoticed by most of the paddock, a small part-time privateer team had debuted the first full-livery sponsorship in the history of F1, a moment of seismic change that would come to change the face of the sport and pave the way for its development into the globe-hopping circus we know it as today.

Gunston cigarettes was founded in the 1950s by South African businessman Dr Anton Rupert. Rupert was a charismatic figure who, in stark contrast to his involvement in the tobacco industry, was a committed conservationist and one of the founders of the World Wildlife Fund.

Rupert was quick to spot an opportunity and shortly after the FIA's lifting of the sponsorship ban, Team Gunston was launched with two Rhodesian drivers, John Love and Sam Tingle, at the wheel.

The team debuted on 3 December at the 1967 Rhodesian Grand Prix in Bulawayo, a non-championship F1 race that was won by Love in a customer Brabham against exclusively local competition. Notably, as well as bearing the words 'Team Gunston' on the side of the cockpit, the cars were painted orange with a wide brown stripe – the colours of a Gunston cigarette packet.

The team's 150mph speeding cigarette packets were within the letter of the FIA's new rules but were certainly not in the spirit of them, a blurring of advert and logo before unsuspecting spectators sitting on grassy banks in picnic chairs. However, when Love and Tingle took the track for the South African Grand Prix they competed without opposition from the authorities.

It appears that the officials simply didn't notice what the team had done. Gunston was a local brand, unknown outside southern Africa, and it is possible that some observers thought it was the name of the team, rather than the sponsor. Love finished last, five laps behind, while Tingle spun off, so there was little reason for anyone to notice the livery.

In earlier years, the orange paint may have attracted attention, but rules requiring cars to run in their national colours had also recently been retracted by the FIA, seemingly in response to the widespread introduction of colour TV. Car colours could now be used by viewers to distinguish competitors, rather than watching a field of British Racing Green with a few splashes of Italian scarlet. The Gunston cars may have been orange but the far bigger news was that the McLarens were also painted orange for the first time, taking advantage of the regulation change to experiment with a more distinct identity.

Ultimately, Team Gunston was a one-off entrant, five laps behind the leaders, and the F1 establishment wasn't very interested in what they were doing. Chapman, however, was a man who noticed everything. He experienced a eureka moment as he recognised the loophole that Gunston had exploited. As the rest of the team headed off to New Zealand, Chapman flew back to London to meet with Imperial.

The tobacco company's promotions manager, Tim Collins, had already been looking at F1 following the UK's decision to ban cigarette advertisements on TV in 1965. He was still smarting after his plan to buy

Silverstone and rebrand it the John Player Circuit was rebuffed by his bosses in favour of an autocross sponsorship. His focus had turned to ways to revive the Gold Leaf cigarette brand, which he told *Motor Sport* magazine was 'perceived as slightly old-fashioned. I was asked to come up with ideas to jazz up its image and make it look more modern.'

Collins introduced Chapman to Imperial boss Geoffrey Kent. The pair had a lot in common and hit it off immediately. Both were charismatic marketeers who had served in the Royal Air Force, although in Chapman's case he had departed after a few months upon realising he much preferred civilian life.

According to Chapman's son, Clive, his pitch was simple. 'We'll paint [the cars] in any colour that you like as long as you pay us some money,' Chapman junior explained to the *Formula for Success* television documentary.

Chapman's timing was perfect. A year earlier, the coloured livery would have been a significantly less attractive prospect. But in July 1967 the BBC had launched its first regular colour programming with a live broadcast from Wimbledon. The prospect of Gold Leaf's red adorning the championship favourites got an immediate yes from Kent. 'Colin offered us a dream team of Graham Hill and Jim Clark,' Collins explained. 'Why would we have wanted to go anywhere other than Lotus?'

Chapman was offered an annual £95,000 ($228,000) to run the branding on Lotus's cars in all series for the next three years. It was almost enough money to cover his entire racing budget for each season and he couldn't say no. There was, however, one sticking point.

Chapman had proposed that the team would be known as 'Team Lotus sponsored by Gold Leaf'. However, Imperial was set on 'Gold Leaf Team Lotus'. 'I felt our brand name had to be an integral part of the operation,' Collins said, adding that it 'would have been a deal-breaker for us . . . We were still debating the point on the night before the scheduled launch. My chairman said everything had to be signed off by 10.30 pm – as Gold Leaf Team Lotus – or telegrams would be sent out cancelling the press conference. It all got rather tense.'

Eventually Chapman capitulated and, as Collins said, 'The rest is history.'

The first two races of the Tasman Series had already passed, but the third was approaching on 20 January. Lotus's mechanics took Clark's car to a local Ford dealer in the New Zealand city of Christchurch who removed the iconic green with yellow trim, painted it red, white and gold, applied a 55-square-inch Gold Leaf sailor boy logo on each side of the cockpit and stencilled 'Gold Leaf Team Lotus' on the side of the car. As the official name of the team it fell outside the restrictions on branding size. As author Mike Lawrence noted in his biography of the Lotus boss, 'Chapman had read his rulebook, found his loophole and had driven a coach and horses through it.'

The paint had barely dried when the car was wheeled into Wigram Airfield for the race. It scandalised many of the observers there, but because it did not contravene the rules, officials decided that there was nothing that could be done. Clark won the race before crashing out in the next round in Teretonga, the southernmost race track in the world. That race was notable for another new development: his car had run in practice with a cut-down helicopter blade mounted at the rear above its gearbox – the first attempt at a wing on an F1 car.

The Gold Leaf livery had raced without consequence, but it was a different story when the cars reached Australia for the fifth round of the Tasman Series at Surfers Paradise. Hill joined Clark but the superstar pairing was abruptly banned from practice and fined £50 each by the strict Australian authorities. With the crowd clamouring to see their heroes, a compromise was reached. The fines were paid and the sailor boy logo was taped over, but the rest of the livery remained. Clark won the race and the following two rounds to take the Tasman title.

At the non-championship F1 Race of Champions at Brands Hatch in March, the first appearance of the Gold Leaf livery in Europe caused 'one hell of a hubbub', according to Collins. Local broadcaster London Weekend Television panicked when it saw the branding as it was worried that it could contravene the TV tobacco advertising ban.

The producer phoned Chapman during practice, threatening to pull the plug on coverage. Hill was black-flagged and the team was forced to paint over the sailor boy with a black question mark in a white circle. However, the Gold Leaf Team Lotus name and the red colour scheme remained. It made little difference to the brand's exposure, as the logo itself was the least prominent part of the livery and would have been barely visible on the television coverage anyway.

Getting even part of the branding past the UK stewards was a triumph, but Lotus's dream season was about to fall apart. The Gold Leaf branding was next featured at the first race of the Formula Two season at

Hockenheim in Germany on 7 April. The two-heat race started on a damp track with poor visibility. Future FIA president Max Mosley, who competed in the race, said, 'I was thinking, "This isn't a good idea." All you could do was steer by looking at the tops of the trees, because you couldn't see where the track went.'

Clark was driving the lead Lotus. On the fifth lap, a suspected puncture caused him to veer off the track and into the surrounding forest. He died before he reached the hospital, aged just 32.

Fellow Scottish driver Jackie Stewart told the BBC that 'Jimmy's death is probably the most tragic thing in my experience of motor racing'. Decades later he would summarise why it had affected everyone so deeply: 'If Jim Clark could die, anybody could die.'

When the news was announced to the 80,000 spectators, they rose to their feet spontaneously in silent tribute. It was left to Hill to phone Chapman, who was at a sportscar race in England, to give him the news. Chapman was devastated. Tim Collins said that the team 'wasn't sure whether Colin would actually carry on after Jimmy's accident'.

Lotus's nightmare didn't end there. One month later Englishman Mike Spence, who had been drafted in as Clark's replacement, was killed in practice for the Indy 500. Chapman returned to England immediately, abandoning the rest of the team in Indianapolis. A statement he issued to the press read: 'I am filled with grief at the loss of my long-time friend and associate, Jimmy Clark, and the additional loss, just a month later to the day, of Mike Spence. As an understandable result, I want nothing more to do with the 1968 Indianapolis race. I just do not have the heart for it.'

It was only three days before the start of practice for the Spanish Grand Prix at the new track in Jarama on the outskirts of Madrid. Chapman refused to attend, leaving Hill as de facto team principal for the event as well as the team's sole driver for the race that would mark the debut of the Gold Leaf livery at a round of the F1 world championship.

There was an oppressive mood in the paddock in the shadow of Clark's and Spence's deaths. The drivers were nervous and it didn't help that the circuit – a rarity for the era in that it had been purpose-built for F1 – was unfinished as money had run out. The drivers' union, the Grand Prix Drivers' Association, tried to get the race cancelled, but the promoter managed to allay their concerns and the race went ahead.

There were gasps among observers as Hill's Lotus left the pits. A number of F1's senior figures weren't aware that the Lotus had been running in the red, white and gold colours of the Gold Leaf tobacco brand at non-championship races. They remembered the team for its distinctive British Racing Green livery and this was the first time it had competed in a championship F1 race without it.

A protest was promptly lodged against the livery and Hill was tasked with dealing with the fallout. The officials wanted Lotus to stick black tape over the logos, but Hill's charm won through. They were eventually forced to concede that the Lotus was entirely within the rules, making the Gold Leaf deal the first big-money team sponsorship in the history of the world championship.

The debut of the livery marked a crossroads for F1 that fuelled its transformation from a sport into the multi-billion-dollar business that it is today. The sponsorship era had arrived and it rocked the racing establishment. But it wasn't the only way that Lotus was making history. Hill took victory in the race, which was enough to tempt Chapman back to the paddock in time for Monaco, two weeks later, where Lotus had another surprise for the rest of the grid.

Chapman had used Imperial Tobacco's money to fund a redesign of the chassis. The 49B was unveiled in the principality and, following on from Lotus's experiments in the Tasman Series, it boasted a small rudimentary front wing. It was the first time the aerodynamic feature had appeared on a car at an F1 race and it was set to have as big an impact on the sport as the Gold Leaf deal.

Like sponsorship, wings weren't Chapman's idea but he was the first person to make the most of them. Jim Hall, a Texan engineer and former F1 driver, had figured out that if wings could make an aeroplane fly, then an inverted wing could be used to stick a racing car to the ground. He engineered the Chaparral 2F sportscar with a huge and ungainly rear wing that was adjustable during a race by the driver pressing on a pedal.

Chapman saw this and responded with his philosophy of 'simplify and add lightness', resulting in the 49B. Hill won the Monaco Grand Prix, giving Lotus its third win of the year.

His Monaco triumph marked the end of possibly the most significant seven-week period in the history of the sport. Three immense events centred on Lotus would change F1 beyond recognition. They affected each of the three pillars of the series – sporting, technical and commercial.

While title sponsorship would transform F1 from a financial perspective, giving the *garagistes* a viable business model, the introduction of wings impacted F1 on a technological front, moving away from the cigar-shaped cars of the 1950s and 1960s to the ancestors of the cars that race today. In terms of transformation on a sporting front, Clark's death was set to have an equally significant impact. Of the 44 drivers who competed in 1968, 13 would die on the track, four of them before the end of the season.

Jackie Stewart was shaken by the death of his friend and it would set him on the path to becoming one of the major players in improving safety in motorsport. 'Jimmy's death at Hockenheim was the beginning of us really driving home the reality that has changed the entire world of Formula One in regards to track safety,' he told *Reuters* on the fiftieth anniversary of Clark's accident. 'He was never a driver anybody would have ever thought would have died in a racing car. And suddenly the sport allowed that to happen because there were no barriers and no protection from those trees that the car catapulted into.'

Changes to safety standards were slow to happen, however. Many saw danger as an inherent part of the sport. Even in old age, Stirling Moss bemoaned the changes, telling *Classic Driver* in 2015 that 'Formula One racing should be demanding. If it isn't, then how can you tell the difference between a really good driver and the rest?'

But others were more cautious. At the 1968 German Grand Prix, Dan Gurney became the first driver to race in F1 wearing a full-face helmet, the Star, which he had developed with equipment supplier Bell. By the following year, they were commonplace.

Although it would take a long time for safety standards to improve, the changes on other fronts were much more rapid. At the next race in Belgium, Ferrari's Mauro Forghieri introduced an improved wing design on Chris Amon's car that made him five seconds a lap faster than his team-mates. Along the pit lane Matra was sporting more prominent branding for its main sponsor, the Elf oil company, that would evolve into one of the sport's most iconic liveries. Chapman had ushered in the modern era of F1.

He had also come up with an innovative way of silencing complaints from the authorities. When F1 returned to Brands Hatch for the British Grand Prix, the sailor boy logo had been replaced with a Union Jack roundel. This just left the 'Gold Leaf Team Lotus' lettering on the car.

'The TV firms couldn't call it cigarette advertising because the altered logo was simply the team's name,' Collins explained. It also reflected Geoffrey Kent's vision of a patriotic partnership between Imperial and Lotus, a British company supporting a paragon of British sporting success. The new design worked so well that it became permanent. Ironically, it meant that the actual 55-inch tobacco logo would no longer be a part of the livery.

Hill and Lotus were crowned champions in Mexico City after an unprecedented season. But not everyone had reason to celebrate. The once-dominant Cooper team had failed to find a major sponsor and finished a distant seventh in the constructors' championship. John Cooper told TV reporters at the race that 'we're in a very, very serious position at the moment. I think we've got to look to people outside the motor industry for support, such as cigarette companies or liquor companies or something like that. The money's got to come from somewhere.'

But it was too late for Cooper. Sponsorship didn't materialise in time and the works team folded over the winter. It had become almost impossible to compete without sponsor-backing, and other teams were stepping up.

After a slow take-up in 1969, the sponsorship boom began the following year with major deals signed by BRM with Yardley perfume and Rob Walker with Brooke Bond Oxo. Faced with an unstoppable tide of commercialisation, the FIA lifted all restrictions on logo size in 1971, leading to a surge in sponsorship. With more visible branding on the table, even struggling teams found that they had an attractive package. It resulted in an influx of competitive new teams into the sport, with March, Hesketh and Williams making their debuts over the next few years. They ushered in F1's most glamorous era, famous for its pin-up stars such as Jackie Stewart and Brazilian Emerson Fittipaldi who lived jet-set lives and drove for increasingly engineered teams like Lotus, Tyrrell and McLaren.

However, some of the teams remained hostile. Enzo Ferrari, who had reportedly been furious to see the Lotuses painted in the red colour usually reserved for Italian marques, believed that pressure from sponsors led to teams taking unnecessary risks. Teams had become beholden to sponsors because their funding covered the squads' accelerating costs and, in order to receive it, they had to race, regardless of the conditions. As Ferrari later explained to *Autocar*, 'If cars were still painted in their national colours instead of the colours of sponsoring companies, then constructors would not say, "I have 60 men to employ and major sponsorship to justify" . . . Racing should never have been allowed to get this far.'

Despite this opposition, in 1971 branding for watchmaker Heuer appeared on the Ferraris as payment for designing a new timing system for the team.

In the eyes of others, however, Chapman had saved the sport. According to John Day, whose model-car company sponsored various teams in the 1970s, Chapman 'found a means of paying his way. In 1968, motor racing was going nowhere, and without sponsorship it was in danger of dying altogether. We all bemoan the loss of national colours on the cars but, to sound an optimistic note, when they were covered in various decals they came alive.' In an interview with *Motor Sport* magazine, he added, 'I never discovered a more effective form of advertising.'

Ironically, despite its impact on the sport, the Gold Leaf sponsorship would last for only four seasons. This was not because Imperial Tobacco had tired of F1 – quite the opposite. Instead, it changed the sponsorship to another of its brands, John Player Special, and the resulting black and gold colour scheme became one of the most iconic racing liveries of all time.

With the addition of sponsorship, Chapman had kickstarted F1 as a business. Having up to this point been handcuffed financially and entirely reliant on meagre prize money or independently wealthy owners, teams were now free to seek out other sources of revenue from businesses looking to attach themselves to the glamour of the sport. For the first time, real money would begin to flow into the sport, and with it would come a feeding frenzy the likes of which the sport had never seen.

2

ENTER ECCLESTONE

The F1 paddock is a hotbed of rumour and gossip at the best of times but when the 1969 season got underway in South Africa, tongues were wagging even more than usual.

As the crews sheltered from a freak storm during the first practice session of the season, rumours blew through the paddock about how much Colin Chapman had paid to tempt Austrian driver Jochen Rindt away from his beloved Brabham team as a replacement for Jim Clark. Chapman was one of F1's most penny-pinching bosses so the question on everyone's lips was: who helped Rindt to get one over him?

One of the last people they suspected was the short, smartly dressed gent lingering in the background of the Lotus garage. If they had known what would become of him they would have been even more astonished.

When the 1968 season drew to a close, Chapman had still not found a suitable replacement for Clark. He had approached Jackie Stewart, but the Scot refused because he thought the Lotus was unsafe. Clark's immediate replacement, future Arrows team founder Jackie Oliver, had underperformed and scored only a single podium. 'It was a terribly difficult year and I'm not sure I was much of a replacement for Jimmy,' Oliver told *Motor Sport*.

In search of the next world champion, Chapman turned his attention to Jochen Rindt. The Austrian had never won a Grand Prix and his unreliable Brabham had retired in 10 of the 12 races in the 1968 season. However, he had scored a podium in the other two, a major feat in the underperforming car.

Rindt was very different from the typical genteel racing driver of the era, such as Clark and Hill. Born in Germany, his parents had been killed in a World War Two bombing raid in Hamburg when he was just 15 months old. He was sent to Austria to live with his grandparents, who spoiled the orphan boy.

As a teenager, he clocked up eight misdemeanour charges from the police and was expelled from multiple private schools, though not before his love of racing was inspired by a trip to the 1961 German Grand Prix with his schoolfriend Helmut Marko, who would himself go on to play a major role in F1 history as Red Bull's head of driver development.

Rindt entered a local race with the saloon car his grandparents had bought him as a graduation present, but was black-flagged for dangerous driving. After learning the ropes in various starter series, in 1964 he used his inheritance from a German spice mill to buy a Brabham F2 car. He won his second race in the series, even managing to beat Hill. The following year he won the 24 Hours of Le Mans for Ferrari.

The chain-smoking Austrian was a distinct figure in the paddock, often accompanied by his elegant Finnish model wife Nina. Rindt had a limp from a skiing accident, and frequently sported aviator glasses with a shaggy fur coat over his overalls. He could be impulsive. On the flight back to London from the 1967 South African Grand Prix he lost heavily when gambling at cards with his team-mate, Mexico's Pedro Rodriguez. He was so furious that when the flight stopped to refuel in Kenya he left the plane and did not return, slipping away alone into Nairobi.

Another of Rindt's quirks was that he was often accompanied by his close friend and gambling partner, a former racing driver and used-car salesman called Bernie Ecclestone. Despite the 12-year age gap, the pair were like brothers. They had met at the 1965 Mexican Grand Prix, when Rindt raced for Cooper and Ecclestone had been visiting his friends John Cooper and team manager Roy Salvadori.

Despite not having a formal role with the team or Rindt, Ecclestone became indispensable. When the team had problems with its radiators, Ecclestone headed off into Mexico City despite not being able to speak Spanish. He returned a few hours later with two gleaming new radiators and a pair of mechanics to fit them. He had bought their services in exchange for tickets to the race. 'How did he talk them into it?' Salvadori later questioned. 'They didn't speak a word of English. How did he do it?'

On another occasion in South Africa, when the team needed to fit in some extra testing, Ecclestone arranged for them to use the roads around an abandoned mountain-top gold mine, which Salvadori described as 'like a deserted town that you see in one of the westerns'. Rindt drove the car through intermittent mist while Ecclestone made tea and played cards with Salvadori.

It was little surprise therefore that it was Ecclestone who Rindt turned to for advice when he was approached by Chapman. Following the Mexican Grand Prix, Jochen and Nina headed off to Acapulco with Ecclestone and his then girlfriend Tuana Tan. Around the resort's gaming tables, Ecclestone and Rindt developed a plan. Using Rindt's fame as a sports star they would launch an international clothing line, a similar concept to the ones from former tennis players Fred Perry and René Lacoste. The only obstacle was that Rindt had yet to achieve the level of success necessary for the plan to be viable – which was where Chapman's approach came in.

Ecclestone could smell the Gold Leaf money like cigarette smoke and he offered to negotiate with Chapman on Rindt's behalf. The Austrian accepted and a contract was drawn up between them by Rindt's 20-year-old Swiss trainee lawyer, Luc Argand, who later became a linchpin in Ecclestone's family trust. Ecclestone knew Chapman from his Vanwall days, when he had advised team owner Tony Vandervell to 'make Chapman the designer, because if he kept driving the car he would only kill himself and that would have been a real waste'.

Chapman was desperate for a new superstar and Rindt was the best chance he had. 'I'm sure Chapman regretted the day he met Ecclestone,' Salvadori told Ecclestone's biographer Susan Watkins. 'The usual contract when Graham Hill was there – as I understood it – was very restrictive. But those restrictions didn't exist once Bernie had been through it.' Although Ecclestone had a lot of respect for Chapman's methods – and the fact he'd managed to upset the apple cart with the FIA – this was business. As Ecclestone negotiated, the numbers kept getting higher and higher.

But the final decision rested with Rindt, who was nevertheless reluctant to leave Brabham, where he enjoyed the family atmosphere. 'I explained to Jochen that you've got a much better chance of winning the world championship in a Lotus,' Ecclestone said. 'But you've also got a good chance of getting hurt.'

Jack Brabham recalled that 'we shook hands and were going to fix up the contract and all the terms were agreed. Rindt was tackled by Colin Chapman who offered him another £10,000 or something.' Rindt suggested he could stay on at Brabham for half of what Chapman had promised, but it was still more than the team could afford.

Rindt is believed to have received around £60,000 ($144,000) to drive for Lotus in 1969. It was a high-octane salary for a driver with no wins and came to almost two thirds of the amount that Imperial was paying. Chapman had opened the door to the commercialisation of F1 but quickly discovered that, while he might be the master of the sport on an engineering front, when it came to business, he had met his match in Ecclestone.

Few F1 personalities had as inauspicious a start in the industry as Bernie Ecclestone. Born in 1930 in the picturesque village of St Peter, South Elmham, in Suffolk, money-management skills were instilled in him from an early age because his family had so little to go round – his father, Sidney, was a Suffolk trawlerman; mother Bertha stayed home to look after their children. Their small home had no inside toilet and no water on tap. In the depression of the 1930s, Bertha demanded that Sidney hand over his wages on pay day and there was little left over for unnecessary spending. They were so poor that Ecclestone didn't get a birthday cake until he was eight. But even though he grew up with few frills, he had grand ambitions and the skills to achieve them, as his brain was as quick as a calculator. He put it to use from an early age. In 1938 the family moved to Bexleyheath in south-east London, just before war broke out. Unlike the majority of the population, Ecclestone saw it as an opportunity.

When bombs began dropping he realised that commodities like cakes and pens weren't as readily available as they had been before, so he hunted down supplies and sold them for a profit to his friends at Dartford West Central Secondary School. Ecclestone got up early for school so that he could stop at the bakery and buy all the best buns, which he crammed into his case. This meant there were none left for his classmates when they arrived there later, so Ecclestone sold his buns to them for a hefty mark-up at lunchtime. They became so popular that he even had to pay a gang of older pupils to guard them.

'I've always been a bit of a dealer,' he told us in an interview for GQ magazine. The cake-selling at break-time honed his negotiating skills from a young age. Showing early evidence of tremendous drive, Ecclestone didn't just have one paper round, he had two. He used the money from them to buy more biscuits and buns to sell in the school-yard. He even traded in his toys to buy more supplies and, in turn, make more profit, which enabled him to buy better toys while keeping the wheels of his business turning.

Ecclestone's immense initiative wasn't just fuelled by his desire to escape poverty. He'd been born nearly blind in one eye and, being on the short side as well – he would grow to be just 5 feet 3 inches tall – felt he had to compensate: 'At school, I was a bit undersized,' he told the *Daily Mail* in 2023. 'When you are a little undersized, or whatever, you have to look after yourself. You have to be a fighter.' This formative experience taught him some of the traits that later made him a billionaire: thinking on his feet and fighting to get what he wanted were essential – likewise, his supreme self-confidence and independence enabled him to outmanoeuvre slow-moving corporate juggernauts over the years.

As a result of his wheeling and dealing, the Ecclestone cupboards were always full of goods that other families struggled to get in the austere post-war period, such as Black Magic chocolates. He treated his sister Marian to expensive toys and bought a projector so the family could watch movies on a sheet hung up in their bungalow.

While studying (briefly) at Woolwich Polytechnic he went on regular visits to the Brands Hatch race track in nearby Kent. Competitive, and fascinated by engines, this was the beginning of Ecclestone's lifelong love of racing. It started with motorcycles as they were easy to tinker with in the family's shed. Bernie's first car was even crossed with a bike – the iconic Morgan three-wheeler that had two wheels up front for steering and stability and a single drive wheel at the rear.

Ecclestone's job (testing gas purity at the local gasworks) gave him more time to devote to his passion and it soon became an obsession. Evenings were spent leafing through classified ads in newspapers, look-ing for motorbike parts that he could sell at a profit. He didn't rest during the day as the deals were done on the gas board's telephone. Soon this side business began to earn him more than his wage, which was when the teenage Bernie decided to combine his passions of racing and trad-ing. He took the bold step of entering the world of car and motorcycle dealing and was soon selling to the industry establishment.

His first brush with motorsport came in the late 1940s when leading motorcycle racer Jack Surtees arrived at the Ecclestone family bungalow to buy an Excelsior Manxman, a motorcycle that had once been popular in racing but was discontinued during the war. Surtees brought with him his young son, John, who would go on to be the only person to win the world championship in both F1 and Grand Prix motorcycling. The younger Surtees later recalled his father speaking about how the teenage Ecclestone would 'mesmerise people' with his business acumen.

By the time he was just 18 Ecclestone realised he needed a more professional sales platform and walked into the Compton & Fuller car showroom in Bexleyheath with a proposal to rent part of the forecourt. At first Fred Compton refused, but Ecclestone persisted and his bike business was soon generating most of the showroom's profits. It enabled Ecclestone to persuade Derek Fuller, Compton's partner, to sell his share of the business to him. Within three years the sign above the door had been changed to read 'Compton & Ecclestone'.

Ecclestone then cast his net wider by selling used cars on London's notorious Warren Street, where he learned to seal deals with an inviolable handshake – a trait he stands by to this day. 'I've done so many deals on a handshake,' he told us. 'The biggest thing for me is people trust me so people rely on me. In what I call the good old days all it took was having a chat with the people that had the money, like Colin Chapman. Now they come along with lawyers and masseurs and they can never agree on anything.'

It wasn't long before Ecclestone started racing motorcycles at Brands Hatch, transported in a van emblazoned with the name of Compton & Ecclestone. Fred Compton later recalled that 'going into racing was a way of getting our name known. It worked. Everyone in the south of England knew us.'

When Ecclestone married telephone operator Ivy Bamford in 1952 his dedication to business was already in top gear, as he took just half an hour off for his nuptials. They had a daughter, Deborah, three years later, but instead of slowing down, his ambitions accelerated. Through dealing in cars, Ecclestone came further into contact with motorsport. A well-liked east London car dealer, Lewis 'Pop' Lewis-Evans, was bankrolling the junior racing activities of his son, Stuart. The younger Lewis-Evans was an affable man who had a great talent for racing. He and Ecclestone became friends and the racer was grateful for the car dealer's savvy advice. 'I used to look after things for him that he didn't do, like contracts. He wasn't up to that. But he was a very good driver,' Ecclestone explained to his biographer, Susan Watkins.

Lewis-Evans was on the verge of making it big in motorsport. He won a non-championship F1 race at Goodwood in early 1957 and on his world championship debut at Monaco in the same year he finished fourth, despite driving an inferior Connaught car.

When Connaught folded later that year, Ecclestone bought two of their cars at auction for £4,050 ($11,340). He believed that the resale value was significantly higher in the southern hemisphere, so he sent them off to race in the Tasman Series over the winter with Lewis-Evans and Roy Salvadori behind the wheel. The drivers were instructed to show what the cars could do on track and then sell them before returning home.

Early one morning, Ecclestone received a call from an excited Lewis-Evans, who was delighted to have been offered a supposedly rare stamp collection by a mysterious foreign gentleman in exchange for the cars. He was just about to sell up when Salvadori advised him to check with Ecclestone first. Needless to say, Ecclestone told him to back out of the dodgy deal. It typified the contrast between Ecclestone's hard-edged business style and the financial naivety of many people involved in motorsport at the time.

To Ecclestone's annoyance, the Connaughts had to be shipped back to the UK unsold. When he still hadn't managed to dispose of them by the spring, he decided to enter one of them in the Monaco Grand Prix, but at the last moment grew dissatisfied with the driver he had hired and decided to drive the car himself. He never made it to the race as he was excluded after he failed to set a qualifying time. Ecclestone's name also appeared on the British Grand Prix entry list but he never even turned the wheel.

His eyesight prevented him from succeeding at the top level and, although he won a handful of races below it, he was never a permanent front-runner. The £100 ($280) a year sponsorship money he received from Shell gave him little incentive to continue and his confidence was knocked in a series of accidents, including one where he was thrown from the driving seat and landed in the car park outside the track. 'I had woken up four or five times in hospital,' he later said. 'I realised that I didn't want to risk lying in bed for the rest of my life looking up at the ceiling.' Little did Ecclestone know that it would only be a matter of time before he walked away from motorsport entirely.

Ecclestone had considered using the Connaughts to build a privateer F1 team around Lewis-Evans. But even the credulous driver was shrewd enough to see that it was a losing game and he instead signed with British front-runner, Vanwall, as Stirling Moss's team-mate. Ecclestone accompanied Lewis-Evans to the races, negotiating his start money.

It seemed like the start of a great career but by the end of the year everything had fallen apart. At the season finale in Casablanca, Lewis-Evans's engine seized, flinging his car into the barriers where it exploded in a torrent of black smoke. In panic, Lewis-Evans ran away from the wreck, his overalls on fire.

'If he hadn't have run away or had rolled over or somebody had been there and grabbed hold of him, he would have probably been all right,' Ecclestone explained. Lewis-Evans was severely burned and was flown back to England to the specialist burns unit at the Queen Victoria Hospital in East Sussex where many RAF pilots had been treated. It was not enough and he died a few days later.

'It was a bad day for me because I was very close with Stuart,' said Ecclestone. 'I went back to one of my businesses not thinking I was ever going to get involved [in motorsport] any longer.'

By this time Ecclestone had a burgeoning property portfolio, which began in 1950 when, at the age of 20, he had bought and sold industrial premises in Greenwich, south-east London. He also became the sole owner of Compton & Ecclestone, adding local Bexleyheath dealer James Spencer's showrooms to his portfolio. The timing couldn't have been better as it coincided with the post-war boom in private transport – and Ecclestone's immaculate showrooms, with their plate-glass windows, stood out in an industry renowned for its greasy and grimy premises.

From his huge desk in the state-of-the-art all-white establishment he could press buttons to spotlight certain cars or even fold back a mirrored wall to reveal a special selection of vehicles only for VIPs. His attention to detail may have bordered on OCD – Ecclestone admitted that he 'was terribly, terribly fussy, probably a bit from my old mum' – but, as ever with Bernie, boosting the bottom line was actually the driving force behind it. Just like when he bought the best buns at school and sold them for the highest prices, Ecclestone could charge a premium for his cars because they were in Britain's best-looking showroom. It made him a millionaire when he was only in his twenties.

By the dawn of the Swinging Sixties, Ecclestone wore fashionable suits from Savile Row and sold cars to celebrities such as Eurovision winner Sandie Shaw, the supermodel Twiggy, the Welsh singer Shirley Bassey and Austrian film director Otto Preminger (who also played Mr Freeze in the *Batman* TV series). Ecclestone became friends with many of them, including the singer Adam Faith, who was a regular travelling companion on trips to the south of France. Ecclestone himself was infamous long before he was famous. He was a regular at the gambling hall of posh Mayfair club Crockfords, which gave him an early taste of the high life. He became famous for his fearless gambling and later said that he feared nothing, not even death. 'Unless you've made the mistake you don't know which way to go,' he added. 'If you're going to take the attitude that you don't think it will work, you will never do anything. You've got to give it a go and hope you've got it right.'

Ecclestone's view has always been that people should be judged on their results, not what they look like, and he lives by this mantra. Aside from some work to his nose when it was bitten by a dog in Las Vegas, Ecclestone hasn't had plastic surgery, despite appearing on TV every other weekend for decades. He has had a deadpan expression for so long it seems to have set in and this makes it almost impossible to read how he is feeling. It is perfect for poker and business negotiations as it can cause his adversaries to underestimate him. 'I don't like others to think I'm sharp,' he once said. 'Then they're more careful and that's a disadvantage.' In contrast, Ecclestone's adversaries are left questioning their own judgement when they realise he is anything but as doddery as he looks.

For such a formidable figure, Ecclestone's voice is strangely soft. He has a slight cockney accent, talks slowly and sometimes mumbles, which often leads to the interlocutor questioning whether they have heard him correctly. Responses are often monosyllabic, which gives the other side little to go on. Ecclestone also frequently litters his utterances with assurances that he has little interest in, or even knowledge of, the subject in question, which often results in the questioner offering their opinion instead.

This tactic was put to great use when a delegation from Disney came to visit him at his London office in 2005, by which time he was firmly in F1's driving seat. Disney was preparing for the launch of its animated movie *Cars*, featuring talking vehicles as its protagonists. The media giant's representatives asked if the director and key members of the cast could have paddock passes to the Spanish Grand Prix because the movie was launching in Europe the following month. Disney's delegation had prepared a detailed presentation about the exposure the movie would give to F1 as it featured voice cameos from several drivers. But they didn't even get a chance to go through it. After shaking their hands, Ecclestone asked who they worked for, to which they replied 'Disney'. Then he looked them straight in the eye and said, 'What's Disney?' The question completely threw them because they had never been asked it before. On that occasion, he took pity on Disney and they ended up getting the passes they wanted. However, it is this kind of behaviour that has often put him on a crash course with corporate America.

Ecclestone is the archetypal nonconformist and doesn't just play hard-ball over deals. Interviews with him often resemble sparring matches as he tests a reporter's mettle. It can put them in a spin while Ecclestone remains in the driving seat. He often achieves this end with statements said for shock value – all of which helps explain why he famously claimed that Hitler was a man who 'was able to get things done', that 'women should be dressed in white like all the other domestic appliances' and why, in 2022, despite the invasion of Ukraine, he described Vladimir Putin as 'a first-class person' who 'believed he was doing the right thing for Russia'.

Ecclestone has often claimed not to care about his outbursts: 'So maybe I upset a few people on the way. Make a few people happy, a few unhappy, but that's how it is.' His approach stands in stark contrast to the scripted cautious statements that F1 drivers and team personnel typically trot out.

'I don't get emotional over situations,' he told us in 2013. 'I always tell people I worry about things when they happen – but don't worry before.' This ability to keep calm under pressure is perhaps the most valuable skill that poker taught him, aside from not giving his hand away. It has served him well.

On one occasion, Ecclestone was flying in a private jet from Melbourne to Adelaide to attend the Grand Prix there when an explosion put one of the engines out of action. With the hydraulics also damaged, the pilot had to make an emergency landing, but Ecclestone wasn't worried. During the commotion the pilot turned round and looked into the cabin only to find Ecclestone reading a magazine. His attitude was pragmatic: 'Well, I said I couldn't fix the engine, what could I do? They were paid to worry about landing the plane, not me. That was their problem.'

His immense composure was put to perhaps the ultimate test in 2016 when Aparecida Schunk, the mother of his charming third wife Fabiana, was kidnapped in her home of São Paulo. Her sick captors sent videos of women being beheaded in an attempt to bribe Ecclestone into paying a record €124m ransom. They picked the wrong person.

Talking about the incident to the *Sunday Times*, Ecclestone said, 'I never intended to pay them,' and joked, 'all my friends know that I wouldn't pay a penny for a mother-in-law.' Fortunately he didn't need to. The kidnappers left an amateurish trail of clues that led police to the rented flat where Schunk was being held and she was released unharmed. 'Mum is strong enough to get over this ordeal,' Ecclestone told us afterwards.

He too needed a thick skin to get over it. It came to light that the mastermind behind the operation was one of his former helicopter pilots, Jorge Eurico da Silva Faria, who was convicted in 2017 and sentenced to 14 years in prison. It was far from the first time that Ecclestone had been betrayed by someone in his inner circle.

As he explained in an episode of the *Lucky* documentary series, when his chain of dealerships took off in the 1960s, he 'bought a car from someone and found out it was financed so the guy didn't own the car. So I stopped the cheque and the guy duly appeared to explain to me how he'd like the cheque cleared and produced a gun from under his sweater to show me.' Ecclestone took a pragmatic approach to that too. 'I explained to him . . . if you shoot me the cheque won't be cleared, let's have a chat.' Ecclestone added that the dispute was then resolved amicably and 'he became a very good customer from then on in'.

This tough-guy approach didn't just build up Ecclestone's reputation for being ruthless, it also built up his wealth. He acquired much more than gambling chips with it.

Moving in London's society circles brought him into contact with Tuana Tan, a sophisticated Singaporean and fellow gambler. They became close, and at the same time Ecclestone had outgrown his homely life with Ivy and Deborah. As he said many years later, 'You know what I was told very early on in my life? "Circumstances change."' It was why he left Ivy and Deborah but ensured they were never left wanting financially. It wasn't the only change.

In 1973, Ecclestone moved into a sumptuous apartment on London's Albert Embankment that was said to be worth £500,000 – a staggering sum at the time. The penthouse in Alembic House, now known as

Peninsula Heights, had 25ft-high plate-glass windows that commanded a panoramic view across the Thames to the House of Commons and the Tate Gallery. Ecclestone bought it from John Barry, who composed the music to his beloved Bond movies. The penthouse itself even appeared in some movies, including *The Italian Job*, though Ecclestone refurbished it to his precise specification after moving in.

Tuana Tan joined him and kitted out the apartment to suit his tastes. She hung paintings on the walls from Italian artist Amedeo Modigliani, installed hand-made Italian furniture and displayed Ecclestone's eclectic sculpture collection. It stretches from statues of snowmen and a decorative Turkish cart to surreal silver skeletons and carved owls, which are his favourite animal. In a quirk that could only apply to a billionaire or a Bond villain, Ecclestone also owns one of the world's largest collections of *netsukes* – finely carved miniature Japanese sculptures.

For decades, right up until the pandemic, he bolstered his bizarre collection by going to Lots Road auctions in Chelsea every Sunday. Even if he walked away empty-handed, Ecclestone saw it as honing his bargaining skills with some of the sharpest minds in the business. It also kept his feet on the ground so that even when he was doing deals worth billions he still didn't lose his sense of value.

Ecclestone might not like to admit it, but he is a control freak. So much so that when he was in charge of F1 he personally selected the crockery given to guests in its corporate hospitality outfit and hired staff for the business magazine he owned. Until 2010, when he was aged 80, he even drove himself to meetings in his Toyota people carrier and walked down busy London streets with no bodyguards despite being instantly recognisable.

On one occasion we travelled with him to an interview and parked in the middle of a residential district a five-minute walk from our destination, the Armani Caffe. No sooner had we got out than Ecclestone had stopped to talk with a seemingly random electrician waiting by his van. 'He works for us,' Ecclestone explained.

When we walked down London's posh Brompton Road with him on the way back to the car, a cigar-chomping dignitary wearing a lapel pin of the Iraqi flag stopped Ecclestone and thrust his business card into his hand. 'I am one of the admirers of Formula One and we wish that one day you make it to Iraq,' he exclaimed, before Ecclestone thanked him and walked on as if nothing had happened.

Ecclestone has a nippy driving style but it was brought to an abrupt halt in 2010 when he was mugged getting out of his car on his way home after a trip to a restaurant for dinner with Fabiana. Around £200,000 of jewellery was taken, including Ecclestone's fancy watch. Ever the salesman, his reaction was to send a photograph of his bruised face to F1 sponsor Hublot so that they could use it for free in an advert complete with the words, 'See what people will do for a Hublot.' As always, Ecclestone had the final laugh as the watch that was stolen was not even a Hublot – it was a Rolex.

Of course, the gang of muggers was apprehended and given a combined 53 years in jail. Nevertheless, it reminded Ecclestone of his frailty and since then a chauffeur has driven him around – usually in a Mercedes or Land Rover with tinted windows. It was symptomatic of Ecclestone's pragmatic approach to business.

When he was in F1's driving seat he famously left the track just after the first lap of a Grand Prix. It is often said about F1 that when the racing starts, the business stops, so it makes sense that the boss of the company doesn't need to be there. Also, the first corner of the first lap is a magnet for accidents in F1, as the cars make a mad dash towards it jockeying for position. If they all emerged safely Ecclestone was safe in the knowledge that the risk was dramatically reduced for the rest of the race. Crucially, while everyone at the circuit had their eyes glued to the action on track, the roads would be empty, which enabled Ecclestone to exit without waiting in a queue. Often he was back at home by the time his staff were still trying to get out of the venue. Time is money, as Ecclestone knows all too well, and everything he does revolves around maximising it.

As such, it wasn't long before Ecclestone was tempted back to F1 after the death of Stuart Lewis-Evans. Roy Salvadori, who had raced one of the Connaughts and now managed the Cooper F1 team, invited him to the 1965 Mexican Grand Prix where he met Jochen Rindt. Ecclestone was instantly fascinated by the dashing Austrian driver's streak of arrogance.

The two became inseparable and flew to European races together on a Beagle aeroplane that Ecclestone had bought at auction after the manufacturer had gone bust. Rindt often visited Ecclestone at his home and walked his bulldog, Oddjob, named after the Bond baddie. When the

Austrian driver married Nina, Ecclestone and Tuana Tan even accompanied them on their honeymoon.

By the time Rindt switched from Brabham to Lotus in 1969, he wasn't in top gear, having finished 12th the previous year. Ecclestone's magic got him the Lotus seat, but it was far from a dream ticket. He retired from the season-opener in South Africa with a broken fuel pump and was even less lucky at the next race.

Chapman had been experimenting with aerodynamic configurations and settled on a design where the wings of the Lotus were positioned five feet above track level on thin struts, more than a foot taller than the ones on rival cars. On the ninth lap at the fast Montjuic circuit, the rear wing of the car driven by Rindt's team-mate Graham Hill deformed, pitching him into the barriers. Hill stood at the side of the track and tried to warn Rindt of the danger, but the Austrian's wing collapsed in exactly the same spot and he crashed into the wreckage of the other Lotus, flipping his car upside-down.

Rindt was taken to hospital with concussion and a broken nose, injuries that would force him to miss the Monaco Grand Prix. When he came round he was furious. He wrote an open letter to the motorsport press, arguing that 'F1 racing is meant to be a serious business and not a hot rod show. Wings are dangerous, first to the drivers, second to the spectators.'

The FIA banned the tall wings and as a result Chapman refused to speak to Rindt except through Ecclestone. Nina Rindt recalled them 'arguing, arguing and arguing, and nothing else'. Such was the lack of reliability of the Lotus that it wasn't until the penultimate race of the season at Watkins Glen in upstate New York that Rindt won his first Grand Prix, taking home F1's then-largest prize pot of $50,000. However, the celebration was marred by Hill suffering severe leg injuries in a crash. Rindt finished the season in fourth, a long way off the world championship that Ecclestone wanted him to win in order to kick-start their clothing line. With Rindt's dreams of superstardom in tatters, Ecclestone sought a solution. Rindt introduced him to Brabham's designer Ron Tauranac, who was due to take over the eponymous team when Jack Brabham retired at the end of the 1970 season. Rindt suggested that Ecclestone could become a partner in Brabham but Tauranac was hesitant.

In the end, the Austrian decided to stay put at Lotus when Chapman offered him and Ecclestone the chance to also run a

Lotus-supported Formula Two team, which became known as Jochen Rindt Racing.

It soon proved to be a bad decision. Rindt retired from the first two races of the 1970 F1 season and after his brake discs shattered in Spain he stormed into the pits, shouting at Chapman that he was 'never going to get into that bloody car again'. But Chapman turned on his charm and Rindt was back in the car for Monaco, which he won. Two races later he was on the top step of the podium again in Zandvoort, but the race was tainted by the death of his close friend Piers Courage who drove for Frank Williams Racing, the forerunner to the Williams team.

Courage's accident came just a few weeks after McLaren team founder Bruce McLaren had been killed in a sportscar testing incident. Unnerved, Rindt was determined to quit racing at the end of the year to set up his businesses with Ecclestone. He scored another three victories in a row, which meant that by September, when F1 headed to Italy, he was favourite to win the title.

But their dreams were about to come abruptly down to earth. During Saturday morning practice at the Italian Grand Prix, Rindt's Lotus suffered a mechanical failure. His car careened into the barriers and fell apart on impact. Rindt died within a few seconds of the accident from a ruptured artery, but to prevent the race from being cancelled he was not declared dead until he reached hospital later.

With no television feed, Ecclestone and the Lotus team were unaware that anything had happened until cars stopped coming past the pits and drivers reported back that Rindt had had a big accident. Sensing that something was terribly wrong, Ecclestone ran down the track and burst through the police cordon to get to his friend, but it was too late. He said that Rindt's body had been transferred to the back of 'what people I suppose wanted to describe as an ambulance'. There was nothing Ecclestone could do but collect his helmet and trudge back to the pits. He drove Nina to the hospital, where they met Chapman, who then left for the airport, fearing the automatic arrest of senior team personnel that often occurred after racing accidents in Italy. Ecclestone was left to pick up the pieces.

Devastated and angry, he took control of the chaotic aftermath of the accident, including tasking 21-year-old Lotus mechanic Herbie Blash with driving Rindt's road car and belongings back to the family home in Switzerland. Meanwhile, the wrecked Lotus was seized by police for the start of an official investigation which would last for six years before eventually clearing Chapman.

Rindt was on top of the standings at the time of his death and his lead proved unassailable. He became F1's first, and so far only, posthumous champion. 'Better he wasn't world champion and he was still with us,' Ecclestone remarked in an episode of *Lucky*.

Rindt's death affected Ecclestone even more than Lewis-Evans's had done. Not only had he lost a close friend, but their business plans were in tatters. Within a few weeks of the tragic accident, he was afflicted with severe flu-like symptoms that confined the businessman to bed. A doctor concluded that it was caused by stress. Ecclestone considered walking away from motorsport again, and spent time developing his property and newly established auctions businesses. But this time he was too much in love with the sport to simply walk away.

In February 1971, Frank Williams was surprised to encounter Ecclestone at an F2 race in Bogota, Colombia, where Jochen Rindt Racing was fielding cars. 'You had to be keen to travel all the way to South America in those days,' Williams observed. But Ecclestone was set on a bigger prize. 'Although Jochen's death was a big, big loss to me, it wasn't going to finish me in Formula One,' he later remarked.

A few months after that, Ecclestone was back at the Monaco Grand Prix, observing proceedings from a yacht in the harbour. One of his guests that weekend was Ron Tauranac, who was struggling following Jack Brabham's retirement. The team hadn't won a race since the start of the previous season and had yet to score any points in 1971. Tauranac later admitted to *Motor Sport* magazine that the financial side of running a team was beyond him. 'I was hopeless,' he said. 'I wasn't going to dress up in a suit and go into London trying to get sponsorship. I just wanted to design cars.'

On a handshake, Tauranac agreed to sell Brabham to Ecclestone for the value of its assets, with the Australian staying on as joint managing director. While Tauranac went away to calculate the team's value, Ecclestone was distracted by an issue with his non-motorsport interests. He had sold Compton & Ecclestone in 1959 and by early 1960 the company was in trouble. When the new owners approached him for help, Ecclestone agreed to pay off its £25,000 overdraft in exchange for a debenture on its assets. Within a few months he had called in an administrator to shut the company down. The administrator found that Compton & Ecclestone was owed £6,134 by its customers, but its debts included £9,700 in unpaid tax owed to HM Revenue & Customs (HMRC), then known as the Inland Revenue.

Ecclestone decided at this stage that he didn't want to close the company after all. He discharged the administrator with a statement indemnifying its representative of all liabilities. The following day Compton & Ecclestone's directors agreed to transfer to Ecclestone the showroom's leasehold, its motorcycles, and the right to the £6,134 in exchange for him waiving the £25,000 he was owed.

A month later the company was shut down again under petition from two of its creditors, although this time it had little left in the way of assets to sell to fund any payments. The complex series of manoeuvres had left the tax unpaid and HMRC with no way of recovering the money from the company.

In 1971 Ecclestone and the administrator were taken to court to recover the £9,700 plus interest and costs. Ecclestone denied that there had been any deliberate trickery but declined to appear in court, despite not normally being one to shy away from a battle.

'The documents themselves and the admissions made out of court cry out for an explanation . . . and [Ecclestone] does not condescend to give one,' said the judge, adding that the situation was 'altogether extraordinary'. Ruling that Ecclestone had breached company law, the court ordered him to pay the £9,700. Ecclestone had no trouble paying it as he was already a man of many means. So much so indeed that in 1971 he founded Pentbridge Properties to manage his burgeoning UK property portfolio.

One of Pentbridge's first deals involved buying 26 acres of woodland behind Ecclestone's home in Farnborough Park. The acquisition was funded with a £95,000 loan from a company called Rochelle in the offshore tax haven of Guernsey – hardly the first port of call for most UK property purchasers. In fact, Rochelle's UK office address was given as 25 Harley Street, London, the same as Pentbridge Properties, as well as that of its auditors. Strangely, Rochelle didn't ensure that it got its money back and by the time that it went into voluntary liquidation in 1980 the loan had yet to be repaid.

The land purchase was far from Ecclestone's only business venture in 1971. Flush with profits from his hire-purchase company Arvin Securities, which had expanded to become involved with commercial properties, he closed the deal to buy Brabham in October 1971. Tauranac had valued the team's assets at £130,000, but at the last moment Ecclestone only offered him £100,000. Flustered and worried that he would lose the money that was on the table, Tauranac agreed, although he would later realise that he had forgotten to include in his calculation a sum of £50,000 in the bank, meaning that he had significantly undervalued the team's assets. 'I gave it away, really,' he later remarked.

Ecclestone, accompanied by ex-Lotus mechanic Herbie Blash, turned up at the Brabham factory in Weylock Works, Surrey, to introduce himself as the new owner. Standing on a wooden box to address the mechanics, he asked them what they thought needed to be improved.

Brabham was outmoded, like Britain itself in the early 1970s when recession gripped the country. Ecclestone recognised this and slashed the team's headcount in a matter of days. He found that junior draughtsman Gordon Murray was about to quit as he had been offered a job designing a Le Mans car. Ecclestone sacked the team's other four designers, making Murray the head of the department by default. He promised the young, long-haired South African that he would have total control over the design of the new car, providing that he didn't use anything of the previous design.

Ecclestone wasn't the only factor in the reduced headcount. Herbie Blash lasted only a morning before he walked out after being yelled at by Tauranac. And it was only a matter of time before Tauranac himself would also get the chop. When the Australian returned from his annual Christmas skiing holiday he found that Ecclestone had installed motorcycle specialist Colin Seeley in his place. Tauranac persisted doing work for the team for a little while longer, but eventually accepted that it no longer belonged to him, so he cleared his desk. Blash returned immediately and was appointed the team manager by Ecclestone, who was collecting a remarkable array of talent. Blash later became a senior advisor to the FIA's race director, a role that he maintains to this day. For years his boss was the FIA's race director Charlie Whiting, who joined Brabham as a mechanic in 1978 and went on to become one of Ecclestone's most trusted allies. Mechanic Nick Goozée later became managing director of Penske racing cars, while another mechanic, Gary Anderson, became a race-winning designer at the Jordan and Stewart F1 teams. Murray went on to design F1 cars that won fifty-six races, five drivers' championships and three constructors' championships. As if that wasn't enough, he was also the man behind the design of the McLaren F1, touted by many as the greatest road car of all time.

And even Brabham's gofer, Tavo Hellmund, ended up making an impact on F1. The American teenager's father Gustavo Hellmund-Rosas was good friends with Ecclestone and, as president of the Mexican Grand Prix organising committee, helped him to steer the country's Grand Prix back to the F1 calendar in 1986 after a 16-year absence. Tavo would follow in his footsteps by bringing the race back to the F1 calendar in 2015 after doing the same with the United States Grand Prix three years earlier.

With so much new talent under its bonnet, Brabham began to tick over nicely. Ecclestone swept the team clean, literally as well as figuratively. Future McLaren boss Ron Dennis arrived at the factory one Saturday to pick up some parts he had ordered and found Ecclestone in jeans and a T-shirt cleaning the building himself. Ecclestone described the factory as 'a bit untidy. Nobody quite knew where everything was and nobody was particularly doing one job. There was a bit of a muddle . . . Everything was upside down.'

Despite this frugality, Ecclestone was willing to spend money where it was needed. When Murray asked for hundreds of pounds to buy a special trolley to hold the mechanics' equipment, Ecclestone signed it off without hesitation as it would keep the factory tidy. Mechanic Kerry Adams recalled that, 'Despite what people say about his ruthlessness, whatever you wanted you would get it if it was going to make the car more competitive, never any question about that. If you couldn't get it, he'd organise it.'

The employees, however, had to be careful to meet his standards. Ecclestone reportedly once returned to the workshop to find that his mechanics had left it untidy, so he ripped the telephone off the wall to get their attention before lining them up and telling them that if it happened again, he would close the factory down immediately. 'And if you doubt me, remember I am not a rational man,' he warned.

Perfection didn't come cheap for Brabham, and Ecclestone reportedly subsidised the team to the tune of $200,000 a year. Tauranac's reluctance to get involved with the commercial aspects meant that the team had few sponsors, although this gave Ecclestone the tidiness of a 'nice, white car'. It didn't stay that way, however, as he inherited a sponsor-friendly driver line-up in the form of Graham Hill and well-funded Argentinian rookie, Carlos Reutemann.

Buying the team was the biggest gamble of Ecclestone's career up to that point. A month after the acquisition he told the *Daily Express* that 'this move is first and foremost a business venture with the objective of selling the finest racing cars available'.

For a used-car dealer, the strategy of making money from an F1 team by focusing on the sale of customer cars made sense, but in the end it would not be the way that Ecclestone made his fortune. Times were changing faster and more drastically than even he had anticipated. The privateer customers were soon to disappear from the sport, and Ecclestone himself would play a major part in their demise.

He turned his attention fully to F1 and not just because he saw the potential in Brabham. In 1973, the UK introduced value added tax (VAT), which would have meant that Ecclestone had to increase his prices and pay the difference to the taxman. Instead, he closed the door to his dealership empire. 'I thought, I don't want to be a tax collector so I'd better get out,' he explained. As the owner of one of the most prestigious teams on the grid, Ecclestone had become a power player in F1. Team ownership gave him entry to an elite club. As he told us, 'The secret to my success is bloody hard work and a bit of luck.' His career had already seen plenty of both by the 1970s but the best was yet to come. The right to exploit F1 commercially was the true grand prize, and within weeks of getting the keys to Brabham, Ecclestone took the first steps that eventually transformed F1 into a multi-billion–dollar global empire.

3

THE SNOWBALL EFFECT

For a sport so closely associated with glitz and glamour, F1 has held meetings in some mundane and unmemorable locations. Ecclestone's induction into the teams' organisation was one of them.

Initially called the Formula 1 Constructors' Association (F1CA), it usually met in the rather drab surroundings of the former Excelsior hotel at Heathrow Airport. The team bosses who gathered there on a cold and rainy day in December 1971 thought that the meeting wouldn't be any different to usual. London was under the threat of power cuts caused by an imminent miners' strike and unemployment was at a 40-year high, casting a depressive atmosphere over the proceedings. Most of the bosses could barely wait to get back to their factories to focus on the more important business of winning.

When Ecclestone arrived for his first ever F1CA meeting he was ushered into an unassuming double room to await his counterparts. F1CA's budget did not stretch to a meeting room, a suite, or even room service. As the other team representatives trickled in, Ecclestone kept a low profile and busied himself pouring tea, leaving the others to grumble about the current state of F1. Engine supplier Alfa Romeo had pulled out over the winter and Matra had announced it would only be fielding a single car to save money in the upcoming season. To make matters worse, a potentially lucrative new Grand Prix scheduled for April on the outskirts of Los Angeles had hit a dead end. Times were hard and many of the team representatives felt they had more important things to do than sit through a list of mostly trivial logistical issues.

No one present, except perhaps Ecclestone himself, could have imagined that they were about to witness one of the most pivotal meetings in the history of F1. At the time, F1CA was little more than a loose grouping of mostly mid-level team managers who met at regular intervals to discuss the arrangements for shipping their cars to races. The group had been founded in 1964 by the bosses of Lotus, Cooper, BRM and Brabham, who thought it would be useful to have a body to represent the *garagistes'* interests to the race promoters, as they often favoured flashier squads such as Ferrari. However, it only interfered in F1 politics sporadically as it was difficult to get the warring teams to agree on a strategy to benefit everyone.

Over the years, the other teams had joined as well, even Ferrari, largely because F1CA combined the teams' shipping to races in order to get good-value freight deals. They each paid a paltry £15 ($37) a year for membership to fund the association's operations, which were run by former Lotus team manager Andrew Ferguson from his cottage on the grounds of Colin Chapman's mansion in Norfolk. To make it easy for all the teams to attend, meetings usually took place either at Heathrow or at races.

For the most part, the team owners did not take F1CA seriously. Enzo Ferrari and the bosses of the other continental teams did not attend meetings in person. Chapman was another absentee, sending senior Lotus personnel while he focused on making his cars go faster. In Ecclestone's words, it 'wasn't a constructors' association at all. It was a group of guys that ran Formula One teams that got together to make some complaints wherever they could.'

So, in 1971, F1CA was barely a player in F1, let alone on the global stage. It was certainly not an organisation that anyone would expect to evolve into one of the most powerful entities in world sport.

On that December day at Heathrow, however, F1CA's fortunes reached a crossroads. As F1's newest team boss, Ecclestone was an unknown entity to many of the personalities present. As they bickered among themselves, he kept quiet and took note of their grievances. His presence was only felt at the end of the meeting when he ceremoniously placed a sealed envelope in front of each team representative and asked them to take a few moments to read through the contents.

The envelopes contained quotations for freight and travel costs to Grands Prix through a special deal that Ecclestone had negotiated with transport company Cazaly Mills. The deal would save as much as $11,250 per car on the long-haul part of the season.

The teams were bowled over but were concerned they might lose the deal as F1CA had no money spare to pay Ecclestone for his efforts. With a shrug of his shoulders, Ecclestone said he would arrange it for 2 per cent of the start and prize money, amounting to a mere $200 at some of the races.

The teams accepted – even Ferrari – without hesitation. As sponsorship money flowed into the sport, and more globally recognised brands such as Marlboro and Elf began to sponsor the likes of BRM and Tyrrell, the meagre amount generated from prize money was no longer a major part of teams' budgets so they could afford to lose a sliver of it.

Ecclestone went off and finalised the arrangements with the Cazaly Mills representative, Alan Woollard, who in years to come he would appoint as F1's logistics director. The deal may have been worth more to Ecclestone than just the share of the prize money. According to his biographer Terry Lovell, Ecclestone also received a 'lucrative percentage' from Cazaly Mills for bringing it the business. Without fanfare and virtually unnoticed, Ecclestone had taken his first step on the road to gaining control of F1. After his first FICA meeting he had gained the trust, support and admiration of the other teams as well as a share of the proceeds. It was a small change that would quickly snowball and have major ramifications for F1. Of everyone present at that meeting, perhaps only one other person had any inkling of what the teams had unleashed.

Max Mosley's background was in stark contrast to Ecclestone's. His father was the infamous extreme right-wing politician, Sir Oswald Mosley, while his mother Diana was one of the Mitford sisters, a family of glamorous aristocratic socialites who were rarely out of the headlines in inter-war Britain. The six sisters' connections were impeccable. Diana's first husband was a member of the Guinness brewing family, while another sister, Deborah, became Duchess of Devonshire, and Nancy was a famous society novelist.

However, Oswald's political connections led to a dramatic fall from grace for the Mosley family. Oswald had served as both a Conservative and Labour politician before setting up his own party, the British Union of Fascists, in 1932. Four years later it was involved in a series of bloody skirmishes in east London known as the Battle of Cable Street.

Just two days afterwards, on 6 October 1936, Oswald and Diana secretly wed in Nazi propaganda chief Joseph Goebbels' drawing room, with Adolf Hitler as a witness. Shortly after Max was born in 1940 the couple was incarcerated by Winston Churchill's government as Britain sought to monitor Nazi sympathisers during the early stages of World

War Two. Neither was released until Max was three years old. The family subsequently settled in Europe and Max was schooled in France and Germany before returning to the UK, where he breezed a physics degree from Oxford University. Following a visit to nearby Silverstone, he began to race in his spare time, scoring a number of victories in the grass-roots Clubmans sports car category in the mid-1960s.

In his twenties, Max had supported his father's postwar Union Movement and was arrested in 1962 after a punch-up with anti-fascists in east London while his father was out canvassing. He later distanced himself from his father's policies but his actions in the early days dashed his hopes of pursuing a career in politics, so he turned to law instead. A supremely skilled and debonair smooth-talker, Max qualified as a barrister but soon became disillusioned with what he anticipated would be a dull and predictable life. Instead, like Ecclestone, he turned his hobby into his career.

Becoming a racing driver seemed far more thrilling than law and enabled him to make his mark in an arena which was far from his fascist upper-class upbringing. Mosley was relieved to find that few people in motor racing had heard of his family. In fact, a rival driver initially assumed that he must be related to Alf Moseley, a wealthy coachbuilder, which amused and delighted Max no end.

Between 1966 and 1967 Max competed in more than 40 races, winning 12 and setting several class lap records. In 1968 he entered four rounds of the European F2 Championship but lost his nerve after two big shunts and the death of Jim Clark. He quit driving altogether the following season and co-founded an F1 team with four colleagues. Called March Engineering, its name was an acronym of the initials of its four founders – Mosley, Alan Rees, Graham Coaker and Robin Herd. Each had a specific area of expertise, with Mosley responsible for the legal and commercial side of the team.

March ambitiously entered F1 in 1970 and finished third in the championship. But Mosley was less than impressed with what he found at F1CA. 'The F1 establishment took me along to one of their negotiations with the organisers because I was a lawyer and they thought that might be useful,' he told *Motor Sport* in 1986. 'I could not believe that a major international sport could be conducted like that. Everybody went, because nobody trusted anybody else, and the level of negotiation was not impressive.'

Mosley said that when Ecclestone joined F1CA, he 'realised in the first few minutes that here was someone of outstanding ability' and 'pretty soon we formed an alliance'. It wasn't just any old alliance.

Within a matter of years Mosley and Ecclestone became the most powerful double act in motorsport and completely transformed F1. Mosley was the silk glove to Ecclestone's iron gauntlet, and they used their unlikely friendship to great effect.

In only Ecclestone's second F1CA meeting, the Brabham boss pointed out to the other team representatives how much easier it would be if instead of each team negotiating prize money individually with the promoters, there was one point of contact representing all of them. The others agreed, but none of them was willing to take on what was a lot of hassle for seemingly little reward.

Ecclestone seemed reluctant to do it himself, until Mosley stepped in to suggest that his share of the prize money could be increased to 8 per cent to reward his efforts. The teams enthusiastically agreed, glad to be rid of the onerous task. They weren't envious of Ecclestone's role. Quite the opposite, in fact. Peter Warr, competitions manager of Team Lotus, remarked, 'If someone had asked me to go and negotiate with twelve or fourteen different race organisers *and* run Team Lotus, I would have said forget it.' But Ecclestone had his eye on the bigger picture and, using his business acumen, he had calculated exactly how much the teams were missing out on.

His first opportunity to negotiate with a race promoter came in March 1972. In hope of joining the calendar the following year, the Interlagos circuit in São Paulo was keen to host a non-championship Brazilian Grand Prix. Ecclestone secured a significant prize fund, but the teams had little experience dealing with Brazilian companies and there were concerns about the race's ability to pay. Strict local currency regulations meant there was not time for the promoter, local broadcaster Rede Globo, to send payment in advance and the teams did not want to spend money freighting their cars to South America only to receive nothing in return.

Ecclestone dispatched Mosley to Rio to meet Globo while the teams waited at their bases in Europe for the go-ahead. Mosley found that, contrary to expectations, the broadcaster was a credible major company and 'entirely serious'. However, Globo could do nothing to speed up the receipt of the prize money dollars from its bank. Mosley took a gamble

and told the teams to fly anyway. The race was a success and coinciden-
tally Ecclestone and Mosley were the biggest beneficiaries, as two
Brabhams and a March made up the top three.

It was only a matter of weeks before Ecclestone and Mosley had to
save the day again. There had been controversy at the previous year's
Monaco Grand Prix when the promoter, the Automobile Club de
Monaco (ACM), had decided to restrict the grid to just 18 cars. This led
to it cutting the five slowest cars, including the Ferrari of Mario Andretti
who was second in the championship. Anxious to avoid a repeat of this
the following year, Ecclestone and Mosley met with the ACM's new
young president, Michel Boeri, at the 1972 Spanish Grand Prix and
persuaded him to accept a 25-car limit.

However, when the teams arrived in Monaco they were told that the
limit had been reduced to 22 cars with the agreement of the CSI, the
sporting division of the FIA that regulated Formula One and other
motorsports. Usually in this type of situation, the teams would each look
after their own interests and support would be quickly whittled down by
the CSI making deals with individual entrants. On this occasion
Ecclestone and Mosley insisted that the teams stood united and they
gathered in the underground car park that was used as the pits and refused
to come out for practice until the 25-car grid was confirmed.

With the spectators growing restless, the ACM sent the local police to
threaten the teams that if they didn't participate their cars would be
impounded and they would be sued for damages. Ecclestone made a
stand. 'I said to get Graham [Hill]'s car out and I'll get in the car and
drive it out of here and show people we are leaving. I couldn't reach the
pedals and charged up the ramp to leave the garage and saw the policeman in front of me. I didn't manage to stop and ran the policeman over.
And then suddenly we had a lot more police arrive and threaten I was
going to be arrested, taken away on the spot. So we said, "Arrest us all."'

At this point, Boeri turned up expecting that the teams would have
crumbled and instead found them more united than ever. As fans started
to boo, he decided that the ACM was willing to compromise but
explained that he could not overturn the limit as it had been set by the
CSI. This confirmed the teams' suspicions that the episode was an
attempt by the CSI to assert its control. They held firm, refusing to prac-
tise until the CSI signed an agreement that Mosley had written resting
on the roof of a parked car. Eventually the ACM managed to locate an

elderly CSI representative who was willing to sign the document and the event went ahead with 25 cars.

It was the first time that the true strength of the teams had been demonstrated and it was a revelation to them. Their unity was bolstered again when FiCA got hold of the FIA's financial records and found out just how much money the governing body was making from the sport.

It showed that the CSI charged $5,000 to list a race on the F1 calendar, generating significant profits for the FIA. It also revealed that the races were hugely profitable businesses, making hundreds of thousands of dollars in revenue. Ecclestone saw dollar signs. The strong revenue stream flowing into the races meant they could afford to pay more prize money, which in turn would increase Ecclestone's take.

It is not clear if he knew or guessed this when he offered his services for a percentage of the prize fund. However, the discovery meant that the teams were even more firmly behind him than before.

'Bernie came down from heaven,' said Frank Williams, who was loaned money by Ecclestone on numerous occasions in order to keep his privateer team going. McLaren team principal Teddy Mayer commented that Ecclestone 'was very good at it, he really was. And he was brave. He would take risks personally that nobody else in FiCA wanted to even get near.' He added that Colin Chapman 'believed passionately in what FiCA was trying to do, which was to gain control'.

Not every team was entirely on Ecclestone's side. While technically a FiCA member, Ferrari remained somewhat uninvolved. Meetings often got heated. On one occasion Ken Tyrrell, boss of his eponymous F1 team, jumped on a table to berate Ecclestone even though he already stood almost a foot taller than him. In response, Ecclestone calmly threatened to throw him out of the window.

Despite these reservations, it is no surprise that Ecclestone's skills seemed heaven sent. He had soon negotiated the prize fund up to an average of $210,000 per race from as little as $10,000 at some of them. This generated $3.2m a year for the teams and $252,000 for himself, even before Brabham's share was taken into account. Ecclestone also demanded that FiCA distributed the money instead of the race organisers or the CSI. This put a stop to a practice where organisers would pay big money to local favourites and almost nothing to everyone else.

Ecclestone appointed former Red Arrows manager Peter Macintosh to replace Andrew Ferguson as FiCA's administrator, and he didn't stop there. He also put his secretary Ann Jones in charge of counting the prize money and dividing it among the competitors. This was done according to an arcane formula devised by the teams, which rewarded both past and current performance as well as consistent attendance at Grands Prix. Teams that had been racing for less than a year were not allowed a share of the money. In return, Ecclestone guaranteed that at least 18 cars would turn up to each race or the fee would be reduced by half. Any team that failed to attend had its benefits docked. It formed the foundation of the prize money payment structure that is still in place today.

Not everyone was happy with Ecclestone's actions. The CSI was furious. Its national member clubs were both alarmed at losing power to the teams and frustrated with the complaints bombarding them from the embattled promoters they represented.

Until Ecclestone came along, F1's business model had been heavily weighted in favour of the promoters and the FIA. The individual promoters had control of most of F1's commercial rights — at this stage, principally the money paid by TV channels and trackside advertisers — as well as income from ticket sales. There was no central organisation of the rights and no formal agreement to confer the rights on the promoters. The FIA benefited by requiring the promoters to pay it a fee to be listed on the calendar. By squeezing the promoters for more prize money, Ecclestone was not only milking their cash cow, he was also jeopardising their ability to pay the FIA high calendar fees.

In November 1972 the CSI set up an organisation called Grand Prix International, headed by Dutch administrator Henri Treu, to represent the promoters against the teams. Treu had been CSI secretary general just six months earlier and was an autocratic and confrontational character. This may be why the CSI thought he was the perfect choice to take on Ecclestone.

Treu's initial salvo was to try to destroy the unity of the teams and he started with Ferrari. As the most prestigious and oldest team, and the one most at odds with the *garagistes*, Ferrari was the obvious weak link. However, Enzo Ferrari saw nothing in Treu's offer that could counter F1CA's hand of cheap freight and increased prize money.

After failing to attract existing teams, Treu's thoughts turned to potential new entrants, particularly ones who might have a gripe with Ecclestone.

Since joining Brabham, Graham Hill had not been able to match his past glories. He had only managed a handful of points finishes and his relationship with Ecclestone had soured. Hill had scored only one more point than his rookie team-mate Carlos Reutemann in 1972.

With Treu's encouragement, Hill launched his own team backed by a $250,000 three-year title sponsorship deal from Embassy tobacco. Treu immediately announced that the new Embassy Racing was the first team to sign up to Grand Prix International's commercial offering. However, Hill's new team was not a big enough name to worry the FICA members and none of them jumped ship. Desperate, Treu petitioned the FIA to change the regulations to allow Formula Two and Formula 5000 teams to compete in Grands Prix, but Ecclestone successfully argued that any such races could not qualify as rounds of the Formula One world championship. Lacking support, Grand Prix International collapsed and Ecclestone's power grew further.

By 1973, prize money had risen to $270,000 for long-haul races such as South Africa, Argentina and the inaugural world championship round in Brazil. Ecclestone and Mosley negotiated directly with the military junta for the Buenos Aires race, meeting stern, uniformed officials at Heathrow to confirm the payment. In June that year Ecclestone also secured a Grand Prix in Sweden through royal heir Prince Bertil, who persuaded electronics firm Hitachi, a major employer in the country, to come onboard as a sponsor.

It wasn't just about prize money. Race weekends were standardised to a maximum of three days of on-track action, meaning that the teams no longer had to foot extra accommodation costs on the whim of the promoter, while qualifying was fixed at two one-hour sessions. Promoters were required to provide tarmacked zones for the teams' transporters near the garages, which had to be fully supplied with water and electricity.

In return FICA conceded that there would be a limit on entries, although it was not quite the sacrifice it appeared. As the FICA teams were automatically included in the entry quota it meant there was no space for most of the smaller part-time privateer entrants. Only the larger FICA-affiliated privateers continued, such as Frank Williams, and the smaller entries were effectively ejected from F1.

'In the old days the FICA's role was to kick these lazy amateur organisers into the 1970s and 1980s and 1990s,' Ecclestone told the *Telegraph* in

1992. 'We kicked them into becoming professionals and running their races efficiently to make money so they could pay.'

The situation was also improving at Brabham. In 1974, Reutemann took the chequered flag in South Africa at the wheel of Gordon Murray's latest design, then won again in Austria and Watkins Glen. 'We had pole position, we had fastest lap, we won the race,' Blash recalled to Susan Watkins. 'And Bernie turned round to me and gave me a bollocking because there were some fingerprints on the car.' The following year he had even more reason for it to look immaculate as Brabham debuted its iconic red, white and blue Martini livery.

Race-winning team principal was not the only new role that Ecclestone took on. After the Spa-Francorchamps track was dropped in 1971 on safety grounds, the decision was made to diplomatically alternate the Belgian Grand Prix between Dutch-speaking Zolder and French-speaking Nivelles.

However, ahead of the 1974 race, the organisation that ran the Nivelles circuit was declared bankrupt. It appeared to be the end of the road for the Belgian Grand Prix there as local businessmen had alternative uses in mind for the track near Brussels, and the noise lobby was also exerting pressure.

At the time, F1 races were ad hoc affairs. Race organisers negotiated with local television companies to televise each Grand Prix individually and the TV companies then sold the race on to other broadcasters around the world. The revenues from ticket sales and trackside advertising were received by the race organisers and paid out to the teams as prize money and start money. It was a pittance, so teams often skipped the races where they didn't stand a chance of winning. Races could be cancelled at the last minute if not enough teams turned up, so television stations refused to broadcast them.

Ecclestone saw tremendous potential for car manufacturers and sponsors to use F1 races as promotional platforms and he knew that TV coverage was the key to this. However, first he had to ensure that all of the races were on a solid footing, and he had a personal motivation for doing so. If the races were cancelled then Brabham couldn't win them and pocket the prize money. Likewise, Ecclestone wouldn't get his share of the prize money paid to Brabham's rivals. It explains why Ecclestone took it upon himself to travel to Brussels in a bid to get the Belgian Grand Prix back on track when the race hit the skids in 1974.

He met with representatives from Marlboro and oil company Texaco but, although they already backed the Belgian Grand Prix, it was not enough. Ecclestone persuaded the Benelux boss of audio-visual equipment manufacturer Bang & Olufsen to join them. He had a vested interest as his son – the fittingly named Bernard de Dryver – was a leading junior racer.

Funding from the three brands just about covered the prize money and the start money but then came the expenses of running the race. Ecclestone calculated that if costs didn't balloon and the race was popular enough it should be able to turn a profit on the tickets plus the proceeds of any advertising and programme sales. He asked his fellow team owners to share the risk and split the reward but they refused. So he took his greatest gamble yet and personally guaranteed both the start money and the prize money and promoted the race himself. As he later explained to *Autosport* magazine, 'Most of [the team bosses] had the attitude, "We want to race, we don't want to be involved in selling tickets to the public or anything like that." When I took things over I offered to do everything for the teams, and run everything, and also more or less support them and make sure they got paid properly. And I was going to take 30 per cent of the risk, but they didn't want to do it. We got stuck with adopting the position of promoter, collecting what money we could and paying out the teams.'

Against the odds, the 1974 Belgian Grand Prix was a success. More than 70,000 spectators turned up and the sponsors got unprecedented exposure. In those dim and distant days, long before the time of online ticket sales, Ecclestone reportedly even collected the cash in a bag and walked it to the nearest bank. His gamble to guarantee all the money had paid off handsomely and, perhaps most importantly, it gave him insight into the business model of a Grand Prix. Over the coming years he also became the promoter of the races in Austria, Germany, the Netherlands, Hungary and France.

By then FICA had expanded its remit again by taking control of passes to the paddock with another Ecclestone sleight of hand. F1's nerve centre at the races, the paddock is an oblong tarmac space between the teams' motorhomes and their transporters that back up to the pit garage rear doors. The area was historically a working environment for team staff, but Ecclestone would make it one of the most sought-after places in world sport.

The motorhomes are where team bosses discuss race strategy and drivers eat, drink and wind down. They are essentially the drivers' locker rooms and today passes to the paddock can cost as much as £8,000 per person at some races. In itself this adds to the allure and exclusivity of the paddock. As interest in F1 accelerated so too did the desire for celebrities and VIPs to be seen at the races – and the paddock is the place to find them.

The crossroads came at the Italian Grand Prix in September 1974. Prior to that, paddock passes had been issued by the promoters, who had a tendency to hand them to their friends, family and associates. However, everyone onboard the F1CA charter flight to the race in Italy was issued with yellow pieces of cardboard marked with the word 'Monza'. The marshals at the circuit were at first flummoxed by the new accreditation but once they realised that the people with the yellow cards were all official team members they started to acknowledge the F1CA passes instead of the ones from the race promoters. Mosley recalled, 'This was an important victory in the battle to control Formula One and led us to make our own permanent F1CA passes valid for the entire season.'

By 1975 Ecclestone was demanding $350,000 of prize money from the organisers of long-haul races. It was the tipping point. The promoter of the Canadian Grand Prix at Mosport Park in Ontario refused to pay the increase, assuming that F1CA would cave in. Ecclestone promptly cancelled the race without negotiation, a radical move that even astonished the other teams. The promoter immediately offered to pay but Ecclestone refused to readmit the event. The Grand Prix crept back onto the calendar the following year after the promoter agreed to the terms but it was subsequently abandoned in favour of racing in Montreal.

It sent a stark warning to the other race promoters. As testimony to this, A. Tracy Bird, president of the Automobile Competition Committee for the United States (ACCUS), complained to *Autocar* that 'something has to happen because the control of motorsport has passed out of the hands of the FIA to the Formula One owners and drivers'.

The FIA agreed with Bird. When the head of the CSI, Prince Paul Metternich, was elected president of the FIA itself in late 1975, the FIA members voted in a new CSI president who was willing to take an altogether more aggressive position than his predecessor. Pierre Ugeux was a former paratrooper who had made a career as a Belgian utilities company executive. His experience in motorsport was minimal.

One of Ugeux's first acts as CSI president was to declare that no race would be allowed onto the calendar until financial terms had been agreed not only between FiCA and the organisers but also with the CSI. This invalidated the two 1976 race agreements that Ecclestone had already signed, with the British Grand Prix at Brands Hatch and the new USA West Grand Prix at Long Beach in California, where FiCA was due to also get a share of the ticket sales.

Ecclestone was furious. His power base within the sport was increasing, and his wily manoeuvres to become the representative of the teams in the paddock had effectively handed him a huge amount of control of the sport. He couldn't tolerate the CSI butting in and chiselling away at his plans. He and Mosley travelled to Brussels to meet with Ugeux and a number of other FIA notables, including Metternich and Jean-Marie Balestre, the president of the French sporting club, the Fédération Française du Sport Automobile.

Balestre was an ambitious and confrontational character who, depending on who you believed, had either been a French Resistance hero during the war or a member of the French division of the Nazi SS. He was famous for having an inflated ego and wasn't ashamed to show it. On one occasion a journalist sent him a request for comment which yielded a brief statement, accompanied by three pages listing his titles and achievements in motorsport.

On meeting Mosley and Ecclestone in Brussels, Balestre launched into a speech on behalf of the European race promoters, arguing that they could not afford an increase in the prize money. As Balestre spoke, Ecclestone got up from the table and started to straighten the paintings on the walls. Balestre was incensed that Ecclestone appeared not to be listening and grew so angry that he snapped his pen in half.

Faced with the prospect of having to tell the promoters that there was no deal, Ugeux panicked and agreed to prize money of $270,000 per European race, which turned into $275,000 when Ecclestone upped the total at the last moment. Ugeux was too tired to argue, much to Balestre's outrage, and the move gained the teams an additional $50,000 across the season.

Ugeux presented the Brussels Agreement as a triumph for the CSI, but it was far from it. To wrest control from FiCA he would have to get the disparate group of promoters to form a united front behind a strong leader, and Ugeux thought he knew just the man.

Patrick Duffeler was a Belgian-born American executive with a mixed history in F1. He had made his name as a key player in the marketing team that brought Marlboro into the sport in early 1972 with a $265,000 two-year deal with the BRM team, announced with a glitzy launch where a newly liveried car burst out of a giant cigarette packet. However, it was a case of style over substance. Marlboro spent a reported $3m per year in promoting the deal, but it received relatively little publicity due to the poor performance of BRM, which failed to even secure a podium in 1973.

Marlboro reacted by hiring young Australian advertising specialist John Hogan, who engineered a switch to the more successful McLaren team. It was a shrewd move that brought numerous world titles and would eventually result in Marlboro becoming the biggest-spending sponsor in the history of F1. But it sidelined Duffeler and he moved on to other projects.

Dubbed 'Laughing Boy' by Mosley because he never stopped smiling, Duffeler had big ideas for F1 that would eventually bring him into direct conflict with Ecclestone. He had put together a deal for the Fuji Speedway to host F1's first Japanese Grand Prix in 1976 and believed that he could secure races in the Philippines and Saudi Arabia. He even took several CSI executives on a visit to meet the Saudi royal family.

Duffeler had a history with Ecclestone, who felt that 'Laughing Boy' had gone back on his word about a Marlboro contract for Brabham that never materialised. Their animosity had spilled over into the arrange-ments for the Japanese Grand Prix. Four months before the event, Ecclestone had approached the Japanese promoter to say that the teams needed more money to cover their costs or the race could not go ahead. With a reception hosted by Emperor Hirohito's brother, Prince Takamatsu, already planned, the promoter caved in, despite Duffeler's protests.

At the 1976 Italian Grand Prix, Duffeler was approached on behalf of Ugeux by Baron Huschke von Hanstein, the CSI member for Germany. He proposed creating a promoters' organisation to rival F1CA's constructors' association, with Duffeler as its head. Duffeler, eager for more power and influence, and a way to unseat Ecclestone, accepted without hesitation.

'Patrick's job effectively was to destroy me and what I represented,' Ecclestone recalled. The promoters were told by Ugeux that Duffeler had been appointed to represent them to FiCA. When some of them questioned this, they were told that they were in danger of having their licences revoked. Boeri suggested that each promoter should pay a $100,000 bond that would be forfeited if they broke ranks. This gave the organisation the nickname of the Hundred Thousand Dollar Club, although it was formally known as World Championship Racing, which was set up by Duffeler as a not-for-profit company in Monaco.

Despite the threats, fewer than half of the 17 promoters came out in full support of World Championship Racing. They were Boeri's Monaco, Balestre's France and von Hanstein's Germany, plus Spain, Austria, the Netherlands, Italy and Argentina, which was represented by five-time world champion Juan Manuel Fangio. FiCA won the support of Brazil, South Africa, Sweden, Great Britain, the new Canadian round in Montreal, the two US events in Watkins Glen and Long Beach and, in a major blow to Duffeler, Japan. Ugeux's home race of Belgium, by then permanently entrenched at Zolder, signed a contract with both sides.

When von Hanstein was questioned by Mosley about why he had joined World Championship Racing he replied, 'It's your friend, the little guy. Each year he wants more and more money and the organisers can't afford it. Now he wants $350,000. Obviously we have to do something.'

Everything FiCA had fought for was under threat. 'If they succeeded, all the hard-won improvements in Formula One that Bernie and I had introduced in the four years since we started working together would be lost,' Mosley explained in his autobiography. 'It would be back to the old ways: race schedules to suit each individual organiser rather than our mechanics, minimal prize money and no say for the British teams on the technical rules . . . They did not understand that it needed to evolve and change, become more professional and modern, or face the prospect of declining to the point where there was not enough money to maintain it.'

Ecclestone's strategy for dealing with Duffeler was simple – he refused to speak to him. This put Duffeler in a difficult position as he could make no progress in negotiations. He had to take radical action. With the start of the 1977 season just two months away, he engaged Fangio to persuade the promoter of the season-opener in Argentina to default on the advance payment of the team's prize money, forcing Ecclestone to cancel the race.

Duffeler and Ugeux accused Ecclestone of endangering the sport and he was forced to defend himself to the press. 'In the past the constructors' association has been likened to the Mafia and people have even called me the Godfather, but that's just not true,' Ecclestone told the *Daily Mail* at the time. 'I wish I was a Godfather. They have millions of pounds, don't they? And travel about in jets instead of railway trains like me. Believe me, if I were a Godfather, I would not be getting involved in wrangles over racing cars roaring round a circuit.'

It was a somewhat disingenuous argument from a man who was one of the lucky few to travel on the first commercial flight of Concorde in 1976. But to win the battle against World Championship Racing, F1CA needed to deflect the argument away from financial discussions, particularly as they needed to keep the support of the most powerful team owner.

Despite being a staunch traditionalist, Enzo Ferrari had remained a member of F1CA throughout its conflict with Ugeux, although he constantly complained about the name because it was too close to the Italian swearword 'fica'. Recognising Ferrari's importance, Ecclestone flew out to Maranello accompanied by Colin Chapman, whose design skills were greatly admired by Enzo, and Mosley, who had learned basic Italian from March driver Vittorio Brambilla.

Mosley explained that 'we wanted to make clear to him that the whole contest was one for control of Formula One; whether we could continue to have practice times to suit the teams or whether they should be scheduled to suit the lunch hour of the local dignitaries; whether we could continue to have our own pit passes or whether we would have to beg for them (perhaps to Mr Duffeler).'

Enzo was one of the few people, along with Mosley, who Ecclestone looked up to. Right up until his last days as F1's boss, Ecclestone had a photo of Enzo in his office.

The Ferrari founder didn't pander to this, however. At the meeting he quickly made apparent his distaste for the financial side of the sport, telling his guests to talk less about money because 'you should never let people know you're running a brothel. You have to pretend it's a hotel and keep the brothel in the basement.' Ecclestone instead focused on safety and the competence of the promoters, topics that were close to Enzo's heart. They left the meeting with Ferrari's unofficial support.

The next stop was London where Ecclestone and Mosley met with Sir Clive Bossom, the chairman of the British FIA member, the Royal Automobile Club (RAC). A former MP, Bossom was alarmed by an article in the *Sunday Times* that alleged there were financial links between World Championship Racing and some members of the CSI, which would have represented a major conflict of interest. As a vice president of the FIA, Bossom was outraged and determined to get to the bottom of it. It gave F1CA yet another formidable ally.

Belatedly, Duffeler himself was now heading to Maranello, taking with him Fangio, who had won the world championship for Ferrari 21 years earlier in 1956. Mauro Forghieri, the team's sporting director, assured F1CA members that Enzo Ferrari would 'tell them that questions to do with money and the Argentine Grand Prix must be dealt with by Ecclestone'. This greatly amused Ecclestone, who imagined Duffeler sitting through a long conversation in Italian about the 'good old days' before being told that there was no business to be done.

However, World Championship Racing still represented a major threat. The press, with a new-found interest in F1 due to the thrilling championship battle between Niki Lauda and James Hunt, was now running scare stories about how the 1977 season might not go ahead.

Ugeux called a crisis meeting with Ecclestone and Mosley at the FIA's headquarters in Paris, preceded by a lunch for sponsors, which Duffeler was invited to but F1CA wasn't. Ecclestone retaliated by demanding that Duffeler was excluded from the meeting, which was agreed, although Ugeux refused his request to start the meeting earlier than 3.30pm. On arriving at the meeting room Ecclestone found no Ugeux, but a *Sports Illustrated* journalist was there who claimed he had been sent to cover the end of Grand Prix racing.

Ugeux arrived late, accompanied by FIA luminaries including Metternich, Balestre and Boeri. For nearly an hour the meeting dragged on – at one point sending Balestre to sleep – until, at Ecclestone's signal, Mosley got out a pile of papers and began to accuse the CSI of abuses of power under the laws of the European Economic Community (later to become the European Union). Mosley claimed that World Championship Racing was 'a cartel of race organisers' and the CSI's support of the organisation breached Articles 85 and 86 of the Treaty of Rome. Ironically, Mosley and Ecclestone themselves would have trouble with the same piece of legislation more than two decades later.

The FIA representatives were stunned but just as Mosley was reaching a crescendo, Ecclestone stood up and declared that he and Mosley were leaving as 'we're going to miss that bleeding plane'.

Chaos erupted. As Ugeux begged them to stay, Mosley pointed out that the short meeting was entirely down to the CSI's actions while Balestre, now very much awake, berated Ecclestone, who told him to 'sod off back to your office'. The situation only calmed down when Ecclestone and Mosley left the room to pretend to change their flight tickets, which had already been booked for a later time. When they returned, Ugeux was conciliatory. Although he would not agree to anything regarding the prize money, they were happy to release a joint statement declaring that the CSI and F1CA were working to resolve their differences.

Soon after, Ugeux offered F1CA a take-it-or-leave-it solution, which gave the teams the same prize money as 1976 but with the addition of a profit share of the gate receipts. Ecclestone leapt at the deal. He knew that very few of the promoters would be willing to open up their books to F1CA, which would be necessary for a profit share. This meant that the deal would inevitably collapse, leaving F1CA's proposal of increased prize money as the only option on the table.

Drawing up the new agreement and getting sign-off from the promoters was due to take several months. To the surprise of many, in the meantime Ecclestone agreed that the teams would race in Argentina under World Championship Racing's terms, which included irregular practice sessions and prize money linked to the level of race attendance.

The teams rushed to get their cars out to Argentina in time and ended up running the first four races of the season under World Championship Racing rules. However, when Ugeux spoke to Ecclestone about finalising the new contract, he refused. With additional opposition from some of the promoters who complained about the profit share, Ugeux was faced with the disastrous prospect of the championship collapsing mid-season. He gave in and agreed to run the rest of the season to F1CA's rules. World Championship Racing was finished.

Duffeler told Ecclestone's biographer, Terry Lovell, that 'when I look back, I can see that World Championship Racing was doomed from the start . . . [Ecclestone] was smarter than the majority of the organisers. He was a very high-pressure salesman and a very good tactician, who out-performed, out-negotiated and out-smarted a great number of the people he dealt with.'

With Duffeler defeated and more than $5.6m of prize money secured for the 1978 season (generating almost half a million dollars for Ecclestone), F1CA could finally turn to other important matters.

One of the main issues was keeping Ferrari onboard. At a press conference in late 1977, Enzo Ferrari – described by the media as a F1CA 'member only under protest' – complained that it was now F1CA and not the CSI that allocated car numbers and opined that F1CA only appeared strong and unified because the CSI was so weak.

Then there was safety. For Ecclestone, improving standards wasn't only about making F1 a more desirable platform for sponsors and broadcasters, it was also a deeply personal campaign driven by the deaths of Lewis-Evans and Rindt. Drivers were still dying at a rate of approximately one a year, with the most recent deaths those of young Welsh star Tom Pryce and a teenage marshal, who had a horrific collision in South Africa. Standards of care were low. When being taken to hospital following a crash at the 1976 US Grand Prix, Belgian racer Jacky Ickx was asked by the ambulance driver, 'Have you got any money to buy gas?'

In early 1978, Ecclestone approached Professor Sid Watkins, a leading London neurosurgeon, and asked him if he would attend races to see where safety improvements could be made. Within days Watkins found himself at Anderstorp in Sweden, where the medical centre was a caravan and the promoters refused to provide a helicopter on Friday because they insisted that 'practice was not dangerous compared to the race'.

When Watkins arrived at Brands Hatch, the medical centre was occupied by two ambulancemen who were drinking a celebratory beer. Hockenheim, despite being one of the most state-of-the-art circuits, had its medical centre in a bus. Neither of the two doctors present was a qualified anaesthetist and the chief medical officer was a gastrointestinal specialist.

Everything came to a head at the Italian Grand Prix at Monza due to an accident with haunting echoes of Rindt's crash eight years earlier. A huge incident at the start involving almost half the grid injured multiple drivers. Watkins tried to reach the crash scene but was held back by a police cordon. Meanwhile Ecclestone was stopped from entering the medical centre by a policeman who pointed a gun at him. Luckily, he had protection of his own in the form of the local chief of police, who drew his own gun on the junior cop. He was allowed to enter.

Watkins arrived some time after and was shocked to find the ambulance carrying Lotus driver Ronnie Peterson was only just arriving due to trouble navigating the crowds. Peterson was conscious and communicating but his legs were badly broken, while Hans Stuck had concussion and Vittorio Brambilla had a severe head injury caused by a stray tyre.

The drivers were taken to hospital but, due to the lack of medical staff, Watkins had to stay at the circuit for the now-delayed race. He finally made it to the hospital that evening with Colin Chapman and found that Brambilla was in intensive care while Peterson was in surgery to pin some of his 27 fractures. Watkins returned to his hotel but he and Ecclestone were called back to the hospital at 4am by Peterson's manager. The Swede had suffered an embolism that left him brain dead. There was nothing that could be done.

Chapman again fled Italy under threat of arrest, although this time it was the standard of medical care rather than the car that was under scrutiny. Peter Varolo, a Swedish-speaking local orthopaedic specialist, had offered his assistance after seeing the crash on TV. Varolo was convinced that the driver's death was caused by the decision to operate on his femur, a procedure with a known risk of causing fat embolisms. 'It was ridiculous,' he later told *Wheels* magazine. 'If the accident had happened in Sweden, I don't think Ronnie would have died.' Watkins called it a 'shambles'. It was estimated that the delay in getting Peterson into the ambulance at the circuit might have been as much as 18 minutes.

Ecclestone acted immediately. He changed Watkins' responsibilities from medical consultant to organiser of rescue operations at every circuit on the calendar. He had one piece of advice: 'If there's an accident to one of my cars and the driver is okay, then don't work too quickly because we want the cameras on the sponsorship!' At the next race in the United States, when the cars left the grid on the opening lap they were followed by Watkins in a specially equipped vehicle, F1's first medical car.

The effect was immense. During F1's first 28 years between 1950 and 1978, 38 drivers were killed in rounds of the world championship, non-championship Grands Prix and testing. Over the next 28 years, there were just six deaths. The chance of being killed or seriously injured in an F1 crash in the late 1970s was one in every ten accidents. Two decades later it was just one in 300.

Technology also played a part in improving safety and spectacle. In order to give the drivers one last chance to check for any glitches in their cars before they race, Ecclestone introduced the formation lap. He also hung traffic lights above the start-finish line to reduce false starts and pile-ups on the opening lap. As he explained to *BusinessAge* magazine in 1999, 'I wanted to have traffic lights to start the race with as opposed to a flag and so we had traffic lights – we didn't have to go to anybody, we just put traffic lights in.'

It was quite some achievement by Ecclestone. By the end of 1978, just seven years after he became a team owner, he had transformed F1 from an amateur pastime into a professional business.

The initial deal to get the teams better-value freight had quickly snowballed to encompass prize money, the calendar and safety. The shape of modern F1 was emerging. F1CA was now responsible for a host of procedures including paddock passes and security, the weekend schedule, car numbers, paddock facilities and even the start procedure. When summarising the early history of F1, Australian driver Frank Gardner quipped, 'There were cars, there were drivers, there were races, there were teams, there was chaos, and then there was Bernie.'

Manoeuvring F1CA into a position of dominance didn't come without sacrifices for Ecclestone, who had to some extent neglected Brabham. 'He seemed to worry about his own team only sporadically,' commented Niki Lauda, who left Ferrari to drive for Ecclestone in 1978, bringing with him not only the status of a double world champion but a hefty title sponsorship deal from Italian dairy company Parmalat.

Brabham had recently moved into a new 28,000-square-foot factory on Cox Lane in Chessington, Surrey, which boasted F1's first in-house wind tunnel. It had been Gordon Murray's idea, but Ecclestone initially rejected it when told it would cost $6m. He relented under the conditions that Murray must design it and Ecclestone would source all the materials himself. It ended up costing just $300,000.

The improvements were necessary: Brabham had finished second in the 1975 championship, but had struggled since then after Ecclestone ditched customer Ford Cosworths for a free engine supply deal from Alfa Romeo.

Murray's genius response was to attach a fan to the back of the car to dramatically increase its aerodynamic downforce, and thereby its performance. Although the regulations banned movable aerodynamic parts, they allowed devices to cool the engine. Murray made sure that the fan achieved this, designing it in such a way that the car would over-heat if it was disconnected.

The fan car hit the track at the 1978 Swedish Grand Prix to the anger of the other teams. As Brabham's rivals made ineffectual protests, Lauda and team-mate John Watson practised with heavy fuel loads while Ecclestone pantomimed anger that his mechanics had let them go out with a nearly empty tank. The pretence worked and the FIA greenlit the cars, which qualified behind Mario Andretti's Lotus on pole. However, once the race was underway Lauda powered past Andretti, driving over an oil slick with ease. Lauda described it as 'the easiest win I ever had'. It was Brabham's first win for three years and Alfa Romeo's first since 1951.

Colin Chapman was furious. When his protest against the fan car looked unlikely to succeed, he went to Ecclestone directly and threatened that the other teams would withdraw their support for him as head of FiCA if he did not drop the fan car immediately. Ecclestone capitulated and Chapman rose higher in his estimation for beating him at his own game. A new rule was drafted to prevent the fan car's future use and the Brabhams were mothballed after reportedly costing nearly $1m to develop.

The Brabham team members were dismayed, especially Murray, who was convinced the car would win the championship. However, he admitted, 'I think it might have been worse for [Ecclestone] than it was for me, because he loved getting the cars on pole position and bringing them in and putting the covers over them.' Blash added that 'Bernie had to think about the future of the sport as well as Brabham. We were desperately upset, but that was Bernie. Bernie was looking at the overall picture and knew that if it continued, Formula One would have been a different place completely.'

FiCA was at a crucial juncture. Ecclestone had persuaded the other teams to formalise his role, as president of administration and chief executive of what had been renamed the Formula One Constructors' Association (FOCA), acting on the linguistic advice of Enzo Ferrari, who was given the honorary title of President of Sport. Mosley, who had sold his stake in March, became the organisation's legal advisor.

With Ecclestone at the helm, some might assume that FOCA was now an unstoppable force. However, there was an immovable object in his way. Ecclestone was not the only F1 personality who had a new job title. Following the World Championship Racing debacle, Metternich had persuaded Ugeux to step down as head of the CSI and in 1978 the FIA elected Ecclestone's pen-snapping foe, Jean-Marie Balestre, as his replacement.

The Frenchman epitomised the bureaucrats that Ecclestone detests – clubbable, upper-class men in blazers who have no skin in the game but love to wield power. Balestre's first move as president of the CSI was to abolish the organisation and in its place establish the Fédération Internationale du Sport Automobile (FISA), an autonomous subcommittee of the FIA that acted as its sporting division but was not restrained by its parent organisation. In his speech to members upon being elected, Balestre attacked FOCA's control over F1 and declared that he would rein in Ecclestone's power.

On the eve of the 1979 season, the FOCA teams met in Maranello and voted to ask the FIA for the complete independence of F1, cutting out the newly established FISA entirely from the organisation of the sport. The teams' desire to break away from FIA control, stoked by an ever more powerful Ecclestone assisted by Mosley's guile, would become a common theme in F1 over the coming years. Ecclestone might have won the previous battle for control of F1's commercial rights, but the real war was just about to begin.

4

WAR AND PEACE

When superstar British driver James Hunt lined up below the slopes of Mount Fuji for the finale of the 1976 world championship, his future television commentary partner Murray Walker was almost 6,000 miles away in a tiny studio at BBC's Television Centre in Shepherd's Bush.

Walker was not yet the household name that he would become in the UK over the following decades. At that time he was a junior commentator who specialised in motorbike racing. He had only been drafted in to cover the Japanese Grand Prix because the BBC's usual F1 expert, Raymond Baxter, was occupied with his more prestigious role as host of the *Tomorrow's World* science programme and didn't want to get out of bed and drag himself to west London at 4am on a cold October morning.

It wasn't even a live show. Walker commentated on the race in real time, but the UK's F1 fans would see only a 20-minute highlights edit, broadcast at a more amenable hour. Even that was a bonus. Many races received no coverage at all and it was only due to a particularly dramatic season and the prospect of a British champion that the BBC had greenlit even those few minutes of footage.

The championship battle read like a work of fiction and would be later immortalised in the Hollywood movie *Rush*, with Hunt played by *Thor* actor Chris Hemsworth. The early races of the season were dominated by the reigning world champion, the pragmatic Austrian Niki Lauda, until his charge was curtailed by a fiery crash at the Nürburgring. Lauda was dragged from his Ferrari with severe burns and was read the last rites before he began the painful road to recovery. His absence left the door open for Hunt, the charismatic English playboy, to take centre stage. By the time Lauda miraculously returned to the grid, just six weeks after his accident, Hunt had reduced the gap to only a few points.

So, while audiences around the world were transfixed, broadcasting footage from Japan was a major departure for the BBC. Brands Hatch chief executive John Webb had previously had to pay the corporation to cover one of the circuit's F1 events.

The lack of exposure was an international problem too. Italian television covered the Italian Grand Prix once a year and nothing else. Max Mosley later explained that 'in the 1970s, to find the results of a major motor race was extremely difficult. Either you telephoned a news agency or looked for the occasional few minutes of TV, tucked between the cricket and the hockey. In those days British TV might show extracts of Monaco, Monza and the British GP, and that was all.'

The non-commercial BBC's reticence was fuelled by the presence of sponsorship logos on the cars, in particular cigarette advertising. This caution was only made worse at the start of the season when the Surtees team turned up with a Durex-branded car. Walker recalled that 'the idea of sponsorship by condom firms was something else . . . There was a crisis.' Although the BBC had been due to broadcast the Race of Champions at Brands Hatch, when they saw the Surtees car they 'packed up and went home'.

However, by the end of the 1976 season the increasing interest forced a rethink, to the benefit of British viewers who were treated to a dramatic conclusion in Japan. In the driving rain, Lauda decided that the championship was not worth his life and quit the race, handing the title to Hunt. It drove up interest in F1 in the UK and around the world and demonstrated the series' strength as a broadcast sport. Walker explained, 'The good-looking and immensely charismatic James was the nation's new sporting hero and with the growth of TV the time was right to exploit Formula One's enormous potential.'

Such was the acceleration of interest in F1 in the UK that the BBC decided it would broadcast the entire season in 1978. The coverage was not live, but instead took the form of a half-hour highlights programme, *Grand Prix*, broadcast on the evening after the race and introduced to the sounds of Fleetwood Mac's 'The Chain'.

Walker would fly out to each race on Thursday, soak up the atmosphere and speak to his contacts, before being flown back to London on Saturday afternoon after qualifying. He would then watch the race at the BBC on Sunday afternoon before providing commentary for the highlights edit. Even when he graduated to broadcasting trackside two years later, the quality of the broadcast facilities was at the whim of the promoter and he might find himself peering at the cars through a tiny window on a far-flung corner of the circuit. At the BBC's first live broadcast of Monaco in 1980, 'there were no commentary boxes . . . just two folding chairs out on the pavement behind the Armco [barrier] and a flickering little TV monitor [showing the race]', Walker recalled. 'We weren't helped by the inferior coverage of the foreign host broadcasters whose standards were, to put it mildly, well below those of the BBC. In Spain, for instance, some 50 minutes of the 100-minute race showed nothing but Mario Andretti going round by himself.'

It was makeshift but nevertheless a significant start for what would one day become one of the world's biggest live broadcast operations, and Ecclestone was in pole position to benefit from it.

The TV rights to races had traditionally resided with the race promoters. However, they saw the sale of TV rights as a major inconvenience and a distraction from their core business of arranging Grands Prix. Each promoter had to either sell the rights to a syndicator or negotiate individually with dozens of broadcasters around the world in multiple languages. Coverage was often sporadic, leaving fans unsure on which channel, if any, they could watch the next race.

But the events of 1976 had opened Ecclestone's eyes even wider to the broadcast potential of F1. When some of the promoters had complained about the rising prize money fees, he had offered to waive increases in return for them signing over the broadcast rights for the races.

Mosley recalled that 'Bernie had realised that it was essential for the future of Formula One to have all the television rights in one basket . . . FOCA would offer to race for a stated fee while also taking over the TV rights to the race, at least outside the country.'

Selling the rights was hard work and no one wanted to do it. The teams were as uninterested as the promoters when Ecclestone first mentioned it to them. Team owner Lord Hesketh recalled to us that 'the founding moment was in a Portakabin at the Österreichring [in Austria]. Bernie came in and we were sitting around the table and he said, "Right, I've paid a million dollars for the world TV rights . . ." And he offered it to us. There were 10 teams and he said you can each have it for $100,000. Everyone turned it down.'

The teams simply did not believe that the TV rights were worth the time and money they would have to invest in them. Frank Williams, who had graduated from privateer to fully fledged constructor by building the car's chassis, told *Motor Sport* magazine that he was glad Ecclestone dealt with commercial matters. 'It takes up his time and makes the Brabhams less competitive. Of course, Bernard makes a lot of money from it and flies to the races by private jet while I go British Airways economy. We're all looking for different things, aren't we?'

It was a costly miscalculation by the team owners that would have major consequences for them and the sport in years to come. However, in the short term, the development of TV coverage was forced to take a back seat as FOCA had far more pressing matters to deal with in the form of Jean-Marie Balestre.

FOCA might have been forgiven for underestimating the French FISA president. After all, at times his behaviour verged on self-parody. Paddock gossip focused on his sudden rages and his self-aggrandisement. On one occasion he scrapped his travel plans because the airline he was booked on did not stock his favourite brand of mineral water. On another, he famously lambasted his assistants when he found that a trip to Australia across the international dateline led to him missing a day. 'Where is my Tuesday?' he complained, demanding that it be returned to his schedule.

'If you wanted to be on good terms with Balestre, you would personally invite him to your Grand Prix and you would send a Rolls-Royce or a Cadillac to pick him up at the airport,' an unnamed race promoter told Terry Lovell. 'The car would have a police escort and display FIA flags. He was not there for the money, but he enjoyed the power and all the trappings that went with it.'

Yet, despite his pomposity, Balestre was a far more shrewd and dangerous opponent than Ugeux or Duffeler had been. He was intensely ambitious and, because of his former career as the publisher of *L'Auto Journal*, he understood how the media worked and what fans of the sport wanted to hear. Unlike Ugeux, the utilities executive, he was well versed in the complex politics of the paddock.

Going into the start of the 1979 season, Balestre was seething. His ego had been severely bruised by FOCA's demand in Maranello that control of F1 should pass from the FIA to the teams. The FIA in reaction issued a statement declaring its support for Balestre and rejecting the idea that control should be ceded to FOCA. The statement had in fact been written by Balestre himself and distributed to key FIA members to sign.

He arrived at the opening race in Argentina determined to exert his authority. On the opening lap, John Watson's McLaren and Jody Scheckter's Ferrari touched, resulting in a six-car pile-up that led to the race being red-flagged. Scheckter emerged from his wrecked Ferrari with a sprained wrist, while Brabham's Nelson Piquet broke his foot. Balestre placed the entire blame for the incident on Watson, without giving the Ulsterman a chance to defend himself at a hearing, and fined him £3,000 ($6,400) – more than the prize money he earned for eventually finishing third.

It wasn't lost on FOCA that a *garagiste* team (McLaren) had been penalised instead of a manufacturer (Ferrari). At Ecclestone's insistence, Watson refused to pay. Balestre retaliated by denying his entry to the following race in Brazil. However, the FOCA-aligned promoter refused to enforce the ban, causing Balestre to back down. It was a minor skirmish but set the scene for the first few years of Balestre's presidency.

The following month Balestre flew to London to engage the British motorsport press in what he called a 'worldwide exclusive' but was actually an extended diatribe against Ecclestone and FOCA. Nevertheless, the media was all ears and dubbed the dispute the FISA–FOCA war.

Balestre claimed that Ecclestone had failed to honour three-year contracts signed with the promoters in 1977 and revealed that the FOCA boss had asked the Argentine promoter for a 27 per cent increase in prize money for 1979, bringing the total to $900,000, plus the television rights. What's more, he claimed that the European Broadcasting Union (EBU, an alliance of Europe's biggest free-to-air channels) and three major American networks all recognised the FIA and not the promoters as the legal owner of F1's broadcasting rights. If true, it would have made Ecclestone's acquisition of the rights void.

It was the first step in a protracted campaign against FOCA. When Ecclestone found a sponsor to revive the cancelled Swedish Grand Prix, Balestre refused to reinstate the race to the calendar, forcing the teams to return a $25,000 advance in prize money. He then turned his attention to Ecclestone's crown jewel races in the US, insisting that they make costly changes in the name of safety. Long Beach was castigated for using concrete blocks instead of Armco barriers designed to crumple on impact, even though they were preferred by the drivers, while Watkins Glen was told to make improvements costing more than $300,000 just a month before its race. Despite a loan from FOCA, the bill proved too much and the circuit held its final Grand Prix in 1980.

It was not too dissimilar to the tactics tried by Ugeux, but with a crucial difference. Ugeux had failed to come close to breaking the unity of the teams. However, with his superior understanding of paddock politics, Balestre knew where to find the cracks in their united front. Ugeux had focused on commercial sweeteners and had ultimately failed because he could not match Ecclestone's financial prowess. Balestre shrewdly focused on a different area of F1 that was certain to cause strife among its participants – the technical regulations.

In 1977 Renault had entered the world championship as a team for the first time at the instigation of Elf executive François Guiter, who thought it would be a good marketing exercise for the two French companies. Although the car maker had been very successful in sportscar racing and had built the car that won the very first Grand Prix back in 1906, it had never competed in the F1 world championship. It was spending a sizeable amount of money on its sportscar effort – resulting in victory at the 1978 24 Hours of Le Mans – but Guiter persuaded it that some of that money might produce better returns in front of F1's large TV audience.

The French manufacturer brought an innovation to the sport in the form of turbo-powered engines, which had cost it more than $2m to develop. Initially the turbos were a disaster. Renault retired from its first seven races and it was more than a year before it scored its first points. However, at the 1979 French Grand Prix a breakthrough occurred. Renault won the race and followed it up with a second place at the British Grand Prix.

Ferrari immediately put its own turbo into production. However, the cost of developing such a radically different power unit went way beyond the budget that Ford had allocated to Cosworth. At the time, Cosworth supplied all of the privateer teams except for Brabham, and Ecclestone was looking to revert to Cosworth in 1980 once he had severed his deal with unreliable Alfa Romeo. Cosworth was charging the teams around $45,000 per unit, but switching to turbo power would have doubled that, putting it beyond the reach of most of the *garagistes*. The cost was not a concern for manufacturers such as Renault and Ferrari which could allocate the spending to the car companies' marketing budgets.

The *garagistes* countered the power of the turbos with innovations of their own. One was the development of ground-effect cars, which had been popularised by Colin Chapman and used aerodynamic skirts around the rim of the cars to increase downforce and make them stick to the track. The British teams employed superior designers – people such as Chapman, Gordon Murray, John Barnard and Patrick Head – who could negate the turbos' advantage.

The manufacturer teams tended to focus their resources on engine development, which had greater relevance to road-car technology, and they couldn't keep up with the *garagistes'* aerodynamic innovations. Renault 'lacked a chassis culture', according to its designer, Jean-Claude Migeot. 'We weren't properly equipped. Renault in those days would never have committed to a moving-ground wind tunnel and that's what was required.'

Balestre knew that changing the regulations in favour of the manufacturers was a sure-fire way to fuel infighting among the teams. In February 1980, he announced that to reduce car speeds, aerodynamic skirts would be made illegal from 1 January 1981. It effectively aligned him with the interests of the wealthy manufacturer teams of Ferrari, Renault and Alfa Romeo and left some of the smaller British teams facing financial ruin.

Ecclestone warned against giving the car makers too much power. 'These manufacturers see that we've built the sport up until it's an incredible success,' he said. 'They just want to use it to sell cars, and then when somebody in their advertising department says to, they'll leave, and all that will be left is rubble.'

To give the teams enough time to design the new cars to specification, major changes to the technical regulations were supposed to have a two-year notice period. However, Mosley recalled that FISA had 'the right to change them at short notice if it could claim this was being done for reasons of safety. Short-notice changes caused major difficulties for UK teams because we lacked the resources to redesign and build new cars quickly. And safety was a very subjective concept in those unscientific days. Public opinion made it extremely difficult for our side to resist a change labelled "safety". As a former journalist, Balestre fully understood this.'

Balestre told FISA member clubs that he would draw up 'a list of measures so that in 1981 the FISA exerts full control over the world championships belonging to it and which, at the present moment, are the object of a takeover by certain private associations foreign to the FISA.' Balestre's plans also involved increasing the minimum weight of an

F1 car from 575kg to 625kg, which would have wiped out the advantage teams gained from using the lighter Cosworth DFVs against heavier turbo units. It was a bold move on Balestre's part, aiming to drive a wedge between the teams and dislodge Ecclestone's power base.

Ecclestone was furious. 'If FISA or anyone else wants to ruin racing, let them get on with it. Why should I spend so much time trying to make racing stronger and more competitive when we go and get a rule like this? What will happen is that my sponsor will come to me at the end of the season and ask what it takes to win races. I'll tell him skirts have been banned, and that we need another £4m ($9.3m) to develop a new turbocharged engine. And my sponsor, like a lot of others, will walk clean out of racing.'

It fuelled the FISA–FOCA war and the winner was far from a racing certainty. FOCA's case was heavily dented a few weeks after Balestre's announcement when popular driver Clay Regazzoni was paralysed from the waist down in an accident at Long Beach, which some observers blamed on ground-effect. A few months later, Patrick Depailler was killed testing an Alfa Romeo at Hockenheim. Although the official cause of his accident was suspension failure, a rumour did the rounds that the actual problem was a skirt that was wedged in the wrong position.

Despite the increasing pressure, FOCA had some powerful allies. Tyre supplier Goodyear was incensed at Balestre's new regulations, which included a drastic reduction in tyre size. The company's motorsport manager called the plans 'lunacy' and threatened to pull out if they were not overturned. However, Balestre was closely aligned with F1's other tyre supplier, the French manufacturer Michelin, and ignored Goodyear's protests.

Meanwhile, Balestre continued to hit the FOCA teams with harsh penalties for minor infractions – and one of his petty schemes was about to escalate.

Several races after the start of the 1980 season, Balestre decided to make the drivers' attendance at pre-race briefings mandatory. The FOCA teams refused to send their drivers on the grounds that the edict hadn't officially been made part of the rulebook. Balestre promptly fined each driver $2,000. Over several races, the fines ticked up until Balestre declared that any driver with payments outstanding would lose their licence for the Spanish Grand Prix at Jarama.

FOCA offered to pay the fines on behalf of the drivers, but Balestre refused as he felt that the drivers should pay personally in order to show contrition for their behaviour. Ecclestone responded by declaring that the FOCA teams would not compete in the race.

FOCA had friends in high places. Spain's King Juan Carlos was a huge motorsport fan and spoke to his cousin, the Marqués de Cubas, who was president of the promoter, the Real Automovil Club de España (RACE). The monarch instructed the automobile club to pay the fines so that the event could go ahead. Balestre again refused.

At 7am on the morning of the race, Balestre turned up at Mosley's hotel room in his pyjamas, insisting that they talk. Mosley arranged to meet with him, Ecclestone and Ferrari's Marco Piccinini in the hotel lobby. When they were sitting around a table, Balestre raged, brandishing a piece of paper which he said included a full list of the automobile clubs that were on his side. Communicating in cockney rhyming slang in order to befuddle the Frenchman, Ecclestone and Mosley arranged to purloin the list. When Mosley stood up he clumsily overturned the table, scattering Balestre's papers everywhere. While Ecclestone was helping to tidy up, he pocketed the important document.

Balestre was mortified. '*Où est ma liste?*' he asked repeatedly, but it was of course nowhere to be found. As Mosley later told us, 'Bernie always says himself, "The old tricks are always the best ones."'

The meeting ended without agreement. However, as Ecclestone and Mosley headed to the circuit they found a solution. Although the Grand Prix was officially sanctioned by FISA through its Spanish member club, the Federación Española de Automovilismo, as a fellow FIA member RACE also had the authority to sanction events. The Marqués de Cubas announced that the event would go ahead anyway. Balestre retaliated by declaring it a non-championship event. FISA officials, including Balestre's spokesman Jabby Crombac, were marched from the circuit by armed police.

Ferrari, Renault, Alfa Romeo and the small Italian team Osella immediately withdrew, but the rest of the grid went on to race. Ironically, it was one of the most exciting events of the season, but the damage it did to both sides in the war was immense. Many of the sponsors were unhappy. Marlboro owner Philip Morris was horrified with what was transpiring, but with one Marlboro-sponsored team in the FOCA camp (McLaren) and one in the FISA camp (Ferrari) it couldn't take sides. Elf, like Goodyear, indicated that it might pull out of the sport.

The fallout from the Spanish Grand Prix and the ever-widening gap between FOCA and FISA were set to form a major part of the agenda of the FIA general meeting the following morning. Unlike many of FOCA's members, Balestre wasn't one for slumming it and the FIA's get-together took place in the Grand Lagonissi Resort, a sprawling five-star hotel nestled in a 72-acre private peninsula in the Athenian Riviera.

Ecclestone and Mosley realised that it was crucial for them to attend, but finding a flight from Madrid to Athens at such short notice was almost impossible. Ecclestone resolved the situation by persuading an American oil tycoon he met in the airport that it would be only a small diversion for him to drop them off in his private jet on his way to Saudi Arabia. Ecclestone and Mosley arrived at the hotel in Greece at 9am on the morning after the race, surprising the room full of FIA delegates at breakfast.

Balestre responded to Ecclestone and Mosley's intrusion by removing their positions on the FISA executive committee. However, armed with the purloined list, Ecclestone and Mosley knew which of the FISA members were sympathetic to their cause. They met with the friendly FISA members and Philip Morris's Aleardo Buzzi in Lausanne a few days later for peace talks. They signed a document declaring that FISA would remain responsible for the sporting regulations while FOCA would continue to have commercial authority.

Balestre, with his eyes still on the commercial rights, refused to sign, despite the agreement receiving the support of a number of powerful FISA clubs. Tom Binford, president of the Automobile Competition Committee for the United States (ACCUS), said, 'I think that the agreement is a good one. But someone who wants to roll things back to the way they were before FOCA existed wouldn't like it. Apparently that's Jean-Marie's goal now.'

Balestre tried to strip FOCA of support from the manufacturers by demanding that Renault and Ferrari leave immediately (Alfa Romeo had never joined). When Piccinini reported this back to Enzo Ferrari, the team owner was unwilling to drop Ecclestone, who had increased Ferrari's take from the prize fund tenfold since he had taken control. Enzo sent his chauffeur to the local post office with a resignation letter, where he obtained a receipt for posting it before asking for the letter back. Balestre was shown the receipt by Piccinini as proof of resignation, but the letter never arrived, leaving Ferrari on both sides of the table. As ever, Ferrari were having their cake and eating it.

Believing he had the manufacturer teams in the bag, Balestre set about trying to divide the other FOCA members. At the Le Mans 24 Hour race, Balestre approached Chapman and offered to rescind the ban on skirts if the Lotus boss usurped Ecclestone as FOCA president. Chapman indicated his assent and was instructed to speak to Enzo Ferrari. To Balestre's surprise, however, the coup never happened. Whether Chapman never intended to follow through or he was persuaded otherwise by Ferrari is unclear. Regardless, at the next race, Balestre's home event at France's Paul Ricard track, Chapman stood side by side with Ecclestone to threaten a boycott.

Balestre had put a great deal of effort into ensuring the smooth running of his home event. He had called on his government contacts to exempt the Ligier team's $750,000 deal with Gitanes from a local ban on tobacco advertising and it would therefore be extremely embarrassing for him if the race didn't go ahead after all the favours that he had called in. Desperate, he consented to discuss a five-year delay to the ban on skirts. Instead, speeds would be reduced by replacing slicks with grooved tyres. The race went ahead.

However, after Michelin rejected the tyre proposal, this too fell through. Goodyear was furious that the rapprochement had been rejected and so were the team bosses. One of the most vocal was Frank Williams, whose cars were leading the championship. Referring to Balestre's beloved over-sized accreditation armband, Williams said, 'All Balestre has is an armband. He doesn't run any cars, he doesn't pay my bills, he doesn't have one penny invested in my business, or any of the other teams. I refuse to be administered by an incompetent. This is my livelihood.'

Not everyone took the teams' business credentials seriously. The anonymous managing director of one of the biggest engineering companies in Europe was scathing, telling journalist Denis Jenkinson that 'I wouldn't give any of them more than a week in the really big world of engineering and big business; they are amateurs really.' Ironically, Ecclestone, Williams and other team owners would go on to become some of Britain's richest men.

By the end of August 1980, FOCA had five separate lawsuits under-way against FISA. Balestre was undeterred. He called a meeting with representatives of Ferrari, Renault, Alfa Romeo and Ligier at his home in Saint-Cloud, one of the wealthiest towns in France. Guy Ligier was a supporter of FOCA, but had recently developed a partnership with French car maker Talbot, which wanted to side with Balestre, particularly after his assistance with the tobacco restrictions. Balestre promised the teams that he would push through the ban on skirts, providing they gave their unwavering support in the battles ahead. They unanimously agreed.

Balestre was preparing to escalate the war. In October, he wrote a column in the French newspaper *L'Équipe* declaring that FISA would take over the running of the commercial side of F1. He added that FISA would soon start organising contracts with races and take charge of the distribution of prize money, with the amounts awarded made public. In return, FISA would retain only 2 per cent of the prize fund, estimated to be around $240,000 per season on a $12m haul.

FISA's new championship rules contained several important clauses that under other circumstances might have appealed to Ecclestone's sense of order. The proposed format obliged teams to take part in every round of the championship, with heavy fines for those that didn't. It homogenised the structure of the events and introduced a 'superlicence' for drivers to ensure that every competitor was worthy of F1.

It also effectively outlawed non-championship races, as Balestre declared that only rounds of the FIA Formula One World Championship could be run to F1 regulations. This was an attempt to avoid a repeat of Spain, but it would have other significant consequences down the line.

Without being able to control the race calendar or how the prize money was distributed themselves, the FOCA teams felt that there was only one option left to them and that was to break away.

At the start of November, Ecclestone and Mosley produced and distributed a detailed dossier entitled 'The World Federation of Motor Sport presents The World Professional Drivers Championship', a manifesto for a breakaway series to rival F1. It included technical regulations drafted by Chapman and a calendar including not only the races already signed by FOCA for 1981 but also new events in Las Vegas and New York. Eight of those races had also appeared on Balestre's FIA calendar announced a few weeks earlier.

There was to be a $10m prize fund, with $1m guaranteed for the champion driver. The World Federation of Motor Sport would be 'an independent, professionally run sanctioning body' with the aim of giving a better return on investment than F1 for 'the $70 million invested each year by the competitors and sponsors'.

Balestre was scathing. 'Those people don't know what they are in for,' he said. 'They don't understand power. They're just little men playing with toys, making cars in garages. Who do they think they are?'

In response, Ecclestone told the *Sunday Times*, 'Who the hell is the FISA?' He added, 'They are a bunch of nobodies. They appointed themselves and they think they own racing, when all they really have is a bunch of clubs around the world and self-important people living off the back of the sport.'

Balestre was pessimistic about the chances of resolution. 'Now things are clear,' he told French newspaper *Le Monde*. 'Ecclestone's mask has fallen. He wants nothing more and nothing less than absolute technical and financial control of Formula One. I believe that he will go all the way and the possibilities of reuniting motorsport are very limited.' He added that the World Federation of Motor Sport was 'a phantom federation trying to build a pirate championship'. Balestre was absolutely right about Ecclestone. That's exactly what he wanted but, pirate or not, his idea for a new championship was no idle threat. He was intent on taking the wheel one way or another.

Just the previous year, team owners in the IndyCar championship in the US had set up their own body, Championship Auto Racing Teams (CART), to sanction the series in place of the United States Auto Club (USAC). One of the key instigators of the breakaway was former F1 driver Dan Gurney, who had drafted a commercial structure for the series based on Ecclestone's work with FOCA. When this was rejected by USAC, the teams decided to go it alone.

However, FOCA would not have it so easy. Ecclestone struggled to find an insurer that was willing to underwrite the breakaway championship. Balestre meanwhile declared that all interested teams must register for the 1981 F1 championship by 1 December and accept the ban on skirts or they would not be able to compete.

The race promoters, many of whom had their events listed on both calendars, made an effort to appear neutral. The Marqués de Cubas said that he would wait until the season opener in Argentina in January before he made a decision on which way the Spanish Grand Prix would go.

The final straw for the World Federation of Motor Sport came when Balestre threatened that any circuit hosting the series would be banned from hosting other FIA events. According to Mosley, a ban 'would be catastrophic for a permanent circuit that needed to run lesser motorsport events all year round in order to be financially viable'. Even the British Grand Prix, FOCA's biggest supporter among the promoters, was worried.

However, Balestre had acted rashly and not thought through the implications of his threat. FOCA immediately launched yet another lawsuit, accusing FISA of interference in its contracts. There was an important consequence of this. FOCA's lawyers pointed out to Mosley that FOCA could not sue FISA for interfering in its contracts for the F1 world championship while simultaneously claiming that those races were in fact part of the World Federation of Motor Sport championship. Only a few weeks after launching, Mosley and Ecclestone held a press conference to call the breakaway series off.

In seeming to accept defeat, Ecclestone consented that the FOCA teams would race in the first three rounds of the 1981 F1 championship – although they would do it with skirts as there was little time left to change the cars. Despite the violation of his deadline, Balestre was forced to accept them or face being seen as the man who brought down F1.

With the breakaway called off, FOCA obtained a series of injunctions against Balestre and the other FISA executive committee members, preventing them from interfering in FOCA's contracts. However, there was now trouble from another camp, as Goodyear had followed through with its threat to quit. 'Goodyear is a victim of the French domination of Formula One rule making,' Ecclestone complained to the *New York Times*. 'You can see who's behind it. It's the French Government. The rules are being written for Renault. It was clear to me eight months ago, but when I said it people laughed at me. What the French Government won't do to win the world championship is unbelievable.'

It was a ludicrous claim that did little to quell the squabbles. Other sponsors looked likely to follow Goodyear out of the sport and replacement partners had dried up. Some of the teams, in a desperate attempt to cut costs, laid off mechanics and introduced a three-day week. As Mosley observed, 'We were going to have trouble getting through the winter, never mind going racing next season.' The situation became so dire that it drew the attention of Parliament. Conservative MP Jonathan

Aitken lambasted Balestre in a speech in the House of Commons, bemoaning the French threat to British livelihoods.

Balestre was unmoved. 'If there will not be a world championship in 1981, there will not be one,' he said. 'After all, Formula One is not essential.'

Unknown to Balestre, however, FOCA still had allies in unexpected places. Enzo Ferrari was more than willing to side with Balestre on technical matters that benefited the Scuderia, but he certainly didn't want the Frenchman running the commercial side of the sport. Long an admirer of Ecclestone's business acumen, he summoned all the teams along with Philip Morris's Aleardo Buzzi to Modena for peace talks.

Together the teams put together the Modena Agreement, which was largely similar to the document from Lausanne that had been rejected by Balestre the previous summer. Skirts would be banned in a two-year timeframe, FISA would govern the regulations and Ecclestone would remain in charge of the commercial arrangements.

It was announced on 20 January 1981, the day before the leading lights of the FIA gathered for the Monte Carlo Rally. 'This put Balestre under intense pressure,' Mosley explained. 'If the Modena Agreement were accepted, it would be a defeat for him; but with every team including Ferrari in agreement, he was becoming isolated. Without the support of Ferrari and the major manufacturers, Balestre realised he was at risk of losing control.'

However, Balestre held his nerve and refused to sign. It was a catastrophe for FOCA, whose teams were still struggling to persuade sponsors to stay onboard. 'What he didn't know was that the financial position of the British teams was now so desperate he only had to wait and he would be able to dictate his terms, at least to us,' Mosley admitted. 'We were very close to collapse.'

The solution came from an extremely unlikely source of inspiration. Mosley, Chapman and McLaren boss Teddy Mayer had been invited to the Hahnenkamm ski race at Kitzbühel in Austria. Following the event they dined in their hotel, where Chapman asked the waitress about an unusual mural on the wall, depicting a cow being painted in different colours by two men in medieval clothing.

The waitress explained that a local town had been under siege and was almost out of food. To give the impression that they were abundantly supplied, the citizens painted their sole remaining cow a different colour each day and paraded it along the city walls. Unable to sustain a lengthy siege, the attackers agreed to spare the city on terms favourable to its inhabitants.

It was a eureka moment for Chapman. 'That's it!' he cried. 'We must put on a race even though we've got no money.' The trio went up to Mosley's room and phoned Ecclestone to explain about the painted cow. They were met with a brief silence before Ecclestone replied. 'You're all pissed,' he said. Mosley explained, 'This was partly true but he saw the point and eventually agreed that we must somehow put on a race despite almost all the teams being broke.'

Ecclestone put the 'cow plan' into action and there was a perfect candidate for the race. The F1 calendar was in chaos following Balestre's manoeuvrings. Due to the considerable uncertainty about the FOCA teams' participation, FISA was only able to guarantee a nine-car grid, so Balestre had decided to postpone the opening two races of the season, Argentina and South Africa, to later in the year.

Argentina happily accepted the switch from January to April but South Africa was determined to keep its 7 February date. The race had significant sponsorship from a local office-supply company, Nashua, which had built a marketing campaign around the date. A significant amount had been spent on printing posters showing the February date and there were also concerns about the weather in late April, which was well into autumn in the southern hemisphere.

Balestre was immovable. Not only did he need the extra time before the start of the season to try to break FOCA, but the South African Grand Prix was far from his favourite event. At the previous year's race he had been bundled off the podium by a burly local security guard and he was still furious about it, complaining that he had been 'the target of physical violence'. Unbeknown to him, the incident had been precipitated by Mosley, who had asked the security guard to help after Balestre had attempted to be the centre of attention at previous podium ceremonies.

FOCA declared that it would be honouring its contract with South Africa, despite FISA's opposition. However, there was a major obstacle. Following Goodyear's departure, the FOCA teams did not have a tyre supplier and Balestre's ally Michelin was certainly not going to provide them. The solution came in the form of one of Ecclestone's other business interests.

With a flash of remarkable foresight, in 1977 he had set up International Race Tire Services (IRTS), a company that supplied tyres for junior race series.

IRTS started out with a supply deal from Goodyear, but following the company's withdrawal from motorsport it had switched to Avon. In order to supply the rebel F1 teams, it had to buy the old tyre moulds from Goodyear and melt its rival's names off the finished product, painting its own logo onto the space.

The pirate race created a quandary for Balestre. Under no circumstances could he recognise the South African Grand Prix as a round of the FIA world championship, but he could no longer declare the race a non-championship event, having outlawed the format in his new regulations. Instead he chose to designate it 'Formula Libre', a format used largely for amateur or historic events, where any specification of vehicle was free to compete.

On site, the race was a disaster. A combination of bad weather and the retirement of local favourite Jody Scheckter resulted in a miserable attendance, which left the promoter in financial difficulty. However, the same was not true from an international perspective. Ecclestone's skilful negotiations meant that the race was broadcast globally, showing people around the world that FOCA meant business. Mosley remarked, 'It destabilised the manufacturers, who realised that we could put on a race but Balestre couldn't.'

Ultimately, however, it was not Ecclestone and Mosley who brought Balestre down but his biggest ally, Renault. The official start to the 1981 F1 season was due to be Ecclestone's flagship race on 15 March at Long Beach in California. Still hoping to break FOCA, a few weeks before the event, Balestre called a meeting in New York with local FIA member, the Sports Car Club of America. He asked them not to sanction the race, declaring that the manufacturers would refuse to participate if it went ahead.

Balestre attempted to get around the High Court injunction banning him from interfering with FOCA's race contracts by sitting motionless as his interpreter read statements from a pre-compiled list, assuming that if his demands were conveyed by someone else the injunction did not apply. It was a bizarre and legally unsound strategy that was likely to see him dragged in front of the court, but in the end it didn't matter.

Balestre's fatal error was that he forgot the reason why manufacturers such as Renault were in F1 – publicity. Renault had recently acquired the American Motors Corporation and planned a marketing campaign for the marque around the race. The French car maker had not been consulted by Balestre before his meeting in New York and was alarmed to hear about his threats that it would withdraw from the event. Renault issued a statement reiterating that it would race at Long Beach and Ferrari followed suit. Alfa Romeo and Ligier soon added their names. According to Jabby Crombac, 'That's when Balestre knew he'd lost.'

For Balestre, it was the worst possible betrayal. FOCA had been on the ropes and he had not imagined that FISA could lose the support of its fellow French organisation. Mosley admitted, 'If Balestre could have held the manufacturers' support for a little bit longer, the constructors would have been on their knees. The outcome then could have been very different.'

But Balestre had also come to a game-changing conclusion. According to Crombac, 'Balestre was clever enough to realise that there was nobody at the FIA who was able to handle the television rights as well as Bernie.'

The only route left for the Frenchman was to save face. He declared the Modena Agreement invalid, but at the same time invited Ecclestone and Mosley to meet him for breakfast at the Hotel de Crillon, next to the FIA's headquarters on the Place de la Concorde in Paris. Balestre agreed to the main tenets of the Modena Agreement providing that FOCA dropped the injunctions against him. Ecclestone said he would, but only when Balestre signed.

Mosley, Piccinini and Renault's lawyers got together to work out the fine details of the agreement. It was finished on 11 March 1981, just days before the Grand Prix at Long Beach. Balestre agreed to sign but he had one final stipulation. The Modena Agreement was no more. It would now be known as the Concorde Agreement.

The Concorde Agreement had finally brought peace to the sport. Somehow, after two years of bitter wrangling, both sides had broadly got what they wanted. The FIA's ultimate ownership of the commercial rights to F1 was recognised in the confidential contract as it stressed that the championship was 'the exclusive property of the FIA', meaning that its position as the ultimate power in the sport was secure. However, the FIA ceded those rights to FOCA for the four-year duration of the agreement, and granted it 'the exclusive right . . . to enter into contracts with the organisers of FIA F1 World Championship events, in the best interests of all competitors'. It's as if a landlord had given their tenant the right to live for free, and also allowed them to make money from sub-letting it.

Ecclestone continued to negotiate with race promoters and broadcasters in return for 8 per cent of the revenue. It was a lucrative deal. The race hosting fees were now worth around $12m a year, with the TV rights adding a few million more to the total. They were on track to overtake the race fees as the most valuable part of F1's commercial rights over the next few years.

The FIA didn't benefit financially from the rights for the duration of the contract but it confirmed its place in the driving seat when it came to framing F1's regulations.

Skirts were banned with immediate effect, but in future there would be a minimum of two years' notice for technical changes. The FIA would continue to control all sporting and technical aspects of F1, but the rules would be drafted by the new F1 Commission, which would propose rules to FISA's World Motor Sport Council (WMSC). The WMSC only had the power to accept or reject the rules, not change them.

The Commission would be composed of three FOCA team principals, three manufacturer representatives, four race promoters, two sponsors and a single representative of FISA. In addition to this, FOCA got two seats on the WMSC – taken up by Ecclestone and Mosley, positions which would prove invaluable in negotiations later down the line – while a seat for the motor industry would be occupied by Ferrari whenever F1 was under discussion.

Crucially, the FIA committed that the F1 technical regulations wouldn't change during the term of the Concorde. The teams required this because they have to build new cars when the regulations change.

The regulations are fixed for multi-year periods to this day, which explains why certain teams tend to dominate F1 for fairly long periods until the rules change, like Mercedes from 2014 to 2021 and Red Bull following that. If one squad gets to grips with the regulations better than the others, its lead can be unassailable. Its rivals can't even copy it to catch up as the F1 technical regulations state that every team has to design its own car.

The calendar they raced in was set by FISA and its ban on non-championship events remained. However, races would only be included on the calendar after the organisers had agreed terms with FOCA, so the teams could reject races that were not worth their while financially.

The Concorde committed them to race in every round of the F1 championship, meaning they could no longer skip events on a whim. The reward for participating in all of them was a guaranteed share of the prize money. The agreement didn't just keep the teams' costs under control, it also gave them guaranteed revenues, which stabilised their financial positions, allowing them to plan ahead with some degree of certainty. It also would provide Ecclestone the ability to negotiate long-term deals for the rights, which would usher in a new era of growth and stability.

Although this structure was Balestre's idea, it was music to Ecclestone's ears. By now he had negotiated the broadcast rights to almost all the races from the promoters and all he needed to turbocharge his return was a way of ensuring that the teams would turn up to them so that the TV channels would guarantee regular coverage. Balestre's manoeuvre gave him just what he wanted and made F1 an extremely attractive proposition for sponsors and broadcasters.

The Concorde didn't just boost Ecclestone's profits, it also reduced his risk. This was because it enabled the prize money to be guaranteed by long-term contracts with broadcasters, so he didn't have to guarantee it himself.

Ecclestone soon got to work and took the Concorde to TV networks. In 1982 the European Broadcasting Union agreed to broadcast the entire F1 season across the continent, safe in the knowledge that the races would go ahead as all the teams would be there. It ensured consistent coverage in F1's biggest markets in Europe and put F1 in the fast lane to becoming the multi-billion-dollar sport that it is today.

The guaranteed TV exposure drove up sponsors' rates, giving the teams more money to spend on cutting-edge technology in a bid to win. Williams' revenue, for example, increased almost sevenfold between 1980 and 1990, from £2.3m to £15.3m, boosted by sponsors including Leyland, Saudia, Camel and Canon. The larger budgets enabled the teams to pay big bucks for top talent, leading to the 1980s being the beginning of the era of professional drivers, racing for professional teams. Niki Lauda came out of retirement in 1982 to race for his former adversary McLaren as young talent such as Alain Prost, Ayrton Senna and Nigel Mansell emerged. These stars made the sport even more appealing to broadcasters and so the fees from TV stations increased. Soon F1 was available in 95 countries with an annual audience that exceeded 1 billion viewers, according to FOCA.

The benefits from the Concorde agreement encouraged the teams not to question its fundamentals or how it had reset the financial model of the sport. FOCA and the FIA agreed between themselves that the latter was the rightful owner of the commercial rights, which are now worth tens of billions of dollars.

The teams were initially pleased to see Ecclestone centralise the operations as it meant they did not have to negotiate prize money and start money with each race organiser. Later, they would come to realise just how much they had given away by surrendering the rights to the FIA.

Meanwhile, with the dispute in their rear-view mirror, the teams could get back to their usual business of racing.

However, it was Ecclestone who benefited most as he now had the power to negotiate with races and broadcasters worldwide. In the words of Mosley, 'The most fundamental change was that the Concorde Agreement had made it possible for Bernie to build one of the most successful businesses in modern sport.' He added, 'Balestre must take the credit for separating the rules from the money in the original Concorde Agreement. And we have seen what a mess other sports have got into when the sporting body also controls the business. Equally, the business must not control the sport.'

Some of the benefits came almost immediately. Ecclestone's race in Las Vegas took place (but his race in New York did not) and was broadcast live by the BBC for two hours during Sunday evening primetime. 'We even put back an edition of *Tinker Tailor Soldier Spy*!' Murray Walker remarked. Although the actual footage was poor, hampered by inexperienced local crews and the race's location in the car park of Caesar's Palace, it was a significant step in making F1 mainstream.

Ecclestone set about improving the aesthetic quality of the coverage as well as its reach. He set up FOCA TV, run initially from the basement of the Brabham factory in Chessington, to produce high-quality broadcast footage of the races. However, one 'thing that wasn't easy, was getting broadcasters and teams to take the onboard camera, if you can believe it', Ecclestone told us. FOCA awarded him $150,000 to develop the cameras, which were introduced in 1985 and greatly improved the show, despite concerns that they would be unwatchable due to vibrations from the car. 'We overcame that and it goes to show you've got to stick at what you believe in,' he added.

Ecclestone also kept himself busy outside F1 and couldn't resist trading when he had a free moment. It was no exaggeration to say that he made more money in his spare time than an average person would make in a lifetime. He proved this with a single currency trade on 15 February 1986 when his company agreed to sell $5m to NatWest and made a staggering £1,092,468 profit on the transaction. However, he didn't drop the ball in F1.

Perhaps appropriately, with the end of the FISA–FOCA war enabling Ecclestone to devote more of his time to racing, it was Brabham's Nelson Piquet who won the 1981 drivers' championship in Vegas, making Ecclestone a championship-winning team principal. He had no more trouble from Balestre and FISA regarding the regulations, although the same could not be said for Renault, which found that technical and sporting decisions were increasingly likely to go against its interests. The French marque continued as a team owner until 1985 without winning a title before, as Ecclestone had predicted, it pulled out to focus its marketing budget elsewhere.

It was a time of change. At the end of 1982, Colin Chapman died from a massive heart attack at the age of just 54. The stress of the FISA–FOCA war, Lotus's deteriorating performance, and the arrest of his business partner John Delorean (who Chapman had worked with to engineer the sportscar that would be made famous in *Back to the Future*) were factors that are unlikely to have done his health much good.

It paved the way for a new group of younger team principals, such as Ron Dennis, who had bought McLaren from Teddy Mayer, and Frank Williams, who had gone from cash-strapped privateer to world champion constructor in the space of a few years. Thanks to the structure created by the Concorde Agreement, team owners like Dennis and Williams would make fortunes of hundreds of millions of dollars from F1.

Ecclestone emerged as important a force in F1 as Enzo Ferrari and, remarkably, at the same time as running the commercial side of the sport, he managed to steer Brabham to a second drivers' championship with Piquet at the wheel in 1983. Ferrari and Renault, which was second in the championship with Prost, accused Brabham of using illegal fuel but Balestre surprisingly dismissed the protests as 'contradictory and unfounded'. Balestre even supported his view with what he described as an official telex from the Institut Français du Pétrole.

From enemy to friend to comrade in a matter of years, the fiercely patriotic Balestre's backing of Brabham against a French team with a French driver showed how seriously he took the entente cordiale of the Concorde Agreement.

Mosley made the most of the moment of rare harmony and left the sport at the end of 1982 to attempt a career in politics. He would of course return but in the meantime the structure that he had written into the Concorde Agreement did its job. It has stood the test of time and the contract is still in place to this day. 'I take a lot of satisfaction in what we achieved in those early years leading up to the creation of the Concorde Agreement. Everything since then has been built from that,' said Ecclestone. It was a memorable achievement. 'What I'm proud of, more than anything, is getting the television sorted out,' he said.

It was a bonus for broadcasters too. Murray Walker later recalled, 'Conditions for broadcasters have improved beyond all recognition and, like virtually everything else in F1, that's Bernie's doing. Yes, he's doing it for very good financial reasons, but when I look at tapes of our early days, the pictures and coverage are just archaic. Now you've got all the telemetry the teams have got, fantastic graphics, pit-lane reporters, an hour's preview before the race, summaries afterwards. Unbelievable when you think how far we've come, and it's all down to Bernie.'

For decades afterwards every aspect of F1 would be defined by the Concorde, and it is clear to see that its signing was, according to Balestre's ally Jabby Crombac, 'the most important date in the history of motor racing'. It gave the impression of fairness to the teams, while at the same time stripping them of the claim of ownership of the rights, which were to become hugely valuable as the sport entered its golden period and Formula One's popularity skyrocketed across the world. The realisation that Ecclestone had yet again outmanoeuvred everyone would come too late for the competitors and lead to many hours in court down the line.

PART 2
THE CONCORDE TAKES OFF

5

BEHIND THE CURTAIN

Five years after the signing of the first Concorde Agreement, Formula One was on a roll. Ecclestone's gambles had paid off handsomely and the burgeoning wealth of the teams meant that the lead *garagistes* had fewer financial worries than ever before in the history of the sport. In another instance of Ecclestone's uncanny luck, the racing was also spectacular, resulting in new broadcasters and race hosts clamouring for a piece of the action. The 1986 season saw four superstar drivers – Alain Prost, Ayrton Senna, Nigel Mansell and Nelson Piquet – challenging for the championship, culminating in a sensational finale in Australia where Prost took the title due to a catastrophic tyre blowout for Mansell.

Nowhere was F1's new wealth and status more apparent than at the inaugural Hungarian Grand Prix, which took place at the newly built Hungaroring on the outskirts of Budapest on 10 August 1986. A dream made reality due to Ecclestone's shrewd negotiating skills, the race was the first world championship Grand Prix in Eastern Europe and the biggest sporting event to take place behind the Iron Curtain since the 1980 Moscow Olympics.

More than 200,000 fans turned up on race day, travelling from across the Eastern Bloc for their first glimpse of F1. It was a Grand Prix attendance record that would not be surpassed for almost a decade. While Jean-Marie Balestre escorted local dignitaries on grid walks, KGB agents lurked in the VIP hospitality lounges, ostensibly to keep an eye on the proceedings. Meanwhile, Ecclestone counted the cash, having negotiated an unprecedented hosting fee of $3.5m, paid for by the government, plus 60 per cent of the revenue from the first 10,000 tickets sold and 2,000 free nights in Budapest's best hotels. The Hungarian politicians were so grateful they even named the road to the circuit after Ecclestone and would eventually commission a bronze statue of the F1 boss at the main gates.

Sponsor logos were everywhere as brands took advantage of the opportunity to reach a usually inaccessible market. West cigarettes even rebranded their logos on the Zakspeed team's cars as 'East' in celebration of the occasion. However, no brand was more prominent than Marlboro, the principal sponsor of the race, with branding that saw its logos emblazoned across the podium and on the uniforms of the grid girls, who channelled the 1980s' zeitgeist with their permed hair and scarlet hotpants.

F1 had transformed from a niche sport to a major player on the world stage. It looked effortless, but behind the scenes a complex structure was being built to keep it in pole position.

Important as the Concorde Agreement was, it was only part of Ecclestone's plan to rev up F1. He also relied on a web of shadowy companies that were all bizarrely named Allsopp, Parker & Marsh (APM). Even though few people in F1 circles ever knew of their existence, the companies were crucial to the development of the sport.

Ecclestone helped to steer the trackside advertising rights for a number of the races to APM and in return it paid the event organisers a fixed fee or share of the revenue. The first APM was founded in 1983 and was run by Ecclestone's friend Patrick 'Paddy' McNally, a former journalist at the weekly magazine *Autosport* who became a marketing director for Philip Morris. One of his first jobs at the tobacco giant was to act as gofer for James Hunt, who won the 1976 F1 title in a McLaren sponsored by its Marlboro brand.

McNally went on to bigger and better things and even dated the Duchess of York, Sarah Ferguson, in the 1980s prior to her marriage to Prince Andrew. McNally made his name selling advertising space for Philip Morris at F1 races so Ecclestone put even more trust in his hands through APM. In an interview with the BBC's *Panorama* programme in 1998, McNally explained that APM started out by working with circuits where 'the promoters wanted a race, but did not have the necessary funds and passed on all their commercial rights'. He added, 'I still have the three-line letter from BCE [Bernard Charles Ecclestone] wishing APM good luck.'

The company had two directors – McNally and Luc Argand, the Swiss lawyer who had worked for Jochen Rindt and later became a director of many of the companies owned by Ecclestone's family trust. Following Rindt's untimely death, Argand helped to set up the

Rindt Trust for the benefit of Jochen's daughter – Ecclestone became a trustee.

Ecclestone could see tremendous talent in the lawyer and the two had many mutual interests. Ecclestone has had a lifelong fascination with law and has said he would like to be a lawyer if he had to start over. Likewise, Argand and Ecclestone both share a love of business and sport, not just motor racing. In 1972, when Argand was training to be a lawyer, he also competed on the Swiss sailing team in the Olympic Games in Munich. He made waves in the world of law after that.

In 1974 Argand was admitted to the Geneva Bar, and he earned an MBA from France's prestigious INSEAD business school two years later, giving him a fast track to the high-flying world of corporate finance. This led to him getting internships with Rothschild and Goldman Sachs before combining his loves of law and sport. He took a position as an arbitrator at the Court of Arbitration for Sport in Lausanne, where one of his most prominent cases was clearing tennis player Richard Gasquet after he tested positive for cocaine that he said got into his system from a fleeting kiss.

McNally was another of his clients and as directors of APM the pair had a responsibility to act in the best interests of the company's shareholders. An investigation in 2000 by the *Economist* revealed that McNally and Argand each held one of APM's 12 shares but the 10 others belonged to a trust in Guernsey, so its majority owner was a closely guarded secret. However, the *Economist* laid bare the company's finances.

The revenue from race advertising gave APM high-octane financial performance right from the start and the more events it worked with, the better its bottom line became. Data from the *Economist* showed that between 1985 and 1988 APM generated $34m of profit on $46m of revenue. That gave the company annual average revenue of $11.5m, with title sponsorship of individual races alone having a $1.5m price tag in 1985 according to filings from Marlboro..

Up until the early 1980s, F1's trackside advertising had been a ragged patchwork of conflicting brands and colours, with obscure local businesses interspersed with global giants. McNally's masterstroke was restricting the number of advertisers per race as well as offering standard-sized panels and limiting corners to single sponsors. Corners present overtaking opportunities for F1 cars as they have to slow down to get round them. The driver who brakes the latest usually has a speed advantage, allowing him to pass his rivals there. It means that race fans focus their attention on corners, which makes them particularly prized slots for advertisers. McNally capitalised on this by giving brands exclusivity in these spots.

McNally's advertising experience wasn't his only strength. There were two other strings to his bow. Ecclestone realised that if F1 was to become a platform to promote the world's biggest brands, their executives would want somewhere stylish to be wined and dined at the races. In the early 1980s, F1's hospitality amounted to little more than a glass of warm beer, a hot dog and a packet of crisps. Ecclestone tasked McNally with transforming it and in 1983 he set up Allsport Management to do this.

APM received the races' rights to organise corporate hospitality, which it licensed to Allsport. McNally worked his magic again and founded the Paddock Club, which operates in F1 to this day. At most races it is recognisable by its sprawling tented structure adorned with fresh flowers and turf. Guests get a gourmet buffet, free-flowing champagne bars, pit-lane walks and talks from drivers for the princely price of at least $5,000 per person.

McNally's other strength was his knowledge of Switzerland – a nation famous for its low taxes and secrecy. Philip Morris's history in Switzerland dates back to 1957 when it signed an agreement with local company Fabriques de Tabac Réunies to produce the first Marlboro cigarettes manufactured outside the United States. In 2001 Philip Morris's operations were moved from New York to Lausanne, and McNally based Allsport just an hour away in Geneva. It moved F1 further offshore and away from Ecclestone's base in Britain.

Allsport is still trading, but the original APM company bit the dust in 1988. Although it was British, APM was initially deemed to be non-resident for tax purposes, so the UK authorities didn't get a penny from its high-octane haul. However, changes to British tax rules in 1988 led to it no longer being non-resident – instead of it continuing to trade, it closed its doors. APM burned up losses of £485,000 in 1988 and was finally dissolved seven years later. Despite this, its work in F1 was only just beginning.

The catalyst for this was the signing of a new Concorde Agreement. The original contract had been due to expire in 1985 but was extended, on substantially the same terms, to the end of 1986. It was then overhauled in a new five-year deal that began in 1987. Having seen F1's TV revenue accelerate following Ecclestone's EBU deal, the FIA forecast further growth and Balestre now wanted a piece of the action. So in the 1987 agreement the FIA was handed 30 per cent of the TV rights revenue, while Ecclestone's take rose to 23 per cent, with the remaining 47 per cent shared by FOCA among the teams as prize money.

In 1987 Balestre became president of the FIA as well as FISA and honoured Ecclestone with the title of the FIA's vice president of promotional affairs. It was Ecclestone's third role for the federation as he also sat on its Senate and the board of its decision-making body, the World Motor Sport Council. He was joined on the body by his old ally Max Mosley, who had returned to the world of F1 in 1986 as president of FISA's manufacturers' commission.

Within the space of 20 years, Ecclestone had gone from driver to team owner to promoter to being at the centre of power. The poacher had become gamekeeper. But there was fallout. The FIA roles kept Ecclestone so busy that Brabham's performance reversed. The team only finished eighth in the standings in 1987, having struggled to recover after its driver Elio de Angelis had been killed in testing the previous year.

Ecclestone explained to us in 2013 that he 'had a decision to make: do I let Formula One splutter along in a very amateurish way and look after my team or do I look after Formula One? I couldn't do both jobs properly. The people who were running the race teams were spending twenty-four hours a day and seven days a week doing that and I had to run the whole business as well.' So in 1988 he sold Brabham to Alfa Romeo and by the end of 1992 the team was gone from F1.

Ecclestone retained an interest in Brabham's factory on Cox Lane in Chessington, which became part of FOCA's headquarters. He got more than his fair share from it, as the UK's tax authority would find out many years later.

Although Ecclestone was F1's golden boy thanks to the boost he had given to its fortunes, Balestre was dismayed to find that the TV revenues didn't rev up as much as he expected. At the time, the money from TV was still relatively modest and, according to the *Financial Times,* the FIA's income from its 30 per cent share was less than $1m a year. This put it far behind race hosting fees and trackside advertising in terms of revenue for the sport.

Although the EBU deal boosted F1's exposure and initially its revenue, it didn't continue to rise. This was because the EBU fixed the buying price then sold programming on to national broadcasters such as the BBC. No one had ever challenged its power but, ever the trader, Ecclestone hatched a plan to demolish the EBU's dominance by approaching each individual broadcaster and doing deals with them directly.

In 1990, as Balestre pondered what would be best for the FIA in the upcoming 1992 Concorde Agreement, Ecclestone shocked the establishment by deciding not to renew FOCA's contract with the EBU. 'The most important decision I ever made was doing deals with television channels directly rather than letting Formula One only be broadcast by European Broadcasting Union stations,' he told us in an interview for GQ in 2013. 'Everyone said there was no way I could ever deal with the companies individually. They are all EBU and you've got to deal with the EBU. But the first people I signed was the BBC. I think that was a big stepping stone for Formula One.'

Balestre didn't see it that way at the time. An aloof and boastful figure, Balestre had little in common with the rough diamond Ecclestone. The Frenchman thought that Ecclestone was taking a gamble by negotiating the TV contracts on a country-by-country basis. Currency fluctuations also preyed on his mind because the FIA was paid in dollars but its expenses were in French francs.

Balestre's concerns were compounded by the bankruptcy in 1992 of La Cinq, the French television company that broadcast F1 in France and was owned by his friend Robert Hersant. It led to the loss of a lucrative F1 contract and was the clincher when he was deciding what to do about the federation's percentage deal. A solution soon presented itself thanks to none other than Paddy McNally.

In September 1988, just weeks after the original APM ceased trading, a second company with the same name was formed in the Republic of Ireland. This allowed APM to continue managing F1's trackside advertising uninterrupted and in 1992 its fortunes hit top gear. Mindful of Balestre's worries about a decline in F1's fortunes, French-speaking McNally approached him with a proposal for a five-year contract that would give the FIA a guaranteed annual royalty payment of at least $3m (between £2m and £4m) in return for its 30 per cent share of F1's TV revenue. Crucially, McNally offered to pay in francs, which eliminated Balestre's fears about currency risk, while the minimum amount addressed his worries about fluctuating interest in F1 on TV.

Investment in the teams had surged thanks to their accelerating income from the Concorde Agreement. It enabled them to build increasingly sophisticated cars, the epitome being British driver Nigel Mansell's Williams, which was bristling with electronic aids and dominated the 1992 season. He wrapped up the championship by mid-August, which drove down audience interest. However, it didn't stay that way for long.

In 1992, when the third Concorde Agreement began, the FIA received its first payment from APM of $5.6m, according to the *FT*. By 1994 it had reached $7m and it hit $9m by 1996, the final year of the contract. But although the FIA's takings increased, it was actually losing a staggering sum compared to the value of the 30 per cent stake it had surrendered to APM. Instead of shrinking as Balestre had predicted, F1's TV revenues surged and between 1992 and 1996 they totalled an estimated $341m, of which $102m went to APM. The FIA's share, however, came to no more than $37m.

This led to a tremendous loss of tax income for France, which was why its tax investigation authority began looking into the situation in 1994. Four years later, the BBC's *Panorama* and the *FT* got hold of its correspondence and put it to F1's leading lights. Few of them knew about the APM deal and many were dumbfounded by it.

One was former banker and businessman Eddie Jordan, who became an F1 team owner in 1991. On learning about the APM deal he told *Panorama* that giving up 'thirty per cent of all television income for two million pounds . . . on the face of it looks strange'.

One of the few who sprang to the defence of the deal was Ecclestone's associate Mosley. He told the *FT* that Balestre 'was always a great pessimist. He hated getting a percentage in dollars, and not a fixed sum in Francs, and McNally was already giving him several times the biggest income he'd ever got.' However, Mosley admitted to *Panorama* that for the FIA, the APM agreement 'turned out badly. But the deal was done in 1990, and that was a contract made in 1990. Now nobody knew in 1990 what would happen. You cannot possibly say that what Balestre did was wrong. On the contrary, the best evidence was that some of these contracts might well disappear and suddenly you're getting no money at all. That income could have collapsed. As it turned out, thanks to Bernie's ingenuity, it didn't.' There is no doubt about that.

In an interview for Terry Lovell's book *Bernie's Game*, Ecclestone admitted that 'what he [Balestre] didn't know was that already at that time I had thought this Channel 5 [La Cinq] was going to get into problems . . . and I got another deal [with another television company].' So although Ecclestone was the FIA's vice president of promotional affairs, he reportedly withheld information from its president that may have encouraged him to retain the highly lucrative percentage share. Instead, it went to APM.

It's hard to say precisely how much profit the deal generated for APM because it didn't file accounts. As the *Economist* revealed, APM was able to keep its finances confidential by claiming an exemption open only to 'a company not trading for the acquisition of profit by [its shareholders]'. To qualify for this exemption, a company's constitution had to include an explicit provision to this effect. The *Economist* added that although APM's constitution 'does contain such a provision, it was clearly trading for profit'.

The tax authorities didn't get a penny from this second APM company either, as it was based in Dublin, where it was allowed to be non-resident for tax purposes. In order to do this, neither its directors nor legal owners could be resident in Ireland. By ticking this box it revealed a surprising connection to its predecessor as its directors (who were nominees for its actual directors) came from the same firm that acted as company secretary for the first APM. This was part of the reason the *Economist* concluded that the two APM companies 'were really the same company. So the beneficial owners of both must have been one and the same.' Accordingly, the identity of its majority owner was safe in Guernsey.

The *Economist* heavily implied that Ecclestone owned APM and Allsport but hadn't declared this to HMRC in the UK where he was based. There is no evidence for this and the *Economist* stopped short of saying it. Ecclestone has repeatedly denied it but the theme continued to dog him for years to come for a number of reasons.

For someone who had no financial interest in APM, Ecclestone certainly helped it a lot along the way. A financial manager for one of the race promoters told the *Economist* that after Ecclestone had taken the wheel of F1 he gave his company no alternative but to surrender track-side advertising rights to the APM companies. It's unclear why he did this but APM was all the richer for it. In return, it paid the race organisers a fixed fee or gave them a share of the revenue, but this arrangement still meant that they missed out on the lion's share of the money. What is clear is that Ecclestone had longstanding ties to the directors of APM and

Allsport. 'I know Luc Argand very well,' said Ecclestone in an interview for Susan Watkins' biography of him, *Bernie*. 'Anything to do with Switzerland we use him.'

Around the time that the Rindt Trust was set up, Argand also introduced Ecclestone to British lawyer Stephen Mullens, who was one of the founding partners of the London-based law firm Marriott Harrison, which was where the first APM was based from 1990 until 1993. Mullens signed off the company's initial regulatory filings, but that was only the start.

Mullens was the top billing partner at Marriott Harrison every year from 1986 until 1999 when he left to become a corporate lawyer for the Ecclestone family's offshore trust. Mullens banked on receiving even richer rewards from the trust and he got what he was looking for.

A grey-haired, slender and softly spoken solicitor, Mullens looks like the archetypal English gent. However, his demure personality belies tremendous ingenuity, as Mullens is the architect of many of F1's most bafflingly complex corporate manoeuvres and the byzantine cat's cradle of companies that still controls the sport. He didn't just file the paperwork for APM but for many of the companies at the heart of Ecclestone's family trust and was its representative on the board.

Of course, simply because Ecclestone was close to Argand it didn't mean he owned APM or Allsport. Despite the closeness of his ties to APM, Ecclestone told the *Economist* that he has 'always understood Mr McNally to be the owner of Allsopp, Parker & Marsh'. But McNally, of course, actually only personally held one of its 12 shares, and the same went for Argand. Although it is possible that Argand added gravitas to the board, it was also possible that he represented the interests of an unknown beneficial shareholder other than McNally.

In an interview with *Panorama*, McNally stressed that Ecclestone had no part in the ownership of APM. Likewise, Ecclestone claimed that McNally also owned Allsport, and although McNally was indeed one of its directors, he was again joined by Argand. It remains to be seen which shareholder he represented on the board of that company too, because Swiss companies do not need to disclose the identity of their owners.

Ecclestone's biographer Terry Lovell attempted to shed some light on this by interviewing one of McNally's contemporaries, Michael Tee, whose family founded the *Motoring News* publication and also funded a company that assisted with hospitality for Philip Morris before the arrival of the Paddock Club. Tee told Lovell that he 'once jokingly asked Bernie where he [McNally] had got the money from, and he looked at me in a way that suggested I should have known better. McNally was just the front man.'

Even Ecclestone admitted that McNally didn't have enough money to get his business off the ground. In an interview with *BusinessAge* he described the driving force behind McNally tidying up F1's trackside advertising. 'The EBU wanted to clear out all trackside advertising – it didn't want silly little banners hanging and flags waving all over the place,' said Ecclestone.

> I was speaking to Philip Morris about it, because it had always been the main advertiser. At that time Patrick was going to leave Philip Morris and they said to me, 'Why don't you take McNally and let him do all this, maybe he knows what he is doing because he's been with us.' For me it was no problem, I didn't care as long as the job was done. So his job was to go to the promoters and make sure they complied with all the rules and regulations. I suggested that if he wanted to start a business (because he hadn't got any money at that time), I knew that people would work with him. I said: 'You go round and take their advertising, I will help you if I can, take it and package it properly in accordance with this and that.

It was a winning formula thanks to McNally's legwork and Ecclestone's network.

Minutes of an F1 board meeting from October 2001 reveal that Ecclestone had a good working knowledge of how much APM and Allsport were worth, because one person present at the meeting referred to 'Ecclestone's assertion that Mr McNally's stake in the business could sell for $600 million to $800 million'. There was good reason for this high-octane valuation. APM didn't just license the hospitality and trackside advertising rights from the race organisers. F1 even handed the company the right to receive revenue from its official sponsors.

These rich rewards were also kept out of the taxman's clutches as a third APM company, Allsopp, Parker & Marsh (Ireland), was founded in Dublin in May 2002. It had the same address as the second APM and its directors were from the same nominee firm that the first APM used to provide its company secretary. This further supported the *Economist*'s conclusion that the companies were all one and the same, and this is reflected by the fact that F1's contract with APM spanned its various incarnations.

In 2014, F1's chief financial officer Duncan Llowarch explained that there was originally no material agreement in place with APM. However, in 1998 F1 signed a contract with it that was due to run until 2008 but was extended to 2010 in 2000. At the same time, the licence fee APM paid to F1 was fixed at a staggering $51.7m annually, as both it and Allsport had turbocharged underlying profits, known in the trade as earnings before interest, taxes, depreciation and amortisation (EBITDA). According to legal filings, 'In 2003, their income totalled $230 million, giving rise to EBITDA of $99 million. By 2005, the companies' revenue had increased to $285 million and their EBITDA to $125 million.'

Despite the huge sums flowing through APM, Llowarch said that as of 2004 the company 'had no budgets, it had no models, it had no management accounts ... I don't believe there were any available accounts.' For whatever reason, its owner was clearly keen to keep the company's details away from prying eyes, even those of F1's senior management. Llowarch added that Allsport filed annual accounts because it was a Swiss company, but 'there were no existing records [for APM] that we could use to be comfortable with'. By then it had taken a step behind the ultimate veil of corporate secrecy by setting up a parent company in the British Virgin Islands, where accounts don't need to be filed and ownership details are kept under lock and key.

That's not to say that APM had an easy ride. In 1997 it would lose its biggest cash cow thanks to one of the most controversial business decisions in the history of F1, which created one of the world's richest men. This was far from the only momentous change.

In 1991 Mosley had stood against Balestre in the election for president of FISA, the FIA sub-committee. Supported by most of the big-name member clubs, Balestre wholeheartedly expected to win. However, under the FIA's electoral system, every member club has a single vote. This means that motorsport clubs from small countries with little racing heritage, such as Fiji or Madagascar, have as much power as major players like Italy or France.

Mosley charmed these smaller clubs, which were flattered that their voices were finally being heard, a tactic later used to great success by the likes of Sepp Blatter and Gianni Infantino at FIFA. Balestre remained completely unaware of his precarious position, particularly as many of the clubs did not dare tell him to his face that they were planning to vote for someone else. He was therefore shocked and bewildered when the result was announced and it turned out that Mosley had won by 43 votes to 29.

Two years later, when Mosley announced his intention to also stand for president of the FIA itself, Balestre had learned his lesson. On the advice of Ecclestone – who else? – he decided to step aside to become the head of the FIA's Senate, a role with no day-to-day power over Formula One. On 10 June 1993, Mosley got the top job and announced his intention to merge FISA back into the FIA. Mosley now had unfettered control of world motorsport – and with Mosley, in through the back door, came Ecclestone. In the space of 20 years of double-dealing, power moves and brilliant manoeuvring, Bernie Ecclestone had taken his place at the very top of the sport. For better or worse, Formula One was now being run by one of the most astute and wily business minds that international sport had ever seen.

6

FOR THE GOOD OF THE SPORT

By the early 1990s F1 was in top gear. Ecclestone's strategy of doing deals directly with the broadcasters had paid off and each F1 race now had an estimated 300 million viewers worldwide. To many, things seemed as good as they could get and even Ecclestone couldn't have imagined what it would take to drive up the exposure of the sport.

F1's age of excess was gathering speed as sponsors were spending an estimated total of $400m a season, with the biggest backers being car manufacturers like Honda, Renault, Porsche and Lamborghini, which supplied engines to the teams. Spending by the teams hit record levels, with McLaren's 1993 season costing it £46.6m, though life was tough at the other end of the grid. Such was F1's popularity, there were more teams than grid spaces and a 'pre-qualifying' competition had to be held to weed out the worst performers.

By this point the top drivers were commanding salaries of between $10m and $12m, which was five to six times what they had been paid just a decade earlier. The world was gripped by the on-track battles between calm, calculating Frenchman Alain Prost and the impulsive and unpredictable Ayrton Senna. The attention on their tense rivalry was magnified by the fact that both drivers had fought for the championship at the same team – McLaren. Senna had secured his first title for the British squad in 1988 while Prost won the following year after colliding with his team-mate at Suzuka.

It galvanised Senna and he steered McLaren to success for the following two years before an era of dominance from Williams began, fuelled by the appointment of up-and-coming aerodynamicist Adrian Newey as the team's chief designer in 1991.

Newey studied aeronautical engineering at Southampton University and wrote his thesis on ground-effect, an aerodynamic phenomenon that determines the design of aircraft. It can also be used to suck race cars to the ground, thereby improving their grip and cornering speed. Having specialised in this field, Newey employed it to great effect at Williams and it powered the team to victory, first with Nigel Mansell in 1992, then with Prost the following year. The Frenchman retired at the end of 1993 and Senna took his place at Williams, putting him on course to win a fourth championship. It was not to be.

To this day, F1's darkest hour is still seen by many as being Sunday, 1 May 1994, when the San Marino Grand Prix took place at Italy's Imola circuit. Thanks to advancements in safety, there hadn't been a death in an F1 race for 12 years, but then there were two in one weekend.

The first involved Roland Ratzenberger, an F1 novice who died while trying to qualify in only his second Grand Prix. Ratzenberger damaged the front wing of his Simtek when he went off track on the Saturday but instead of coming into the pits he continued to push for a quick lap. Eventually the front wing broke and launched his car head-on into a concrete barrier at 180 miles per hour. The Austrian suffered fatal head injuries but the race weekend carried on regardless, largely because Ratzenberger's incident was of his own making. His rivals thought they would have done things differently. However, despite the huge sums being pumped into research and development, F1 cars were far from infallible – the risk of danger that was ever-present in F1's early days still hung over the sport.

Then, ominously, the following morning, Senna placed an Austrian flag in his Williams. The Brazilian was in pole position and planned to wave the flag as he passed the finish line in victory. Senna wanted to celebrate Ratzenberger in triumph but ended up joining him in tragedy: on just the fifth lap, his car veered off the track and ploughed into a concrete wall at 200 miles per hour while he was leading the race. Debris pierced his helmet, leaving the 34-year-old with multiple fractures at the base of his skull. He was airlifted to a hospital in nearby Bologna but, remarkably, this didn't bring the red flag down on the race.

On its path to institutionalisation F1 had become beholden to new paymasters, as Ecclestone explained in *Lucky*: 'I [said I'm] not stopping the race and eventually it became quite clear that it would be the worst thing for the promoter in Italy for the race to be stopped. By law it would be bad if we did that because we would be completely responsible.' Up-and-coming German driver Michael Schumacher eventually won the Grand Prix at the wheel of his Ford-powered Benetton car, though the podium was a sombre affair as the world awaited news on Senna. The Brazilian died three hours after the race, and grief quickly led to recrimination when his steering column was identified as the potential cause of the crash. (Senna had wanted the position of the steering wheel changed, and the welding and reinforcing of the additional length of the existing column had been greenlit by Newey and Williams' director of engineering Patrick Head – it would take three years of investigations by the local authorities before all of the defendants were acquitted.)

Senna's life had been cut short suddenly and brutally on live television beamed all over the world. The unexpectedness of the incident magnified the shock, as many saw Senna as being almost unbeatable. Instead, he became the first, and to date the only, F1 champion to die in a world championship Grand Prix. F1 had experienced many driver deaths before but none had been as public as Senna's. Fittingly, his state funeral was broadcast on live TV in Brazil, while the government declared three days of national mourning.

F1 went into a spin at a time when more eyes than ever before were on the sport. 'Immediately after Ayrton's death, the viewing figures increased dramatically,' said Ecclestone. 'He lifted the sport more after his accident than before. It was really probably the first time that generally news worldwide had got out about [F1].' All that was missing was its poster boy – and one man was in pole position to take over that mantle.

Famous for his lantern jaw, determination and steely stare, Michael Schumacher was the very personification of a *wunderkind*. He won the first of many kart championships aged just six, competing against much older children. He made the move to single-seater race cars when he was 19 and won several junior championships, earning him a place on Mercedes' young driver development scheme. Nevertheless, he was largely unknown when he made his F1 debut at the 1991 Belgian Grand Prix in Spa. It took more than a bit of luck to get him there.

The fledgling Jordan team needed a replacement for Belgian driver Bertrand Gachot, who had been jailed for assaulting a London cabbie. Schumacher got the drive on the strength of an impressive test and a cheque for £150,000 per race, which ultimately came from Mercedes. Eddie Jordan later said on his *Formula for Success* podcast that 'Bernie came to me and Bernie said, "Listen, Jordan, you're going out of business. I can't possibly see how you're going to survive. Take the money, go. Just take as much as you can off the table."'

Mercedes had won two drivers' championships in the mid-1950s before it quit F1 in the wake of the 1955 Le Mans disaster. It was not until the early 1990s that the marque considered a return as an engine supplier and began to support the careers of young drivers with a view to eventually seeing a German driver win in a German-powered car. However, its F1 engine programme was behind schedule, so it needed to find other ways to get Schumacher the necessary experience to be a future winner, which was why it decided to fund his Jordan outing. It was a move that the German car giant would regret over the coming years once it started supplying engines to F1 teams that were routinely beaten by Schumacher.

Despite his lack of experience, Schumacher qualified seventh for his first Grand Prix, equalling Jordan's best grid slot of the year. Although his car's clutch gave up after only two corners in the race, he had already done enough to grab Ecclestone's attention. Germany was a major untapped market for F1 and Schumacher was a potential solution to that problem. However, it was unlikely that the young German would become a national hero at the wheel of an uncompetitive and unreliable Jordan.

Ecclestone was close to Eddie Jordan, but he was even closer to the top brass at the Benetton team, which had finished third in the championship the previous year. Perma-tanned playboy Flavio Briatore ran Benetton, while Tom Walkinshaw, the burly businessman who founded car maker TWR, was its engineering director. The team's ranks were filled with technical and engineering experts, several of whom ended up working for F1 itself, including its former technical director Ross Brawn and its chief technology officer Pat Symonds.

Jordan reportedly had an agreement to retain Schumacher for the rest of 1991 and the following two years, as well as an option on 1994. It meant that Jordan had to be paid off and Ecclestone explained that 'Eddie got a few dollars to help him along the way'. According to an interview Jordan gave to Rupert Murdoch's now-defunct *News of the World* newspaper, Ecclestone 'was keen to get a German driver into F1 to bring in TV money from that country'. It was no exaggeration.

At the time, F1 was broadcast in Germany by media giant RTL and its contract is believed to have stated that if a German driver entered the sport permanently it would double its estimated $10m fee, with a further increase if another one signed up. Ecclestone's company Formula One Promotions and Administration (FOPA) kept 23 per cent of the revenue from the broadcast contracts so he had a personal reason to engineer Schumacher's switch to Benetton.

In Schumacher's first race for Benetton he finished fifth, 11 seconds ahead of his new team-mate, triple world champion Nelson Piquet. Against strong opposition he regularly shone and on the anniversary of his F1 debut he took his first victory in the pouring rain at Spa. It was the first demonstration of his supreme car control in the wet, which would earn him the title *Regenmeister* – the Rain Master.

In 1993 Mercedes started supplying engines to newcomer Sauber, marking the German car giant's first involvement with F1 for nearly 40 years. Mercedes invoked a clause in its agreement with Schumacher stating that if it entered F1 he would drive for its team. However, Schumacher showed early signs of the defiance he would later become famous for as he reneged on the agreement and stayed put at Benetton. The team was getting into its stride, whereas Sauber was spluttering. Its owner Peter Sauber confirmed that Schumacher 'didn't want to drive for us. Why would I have forced him?' The defiance paid off as Benetton began a meteoric rise through F1's ranks in 1994. It started with Schumacher winning the first four races and was followed by some of the most unusual manoeuvres that F1 had ever seen.

Eyebrows were raised by the huge performance gap between Schumacher and his team-mates at Benetton – JJ Lehto and Jos Verstappen, father of future F1 champion, Max. This kind of disparity between team-mates in F1 was virtually unprecedented at the time and raised the question of whether something was different about Schumacher's car. One of the easiest aspects to change was the software, especially as electronic driver aids, such as traction control, had been banned by Max Mosley in 1994 to put more emphasis on driver talent than technology and encourage closer racing.

In just the second Grand Prix of the season, Senna concluded that Benetton was using traction control after he spent time closely watching the team's cars following his exit from the race, which was won by Schumacher.

Even Verstappen suspected that Schumacher had an unfair advantage. 'I know what happened when we were together at Benetton,' he later said. 'People think I'm looking for excuses but I know that his car was different from mine. I always thought it was impossible; I braked at the limit and took the corners as hard as possible, so how could Schumacher do it? There was something wrong. There were electronic driver aids. It was never mentioned, but I'm convinced and when I later asked Flavio Briatore he replied, "Let's not talk about it."'

The FIA took matters into its own hands in May 1994 and demanded to see Benetton's engine management system source code. However, the team missed the deadline for supplying it because its engine supplier, Cosworth, considered it to be their property. Benetton was fined $100,000 for this but eventually complied. When it did, the FIA made the remarkable discovery that Benetton's software contained a prohibited 'Launch Control' system designed to give its drivers an automated optimum start in races. What made it particularly remarkable was how deeply it was buried in Benetton's software.

The FIA's investigation revealed that the system could be switched on by a laptop and was not labelled as 'Launch Control' in Benetton's menu but was hidden under the shadowy name of 'Option 13'. The discovery lifted the lid on the lengths that teams were going to in order to gain an edge and it was a stark reminder that the days when *garagistes* would turn up to races with cars they had built in their backyards were long gone.

Benetton claimed that the system was deliberately hidden to prevent it from being activated accidentally. It added that Schumacher himself could not turn it on and it had not been used in races. However, it did admit that it had been used in testing, so clearly it had some benefit to the team.

In the end it didn't matter as the FIA's rules only prevented the use of such systems, not the existence of them in the teams' software. As the FIA had no proof it was being used in races, it announced in July that no action would be taken against Benetton. It was a different story for Schumacher. At the British Grand Prix on 10 July, the German made three illegal overtaking manoeuvres, landing him with a two-race ban and Benetton with a $500,000 fine.

In the wake of Senna's death, the FIA made it mandatory for the teams to install a thin piece of wood under their cars in a bid to reduce their cornering speed. The wood increased the ride height of the cars, thereby preventing ground-effect from sucking them to the track, which was how they managed to get round the corners so fast. However, at the

Belgian Grand Prix in August 1994 the skid block underneath Schumacher's Benetton was found to have worn down so much that it gave the car a ground-effect advantage. Benetton claimed it was due to Schumacher running over a kerb during the race but the FIA disagreed and disqualified him from it.

The controversy kept F1 in the public eye after the sport surged in exposure following Senna's death. However, Benetton went too far. The moment it pushed its luck had come during the German Grand Prix at Hockenheim on 31 July.

As Verstappen pulled in for his first pit stop on lap 15, the refuelling hose failed to connect properly to the car, spraying three litres of fuel all over it and the mechanics. Nothing happened for a few seconds before the heat from the car's brake discs suddenly ignited the fuel while Verstappen was trapped inside it with his seatbelt fastened, his steering wheel locked in place and his visor slightly open. A fireball engulfed the car. The flames didn't just endanger Benetton's crew but also their counterparts in the neighbouring McLaren garage, and they rushed in with their own extinguishers.

It took around seven seconds to put out the blaze and a few seconds more for the fire on the Benetton mechanics' overalls to be extinguished. Seven members of the team, including Verstappen, were rushed to F1's medical centre. Three of them were then airlifted to the same burns unit in Mannheim that had treated Niki Lauda after his fiery 1976 crash at the Nürburgring. Verstappen was one of them along with Benetton's mechanic Dave Redding and its junior refueller Simon Morley, who was kept in hospital for several days to receive further treatment.

Following an investigation by Intertechnique, the refuelling rig manufacturer, the FIA released a statement confirming that the fire had been started by a fuel spillage 'caused by a valve failing to close properly'. It added that 'the valve was slow to close due to the presence of a foreign body'. Crucially, the FIA concluded that 'the foreign body is believed to have reached the valve because a filter designed to eliminate this risk had been deliberately removed'.

After a decade-long absence on safety grounds, refuelling had been reintroduced to F1 in 1994 to add an additional layer of strategy. Teams had to decide whether to conserve fuel and stay out on track for longer or pit earlier because they had burned fuel by pushing for faster times. The quicker the pit stop, the sooner the teams could get back in the race.

They had been specifically told that the filter was essential in such a fast-paced environment to ensure that debris didn't enter the valve of the refuelling rig.

However, the filter also slowed down the flow of fuel. Removing it increased the fuel flow rate by an estimated 12.5 per cent, giving a one-second saving over an eight-second pit stop. It could mean the difference between winning and losing.

Timing is everything in F1 pit stops. Although they only usually last for a matter of seconds, if one team can do it quicker than its rival it can get back onto the track ahead of it. This is exactly what happened at the first race of the 1994 season in Brazil when Senna, who was leading in his Williams, made a pit stop with Schumacher close behind. The Benetton pit crew were faster than their counterparts at Williams, so Schumacher got back out on track in the lead and went on to win the race.

There is no evidence that Benetton removed the refuelling rig filter before the German Grand Prix in July, despite widespread allegations of cheating. It was driven by the team's turbocharged performance that gave Schumacher a 27-point lead by the German Grand Prix, putting him on course to be F1's youngest-ever champion. This was just what was needed to drive up interest in the sport from Germany and put the dark days of Imola behind it. However, Benetton's chicanery drove the FIA into a tight spot.

Before the 1994 season began, FIA president Max Mosley had proclaimed, 'If anybody is found deliberately cheating, as opposed to making a wrong interpretation of the regulations, then draconian penalties would be appropriate.' He added that 'in these circumstances teams can be expected to be stopped from racing'.

The thought filled Ecclestone with dread, and he wasn't the only one. Benetton released its own statement that included the results of a report by the experienced firm Accident and Failure Technical Analysis, which concluded that Benetton had removed the filter 'for the Hockenheim race after a lengthy period during which no debris was collected'.

Benetton added that prior to the race, its fuel rigs 'had been thoroughly stripped and cleaned and there was no risk of debris entering the valve assembly. Benetton also pre-filter their fuel twice before it is placed in the fuel rig.' Then came the bombshell. The statement added that 'Benetton Formula concluded the filter was unnecessary and it was removed with the full knowledge and permission of the FIA Formula

One Technical Delegate, Mr. Charlie Whiting. This permission was given on the afternoon of Thursday 28 July.'

An F1 veteran, Whiting was one of Ecclestone's most trusted lieutenants and spent a decade at Brabham before switching to the FIA's predecessor, the Fédération Internationale du Sport Automobile (FISA). In an interview with *GP Week*, he said that Ecclestone 'suggested that I should go to work for FISA as I was familiar with the things teams could do to cheat and he thought that I was probably a good person to try to catch them.' Briatore insisted that removing the filter was not one of these things, as Whiting had given it his blessing. 'We have proof and we could prove it in court if we had to,' said Briatore.

Controversially, Benetton claimed that the removal of the filter didn't cause the fire. Instead, it claimed that there was a fault in the equipment provided by Intertechnique. This seemed hard to comprehend, as Intertechnique was one of the world's leading experts in aircraft refuelling systems, which was precisely why it won the F1 contract. That said, in the wake of the fire, Intertechnique issued all F1 teams with revised refuelling rig couplings – though it didn't admit there was any fault with the existing ones, so it may have been a precautionary step.

Intertechnique did however release a statement saying that no proposal to remove the filter was received from Benetton, which would have had to lodge that via the FIA. And if it had been made, 'it would have been refused for technical and safety reasons'.

The FIA corroborated this. 'Permission was certainly not given,' said its communications supremo Francesco Longanesi. 'Any query on technical regulations should be addressed to FIA in writing and we have not received a letter from Benetton on this matter.' The FIA summoned Benetton to a disciplinary hearing of its World Motor Sport Council (WMSC) on the grounds that the team had breached Article 6.5.1 of the F1 Technical Regulations, which stated that its 'equipment must not be modified in any way whatsoever'.

Reflecting Mosley's original threat, Longanesi ominously added that Benetton 'face sanctions ranging from a reprimand to their disqualification, which would mean their exclusion from Formula One'.

Benetton's future, Schumacher's title hopes and Ecclestone's expectations of riches were all at stake in the WMSC showdown on 7 September 1994.

If the WMSC had found that Benetton was innocent because Whiting allowed it to remove the filter, the FIA itself would have been responsible for causing the blaze. That would have opened the door for Verstappen and Benetton's mechanics to sue the FIA over their injuries.

Excluding Benetton would have been a catastrophe for F1 and not only in terms of its effect on the German audience. The Monaco Grand Prix, the event immediately following Senna's death, had been the first event since 1959 where no world champion had competed. F1 desperately needed a new star and Schumacher had the most potential.

Ahead of the WMSC hearing, Benetton claimed that the evidence was overwhelmingly in its favour. In contrast, the FIA needed the team to be found guilty without being excluded from the championship. It got what it wanted.

At the hearing, Benetton pulled a surprise eleventh-hour U-turn and blamed a junior employee for removing the filter on their own initiative without informing the team's management. It was well received by the WMSC and, far from banning Benetton, it didn't even fine the team.

Benetton excitedly sent out a statement saying that it was 'very pleased with the result of today's hearing in Paris, which has completely cleared its good name from any allegations of cheating'. It added that the team had been 'completely cleared of the charge of removing the fuel filter illegally. This should put an end to unfounded and wild speculations in the press that the removal of the filter caused the fire at Hockenheim. Before the hearing, the FIA conceded that it was not alleging that the removal of the filter had caused the fire. In giving the World Council's decision, the President stated that its unanimous view was that the filter was removed in complete good faith and that it would be inappropriate to impose any penalty whatsoever.'

Mosley explained, 'The moment that Benetton pleaded guilty, the situation changed. Instead of being out to [prosecute] Benetton, we listened to what they had to say [in mitigation].' He added that 'we never had to consider the guilt or otherwise, because they pleaded guilty'. A former barrister with a silver tongue, Mosley was famous for his clear, calm and collected delivery. However, on this occasion he seemed flustered and his responses verged on the incomprehensible. He shed little light on the reason for Benetton's unexpected change of heart, which became all the more difficult to understand when it was revealed that the team's original defence had been corroborated by one of its rivals the night before the WMSC hearing. This came when French outfit Larrousse notified the FIA that in May Intertechnique had asked it to remove its fuel filter. 'Benetton did produce a letter from Larrousse saying this, and they also produced a drawing from Intertechnique showing how the filter could be removed,' said Mosley. 'I think the junior employee thought, because of the Larrousse business, that Intertechnique had said it was alright. Or that was what was presented to us in Paris. And the whole confusion at that level [was] unknown to Briatore and to Benetton Formula. The problem we were faced with here is that it became apparent on the facts placed before us that this knowledge, which is the essential element in deliberate cheating, was missing.'

By concluding that Benetton's management weren't aware that the filter had been removed, Mosley managed to reconcile his decision not to punish a guilty party with his comments earlier in the year that anyone caught deliberately cheating would be stopped from racing. He added that 'it was said by [Benetton] that Charlie said they could [remove the filter]. What Charlie said he said was, "It's OK by me if it's OK by Intertechnique." In other words, [Whiting was saying] "Go and ask Intertechnique, because it is not within my competence."'

Mosley continued, 'On the basis of the facts in front of us it would not be appropriate to impose a penalty. That was how it happened.'

Not quite.

At the time, the World Motor Sport Council was comprised of 17 representatives of national motorsport clubs as well as the deputy president and seven FIA vice presidents, including Ecclestone. Together, they were the equivalent of the jury, with Mosley sitting in the judge's seat. Both Benetton and the FIA brought their own barristers, though there was a gulf of a difference in their standing.

Representing the FIA was Ian Titchmarsh, a lawyer and part-time racing commentator who had defended Jordan driver Eddie Irvine earlier in 1994 after he triggered an accident at the Brazilian Grand Prix that launched debutant Verstappen's Benetton into the air. Irvine was given a one-race ban, which was increased to three when Titchmarsh appealed it and lost. Despite this, Mosley claimed that 'perhaps Eddie was rather harshly dealt with, but that was not for want of any ability or endeavour on the part of Mr. Titchmarsh . . . I decided next time we needed a good lawyer, to have him on our side and not the other side.'

In the other corner, Benetton was represented by George Carman, one of the world's most feared QCs. His client list read like a roll call of the rich and famous, ranging from billionaires like Richard Branson and Mohamed Al-Fayed to megastars such as Tom Cruise and Elton John. Although he was primarily a libel barrister, Carman often took on tricky and difficult quasi-legal hearings as well as commercial work, which was particularly lucrative. Carman didn't come cheap and is believed to have charged Benetton around $50,000.

Clients don't pay that kind of money to plead guilty without putting up a fight, which made Benetton's last-minute change of heart all the more astonishing. Carman wasn't hired for his specialist knowledge as he had never acted in a WMSC disciplinary hearing before. Mosley appeared to shed light on the reason Benetton hired him in an interview for the 1998 book *Grand Prix Men* when he said that, while he had never met Carman before the WMSC hearing, they had many mutual friends in London's Lincoln's Inn legal district. 'They all had the same respect and regard for his talent and reputation. He was a really big gun for Benetton and Flavio Briatore to wheel out. Just what we would have expected from them under the circumstances.'

In other words, Benetton hired Carman to escape punishment, even though it had pleaded guilty. That sounds perfectly logical and doesn't stand in need of further explanation. It would have remained that way if it were not for an extraordinary coincidence.

At the outset of our career in journalism we worked for Carman's son, Dominic, and, knowing our interest in F1, he told us about his father's involvement with the sport. It was a very different account from the one given by Mosley.

Dominic revealed that the night before the WMSC hearing, his father met Mosley and Ecclestone in the bar of Paris's palatial Hotel de Crillon, next to the FIA's headquarters on the historic Place de la Concorde. 'My father was staying at the Crillon and so they met for a drink the night before for an hour or two. My father said that Ecclestone was very cunning, very capable and Mosley very suave. But the essential message that came across was that for all of Mosley's intelligence and integrity, there was nevertheless part of him that was an agent to Ecclestone.'

Carman said that his father thought the meeting the night before the hearing was a 'bit of a set-up' and he explained that Ecclestone and

Mosley 'were trying every conceivable way to finesse it so they were seen to be doing the right thing but nevertheless not disrupting the sport'.

With Mosley's position equivalent to that of a judge, Ecclestone a jury member and Carman the defending barrister, Titchmarsh was unaware that the meeting was even taking place and wasn't there, despite being Carman's opposite number in the hearing.

Carman told his son that his aim was to get Benetton a 'rap on the knuckles rather than anything more serious', because in Schumacher they had a 'rising star' and if the WMSC had come down hard on his team, 'that would have meant the end of Benetton and Schumacher for the season'.

Dominic added:

If you compare it with English court, normal proceedings, it would not have been normal for a barrister to have a chat with a judge, over a drink, about the case they had coming up the next day. In fact it would be extremely abnormal. That would never happen. It would be construed as improper were it a criminal matter in front of a judge. They would never discuss a case before or during. But in this case, it's not a court in the conventional sense. It is extremely different. A judge in court sits there impartially completely because he's not involved. If, for example, a judge is a shareholder of a company that's involved in a case on trial, for obvious reasons, he might be partial. It's very difficult in any sport and it's particularly tough, I think, in motor racing to be completely impartial. The FIA is not a court in the conventional sense, they make their own rules . . . My father believed that bodies such as the FIA and the Rugby Football Union, as good and capable as they are at discipline and regulating sport, they were pretty poor, compared to a normal court, when it comes to disciplinary hearings and acting as a quasi-court, even though they may do this with the best will in the world. In other words, their intention may be noble but their execution and their methodology was terribly flawed.

Several years before Mosley passed away in 2021, we informed him that we knew about his meeting with Carman and sent him a series of questions about it.

Mosley initially responded that the questions related to events which were so long ago that 'as a matter of practicality alone, it would be difficult for me to review reliably the material you have sent to me. Moreover, the FIA's relevant papers may have been destroyed and are certainly not readily accessible.'

It was a different story after we sent him the quotes from Dominic Carman. This yielded a detailed letter from Mosley's advisors revealing chapter and verse about what happened.

It said:

> Mr Mosley recalls, and is clear that, it was Mr Carman who had requested the meeting. It never occurred to Mr Mosley that there was anything improper in agreeing to meet as suggested. Mr Carman had never been instructed to act in a World Motor Sport Council disciplinary hearing and asked how it worked. Mr Mosley gave an account of the procedure. He then said that Benetton appeared to have no defence to the charge of removing the filter. Mr Carman suggested that there was no evidence of a deliberate intent to cheat. It appeared to Mr Mosley that Mr Carman was taking the opportunity to probe him as to the way in which the World Motor Sport Council might react to Benetton's case. Mr Mosley gave Mr Carman his view that it was best to keep the matter of the filter simple and not to seek to blame any FIA personnel.

It was a sensational admission. Mosley was the judge of the hearing and was a barrister by profession, so it seems extraordinary that it never occurred to him there was anything improper about the meeting. Not only did Mosley advise Carman what to say, he told him not to blame the organisation that he ran.

Carman followed the advice to the letter and changed Benetton's plea to guilty on the grounds that a junior employee removed the filter on his own initiative without telling the team's management. Carman was duly rewarded as Benetton got off scot-free. It was a different story for the junior employee, who was named in the media as being Simon Morley, the refueller who ended up in hospital. According to *Motor Sport* magazine, Morley never worked on another pit stop and this wasn't just because the fire had put him off. He was also frustrated at being singled out as the junior employee who allegedly caused the incident, so he left F1 to work in America.

When we asked Ecclestone about Mosley's admission he corroborated it and said:

Max didn't ask to meet the guy before – I spoke to Carman. I met him and talked to him about how the FIA works. I said: 'This isn't a trial, you haven't got a jury, you haven't got anything. You've got Max who would probably like an argument if he can have one. In a nice way, not so much an argument, but Max would point out the facts. These are the facts and your job would be pleading with the World Council, who is basically like a jury, and getting them to agree something that you think there should be rather than maybe what Max [wants].' I told him, 'You're going to have a hell of a job.' Then I said, 'Let's call Max in his room and have a drink and talk about the world,' because Carman was an interesting guy. There was a question mark about whether the FIA told Benetton to take the filter off. Did they do something that was contrary to the regulations or not? That's what it amounts to.

Mosley took that decision out of Carman's hands when he advised him not to blame any FIA personnel, even though Benetton's defence depended on blaming them.

It raised questions about Mosley's joint positions as FIA president, which required him to act in the best interests of the federation, and chairman of the WMSC, which may have needed him to side against the FIA. Likewise, it shone a spotlight on Ecclestone's position as a WMSC member voting on sporting matters that could be of great financial consequence to the company he ran.

Finding Benetton guilty but not punishing it was ideal for Ecclestone and Benetton but not for the team's rivals. If Mosley had stuck to his word and stopped Benetton from racing, it could have saved Britain's Lotus team, which collapsed the following year. Had Benetton been retrospectively removed from the results of every race, on the grounds that it cheated, Lotus would have gained more points and would have moved up the standings, thereby boosting its prize money and making it more attractive to sponsors. In turn, this could have helped to keep its wheels turning.

At the other end of the spectrum, winning the championship usually enables a team to secure millions of dollars of additional sponsorship. This would have gone to second-placed Williams if Benetton had been disqualified. It would have put the team on an even firmer financial foot-ing as its revenue, which consisted primarily of sponsorship, only increased by an estimated 1.1 per cent the following year in contrast to a 20 per cent rise at Benetton.

Disqualifying Benetton would have also crowned Britain's Damon Hill world champion, which no doubt would have increased the value of his personal sponsorships and salary.

When we put this to Hill he declined to comment on his career but stressed, 'It is very important that the judicial process of the governing body of any sport is impartial and objective.' Talking about F1, he added, 'The claim that justice is applied fairly is, for people who have been around the sport for a long time, quite frustrating.'

It was particularly frustrating for Hill as the championship was within his grasp right up until the season-ender in Adelaide. He went into the race trailing Schumacher by a single point and momentarily seemed to seal the lead when the German made a mistake on lap 36 by scraping the wall. Schumacher then drove back onto the track into Hill's path, forcing both drivers out of the race. The German was crowned F1's youngest-ever champion. Although the FIA held an enquiry into his incident in Adelaide, it concluded there was insufficient evidence to bring him before the WMSC.

Following Schumacher's championship victory, F1's TV audience soared, particularly in Germany. The average number of viewers per race in the country accelerated from just 1.8 million in 1992 to 5.6 million in 1995. By 2001, it would hit 10.4 million.

German companies flooded into F1. In 1999, Mercedes went from engine supplier to team owner when it bought a 40 per cent stake in McLaren. The following year BMW entered F1 to provide Williams with engines. Siemens, DHL, Allianz and Mercedes itself all became advertisers in the next few years and by 2004 German sponsors were contributing more than $400m to the sport annually. None of this may have been possible had Mosley not stepped in to rescue Schumacher from disqualification in 1994.

Schumacher made the most of it. His manager Willi Weber renegoti-ated his contract to allow his release from Benetton at the end of 1995, rather than the following year, as a result of the persistent allegations of cheating. 'The contract had to be changed in several areas,' Weber told German newspaper *Bild*. 'Michael's image was damaged, there is no question of that, and we had to do something about that.'

Proving that he wasn't a flash in the pan, Schumacher won back-to-back championships, dominating 1995 with nine victories and equalling the record for the number of race wins in a season. This led to him joining Ferrari in 1996 on a previously unheard-of $20m salary. It paid off. Schumacher won a further five titles for the Italian team, giving him a total of seven, a record he now shares with Lewis Hamilton. However, the biggest winner was Ecclestone. In 2004 RTL signed F1's biggest ever broadcasting deal when it paid an estimated $360m for a four-year run of the sport. But this was far from F1's biggest payday. That was yet to come and, again, Mosley held the keys to it.

7

THE GRAND PRIZE

Senna's death and Schumacher's success thrust Ecclestone into the lime-light more than ever before. To millions of TV viewers around the world he was Mr F1, almost synonymous with the sport. Little did they know that he didn't own a single share in Formula One. It was a roadblock he needed to navigate.

In 1994 the teams – with huge sums of their own money tied up in their businesses – started to get jitters when, in the hotbed of rumour that is the F1 paddock, they heard that the now 64-year-old Ecclestone had health worries. The bosses of the most prestigious teams were the most concerned, chief of whom were Ron Dennis, Luca di Montezemolo, Ken Tyrrell and Frank Williams who ran the McLaren, Ferrari, Tyrrell and Williams squads respectively.

They drew up a document that said if Ecclestone died, the teams could buy his business from his heirs for 30 per cent less than its market value. It was a morbid model and it had a suitably grim name, as Ecclestone explained to *BusinessAge*: 'Eventually [the teams] came up with an agreement they called 'The Dying Agreement'. It was quite comforting actually. Every six months we would have the company valued. Whenever I became deceased they go back to the previous six months, take the value of the company, get 30 per cent discount for cash and pay the shareholders and that was it.'

The first draft of the agreement was circulated in January 1995 and was drawn up by Ecclestone's lawyers and their counterparts acting for the teams. However, Ken Tyrrell couldn't afford to contribute as the glory days were a long way behind him. The man who had powered Jackie Stewart to his three world championships hadn't won a race since 1983. The negotiations were therefore left to Ferrari, McLaren and Williams, which planned to form a company that would buy Ecclestone's business and be owned by all the teams. The exact shareholdings in it were calculated according to a complex formula based on seniority among them. It gave Ecclestone a good indication of their business acumen. 'It was all rubbish,' he said. 'When Ron and his lawyer came here, it was painfully obvious they had made a mistake with the figures because it didn't add up. I said, "Hang on, we've got a bloody good accountant here." So we added it up for them.'

In the end, the Dying Agreement died when di Montezemolo realised that the company would be controlled by the three British teams – McLaren, Tyrrell and Williams – which were some of the oldest competitors after Ferrari. In early 1996 the suave Italian suggested to Ecclestone an alternative way of giving the teams a share of his business and feathering his family's nest at the same time.

This was to float Ecclestone's company, FOPA, on the London Stock Exchange in an Initial Public Offering (IPO) of its shares. There was just one problem: the vast majority of FOPA's revenue was generated by the F1 rights – but it didn't directly have a contract to lease them. Instead, it was the teams that had been guaranteed the revenue share by the FIA. FOPA merely sold F1's commercial rights on their behalf, including the extremely lucrative television and race hosting contracts. The teams could in theory have replaced Ecclestone's company with another organisation, which would have made the company a risky prospect for investors. With Mosley's help, Ecclestone soon navigated that hurdle.

'All of a sudden Bernie wanted to float, and as soon as he wanted to float, that meant renegotiating our contract with him,' explained Mosley. This time, the FIA decided to lease F1's commercial rights directly to another company owned by Ecclestone, F.O.C.A. Administration. He had founded the company in February 1981, six days after the similarly named teams association, FOCA, had held its unsanctioned Grand Prix in South Africa. Ecclestone may have set up F.O.C.A. Administration envisaging that it would hold the commercial rights to FOCA's breakaway series. After peace was declared, Ecclestone did little with the company until it signed the deal with the FIA on 19 December 1995.

The deal gave F.O.C.A. Administration control over F1's commercial rights for 14 years in return for an annual fixed payment to the FIA. As part of the deal, F.O.C.A. Administration agreed to pay the teams their prize money, which would be equivalent to 47 per cent of F1's TV revenue, but it had now replaced them as the signatory on the rights agreement. The company banked 100 per cent of F1's revenue including the FIA's 30 per cent share of the TV takings that had previously gone to APM.

After many years of negotiations and wheeling and dealing, Ecclestone had gained control of all of F1's commercial rights for the very first time. The contract didn't begin until 1997, but no sooner had Ecclestone signed it than he began putting plans in place to make the most of the F1 rights.

The annual fee F.O.C.A. Administration paid to the FIA for the F1 rights started at just $9m (index-linked to inflation), even though they generated nearly 40 times that in revenue every year. In 1997 alone it gave F.O.C.A. Administration a 900 per cent return on investment as it made a $90.7m (£55m) net profit on $360.6m (£218.6m) of revenue. The following year its revenue rose to $404.6m (£243.9m), with fees from TV broadcasters representing more than half of this at $213m. If the FIA had retained its 30 per cent share of the revenues it would have received $63.9m that year rather than a fixed fee that was around seven times lower. The impressive returns gave Ecclestone's planned flotation a valuation of $3bn.

'I explained the figures beforehand to Balestre, so he wouldn't be surprised, and he kept explaining to me that I got it wrong, that I was talking about francs, not dollars,' said Mosley. 'When I said three billion, you know, he said, "It's not possible, it's not possible,"' When Balestre realised the figure was in dollars he was flabbergasted.

The FIA was set to be rewarded in the planned flotation. In a 1998 interview with the *FT*, Mosley said that in return for doing the deal, Ecclestone had agreed to grant the FIA a 10 per cent stake in his F1 rights business when it floated. It would have been worth around $300m, which would have compensated somewhat for the FIA forgoing its 30 per cent share of the TV revenues for a low annual fee. However, it would not cover it entirely; in 1999 alone the FIA would have got as much as $72.3m from its 30 per cent share of the TV revenues, as F1's 56 broadcast contracts generated $241m.

At this rate it would have only taken four years for the FIA to make more than $300m from the 30 per cent, but the federation gave it away for 14 years on the promise of getting that sum. Mosley knew there was a chance that the float would not get off the ground so he had to lather it on when the *FT* quizzed him about the reasons for the deal with Ecclestone. He told the paper that it would have been 'fantasy land' for the FIA to retain its 30 per cent share of F1's TV revenues as it would have left Ecclestone's company with 'only' 23 per cent of F1's TV rights revenue. By Mosley's argument, this would not have provided enough money to cover the enormous costs of running and developing F1 – a global circus involving two jumbo jets carrying the teams, their 22 racing cars and all the equipment around the world.

This was somewhat misleading as it incorrectly implied that Ecclestone's company paid to transport the teams' equipment when it was (and still is) the teams themselves that pay for the majority of it. F1 company filings revealed that, at the time, Ecclestone's company only transported the teams at zero cost to five of the seventeen races – the long-haul ones that were held outside Europe. Even then it capped the number of personnel and amount of equipment it would transport and only provided the benefits for the top 10 teams, at a time when 11 were competing.

FOPA owned an F1 travel agency that was used by the teams but they paid for its services. Indeed, in 1995, when the rights deal with the FIA was signed, it made an operating profit of £40,232. So Ecclestone's company made a profit on the teams' travel arrangements rather than purely incurring costs on them as Mosley suggested. As Ecclestone's company didn't cover all of the teams' transport costs, this perhaps shouldn't have been used as justification for why it needed the FIA's 30 per cent share of F1's TV revenues. Even if it did need the 30 per cent, it would not explain why the FIA sacrificed its own revenue to line Ecclestone's pockets.

There is no doubt that running F.O.C.A. Administration was not cheap. In 1997, the first year of its deal with the FIA, its costs hit £142.2m, including a staggering £538,663 spent on aircraft, £66,988 on printing, postage and stationery, and £52,758 on cleaning and laundry.

The company spent 70 per cent more than FOPA did in 1996, though both companies' costs were largely concentrated in one area as they were actually very lean businesses.

This is because the key costs of putting on the F1 circus are the responsibility of the teams and race organisers. The former pay for the F1 cars, motorhomes, transporters and their staff while the latter market the races and take all the money from ticket sales. Trackside advertising continued to be handled by APM and, although corporate hospitality is cost-intensive, it was run by Allsport, which was also responsible for the podium ceremony, the grid girls, safety cars and the race timing systems.

However, both FOPA and F.O.C.A. Administration arranged F1's TV coverage and this came at a significant expense. It accelerated around the time that Mosley awarded the F1 rights contract and it was driven by an estimated $80m investment made by Ecclestone's companies in digital TV.

Ecclestone's new platform, called F1 Digital+, was groundbreaking in that it allowed viewers to switch between the cars' onboard cameras. It was years ahead of its time and, perhaps surprisingly, this didn't help it.

The service started in a limited number of markets in 1996 following preliminary tests the previous year at the Belgian Grand Prix – a trial run that had enabled Ecclestone to sign a broadcast deal, covering Austria, Switzerland and Germany, with DF1, a digital TV network owned by German media giant Kirch.

A total of 20 track cameras, 14 onboard cameras and six pit-lane cameras were required to produce six different channels for F1 Digital+ – main race action, secondary race action, pit-lane action, onboard cameras, highlights and live timing. The service gave subscribers the opportunity to switch between them in real time and direct their own race, addressing concerns that F1 broadcasts were missing some of the action by focusing only on the race leaders.

Four months after the DF1 service began, F1 signed a five-year deal with Canal+ to broadcast F1 Digital+ in France and Italy. However, by the end of 1997 the German coverage had been unable to meet its target of 700,000 subscribers. It was a similar story in France, where it had been predicted that the service would be taken up by around 75,000 people – 15 per cent of the 500,000 subscribers to Canal+. Instead it got just 30,000 and, by the end of 2000, only seven countries had signed up to the service.

The problem seemed to be the high quality of the free-to-air coverage of F1, which was essential to the sport as it generated the big TV audiences that made it attractive to sponsors. While some fans had gripes about the lack of coverage of a certain driver or an advertising break cutting into the broadcast at a crucial point in the race, not enough of them were sufficiently disgruntled to pay more than $20 a race and still run the risk of missing a key moment while they were flicking through one of the other five channels.

The programming also suffered from being so far ahead of the curve that the idea of paying for television channels had not yet been widely adopted in Europe. Consumers were not accustomed to paying so much for content; in 2000, the average subscriber to Sky television in the UK paid only around $35 (£23.91) per month for access to a suite of channels. F1 Digital+ became a casualty of this and in 2002 it was shut down. Unaware that this would happen, Mosley said that 'it was the FIA which made these investments feasible by swapping its percentage for a fixed fee'.

That too seems somewhat misleading because at the same time that Ecclestone invested $80m in digital TV, he was also the world's highest-paid executive. In the year to 31 March 1996 he took home an astonishing £54.9m ($83.7m), which still dwarfs the pay given to many FTSE 100 CEOs. Crucially, it was more than the reported start-up costs of F1 Digital+, so clearly Ecclestone didn't need the 30 per cent to fund it as he could have simply cut his own salary.

Nevertheless, Mosley made the deal look like a winner, which was a skill of his. The FIA had leased the rights to Ecclestone's company for 14 years but had not actually surrendered ownership of anything. As Mosley said to *BusinessAge*: 'The thinking of the other people in the Senate was that if we do this deal with Bernie and he does make this enormous investment in digital television, it will either work or it won't. If it does work then the whole business reverts to us at the end of the contract . . .' The 'clinching' argument, Mosley said, was that when all the rights reverted to the FIA in 2010, it could then attempt to sell them for a higher amount. But not only did F1 Digital+ fail, later manoeuvres meant that the FIA is still waiting to get its rights back to this day.

Over the decades since, it has never been revealed why Mosley was so supportive of Ecclestone. The fact that the FIA members didn't try to stop the deal, even though it ended up being highly disadvantageous to the federation, is testament to how much respect and power Mosley wielded. However, although, at least publicly, he made statements on why the FIA should sell its 30 per cent stake in F1's TV revenue, he was less clear on why it should be sold to Ecclestone's company. He steered clear of this subject because his arguments in favour of it were flimsy to say the least, muttering about Bernie being 'an agent of the FIA' and doing the best deal they could with him.

Calling Ecclestone an agent of the FIA was no exaggeration. Not only was he the FIA's vice president of promotional affairs, he was also a member of its decision-making body, the World Motor Sport Council, as well as the FIA Senate. Its decisions were based on a majority vote by its ten-strong team, with Mosley having the casting vote in cases of a stalemate. It was the Senate that signed off the sale of the rights to Ecclestone's company and, as Mosley revealed to *BusinessAge* several years later, Ecclestone wasn't even excluded from the proceedings. He was allowed to participate in discussions about whether the rights should be put to tender because 'it's very useful to have him there'.

The FIA wasn't the only entity to lose out. APM's right to a 30 per cent share of F1's TV revenues had generated around $66m in 1996 and would have dramatically increased over the following years thanks to the popularity of Schumacher. But it was not to be.

The company's income dried up abruptly in 1997 when Ecclestone's contract began. It was a 14-year agreement, so it ran all the way up until the end of 2010. If McNally was the majority owner of APM then he lost hundreds of millions of dollars in revenue due to Ecclestone's decision to acquire F1's commercial rights in their entirety. It seems hard to believe he would treat a close friend like this – unless, of course, he wasn't actually the owner of APM, or Ecclestone compensated him for his manoeuvre.

Despite APM suffering a devastating loss of revenue as a result of Ecclestone's deal, its owners don't appear to have ever publicly voiced their annoyance at it. The closest that has come from McNally was a cryptic comment published by *Forbes* in 2001. According to the magazine, after Ecclestone's family trust banked $3.4bn from selling stakes in F1's rights holder, McNally was overheard 'grousing' over lunch, 'that billion dollars should have been mine'. If McNally owned a 30 per cent stake, which was indeed worth $1bn, he would have had good reason to be doing more than just 'grousing' about Ecclestone and Mosley's deal. However, if McNally was just the front man for Ecclestone's money, as the *Economist* claimed, then he wouldn't have had much reason to complain at all.

McNally might have been willing to suffer in silence, but not everyone felt the same way, and the teams certainly had a lot to say.

Although F.O.C.A. Administration's name sounded remarkably similar to that of the teams' association, the other FOCA had no involvement in the deal. When the team bosses found out that Ecclestone had gone behind their backs to get the rights they were apoplectic.

The three most vocal were the sole survivors of the first Concorde Agreement in 1981 – Ron Dennis, Frank Williams and Ken Tyrrell. They refused to sign a new agreement in 1996, though the other eight teams promised their support. However, little did the rebels know that their commitment was even more crucial than Ecclestone made out – it being essential for his plans to float his company.

Tyrrell, who was FOCA's vice president, was so incensed about Ecclestone's deal that he sent a letter of complaint to the FIA, saying: 'Were we not entitled to expect the FOCA President would represent our interests above his own?' Tyrrell was either wilfully ignoring his previous dealings with Ecclestone or had yet to realise quite how much he was working both sides of the deal.

The teams were furious that the rights had been handed to a company owned by the president of the organisation that represented them. Some of the teams reportedly even felt that Ecclestone had breached his legal obligations towards them, though they stopped short of taking legal action against him.

When the teams had negotiated previous Concorde Agreements they'd given permission for the rights to be managed by Ecclestone's company, but this time they claimed not to have been consulted about a deal that bypassed them entirely.

In response, Mosley bizarrely pointed to the Dying Agreement as evidence that the teams knew Ecclestone's company would get the F1 rights contract. Mosley claimed that in 1994, long before he signed the contract with F.O.C.A. Administration, he was negotiating with the teams about what would happen after Ecclestone died. 'They knew we were going to do this deal,' Mosley explained to *BusinessAge*. 'That's why they needed the Dying Agreement.'

As was often the case with Mosley's rhetoric, it initially seemed highly persuasive but didn't stand up to close scrutiny. In *BusinessAge*, he claimed that he only decided to award the rights to F.O.C.A. Administration after Ecclestone decided to float his company. However, the proposed flotation was a direct consequence of the collapse of the Dying Agreement, so the teams couldn't have known about the rights transfer to F.O.C.A. Administration during those negotiations.

It wasn't the only area of confusion. The similar-sounding company names made it tough for observers to follow the money. To add an extra challenge, Ecclestone frequently changed the names of the many companies in charge of the different divisions of F1. By the early 2000s, most had mysteriously changed their names at least three times since being incorporated. Sometimes the changes lasted for less than a week. And, unlike common cases where a company changes its brand name for marketing reasons, Ecclestone often interchanged the names of two of his companies, suggesting an ulterior motive rather than corporate aesthetics. The similarity of the name to FOCA was also a source of befuddlement and the fact that F.O.C.A. Administration seized the rights from the teams added yet more fuel to their fire. It was impossible for all but Ecclestone to know exactly who owned what, and when.

Tyrrell was by far the most vocal critic, as he still saw Ecclestone as an on-track rival and was hugely jealous of his commercial success. To Ecclestone, Tyrrell represented the old generation of amateurs with rusty cars rather than the slick sponsorship vehicles he wanted in order to attract new brands to F1. As Ecclestone said to *BusinessAge*, 'We have built up a standard, and it's hard to keep it like that. People are in an environment, which we have created, which is very upmarket. All the dirty, scruffy teams, including the scruffy Tyrrell, started to bring themselves up to a better level because they realised they stood out so badly.' He added to *F1 Racing* magazine:

> Ken always wanted a big slice of a small cake. He was always more concerned with what I was getting than what he was getting . . . If I hadn't done what I did, commercially, with Formula One, Ken wouldn't even have been in business. I didn't 'get hold of' anything. Many years ago, when I started putting things in place commercially, I said to the team owners, 'Let's form a company. I'll run it. I'll pay all the expenses and all the costs, and in return I want a percentage of our generated profit.' And they said, 'Okay. We'll just run our teams – and, as long as you pay us, you can do what you like with the rest.' That's what they all said. All of them. Without exception. I took the risks, I took big risks. And they did very well.

They didn't see it that way when they found out that Mosley had awarded Ecclestone's company the F1 rights. At an explosive meeting in the paddock at the German Grand Prix in July 1996, the three rebel teams – Williams, McLaren and Tyrrell – insisted on a substantial increase in their share of the television revenue as well as a wedge of the money from advertising, corporate hospitality and race hosting fees. Ecclestone refused to yield. He then cleverly excluded Ron Dennis, Frank Williams and Ken Tyrrell from a crucial meeting that he called with the other team bosses on 7 August 1996. Ecclestone planned to hit the three rebels where it hurt – the wallet.

The rebels' share of the television revenue for 1996 couldn't be touched as the parties were still bound by the 1992 Concorde Agreement that expired at the end of that year. Accordingly, Ecclestone offered their share of the 1997 revenue to the other eight squads on condition that they signed a new Concorde Agreement. His age-old trick of divide and rule was coming into play yet again.

On 5 September 1996, a Concorde Agreement lasting for five years from 1997 was signed by the eight compliant teams, including big names such as Ferrari and Benetton as well as the likes of Jordan and a host of smaller teams.

Within weeks, Frank Williams, perhaps fearful of the financial pinch to come in 1997, indicated to Mosley that he might be prepared to sign on equal terms and it was also hinted that Dennis and Tyrrell might do the same. Dennis, Williams and Tyrrell told Ecclestone to allow them back in on equal terms by 26 March or face a complaint to Brussels under the competition rules of the European Commission (EC).

Ecclestone had yet to come toe-to-toe with the bureaucrats in Brussels but the last thing he wanted, given his hopes of flotation, was a protracted and highly public dispute, with three stars of his show as witnesses for the prosecution.

After the proposed flotation, and the huge amount of money it would pay out, Ecclestone planned to create a new company (with yet another acronym) called Formula One Holdings (FOH), which would own F.O.C.A. Administration. The flotation plans were leaked to the *Sunday Times* on 9 March 1997, revealing Ecclestone's hand to the teams.

He was livid with Salomon Brothers, the investment bank behind the float and allegedly behind the leak. 'The more they talk, the less interested I am,' he said.

At the end of March 1997 Ecclestone finally put together a package for the three rebel teams that would put them on equal terms with their rivals. Although their respective shares of the television revenue would still not be restored until the following season, they were offered a multi-million-pound incentive plan.

However, the news of the float had revealed to the rebels that their signatures were crucial to Ecclestone's plans. So when his package to pacify them arrived, they already wanted more and still refused to put their names to the Concorde. By then the 1997 season had begun so Williams, McLaren and Tyrrell raced without being bound by a Concorde for the first time in 16 years. It made little difference. The three teams could have been kicked out by Ecclestone at any moment, but that would have dented confidence in F1 and his aspirations for a flotation. Likewise, the teams couldn't pull out because together they had hundreds of millions of pounds and hundreds of staff on the line.

It taught Ecclestone a lesson that would later become very valuable – teams won't leave F1 out of spite, no matter how much they threaten to do so and no matter how angry they are. The events of 1997 illustrated this perfectly. Not only had Ecclestone's company seized the F1 rights from the teams behind their backs while he represented them, but he also planned to float it and hadn't told them that either.

While all this was transpiring, there was another significant development going on behind the scenes. Between 1997 and 1999 F.O.C.A. Administration changed its name six times, with one of them lasting less than a week. On one occasion, it had no dots between the letters and on another it switched names with a different company in the F1 empire, suggesting an ulterior motive rather than corporate aesthetics. The name changes may well have been part of Ecclestone's flotation preparations, which involved creating an empire of companies with the 'Formula One' prefix. But they also showed that once F.O.C.A. Administration had acquired the commercial rights and the teams had signed the Concorde Agreement, Ecclestone wanted to create a new organisation to administer the sport, and one that would exclude the constructors from its name. The company that started as F.O.C.A. Administration was now called Formula One Management (FOM) and this is what it is known as to this very day.

8

DEATH AND TAXES

In June 1997 news broke in the media of Ecclestone's record-breaking salary, which made the three rebel teams even more angry. It didn't put him in good stead when he returned to the negotiating table with them over the flotation later in the month. Ecclestone proposed to give them either a 10 per cent shareholding in the company he intended to float or an increased cut of the television revenues, but they demanded 20 per cent as well as an increased cut. Predictably, Ecclestone refused outright and stormed out of the meeting. 'The teams can go to hell. Some of them think they have me by the balls but their hands aren't big enough,' he said. 'Formula One is bigger than the teams and it could float without them.'

By then, even the other eight teams smelled money. Although they had loyally backed Ecclestone by signing the Concorde Agreement in September 1996, they now wanted a piece of the flotation too. So, in October 1997, Ecclestone proposed a compromise. The teams were offered a 10 per cent equity stake to be split between all of them. This would be placed in a trust giving them the right to dividends without actual ownership of the stake in order to prevent the shares from ending up in possession of teams that might subsequently leave the sport or try to sell them on to unapproved buyers. The teams would also have an annually rotating presence on the board of the floated company to ensure that no one team was more powerful than another. In return, they were expected to sign a new Concorde for ten years rather than the previous five, and this one would take effect from 1998.

Even an offer of dividends and directors wasn't enough to get the contract across the line. The teams wanted more money, and this ended up being a costly manoeuvre for Ecclestone in more ways than one.

Although he was handling the discussions with the teams about their future in F1, the money they were offered didn't come from his own pocket. Following a complex corporate shuffle, F1 had moved into the

hands of one of Ecclestone's family trusts – of which there were numerous – and it committed to paying the teams so they would sign the
Concorde. According to Stephen Mullens, the trust's legal advisor, it
'negotiated with each of the teams separately in order to obtain their
agreement to the proposal, by offering them each a share in the IPO, or
of the proceeds from an IPO'.

It took the teams aback as they were used to dealing with Ecclestone
and receiving financial offers from his company. Most of them thought
nothing more of the involvement of the trust but it attracted the suspicions of the trio of renegade teams, which were still aggrieved over the
transfer of the rights to Ecclestone's company. Williams, McLaren and
Tyrrell turned their attention to Ecclestone's interaction with the trust.

On 23 February 1998 Mullens wrote to all of the team bosses to say
the trust had confirmed that, if they signed the 1998 Concorde Agreement
within the next seven days, 'it will make available to you or to your
order, out of the proceeds of flotation, USD 10 million'. The trust also
offered the teams the alternative of taking shares in the flotation, but four
of them – Prost, Jordan, Arrows and Benetton – went for the cash.

Minardi, Stewart and Sauber were the minnows of the grid and took
shares, as it didn't matter to them whether F1 floated or not. They had
voluntarily signed the Concorde in September 1996, which meant they
were already signed up and committed to race, so they were of the opinion that if they later benefited from the shares it would just be a bonus.

Ferrari kicked up a fuss, though not as much as the three rebels, and
was duly rewarded for doing so. As we revealed in the *Daily Telegraph,* 15
years later the famous motor marque was handed a 0.25 per cent stake in
F1 and later cashed it in for $8.7m.

That left the three rebels. Williams and McLaren agreed to sign the
1998 Concorde only on condition that they would each get 1 per cent
of the proceeds of the float or a sale of FOH. After years of battling, the
duo went to great lengths to guarantee this. Williams hired so-called
Magic Circle law firm Linklaters, while McLaren was represented by
international grandee Baker McKenzie in the drawing up of the contract.

Tyrrell, however, was on the back foot. Going without a share of
television revenues in 1997 had brought it to the brink of bankruptcy,
but in its dying days, Ecclestone gave the team a helping hand. He set up
the sale of the company to tobacco giant British American Tobacco
(BAT) for an estimated $30m. Although Tyrrell was in strife, it was sitting

on a valuable entry right to compete as an F1 team. If BAT had set up its own squad it would have had to pay a $48m bond to the FIA just to receive its entry right. That was without even incurring the construction cost of the factory, hiring the staff, buying an engine and designing and building the car. Buying Tyrrell swerved around all that.

It was also convenient for Ecclestone, who replaced a team owner who had often vocally opposed him with an owner that was delighted with his help. BAT was so impressed with his assistance that the company presented him with an ornamental sculpture, which he proudly displayed in his office.

After Ken Tyrrell stepped down, his replacement, Craig Pollock, soon showed his readiness to sign the Concorde Agreement on behalf of the team, which began competing as British American Racing in 1999. It took around 50 drafts but all the teams finally put pen to paper at Monaco in May 1998.

Ironically, although Ecclestone had finally navigated the hurdles that the teams presented it was too late to rescue the float. It was put on hold as he now had more pressing concerns of a personal nature that were about to intrude on his work in F1. Unbeknown to the teams, the heart problems that had led to the drafting of the Dying Agreement had worsened and Ecclestone now had to consider what would happen to his family in the worst-case scenario.

Back in 1982, at the Italian Grand Prix, Bernie had met his second wife, the statuesque Slavica Radic, a raven-haired 6 feet 1 inch Croatian Armani model. The pair wed at Kensington and Chelsea registry office three years later, with just two people present. Like Ecclestone's first wife Ivy, Slavica came quickly to understand that her new husband didn't stand on ceremony: he went straight back to the office after the wedding rather than take a honeymoon. The year before they were married their eldest daughter Tamara had been born, and she was followed by Petra in 1988. Often described as 'It' girls, both have become famous for spending their father's fortune.

Despite the marriage, Ecclestone had discovered that if he died, Slavica would have had to pay 40 per cent tax on any of his assets that she inherited. Inheritance tax isn't usually charged on spouses in the UK but Slavica couldn't benefit from this, being Croatian and not having lived in the UK for long enough to be domiciled there.

To solve that problem, in February 1996 Ecclestone gifted his shares in F.O.C.A. Administration to a Jersey company called Petara, which was named after his daughters and was wholly owned by Slavica. The intention was that if he died, they wouldn't have to inherit the company and pay tax on it. The process involved the creation of a frightfully complex cat's cradle of offshore trusts and companies in locations stretching from snowy Liechtenstein to the sunnier climes of the British Virgin Islands.

In simple terms, thanks to Ecclestone's manoeuvre in 1996, his shares in F.O.C.A. Administration became ultimately owned by his family trust's Bambino Holdings company, which was based in Jersey where no capital gains tax was levied on the proceeds from selling its subsidiaries.[1] As Ecclestone was a UK taxpayer, he was not allowed to be a beneficiary of any of the trusts or exercise any control over their assets. If he was found to be doing so it could have made him liable for tax on any of their assets. As he later explained to us, 'I cannot even speak to the trust. I was told quite clearly, if you speak to the trust it's bad news for you, revenue wise.'

Ecclestone did not transfer his shares directly to the trusts and therefore did not set up or 'settle' the trusts in financial parlance, so there was some distance between them. HMRC allowed him to continue running F.O.C.A. Administration even though he had given it to an offshore company ultimately controlled by his wife and wouldn't pay any tax on the proceeds when she sold it.

A die-hard control freak, this situation suited Ecclestone to a tee and blurred the lines between him and the trust from the start through no fault of his own. What's more, one of the directors of Bambino Holdings was Ecclestone's old friend Luc Argand. Furthermore, one of its first investments had a strong F1 pedigree and came in 1999 with the acquisition of the Paul Ricard circuit near Marseille, which hosted the French Grand Prix 14 times from 1971 to 1990.

With the flotation on hold due to his health, Ecclestone gave the green light to a simpler way of raising money from F1. It was a precursor to a possible future flotation, which helped financial institutions familiarise themselves with the business. The scheme saw F1 borrow billions from banks, which then sold the right to repayment with interest to investors. It is known as a bond and part of the process involved the creation of a new company called Formula One Administration (FOA), which was ultimately owned by the trust and became the new owner of F1's commercial rights when F.O.C.A. Administration transferred them to it in 1999.

The fund-raising for the bond was led by Salomon Brothers, which originally hoped to raise $2bn and repay it over 20 years. However, potential investors baulked at the level of risk as F1's financial horsepower was still unproven. Although the sport had nearly 50 years of history under its bonnet, its status as a corporate behemoth was a relatively new phenomenon. F1's popularity accelerated in the late 1990s thanks to Schumacher's switch to Ferrari, but potential bond investors were concerned about its long-term staying power, especially in the face of rebellious teams. Likewise, there were questions about why a 20-year term was needed if F1 really was in top gear.

Salomon Brothers failed to find enough investors to get the bond off the starting grid and Ecclestone's plans of giving his young family a nest egg seemed to have gone up in smoke. Then blonde American banker Robin Saunders stepped into the driving seat of the bond issue. She worked for state-owned German bank WestLB, which saw an opportunity to cash in on its countryman Schumacher's success. Working with Morgan Stanley, Saunders attempted to steer the bond back on track.

A financial wonder woman dubbed the 'Queen of the City', Saunders cut the size of the bond issue from $2bn to $1.4bn, requested that $300m should be held in security and reduced the duration from 20 years to 10 years. It had a magic touch, as the top four rating agencies rated the bonds and Morgan Stanley proclaimed that there was a 'strong investor appetite'. Nevertheless, it ended up buying a good deal of the bonds with WestLB to ensure that the full $1.4bn was raised. It came at just the right time.

Ecclestone's health fears were eventually confirmed when his close friend, the FIA medical delegate Sid Watkins, advised him to have a precautionary triple heart bypass. Knowing that it could spook bond investors, Ecclestone waited until the day after the transaction had closed in May 1999 to tell Saunders that he was having the risky medical procedure.

The morning after the bankers celebrated finalising the transaction, Ecclestone telephoned Saunders and reportedly said, 'I've been a naughty boy.' He went on to explain that he was having the operation later that day, to which she exclaimed, 'I want to jump out of the window.' Saunders later admitted that it was the 'worst day of my life' because if Ecclestone hadn't made it through the operation someone would have to be held legally liable.

She had assumed that Ecclestone's health issues were nowhere near as serious as the reality, and that the due diligence process for the bond had included the health of the man running the business, but this crucial detail had been overlooked. Later that day Saunders was reassured that Ecclestone had made it through and he later described it as a 'little' operation. Showing a flash of his wicked wit, he added, 'I disappointed so many people. I stayed alive.'

Ecclestone took a mere ten days off work to recuperate on his first ever holiday with his family. They could certainly afford it.

The net $1.4bn was paid to the offshore trust via FOA, making Slavica richer than the Queen. As the proceeds ended up offshore, no tax was paid on them, and this didn't escape HMRC's attention.

In November 1999 HMRC opened an investigation into Ecclestone's affairs dating back to 1996 when the estate planning process had begun. Two months after the start of the investigation into Ecclestone, HMRC also began looking into Slavica's tax affairs.

The following year the *Daily Express* newspaper found out about the probe and reported that officers from HMRC's feared Special Compliance Office, nicknamed the Ghostbusters, had begun trawling through company documents linked to Ecclestone.

It was hardly surprising that Ecclestone was under investigation given his wealth and links to foreign funds. An insider linked to the Ghostbusters spelled it out to the *Express* by saying, 'Ecclestone is the head of a huge empire and there are some interesting overseas aspects and investors. Let's face it, Britain's biggest taxpayer will always be under constant scrutiny. Most of his UK companies are ultimately controlled by offshore companies.'

Little did anyone know that it wouldn't be until 2023 that the chequered flag would finally fall on the probe. Ecclestone himself, however, seemed to have a good idea back then of who would be the chief antagonist of his life story. The *FT* reported that when Ecclestone was asked in the late 1990s when his autobiography would be published, he responded, 'The morning after I die. And the first 12 copies go to the Inland Revenue.'

9

EUROPEAN DISUNION

By the turn of the millennium Ecclestone's family trust had pocketed $1.4bn from the bond but he wasn't satisfied. He still wanted to float F1 to raise even more money for his wife and children. This time F1's teams weren't the obstacle in his way. Instead, he found himself caught in the headlights of the European Commission (EC) after several championship promoters outside F1 lodged anti-competition complaints against the sport. The wheels had begun turning four years earlier and, yet again, Mosley had been the catalyst.

The chief antagonists were Patrick Peter, a partner in the BPR sports car series, and German businessman Wolfgang Eisele, whose company AE TV filmed FIA-sanctioned truck races in Germany. Ecclestone quickly established what was driving it: 'The motive for those complaints seemed to me to be to extract a large sum of money to go away and stop complaining when they knew I was vulnerable.'

That's as may be, but the complaints from Eisele and Peter were hardly spurious. Starting in 1996, the FIA had seized the broadcasting rights to their series and transferred them for 15 years to International Sportsworld Communicators (ISC), another company founded by Ecclestone and owned by one of his family trusts. Mosley justified this audacious hijack on the grounds that the FIA's name was in the official title of both series so it owned the rights to them and could therefore do with them as it wished.

ISC already managed the commercial rights to the World Rally Championship (WRC) as Mosley had appointed it the promoter of the series in 1993 with the reluctant agreement of its teams. Three years later the FIA began to take over the rights of 17 other racing series in the same way and handed them to ISC too. It gave Ecclestone control over the commercial rights to every major motorsport series on every FIA calendar. Mosley claimed he had done this so that Ecclestone could boost their visibility, but it also had the consequence of lining the pockets of his family trust. The manoeuvre triggered a series of events that would transform F1 and which Ecclestone is still paying the price for to this day.

This wasn't the first time that Ecclestone had commercialised championships outside F1. In fact, from the mid-1980s, he managed the TV rights to F1's two-wheeled counterpart, which is now known as MotoGP but was then called the Road Racing World Championship. It was an area Ecclestone knew well thanks to his early days dealing in motorbikes.

Ecclestone's UK-based company Two Wheel Promotions bought the rights to the Road Racing World Championship from the FIA's equivalent in motorcycle racing, the Fédération Internationale de Motocyclisme (FIM). Ecclestone developed the commercial foundations that still underpin MotoGP and planned to turn the Road Racing World Championship into a two-wheeled version of F1. He made an immediate impact.

This was documented in detail by *Motor Sport* magazine in 2020 in an interview with Mike Trimby, the late head of the International Roadracing Team Association (IRTA), the equivalent of the F1 teams' FOCA. In the 1980s, there was so little money in top-level motorbike racing that the teams had to adapt light fittings to get electricity in the paddock and used gas water boilers with naked flames just steps away from their petrol tanks. Thanks to Ecclestone's financial wizardry, the world championship became a cash-generating engine; Trimby said the amount Ecclestone paid out was 'split between the FIM, IRTA and the organisers. We spent IRTA's share on on-bike cameras, so the first on-bike cameras were paid for by us, to improve the TV show.'

At the start of the 1992 season Spanish sports management company Dorna arrived on the scene and wanted to buy the TV rights. It was on a roll, having recently bought the rights to the women's tennis Fed Cup, Spain's Professional Basketball League and exclusive courtside signage at NBA games. Dorna was financed by the Spanish banking giant Banesto and Ecclestone sensed an opportunity for a turbocharged payout by selling Two Wheel Promotions to Dorna. According to Trimby, he had a helping hand who ensured the FIM would wave the deal through: 'One of the reasons Bernie got his deal done was that he persuaded his big mate Max Mosley to change the statutes of the FIA, so they could sanction any form of motorsport, not just four wheels. That rattled the cages of the FIM and helped secure the deal. That was the sort of power Bernie had.'

Trimby said that, with the FIA on his side, 'Bernie played everyone off against everyone, as was his skill. Within 12 months he had hypnotised Dorna into buying out Bernie's interest for $50 million. Bernie cashed in big time.'

MotoGP went from strength to strength and, coming full circle, in 2024, F1's owner Liberty Media made a €4.2bn bid for Dorna in an attempt to bring the top two- and four-wheeled motorsport series under one roof.

Back in 1996, Mosley had hoped that Ecclestone could transform the fortunes of the other FIA motorsport series in the same way he had done for MotoGP. Many of the series got little TV exposure and the ones that did were sometimes funded by sponsors in return for product placement, which was a particular problem for truck racing as it often looked like an advert for Mercedes. 'We were not happy,' explained Mosley to *BusinessAge*. 'We wanted two things: we wanted more coverage, which we thought Bernie could get, and we wanted to stop it being a commercial.'

It was an approach that Ecclestone had made great efforts to tackle in F1. At the time, François Guiter of Elf filmed news footage of the races, which was then edited in favour of his employer before the reports were supplied to broadcasters. As Ecclestone explained, 'François used to look after all the news edits, so every bit of news that went out you could bet your life it featured Elf and Renault . . . a person being interviewed who just happened to be sitting on a 50-gallon oil drum with Elf written on it. It was bloody strange until we stopped him.'

Mosley wanted Ecclestone to put the brakes on this in other racing leagues as well, which was one of the reasons he gave for transferring their broadcasting rights to ISC. As Mosley explained, 'Formula One is right up there with the Olympics and the Football World Cup so it seemed completely logical to ask Bernie if he would deal with other forms of motorsport as well.'

As these series used the FIA's name in their titles, it opened the door to the federation seizing their broadcasting rights. In order to do so it had to alter its own rule book by insisting that any series wanting to use the FIA's name had to give up its television rights. This change was initially proposed by the WMSC and approved by the General Assembly, the FIA's supreme decision-making body, in October 1995.

That was the easy part. Transferring the rights to ISC proved to be much more problematic, as it fuelled criticisms that Ecclestone was monopolising motor-racing TV rights and deliberately suppressing them to prevent competition for F1. Wolfgang Eisele was the critic in chief. The usually quietly spoken German businessman was left fuming by Mosley's manoeuvre. Eisele had filmed truck races for a decade but his livelihood was suddenly in jeopardy. 'Eisele was invited to tender for doing the television,' said Mosley. 'He did, but the amount of money he asked for was two or three times the next highest bid. So not unnaturally Bernie gave the deal to the next-highest man.'

It was the final straw for Eisele.

After losing the bid, Eisele complained to the European Commission and found that he was pushing against an open door. 'The fable got around that [the TV rights transfer] had been done in order to suppress these other forms of motorsports for the benefit of Formula One,' said Mosley. 'The truth is there was no coverage at all.'

Ecclestone added that these other motorsport leagues had been around for decades but had 'done absolutely nothing – they've not increased their audience one bit. The idea that the FIA gave them to me in order for me to suppress them is not credible. They were already suppressed.'

Ecclestone managed to turn that round somewhat by using F1 as leverage to get these other series on TV screens. In December 1995 he stunned the world of sports broadcasting by announcing out of the blue that, after 19 years on the BBC, F1's UK coverage would switch to rival ITV from 1997. Executives at the Beeb were furious as they thought they were still in the running, but ITV had offered a reported $20m a year for the rights – 10 times more than the BBC was paying.

Soon afterwards, Ecclestone said, 'I got my balls squeezed when we changed BBC for ITV and everybody said the reason I did it was for money – honestly, primarily yes, but the BBC wouldn't do anything for the rest of motorsport – it wouldn't come on half an hour before the show and stay afterwards.' As part of the deal, Ecclestone managed to get ITV to broadcast one hour of other forms of motor racing for each of the 17 F1 races, and he used the same strategy elsewhere in Europe. 'It was what we wanted. Exactly the same thing happened in Austria,' Ecclestone said.

Ironically, although ITV has long since lost its F1 coverage, it is still showing many smaller championships, so Mosley's strategy was a success. Other series didn't see it that way at the time. There was a spat over declining viewing figures for the International Touring Car Championship in Germany, which caused the EC to take an even closer look at F1. On doing so it uncovered Ecclestone's dual roles with the FIA and as the rights holder. It was also concerned that the FIA had repeatedly sold the F1 rights to a related party and that there had not even been a tender when Ecclestone's company bought them. The icing on the cake was that some of F1's contracts with broadcasters gave them a 33 per cent discount if the broadcasters committed to not showing any other open-wheel racing series, such as the American CART championship, while the agreements with race organisers prevented any rival series from taking place on the track.

Eisele had so much on the line that he didn't just leave it to the EC to take on Ecclestone. The German began his own investigation into him, as he stood to lose everything if ISC kept the rights to truck racing. 'It would have been an absolute disaster for me, I would have lost all my contracts which I had built up for the last eight, nine years,' Eisele said at the time. 'I would have lost all my distribution to the TV stations and my employees. I would have been bankrupt.'

Eisele became so obsessed with his crusade against F1 that he even changed his email address to '*sportmonopol*' meaning 'sport monopoly' in German. Through his research, Eisele amassed a stash of purportedly compromising financial information about Ecclestone that he used to his advantage to play hardball – an approach Ecclestone wasn't used to. It made him wary of Eisele and he wondered where his information was coming from. Ecclestone and Mosley suspected it was Mercedes. The German manufacturer provided the trucks that Eisele filmed and had recently begun supplying engines to the McLaren F1 team run by Ron Dennis, who had become an arch-enemy of Ecclestone and Mosley – Dennis was still seething that, with Mosley's help, Ecclestone had snatched the F1 commercial rights from the teams.

'Bernie effectively stole Formula One from us,' Dennis later claimed. He added that Ecclestone used his commercial position to 'persuade the teams to accept a contract that eliminated them from the passing of rights as had previously existed . . . The way [Ecclestone] swerved the situation, I mean some people would say it was brilliant, but in essence it was pretty deceitful because the teams were trying to say, "Hold on, Bernie, we own these rights."'

Eisele was much more than just a thorn in Ecclestone's side, as the EC investigation had the power to dent both the chance of a second attempt at a flotation and the alternative option of selling stakes in F1. The incensed German also sued ISC and the FIA in Germany, arguing that it had no right to the truck-racing rights. However, he was no match for Mosley's guile.

In June 1997 Eisele won his initial case, provoking a sharp response from the FIA. On the same day as the verdict it distributed a press release saying it would cancel the 1997 European Truck Racing Cup. The FIA justified it on the grounds that the races were little more than glorified adverts for the truck makers, as footage was turned into a highlights programme and given free to anyone prepared to show it. 'You cannot put yourself in a position where somebody's running something as a product placement advertising series and it's described as an FIA Championship,' Mosley told *Panorama*. However, in truth truck racing was steadily growing in popularity, which was, of course, the very reason Ecclestone wanted it. Indeed, some of the races reportedly attracted as many as 240,000 spectators – more than many F1 events.

With Eisele digging in his heels, Ecclestone did what he does best and turned to deal-making. Ecclestone paid $2m to put the brakes on a similar battle in France over the rights to the BPR Sportscar Series and while he was navigating this, the details of his new F1 flotation plans were leaked to the *Sunday Times* in what was a godsend for Eisele. Although Mosley and Ecclestone believed that the German had no case, investors would not let the flotation proceed without a settlement.

The resolution of Eisele's dispute with Ecclestone reads like a scene from a James Bond movie. It began with Eisele asking Ecclestone for $5m, which he considered to be in line with the costs he had incurred. 'In return he was going to withdraw his complaint to the Commission, which was a nuisance action,' said Ecclestone.

In America you have these nuisance actions, where you could sue people and get paid off for pulling out. He would pull out with the complaints against the FIA and us in the German courts. He told me he wanted a few quid for just trust, so asked if I would send him half a million dollars on account. We were going to sort the details out later. I would give him another $2 million and the balance of $2.5 million when the Commission gave us the clearance, which he said he could engineer for us – he actually said that. He said to me, 'Trust me.'

Ecclestone also wanted to know who had helped Eisele in his German court case, along with all of the relevant paperwork he had amassed. Eisele gave him his Swiss bank account number and Ecclestone transferred the money.

Ecclestone had agreed the deal verbally with Eisele and expected it to be followed through. However, Ecclestone said that after Eisele received the $500,000 he started to change the terms, which made Ecclestone uneasy. He had sent him a $500,000 deposit on a handshake and it was feeling increasingly flimsy. Eisele suddenly demanded the whole $4.5m balance upfront, so Ecclestone said to him: '"If you are so sure you can do it, what's the difference?" He kept varying proportions in the way he wanted the money upfront but at one point it actually came to the point where he didn't want any of it to be contingent with the outcome in Brussels – he just wanted the money.' The whole affair turned into a farce as Eisele demanded that Ecclestone deliver the money in cash in two briefcases to a private bank in Switzerland. As Ecclestone told *BusinessAge*, 'It became a joke. We obviously wouldn't agree to it.'

Then came another curve ball. The district court in Frankfurt made the surprise ruling that if there was a violation of television rights or European competition law, an action could only be brought by the series organisers, not by a third party such as Eisele's AE TV company.

Eisele immediately lodged an appeal, though it was to no avail. In a last-ditch effort he appealed to Germany's Federal Court of Justice – in return for dropping the appeal, Ecclestone let him keep the $500,000. It left Eisele with a sour taste, as he never received the additional $4.5m he had hoped for.

However, Eisele's complaint had already triggered change by the time of the ruling in Frankfurt. In an attempt to appease the EC, the FIA had agreed to return the TV rights and marketing of most non-F1 championships to the event organisers, which opened the door to truck racing doing a deal again with Eisele. As Mosley explained to *BusinessAge*, 'We just said, "Well, OK, we will go on looking after the Formula One, rallying, GT and Formula 3000, all the rest we will give that to the organisers." Bernie said with some justification he had spent $3 million in 1997 trying to do this and that there was no point doing it if we could not guarantee he would be able to go on doing it for any length of time. So as a result of that we gave it all back to the organisers.' He added that, 'If we find any more product placement we would simply say it's no longer an FIA Championship, which is the only thing we can do.'

Ecclestone remained in control of WRC as ISC had been validly appointed as the promoter, though even that didn't last for long.

Eisele ended up in the driving seat of truck-racing TV production again but, ironically, the series was worse off because of it. Ecclestone had persuaded Eurosport to televise truck racing regularly live and added that he would even pay the TV production costs if necessary. However, Eurosport's coverage stopped after Ecclestone relinquished the rights. It added insult to injury for Eisele, and he didn't forget it. Unbeknown to Ecclestone, this wouldn't be the last he would see of the German.

It was somewhat ironic that so much trouble had been caused for F1 by the promoters of two relatively minor racing series that were certainly not a significant challenge to F1's global popularity. The planned flotation was almost irrevocably damaged – F1 was now firmly on the radar of the European Commission's Competition Authority, which would put off potential investors and stockholders. F1's TV coverage could no longer be bundled with the other series to make an attractive package for broadcasters, and Ecclestone had made an enemy who would cause a great deal of grief for him in years to come.

And although Eisele's EC complaint was no more, the main problem for Ecclestone was that the wheels were still turning in Brussels, which left the F1 float stuck at the lights. After several years of investigations, the EC opened formal anti-competition proceedings into F1 in June 1999. They didn't last long. Knowing Mosley's political acumen, Ecclestone turned to him for help.

Mosley immediately took a hard line. First the FIA asked the EC to confirm that the 14-year rights contract it had signed with Ecclestone was lawful and not anti-competitive. The reason for this was simply that the company couldn't be floated while its key contract was in doubt.

In an effort to move things forward, Mosley wrote to the EC asking for a letter of support to be issued within two weeks. If it refused, he said one option would be to 'relocate both the FIA and Mr Ecclestone's company outside of the EU and severely limit the number of Formula One races in Europe'. That didn't go down well. Karel Van Miert, the EC's Competition Commissioner, responded angrily that 'threats against me will not prevent assessment of all the relevant issues in the proper manner'.

There was no option left for F1 except compromise. Moving F1 and the FIA out of the EC would be far from simple. Both organisations, with their hundreds of staff, were headquartered there and in 1999, 9 of the 16 races were held within the EC's boundaries. As F1 circuits have to meet stringent safety and logistical standards to be included on the calendar, as well as paying a hefty hosting fee, there were doubts that there would be enough suitable circuits worldwide to make up the numbers.

F1 and the FIA agreed to make sweeping changes, leading to the EC finally agreeing to close its probe. F1 quashed the concerns that it had a monopoly on racing by removing the clauses from its contracts that hindered rival series. Former rally co-driver David Richards bought ISC from the Ecclestone family trust and thus acquired its main asset, the broadcasting rights to the World Rally Championship. The EC also tackled concerns that F1 and the FIA were too close by insisting that Ecclestone step down from his role on the FIA Senate and relinquish his role as the vice president of promotional affairs. His only remaining FIA role was on the World Motor Sport Council, where he was a member by right as the representative of F1's rights holder.

These measures were a complete change of gear for F1 but they were still just preludes to the main event. On the surface, it appeared that F1 and the FIA had surrendered to the EC; however, Mosley had found a way to turn the capitulation into a bonus for Ecclestone that would change the face of F1 forever.

One of the EC's main concerns about the way the FIA operated was that it had a financial incentive to favour F1 over other motorsport series. Because F1's commercial rights would revert to the FIA once Formula One Administration's contract expired in 2010, the FIA had a stake in the success of F1, so it might favour it in any potential dispute with other series in order not to damage its value.

Other governing bodies own stakes in the sports they regulate, so it would seem strange to force the FIA to sell up. However, as Mosley later revealed, the situation was actually of its own making.

> If all the FIA did was regulate F1, there would be no problem with ownership. Other regulators could have regulated other branches of motorsport. This is the so-called American model – different forms of motorsport, each with its own regulator ... The difficulty was we wanted total control of all international motorsport worldwide with no rival regulators. We wanted the Commission to accept our sporting code with its provisions that prevent anyone running any form of international motorsport not regulated by the FIA. In the end, the deal was, 'OK, you can keep your draconian powers to stop anyone setting up a rival regulator, but you must have no incentive to favour one branch of motorsport over another.'

As a result, the sporting code still allows the FIA to stop motorsport activity on a circuit should it run an event not regulated by the FIA. This would have been decisive had the F1 teams (or some of them) tried to run outside the FIA. 'Many people fail to understand that the FIA is not like the governing body of, say, tennis, football or basketball,' continued Mosley. 'It is like a federation of all known ball games. Just think of the vast variety of competitive activity involving four or more wheels ... Our problem with the Commission was we wanted to retain that total control.'

Mosley's masterstroke came in suggesting to the EC that the FIA would sell a 100-year lease on F1's rights in order to remove the conflict. If the FIA would not have the opportunity to sell F1's rights again until the 22nd century, then there was little incentive at the present moment for it to favour it over other championships.

The EC stressed that Formula One Administration (FOA) 'will not be automatically named as successor' under the new contract. However, there was no auction for the rights and instead, on 28 June 2000, SLEC Holdings, a Jersey-based company owned by the Ecclestone family trust, was the only bidder when the FIA's General Assembly voted to award it the commercial rights to F1 for 100 years from 2011. It paid the staggeringly small sum of $300m, amounting to just $3m for every year of its deal. It was one of the most significant deals in the history of F1 and the most significant deal that is still operating today. It gave the Ecclestone family companies complete control over the sport's lucrative commercial rights for as good as forever and prevented the teams or Mosley's eventual successor as FIA president from wresting them away. In turn, this made F1 a viable prospect for investors, who did not want to pay big money for an entity that had no guaranteed way of making money after a few years.

It also eliminated one of the EC's biggest objections. It closed its investigation and concluded that 'the role of FIA will be limited to that of a sports regulator, with no commercial conflicts of interest . . . To prevent conflicts of interest, FIA has sold all its rights in the FIA Formula One World Championship.'

The EC could have ordered the FIA to put the 100-year rights out to tender, and it is likely that this would have considerably raised the returns for the FIA. It would also have led to SLEC paying a lot more, had the bidding process been competitive. It's tempting to ponder why Mosley was so accommodating to Ecclestone's wishes. There's no evidence to suggest that he ever received money from Ecclestone, or indeed any other favours. So why, then, was he so supportive? According to people who worked with both of them, Mosley viewed the teams as in effect customers of Ecclestone's 'restaurant'. Ecclestone had done the hard work and taken the risks to build the business up, so why should it be the diners who benefited? Also, Mosley loved the cut-and-thrust of board-room dealings, playing off his intellect against others, and was more than happy to use his expertise to continually get one over his opponents in the teams.

Paolo Cantarella, chief executive of Fiat and chairman of the European Automobile Manufacturers' Association, met Mosley twice to discuss buying the rights. He offered $500m in principle but Mosley said he produced nothing concrete. He was invited to make a formal bid and was told that he had to put it together in a month. Unsurprisingly given the tight timeframe, the manufacturers didn't place a bid and asked for an additional four months. Mosley refused on the grounds that there was no guarantee they would even make an offer then. As he put it, Ecclestone's 'bird in the hand was worth more than the one in the bush'.

According to Ecclestone, the decision was made at 'an extraordinary FIA meeting somewhere. All the members of the FIA board were there. Fiat had offered half a billion for the shares. All the board sat at the table, not me, and agreed that it's better to take Bernie's cash because Fiat had made an offer but [it was] in principle.' He added, 'I remember Otto Flimm, the president of the German club ADAC, said, "How can you do that? We could lose the deal on the table that we know about." That's why they sold the shares and nobody else wanted to buy them. Now it is worth a hell of a lot more than $300m, it wasn't at the time.'

Regardless of whether or not the 100-year deal was legitimately granted, the $300m price was an absolute scandal and Ecclestone had Mosley to thank for that. In comparison, in June 2000, nearly a year before the F1 rights deal was signed, BSkyB paid £1.1bn for the broadcast rights to one season of the Premier League.

Under the terms of the 100-year contract, SLEC switched FOA for a new F1 operating company called Formula One World Championship (FOWC). In 2011, the first year of the 100-year rights agreement, it made a $229.5m net profit on $1.2bn of revenue, enough to cover most of the $300m price of the rights. By 2024, the fee for the entire 100 years of rights represented just 9.2 per cent of the combined Formula One Group's annual revenue.

As Ecclestone later explained, 'Could I have done it all without Max? Probably not. Put it this way. It's been a great deal easier with him than it would have been without.' He added that 'the bottom line is that we've not cheated anyone in business, and never gone against our word. What we have done is taken advantage of situations, but that's what people do daily in politics and business.'

PART 3
GLOBALISATION

10

SELLING THE FAMILY SILVER

As the new millennium dawned, Formula One was fittingly going through a period of unprecedented change. Its new era started a few months before the world gathered to see in the new year, on 17 October 1999 at the newly minted Sepang International Circuit near Kuala Lumpur.

The cars lined up to start the first Malaysian Grand Prix in blistering heat against a glorious backdrop. The $180m circuit had been designed to the specification of the government by sportscar racer turned architect Hermann Tilke and featured an elaborate hospitality tower inspired by the country's national flower, the hibiscus. It was a spectacle the likes of which had never been seen before in F1.

Malaysia had the least significant Grand Prix heritage of any country ever to grace the calendar. There had never been a Malaysian F1 driver or team and, until national oil company Petronas partnered with Sauber in 1995, there had never been a major Malaysian sponsor. There wasn't even a big fanbase for the sport in the country and only 80,000 fans turned up across the entire three-day event – less than many of the top circuits attracted on race day alone.

But that wasn't what it was all about. The promoter's target audience wasn't local petrolheads, but the myriad fans watching on TV around the world. In 2001, F1 reported a cumulative 54 billion viewers of its race and news broadcasts. For Malaysia, F1 was much more than just a sports event. It was a chance to be seen on screens around the world and to have its name associated not only with glitz, glamour and fast cars but also with high-tech modernity and big business.

The F1 circus brought with it not only cars and drivers but ultra-high-net-worth fans and top executives from blue-chip sponsors and team owners. For the government and companies such as Petronas, it was an extraordinary networking event that gave them the opportunity to sell Malaysia to the world.

It didn't come cheap. Race hosting fees had been the poor relation to TV rights revenue since the late 1980s, but that was about to change. In a major coup for Ecclestone, Malaysia paid an estimated $17.5m to host its first race, a record fee that would hit $41.3m by the end of the event's 10-year contract due to an annual compound escalator averaging at 10 per cent.

It was a price that Malaysia and many other countries were willing to pay. Within a few years, other emerging markets with little racing heritage had joined the calendar, including Bahrain, China, Turkey, Singapore and Abu Dhabi. When Malaysia launched in 1999, more than two thirds of races took place in Europe. But by 2013, 42.1 per cent were in Asia, surpassing Europe for the first time.

More recently, the strategy has been refined further and many of the latest additions to the calendar, such as Baku in Azerbaijan and Las Vegas, have been street races, which can make local landmarks inseparable from the racing action. This isn't the only benefit. Purpose-built tracks take years to build; it is far quicker to prepare races on existing streets. The inaugural Saudi Arabian Grand Prix in 2021 would prove how quickly it could be done as the race took place on the streets of Jeddah just 13 months after it was announced. Street races give their hosts quick access to the attractions of F1 and eradicate any fears of being left with a white elephant if the organisers decide to quit when their contracts expire.

Malaysia, and the races that were modelled on it, transformed the face of F1 – but not everyone felt it was for the better. The top hosting fees would eventually hit more than $70m a year, pricing out not only many popular traditional venues, such as Germany's Nürburgring and France's Magny-Cours, but also eventually Malaysia itself, something that was unthinkable when F1 raced at the slick new circuit for the first time.

Approaching its 50th anniversary, the 'world' championship had finally gone global and the really big money was about to roll in.

The sport's growing revenues were a boon for Ecclestone and his family trust in more ways than one. The EC investigation may have prevented F1 from floating but it didn't stop the trust from looking for a buyer for its shares in SLEC, the parent company of F1. It was all the more important to find new investors, given Ecclestone's advancing years.

Fresh from her success with the bond issue, Robin Saunders tried to do the double by finding an investor for F1. Famous for her friendship with celebrity chef Marco Pierre White, Saunders had a bristling book of contacts, including flamboyant British tycoon Robert Tchenguiz, who had first approached her about F1 in May 1999 having heard about her work on the bond.

Tchenguiz, who made his fortune in property, wanted to buy a 12.5 per cent stake in SLEC but struggled to rustle up enough money, so he got the private equity firm Morgan Grenfell to take over the wheel.

Owned by Deutsche Bank, Morgan Grenfell too had been beguiled by Schumacher's continuing success and in October 1999 its Jersey-based subsidiary Speed Investments paid the trust $235m for the 12.5 per cent SLEC stake. Tchenguiz persuaded Morgan Grenfell to take an option on a further 37.5 per cent of SLEC but it failed to find investors who were prepared to stump up the $700m to buy it. Despite this, Ecclestone was so impressed with Tchenguiz that four years later he reportedly committed £100m to the property mogul's £550m bid to buy famed London department store Selfridges, though that too ultimately hit the skids.

One of Morgan Grenfell's potential co-investors was Entertainment München, Merchandising, Film und Fernseh, or EM.TV for short, a German media firm that had recently bought the Jim Henson Company, maker of *The Muppets* and *Sesame Street*. Founded by brothers Thomas and Florian Haffa in 1989, EM.TV started by buying the rights to distribute cartoons from Warner Bros. and soon had a lucky break.

One of its earliest deals was acquiring the German rights to *Teenage Mutant Ninja Turtles* from Fox before the craze started. It sold the rights to German TV channel RTL when the phenomenon was in full swing and generated huge profits, which were ploughed into buying a library of German and European children's programmes at sale prices in the recession of the early 1990s. Along the way EM.TV acquired the rights to such storied characters as the Simpsons, the Flintstones, the Smurfs and Charlie Brown.

Each deal was a springboard for a bigger acquisition, with the ultimate aim being to launch a kids' TV channel with an accompanying range of merchandise and stores to sell it in. The investment community was charmed by the plan and EM.TV became a darling of the now-defunct Neuer Markt, Germany's equivalent of the Nasdaq exchange for tech stocks. EM.TV was one of the first stocks to float on it in October 1997 and its market capitalisation rose from barely €50m to around €9bn in less than three years.

After acquiring the Jim Henson Company, EM.TV then set its sights on SLEC. The helping hand that Mosley had given to Benetton and Schumacher in the bar of the Hotel de Crillon was continuing to pay off. Like many Germans, Thomas Haffa was dazzled by Schumacher's success, although he didn't partner with Morgan Grenfell as he believed he could negotiate a better deal for the SLEC stake once the option expired at the start of February 2000. Bernie's buddies beat him to the finish line.

Australian Grand Prix boss Ron Walker introduced Ecclestone to businessman Brian Powers, who he knew because he was a former chairman of Fairfax Media, publisher of both *The Age* and the *Sydney Morning Herald* newspapers. 'Certainly Bernie is one of the closest friends I have on earth,' said Walker, adding, 'Brian Powers is a dear friend of mine and I was able to introduce them.' After his time at Fairfax, Powers went on to run San Francisco-based private equity firm Hellman & Friedman and it bought the 37.5 per cent SLEC stake for \$712.5m in February 2000.

The Jersey-based Ecclestone family company, Bambino, loaned Hellman & Friedman around half of the money for the purchase and when it was repaid it hit the trust's offshore coffers, so no UK tax was paid on it.

Losing out on the deal made Haffa even more determined to get his hands on F1 and this led to him eventually over-paying. Morgan Grenfell and Hellman & Friedman amalgamated their shareholdings in SLEC for the purpose of maximising the value. This gave Speed Investments a total 50 per cent stake in SLEC and in March 2000 Haffa's EM.TV bought it for a whopping \$1.7bn. It was 79.4 per cent more than the two investment firms had paid for it, but Haffa was still in his element.

In an interview for the *Formula 1 Opus* book in 2013 Mosley recounted a meeting he had with Ecclestone and Haffa, who appeared to be like a kid in a sweet shop. The three powerbrokers met in Ecclestone's motorhome at the Nürburgring during the weekend of the European Grand Prix in 2000. Nicknamed the Kremlin, as it was the seat of F1's power, the silvery motorhome had blacked-out windows and dark, futuristic furniture. In its inner sanctum was Ecclestone's mobile office where a long desk was set against a bank of TV screens showing views from all over the circuit. 'We told [Haffa] he was very welcome to stay right where he was and enjoy the rest of the race. But then as we were leaving I told him not to touch any of the buttons under the table. He said: "What do you mean?" I told him that they were the blow-up buttons. If Bernie wanted a race to suddenly change he'd press a button and get a car blown up. He actually believed me. That says something about the ultimate power people believed Bernie had.'

EM.TV's 50 per cent stake came with an option to buy a further 25 per cent, which had the high-octane price of $987.5m as it would give the owner control of F1. The trust originally inserted the option into the SLEC shareholders' agreement to put a value on the business in the event that the flotation finally managed to rev up. Although the trust didn't expect the option to be exercised, it fuelled the most seismic ownership change in F1's history.

The F1 sale was a major success for Hellman & Friedman. EM.TV's payment for the 50 per cent stake comprised 10 million shares in EM.TV and $725m in cash that the German media company had borrowed from the bank Credit Suisse. With EM.TV's value climbing following its F1 purchase, Hellman & Friedman sold on its shares quickly and made a tidy profit. Bambino was so impressed that it appointed Brian Powers to its board as its investment advisor.

In contrast, Morgan Grenfell chose to hold on to its shares, but the gamble didn't pay off. EM.TV was weighed down with debt and when the dot.com bubble burst, its share price nosedived, leaving Morgan Grenfell with a reported loss of more than $250m. This embarrassment was enough to put Morgan Grenfell off F1 for good and neither it nor its owner Deutsche Bank have had any significant involvement with the sport since then.

With EM.TV's share price in free-fall, it couldn't persuade anyone to loan it the $987.5m it needed to buy the additional 25 per cent stake in SLEC. Having to make more loan repayments would have driven EM.TV under so it was bailed out by Kirch, another German broadcaster. Kirch was well acquainted with F1 and not just because of Schumacher's superstar status.

Kirch had partnered on Ecclestone's F1 Digital+ since its launch in 1996 and although the service hadn't been a success this was because it was far ahead of its time. Kirch knew there was nothing wrong with F1's fundamentals. In fact, the value of sports to pay-TV broadcasters was accelerating, as they have a fervent fanbase prepared to pay a premium subscription price to watch live events.

Kirch was a giant of pay-TV broadcasting, so not only did it put together a rescue package for EM.TV but it also wanted to take over its shareholding in SLEC. The media giant was run by its founder Leo Kirch and deputy chairman Dieter Hahn, who had big ambitions. This put them on a collision course with Ecclestone. The trust had made a great deal of money from selling half its stake in F1, but Ecclestone now had to come to terms with the consequences of offloading it – having to deal with new owners he could neither choose nor control.

In a bid to prevent Kirch from taking the wheel, Robin Saunders came up with the innovative idea of the trust exercising a trigger in the bond contracts. This would have forced F1 to repay the bond early and would have hugely reduced the sport's value as it would have exhausted its cash reserves. With less money in the bank, it would have made it less attractive to any potential investor, so the trust could have bought EM.TV's 50 per cent stake back for a discount.

It is highly unusual for an owner to want to reduce the value of its own company and is a risky strategy, so much so that the trust came up with a Plan B that involved the teams.

F1's new-found wealth had led to some of the world's biggest companies joining the series. Chief among them were car manufacturers, which could promote the transfer of technological developments from the race track to road cars. In the wake of the safety improvements introduced after Senna's death, F1 was more attractive to car companies, which had previously been cautious about associating their brands with high-speed accidents. By early 2002 seven of them, including the ever-present Ferrari, would be involved in the sport. The era of the *garagistes* was coming to an end.

It started in June 1999, when Ford bought Jackie Stewart's team for $100m and renamed it after its Jaguar brand; then a month later Mercedes owner DaimlerChrysler spent a reported $400m on a 40 per cent stake in the company that owned both the McLaren team and its sportscar spin-off. In March 2000, Renault bought Benetton for $120m; the French marque had last been a team owner in 1985 but had won six constructors' championships as an engine supplier since then. In that same year, BMW and Honda returned as engine partners, with Williams and British American Racing respectively, then in early 2001 came the biggest coup of all. At a glitzy launch at the trust's Paul Ricard circuit – attended by Ecclestone and Mosley as guests of honour – the world's third-biggest car maker, Toyota, presented its plans to enter F1 for the first time, by building a new team that would compete from 2002.

The car manufacturers had deep pockets. They brought big marketing budgets to F1 that helped to promote the sport worldwide, but they were also spending huge sums on their teams and, in particular, their engine programmes, which by then cost around $100m a year per marque. F1 had come a long way from the $280,000 Cosworth had requested from Ford in 1967 to fund Lotus's engine supply. The level of spending made it difficult for small independent teams such as Jordan and Minardi to compete and by the end of 2002 both Prost and Arrows would fold.

The car manufacturers felt that their financial commitment should entitle them to more say in the sport and inevitably this brought them into conflict with Ecclestone and Mosley. To try to pacify them, the trust came up with an idea that involved it buying EM.TV's SLEC shares along with five of the car manufacturers. It was a logical way to protect their investment in the business and the car manufacturers' investment in the teams.

Owning a stake in F1 wouldn't have just increased the manufacturers' take, it would have also headed off the threat of Kirch taking it over and moving the sport on to its pay-TV networks, which had a smaller audience than the free-to-air stations that were already broadcasting it. That could have dented the teams' fortunes as their single-biggest source of revenue at the time came from sponsors and the amount they paid was largely proportionate to F1's TV audience. The wide TV coverage was also crucial to the manufacturers, which were using F1 as a marketing tool. It explains why the then head of Renault Sport told French newspaper *La Tribune* that 'it is out of [the] question for us to participate in a competition broadcast over pay-television channels'.

F1's TV exposure was far from the only concern for the teams. Kirch was also planning an IPO of its own business on the stock market, so if it bought F1 there would have been no need for the sport itself to float. The lack of a float was a particular concern for Benetton and the financially insecure teams Arrows, Jordan and Prost, as they had each been promised a $10m share of the proceeds of a float in return for signing the

1998 Concorde Agreement. As Stephen Mullens later explained, the teams' annoyance was 'brought about by the involvement of Kirch in Formula One. They [Kirch] were interested in doing an upstream IPO which would frustrate the teams from participating in the IPO that was envisaged under the agreements that SLEC had entered into with various teams.' He added that 'four of the smaller teams threatened to claim for compensation for the "lost" IPO, and SLEC concluded that it made commercial sense for it to make payments to extinguish any potential liability.' The payments came to a total of $40m in line with the original stakes offered to the teams. They were made in May 2001 by the trust's subsidiary Valper Holdings to the bosses of the teams, some of whom also owned their squads, either partly or entirely. The lucky four were Benetton's Flavio Briatore, Arrows boss Tom Walkinshaw, Eddie Jordan and Alain Prost. It came with the condition that they would each drop their complaints about losing out on the IPO against F1 and the trust.

They weren't the only teams that needed to be pacified, however. As Mullens explained, 'The agreements of Williams and McLaren were more complex because they wanted more.' There was good reason for this.

After the two teams had held back on signing the 1998 Concorde Agreement, they were mollified with the promise of 1 per cent of the proceeds of a float or of the sale of shares of F1's holding company, FOH. In the end, it was not FOH that was sold but its owner SLEC, and that left the teams with nothing.

Frank Williams and Ron Dennis were livid. 'The teams had met with me. And they had indicated that they were going to initiate proceedings against SLEC in relation to the documentation which had been issued at the time of the IPO,' said Mullens. 'McLaren and Williams brought a claim by way of an arbitration, and Ferrari made some informal claims.' The teams didn't hang around.

The arbitration took place in Geneva in June 2002 and Bambino came in all guns a-blazing. The trust appointed external lawyers as both Mullens and Luc Argand's wife Emmanuele gave evidence along with Ecclestone.

It was a car crash for Williams and McLaren as it became clear that, although they had appointed two heavyweight law firms to negotiate the contract that was intended to give them a share in the sale of F1, the agreement specifically applied to a sale of FOH, which left them with nothing. FOH itself had neither been floated, nor had its shares been sold. Ecclestone's byzantine corporate nomenclature had finally paid off as it appeared to have bamboozled even the teams' high-level lawyers. It made their bosses even more determined to get justice.

With McLaren and Williams seen off, and the other teams paid off, Kirch had a clear road ahead and in the middle of February 2001 EM.TV's lenders approved the deal with it. The poison pill Kirch inherited was EM.TV's option to buy a further 25 per cent of SLEC, which expired at the end of the month. In order to meet this tight deadline, Kirch gave EM.TV the funding it needed to take up the option and committed to buy the SLEC shares from it in stages.

The $987.5m asking price for the 25 per cent stake was almost as much as had previously been paid for 50 per cent of SLEC. To fund its subsequent purchase of the 75 per cent of SLEC from EM.TV, Kirch obtained a $1.6bn loan from a trio of banks secured on the F1 shares. Lehman Brothers loaned around $300m, while $282.7m came from a Kirch company that then assigned its entitlement to the money to JP Morgan. Kirch's biggest creditor was provincial German lender Bayerische Landesbank (BayernLB), which was part-owned by the state of Bavaria and loaned the $987.5m. It was a seemingly routine financial manoeuvre that was set to have a colossal impact on the future of F1 in years to come. In order to buy SLEC, Kirch had mortgaged itself to the hilt, betting that the sport's future growth would give it the ability to repay this colossal loan. Things didn't pan out as it planned.

11

BURN-OUT

If ever there was an acquisition that came with a sting in its tail it was Kirch's purchase of F1.

Soon after buying the sport, another big bill landed on Kirch's doorstep. It was time for F1 to pay the FIA its $300m to acquire the 100-year rights and, as its 75 per cent owner, Kirch had to rustle up the money to cover three quarters of it. Ecclestone's family trust would cover the other 25 per cent.

According to Mosley's autobiography, there was good reason for the hold-up: 'Bernie, it seemed, was waiting for [Leo] Kirch to find the $1 billion to complete the deal and expected him then to contribute his 75% share of our $300 million.'

There were limits to Mosley's patience so in February 2001, just as Kirch was stepping into F1's driving seat, he issued a statement saying that F1 'must pay the sum by March 22nd or we may decide to make other arrangements'. The deadline coincided with an extraordinary meeting of the FIA's General Assembly, which agreed to give Ecclestone one more opportunity to pay up. He duly did this, a month after deadline, on 24 April 2001 when the 100 Year Agreements were signed by the FIA and what was now the F1 Group of companies.

Mosley seized the opportunity to extract more money from F1's wealthy new owners. He charged interest on the $300m, bringing the total fee for the 100-year rights to $313.6m. There was more to come, as the FIA also received a further $7.4m to cover 50 per cent of a Swiss tax liability which arose on the original transaction. Separately, F1 agreed to pay it an annual regulatory fee, which came to around $11.5m before it was sharply increased in a renegotiation in 2013. Mosley put the money to good use, using it to launch the FIA Foundation, a UK-registered road safety charity based at London's historic Trafalgar Square.

In line with its 75 per cent ownership stake, Kirch provided $235m of the $313.6m in the form of a loan to SLEC. A total of $115m came from its cash reserves, while it took out yet another loan to pay the remaining $120m, this time from Swiss bank Credit Suisse. Following the bailout of EM.TV, Kirch was considered to be an extremely risky bet. Accordingly, Credit Suisse required a $120m deposit from Kirch's family trust, Faller-Stiftung, as well as the right to repayment of the entire $235m from SLEC itself. This meant that if Credit Suisse didn't get the $120m back it could keep the deposit and try to recover the loan from SLEC. It mitigated the bank's risk, and its prudence proved to be well founded.

Just as Kirch was making preparations for its F1 ownership, all its grand ambitions came to nought, overtaken by world events. Months after it bought EM.TV, the terrorist attacks on 9/11 caused a deep advertising downturn that hit the media giant's main source of revenue. In April 2002, Kirch collapsed under the weight of its huge debt pile and was taken over by administrators. The media company defaulted on its loan repayments to the trio of banks. As collateral, the banks took over Speed Investments, which held its SLEC shares. F1 was on its fifth set of new shareholders in two and a half years and this time they had no long-term aims for the development of the sport. They would, however, leave a long-lasting impression in other ways.

The objective of the banks was to sell Kirch's SLEC shares as soon as possible in order to recoup the money from the loan they had provided. They soon found out that it might not be that simple. When the banks came to take over the shares they discovered that they needed approval from the FIA. The reason for this was buried in the contract that SLEC signed with the FIA when it bought the 100-year rights to the sport, known as the Umbrella Agreement. As the F1 rights will return to the FIA in 2111, it has a say in who holds them in the meantime.

According to the Umbrella Agreement, the FIA has to approve any change of control of SLEC unless it is through a flotation on a stock market. The FIA approved the banks' takeover but they then had to get anti-competition clearance from the European Commission, which took time. Even after that, the banks didn't own the full 75 per cent of SLEC. Kirch had agreed to buy SLEC from EM.TV in stages, but had collapsed before acquiring the final 16.7 per cent. Kirch had paid for this using the loan from the banks that was secured on the shares, so the banks assumed that they would just replace Kirch on the agreement. But EM.TV countered that the banks did not have any claim on the 16.7 per cent as it wasn't yet Kirch's property. This led to a lawsuit in Jersey, which was won by the banks: although they had to buy the 16.7 per cent from EM.TV, they didn't have to pay top dollar.

The stake was transferred for the bargain-basement price of €8.5m and BayernLB got it all as it was the biggest lender to Kirch. This gave it a 62.2 per cent stake in Speed Investments, which now owned 75 per cent of SLEC. BayernLB therefore held 46.7 per cent of SLEC, making it F1's single-biggest shareholder. Being the majority owner of SLEC's majority owner meant that BayernLB, a bank with no motorsport or media experience that had never intended to own the company, now had the legal right to control F1.

BayernLB's cut-price acquisition of EM.TV's shares led to the struggling media company revising the value of its F1 stake by €195.8m, causing it to make a €310m net loss in 2002. However, EM.TV had a chance to make it back, as BayernLB also agreed to give it a cut of the proceeds when it sold its SLEC stake, after the bank had made its own money back. BayernLB's total outlay came to $1.057bn because it had loaned Kirch $987.5m to buy the SLEC shares and invested a further $69.5m during its time as an owner of them.

Although Ecclestone had no idea about BayernLB's deal with EM.TV at the time, it would later prove to be one of the most pivotal manoeuvres of his career as it would ultimately lead to his exit from F1.

However, for the moment, his attention was focused on other things. During the vacuum of power between the collapse of Kirch and the takeover of its F1 shares by the banks, his family trust had swamped the boards of FOH (Formula One Holdings) and its subsidiary FOA (Formula One Administration), which ran the sport, with its own directors.

A shareholders' agreement filed in May 2000 by SLEC's then-owner, Bambino, included various rights for Speed and Bambino to appoint directors to SLEC and the tangle of F1 companies that cascaded from it. It limited the number of directors of FOH to eight, with 'A Directors' representing Speed Investments and 'B Directors' representing Bambino. Crucially, the agreement did not exclude the possibility of neutral parties on the board, who were known as ordinary directors.

Legally, Bambino only had the right to install two directors on FOH and it added Luc Argand along with his wife Emmanuele, who was also a lawyer. By now Argand was a member of the Geneva Magistrates' Upper Council and was a former president of the Geneva Bar Association. That didn't stop him from racing into controversy. Even though Bambino was only allowed to have two directors, by the time that the Argands were appointed to FOH, Bambino's legal advisor Stephen Mullens was already on the board. So too was Ecclestone, who the banks believed also represented Bambino, although he has always strongly denied having any influence over it or receiving any benefit from it. Nevertheless, the Argands' names were entered into the FOH register of directors, so when the banks finally got their hands on the SLEC shares they couldn't appoint their own two representatives to the board as the maximum number of eight directors had been reached. F1's chief legal officer, Sacha Woodward Hill, was one of them, as was Ecclestone's financial fixer Robin Saunders, who was overseeing the interest of the German bank WestLB, which had arranged the $1.4bn bond. The banks already had two directors of their own and – rightly – claimed that Bambino had four – the Argands, Mullens and Ecclestone, although it was legally only allowed two.

When the shareholders' agreement had come into effect in May 2000 Mullens spotted that it didn't exclude the possibility of ordinary directors, and Bambino's lawyers made the most of it. They argued that Ecclestone and Mullens were ordinary directors as they were already on the board of FOH before the shareholders' agreement came into effect. Therefore, they claimed that the Argands were Bambino's only representatives on the board.

It was a particularly ludicrous claim to make about Mullens as he was the trust's legal advisor. He later acknowledged that there was actually a strategic reason for this argument. He later admitted in court proceedings that the hijack of the FOH board was 'a tactical procedure' and clarified that 'we thought it would be a catastrophe if the banks had too much to say in the negotiations with the constructors. We did this in order to give Ecclestone time to reach an agreement with the constructors.'

As Ecclestone was continuing his quest for control over F1, all was not well in the paddock: still frustrated by the division of money, the manufacturers had now threatened to launch a breakaway series.

In November 2001, five of the biggest backers of F1 teams (BMW, DaimlerChrysler, Ford, Ferrari and Renault) had set up a Dutch company called Grand Prix World Championship (GPWC) and announced they would launch their own racing series when the Concorde Agreement expired at the end of 2007. It was a classic case of poachers turned game-keepers, as it was Ecclestone and Mosley who now had to prevent the rebel teams from breaking away. Despite the change in their role since the FISA–FOCA war, they were once again the underdogs in the fight, coming up against some of the world's biggest car companies, which had incredibly deep pockets.

A grand prize was at stake as F1 had begun to tap into the lucrative new source of revenue that came from race hosting fees and the teams had the power to throw a spanner in Ecclestone's expansion plans. As is still the case today, the majority of the teams were based in the UK in an area of talent concentrated in the Midlands nicknamed 'Motorsport Valley', so the more races they had to attend outside Europe, the greater their travel costs and the more time they had to spend away from home.

Accordingly, they were reluctant for the calendar to continue growing and this ultimately led to the Concorde Agreement requiring the consent of 70 per cent of the teams if there are more than 24 races in a season or if there are fewer than eight across Europe and North America combined. It is designed to stop the teams' travel costs surging; Ecclestone could see this coming in the late 1990s as F1's popularity accelerated and more countries wanted to host races. Faced with opposition from the teams he employed the smart strategy of pitching F1 to emerging markets, which were prepared to pay top dollar to snag a spot on the calendar alongside developed countries like the UK, the US and Australia. The limited number of slots fuelled an arms race in the amount countries were prepared to spend.

In the early 2000s, the teams shared in none of this as their prize money was restricted to 47 per cent of the TV rights revenues. This represented just 25 per cent of the sport's overall profits. At the same time, the top annual team budgets had risen to more than $400m, including engine development, as F1 had become a data-driven, high-tech, manufacturer-led sport.

The teams wanted 60 per cent of the profits. Ecclestone was only reportedly prepared to consider this if the car manufacturers that owned the teams directly signed the Concorde rather than their subsidiaries, which ran the squads. Ecclestone remembered how Balestre had made major concessions to Renault, only for it to shut its team when the going got tough, and was also wary of Honda's commitment as the Japanese manufacturer had pulled out of the sport on two previous occasions. Getting the manufacturers' signatures on the dotted line would give F1 the ability to make a claim from the teams' parent companies if the agreement was breached. In contrast, a car manufacturer could easily just shut down its team in times of trouble, leaving F1 with no legal recourse.

Hammering home the threat, in February 2003 Ferrari chairman Luca di Montezemolo told *The Times* that 'without us, in 2008 the banks will own 100% of nothing. We are preparing a new championship without banks, without Bernie, and with a far bigger cake.' F1 company filings admitted that without a Concorde Agreement it could be very difficult for it to renew its TV contracts. Ecclestone took di Montezemolo's challenge in his stride. 'There's been an offer on the table which [the teams] shouldn't refuse,' he told the *Guardian* without giving any details. 'This would be more than they had ever dreamed of.'

Ecclestone also threatened the dissenters with legal action, pointing out that they were all bound by the Concorde through to the end of the 2007 season. Crucially, one of its clauses stated that only in the last year of the contract could the teams 'promote or make any preparations whatsoever to promote, or solicit any broadcasters or circuits' for a rival series to F1. Ecclestone added to *Autosport* that if the complaints continued before then, 'writs will fall like autumn leaves'.

It kept the teams on their toes but added to the banks' worries. According to Mullens, the banks' view had been polluted by Dieter Hahn, who was deputy chairman of Kirch when it collapsed after taking on debt to buy F1. 'Dieter Hahn wanted to get rid of Bernie Ecclestone,' Mullens said. 'The attitude of Dieter Hahn also transferred to the banks, who were of the opinion that Ecclestone should remedy the existing problems and then disappear.'

With Bambino in control of the board of FOH, however, there was little chance of Ecclestone going anywhere. The banks' lack of control over the company's board also significantly reduced the value of their SLEC shares, opening the door to the trust buying them back at a discount. In February 2003 Ecclestone told *The Times*, 'I believe the family trust would buy back F1 from the banks if all the F1 teams extended until 2015.' But the banks didn't let the trust take the wheel, not just out of principle but also because of the rich rewards at stake.

In November 2003 Ecclestone joined celebrities such as Jodie Kidd and Jeremy Clarkson on the last flight of Concorde from New York to London, more than 25 years after he was a passenger on its inaugural commercial flight. He had good reason to treat himself; F1 was firing on all cylinders. Its total revenue crossed the billion-dollar mark for the first time in 2004 driven by contracts for new races in Bahrain and China as well as a $93.1m severance payment from marketing company Interpublic for breaking its contract to promote the British Grand Prix. It made the banks even more determined to get control and in March 2004 they sued Bambino in London's High Court for control of FOH.

Ecclestone claimed he was not worried by the banks' legal action. He told the *Sunday Express* that 'this is a dispute about the nomination of directors and what will eventually come out of this will be a clarification of my position and the type of shareholder I am . . . the writ is nothing to do with me. I haven't even bothered to find out what it's about.' He added, 'I am not involved in or concerned with it.' Given his pivotal role in the legal action, his denial suggested that, for the first time in his life, he was actually on shaky ground.

Even though Ecclestone didn't own shares in any of the F1 companies, he claimed he represented himself on the board of FOH while the banks believed that he represented the trust. Ecclestone denied this, as if he was found to be the trust's representative it could have made him liable to pay tax on the billions it had raised from F1.

12

A TIME BOMB STARTS TICKING

Few would have expected that a burly balding banker would be Ecclestone's greatest nemesis but this description perfectly fits Gerhard Gribkowsky, BayernLB's chief risk officer.

Gribkowsky was tasked with getting back the money the bank had lent to Kirch. This meant selling its stake in F1, but first it had to get control of the companies that ran the sport, FOH and its subsidiary FOA. Bambino stood in its way as its directors had swamped the companies' boards. Ecclestone insisted that he wasn't one of them and wasn't allowed to be. Gribkowsky sensed an Achilles' heel.

The banker was cut from a different cloth to Ecclestone. Born in 1958, he came from a wealthy family in Bremen. Son of a board member at Beck's Brewery, Gribkowsky has a doctorate in law. After completing a trainee programme at Deutsche Bank he worked his way up to become one of its senior credit executives before moving to BayernLB in 2003. His experience gave him tremendous tenacity and drive. He could smell the money in F1 and soon realised that Ecclestone was the gatekeeper of it.

Instead of believing Ecclestone's every word, Gribkowsky investigated him and approached his opponents, including the group of rogue car manufacturers, led by Mercedes. The group's spokesperson Xander Heijnen was a former Mercedes employee and during his time there he had come into contact with Wolfgang Eisele, the truck racing entrepreneur who had triggered Ecclestone's battles with the EC. Knowing that Eisele had managed to get one over Ecclestone in that dispute, Heijnen went to his house in Heidelberg to introduce him to his friend Alexandra Irrgang, who worked alongside Gribkowsky at BayernLB.

'In that meeting Eisele gave us a document which I remember at the time, it was important to the banks,' says Heijnen. 'Gribkowsky was not at the meeting. It was just me, Irrgang and Eisele. I set up the meeting because I knew he had issues with Bernie and he had a huge database of documents. He was always looking for ways to prove that for instance the FIA, with Bernie as the vice president, [was] interfering with other series, making them smaller than they wanted to be so that they couldn't compete with Formula One.'

One possible option the manufacturers were considering was buying F1 from the banks. They were therefore keen to see what Eisele had unearthed, but not as keen as Irrgang. Sensing an opportunity to get revenge on Ecclestone for not paying the remaining $4.5m he thought he was owed, Eisele handed over the highlight of his collection. 'At the end of the meeting he gave her a document which I think showed the structure of the company. I didn't think much of it at the time but I do remember that she was happy with it,' continued Heijnen.

The document was said to be explosive and the information held within it led Gribkowsky to believe that Ecclestone did indeed have connections to Bambino. The kind of details the banker is thought to have found out include claims that Ecclestone had shaken hands with property owners on deals for the trust to acquire their assets.

Famously, in 2001, the trust paid £50m for 18–19 Kensington Palace Gardens on London's so-called 'Billionaires' Row', making it Britain's most expensive house at the time. The 55,000-square-foot home had an indoor pool, parking for 20 cars and Turkish baths made with marble from the same quarry that supplied the stone for the Taj Mahal. The property was sold by eminent art collector Sir Nasser David Khalili, who revealed that after showing Ecclestone and his then-wife Slavica around it, 'I had a meeting with Mr Ecclestone in mid to late July 2001 and we shook hands on a deal.'

Likewise, Dieter Hahn claimed at a breakfast meeting in October 2005 that Ecclestone indicated the trust might be willing to pay $100m for the right to repayment of the loan used to partially cover the purchase of the 100-year rights to F1. Ecclestone also helped to co-ordinate 1,200 workers who renovated Paul Ricard after the trust had purchased it. Then there was his relationship with the trust's director, Luc Argand. Even Argand himself admitted that the closeness of their relationship was not ideal when it came to these roles.

In 2011 Argand revealed that he was 'one of numerous lawyers' who work for Ecclestone. On being asked why he nonetheless also had the formal functions with the trust and its subsidiaries he replied, 'If I'd been involved on a daily basis, written letters, travelled to London, carried out negotiations, this would have meant a close connection between Mr Ecclestone and the trusts.' However, it was put to him that he still remained on the letterheads as trustee and director, which caused him to admit that 'this situation was not ideal'. In short, Argand's name was on letterheads as Bambino's trustee at the same time that he acted as Ecclestone's lawyer.

Gribkowsky's treasure trove of information was crucial to the banks' court case, which centred on whether or not Ecclestone was a director representing Bambino. Gribkowsky knew that Ecclestone wouldn't want this to be probed further in court, especially as the investigation that HMRC had started back in 1999 was still ongoing.

The banker had Ecclestone's back against the wall and seized the opportunity to line his own pockets. Gribkowsky started by suggesting business opportunities to Ecclestone; when he was rebuffed he stepped it up a gear. The banker began to insinuate to Ecclestone that he believed he was in control of the trust and that he could inform HMRC about it. In the same breath, Gribkowsky suggested property ventures and business opportunities to Ecclestone before asking him for a loan, which the F1 boss saw as an attempt to extract money from him.

According to Ecclestone, Gribkowsky 'wanted to leave the bank and he wanted to start up in his own business. He wanted me to be a partner with him in his own business. He wanted to borrow money to start the business.' He added that Gribkowsky said:

'In the event that someone had asked me: do you control the trust? I'd say "yes".' I said, 'Why would you say that?' He said, 'Well, they own a race circuit in the south of France and you help this race circuit quite a lot.' 'Yes,' I said, 'and you know the reason why,' because we had, at that time, I think, 17 race circuits which I looked after and that was the reason I helped.

Ecclestone said that 'the threat was in any case at a time the bank was still a shareholder. It was a gradual process. Back then, when the first threat came from Mr Gribkowsky, I asked Stephen Mullens. He said that major problems could result. In terms of tax, everything was actually correctly regulated but Mr Gribkowsky could cause aggravation anyway.'

Ecclestone said that if he had reported the threat to the police it could have led to HMRC finding out and digging deeper, which was the very thing he was trying to avoid. 'What would [the police] have done? I informed them about a burglary we had. They did nothing.' He added, 'I was trying to keep all of this out of the tax people. That was the whole point of paying him. If I hadn't have wanted to do that, I wouldn't have paid him.'

Summing it up, Ecclestone told us, 'I gave him some money to shut up because he was sort of blackmailing me actually.' He revealed that Mullens came up with the idea. 'When I asked Mullens what is the best thing to do he said, "The best thing to do is get rid of the guy." He said, "What is he after?" And I said, "He wants to borrow money and wants to be partners in property. He wants money." He said, "Can't we pay him off?"'

Explaining this further in an interview for *Pitpass*, the leading independent F1 website, Ecclestone said that Mullens told him, 'you need to get rid of this bloody guy because if he had written a letter and said "Ecclestone runs the thing", which I didn't and don't, [HMRC] would have had to assess me.'

This risk partly explains why Ecclestone later said, 'Out of all the mistakes I have made in this world probably the worst was giving everything to my ex that she put in trust.' He did it as Slavica was a non-domicile so would not have been subject to the usual inheritance tax exemption on spouses if she had inherited his assets when he died. The irony is that just four years after he gave his assets to her, Slavica became domiciled in the UK for inheritance tax purposes so he could have avoided a lot of headaches if he had just waited. Ecclestone wasn't inclined to do that as he didn't know how long he would be around given the health scare with his heart. It ended up only being a brief setback but, of course, he didn't know that at the time.

On 6 December 2004 came the judgement Ecclestone had been dreading: the banks won control of FOH in court and, embarrassingly for Bambino, they hadn't even needed to go to a full trial. Bambino claimed that as Ecclestone was already a director when the shareholders' agreement came into effect he had not consented to being its representative. It added that he would have declined if he had been asked, but the judge ruled that his consent was not needed. He said that Ecclestone and Mullens had indeed been appointed by Bambino when the shareholders' agreement began and had remained so ever since.

The judge added that the trust had 'no real prospect of successfully defending' the banks' claim. Even in the face of defeat, Bambino persisted with its delaying tactics. Not only did it say it would appeal to the lawmakers in the House of Lords, but it also requested for judgement to be suspended until then, though this was refused.

It was a disaster for Ecclestone. Not only was the trust's tax-exempt status now under threat, but his control of F1 was slipping through his fingers. The banks were now in charge of F1's holding company, FOH, and he could not stay on its board as the judge had ruled that he was there because he was the trust's appointee. In order to demonstrate to HMRC that this was false, he had to resign from the board. Ecclestone had fought to rule F1 for more than three decades, but everything was now in danger of collapse.

Gribkowsky sat in the court beaming when the judge ruled that Ecclestone had indeed been appointed by the trust. The F1 boss went into crisis-management mode.

Just one day after the verdict, he told *The Times* that he would offer F1's teams $500m over the next three years in a bid to put the brakes on the rival GPWC series. Ecclestone's announcement reminded the banks that he held the keys to resolving the dispute. Although the plan wasn't developed enough to convince the teams to call off their threat, it got their attention, which was the desired effect.

If the banks had ejected Ecclestone from the driving seat and not offered the teams as much money it could have driven them away from F1. To make matters worse for the banks, Ecclestone would then have been free to run the breakaway series. The teams might have had their issues with Ecclestone, but his contacts book and supreme deal-making skills meant that a new series under his administration would be a powerful force in world sport.

Offering the teams an additional $500m would have doubled their income from F1 immediately and was a classic Ecclestone strategy, as it distracted from the brutal court loss. It was clearly on his mind. A few days after the verdict Ecclestone told the *Guardian* that 'the judge is totally out of order, talking about me being appointed by a company called Bambino, which I am not'. Just a few days after that he resigned from the board of FOH in an attempt to avoid the suggestion that he was the trust's representative, though he remained on the board of its subsidiary, FOA, the company that owned F1's commercial rights, and crucially he was still chief executive of F1.

Nevertheless, as BayernLB was the largest of the three lenders to Kirch, this put Gribkowsky firmly in the driving seat of the owners and he used the banks' control of F1's holding company to its full effect. Gribkowsky told the media that the banks now had the power to fire Ecclestone, and it was no exaggeration. By controlling FOH, the banks could even remove Ecclestone from the board of its subsidiary FOA that ran F1.

The banks planned to use their victory in the FOH case as a springboard to launch further legal action aimed at gaining control of FOA, as the two circumstances were substantially the same. The key difference was that the FOA claim was set to go to a full trial, which would give ample opportunity for the court to probe Ecclestone's links to the trust. This was crucial to determining whether he was actually its representative on the board or was an ordinary director as he claimed.

The FOH case had only begun to explore this, with the judge asking, 'Who has the real authority to take decisions for Bambino?' He added, 'If the directors look for guidance and suggestions to others, who are those others? Mr Ecclestone is adamant that he is not one of them, but neither he nor anyone else says who is.' Gribkowsky wasn't the only one who claimed to know the answer to this question.

Still seething from their failure to benefit from the sale of F1 and then losing the 2002 arbitration about it, Frank Williams and Ron Dennis were out for revenge. Like all of the F1 teams, the duo had hitherto been reluctant to openly challenge F1's power structure for fear of being reprimanded. However, after the F1 sales left them empty-handed, they finally snapped.

The arbitration had confirmed that Williams and McLaren were the architects of their own demise because their contract had specified that while they would get a share of the proceeds if FOH was sold, of course it was actually SLEC that changed hands. The two teams therefore turned their attention to their lawyers – Linklaters and Baker McKenzie respectively – as they were the ones who had drafted the questionable contract.

In May 2004, as Ecclestone's dispute with the banks hit top gear, Williams and McLaren had sued their former lawyers for negligence. Although Ecclestone and the trust weren't parties to the claim, they kept a close eye on it and there was good reason for this. In a move that had striking similarities to Gribkowsky's recent tactics, the two teams dropped a bombshell on Ecclestone by claiming in their witness statements that he controlled the trust and/or SLEC 'at all material times' from 1997 onwards – and that the separation between Ecclestone and SLEC/the trust and its advisors 'was, in effect, a charade or window dressing'.

Perhaps the teams had got a whiff of Gribkowsky's strategy, as this blockbuster allegation was as core to their case as it was to the banks' argument. In order to determine whether the lawyers had indeed been negligent it was essential to know who the teams were negotiating with, so the teams' dealings with Ecclestone and the trust would have to be analysed in detail in court.

The teams had been negotiating their continued participation in F1 with Ecclestone while the incentive they were offered came from the trust's subsidiary Valper Holdings, another strand in the labyrinthine web of Ecclestone's family trusts. Just like with the banks' case, the teams knew Ecclestone wouldn't want these kinds of matters to be probed in public, so he had an interest in it not coming to court. 'I can confirm that such suggestions or allegations are a nonsense,' Ecclestone said in a letter to Linklaters' lawyers. 'In particular, I confirm, as I stated in evidence during the arbitration, I do not control the trust or SLEC. I have never controlled the trust or SLEC. Never attempted to influence or control the trust. Never attempted to influence or affect the conduct of the trust.'

Proving that he could either be Ecclestone's worst enemy or his best friend, Gribkowsky even endorsed this view in the Williams and McLaren litigation while threatening Ecclestone privately around the same time.

In multiple interviews after the banks' court victory Ecclestone had stressed that he wasn't doing the selling when F1 changed hands. 'Let me make this clear,' he told the *Independent*. 'I didn't sell anything myself. I gave the shares to my wife, who put them in trust as she was advised to do, and the trust sold them. I wish it hadn't.' He told the *International Herald Tribune* that 'they do what they like, the trustees, and they thought they should sell them because they thought maybe if I'd died they're going to be worth a lot less'.

It contradicted comments from him in interviews prior to the banks' litigation. In March 2000 Ecclestone had told the *Sunday Times*, 'I sold the shares so there would be money there for Slavica and the girls if anything happened to me.'

Even the EC, which spent years investigating F1, concluded that Ecclestone sold the trust's assets. When discussing ISC, the company that held the commercial rights to the World Rally Championship, it had said, 'Mr Ecclestone sold the company to Mr David Richards.'

This throwaway line in a dense document didn't attract Ecclestone's ire as much as the ruling in a court case that the world was watching. Williams and McLaren planned to seize on that platform. While their legal claim form left open the question of who was actually in charge of negotiating their deal to sign the Concorde – it referred to the teams' 'negotiation of an agreement with Mr Bernie Ecclestone and/or the Ecclestone Family Trusts' but didn't go any further – the process was due to be explored in detail in court. It was not to be.

Linklaters settled with Williams in late December 2005, while Baker McKenzie did the same with McLaren the week before the trial was due to begin on 16 January 2006. Both teams have been treated favourably by Ecclestone since then, with Williams getting additional prize money payments from a dedicated heritage fund in the 2013 Concorde Agreement while McLaren was also handed a hefty bonus and even a seat on F1's board, which it held right up until the end of 2020 when the contract ended.

The legal settlement was a big boost for the teams at a crucial time. Neither team had a title sponsor for the following season, and Frank Williams had recently rebuffed an approach by his engine supplier BMW to buy the team. It decided to buy Sauber instead, which left Williams paying for Cosworth engines in 2006. Following the acquisition of British American Racing by Honda in 2005, six of the car manufacturers were now team owners, giving them control over the majority of the 11-team grid (Ford had quit F1 at the end of 2004, following a string of disappointing results).

It was yet another issue troubling Ecclestone, who still hadn't managed to shake off Gribkowsky and the banks.

Although the settlement with the lawyers put the brakes on the teams coming out with further allegations about Ecclestone in court, Gribkowsky was still on the loose. The banks were an even more imme- diate threat and at the end of 2004 they were preparing to cut right to the heart of Ecclestone's fiefdom by using their victory in the FOH case to launch a lawsuit for the control of F1's operating company, FOA.

But before the banks even had a chance to file the writ, the trust had already taken desperate measures to delay it. Just 11 days after the court verdict in the FOH case, Mullens summoned an FOA board meeting 'to consider all appropriate steps to ensure that [Mr Ecclestone's] position as a director and CEO is maintained and to take whatever action may be considered necessary by the board to achieve this'.

At the meeting on 20 December 2004, Ecclestone and Mullens caused a resolution to be passed for a single share in FOA to be issued to Ecclestone giving him 50 per cent of the company's voting power for just £1. In a nutshell, this meant that FOA couldn't make any major decisions without Ecclestone's approval.

Mullens explained the reasoning behind the decision in a letter to the banks that said:

> In view of the serious possibility of damage to the interests of [FOA], its business and the group, we felt that it was in the best interests of FOA and the group to remove all doubt as to Mr Ecclestone's position which we felt had been seriously undermined in the run up to and subsequent to the recent [FOH] decision in the High Court.
>
> Suggestions that he might be removed as a director of FOA and no longer have authority to negotiate on behalf of the group's business, have threatened seriously to undermine his position and damage the interests of FOA and the group. Accordingly the ordinary share in FOA has been issued.

The paperwork was filed just five days before Christmas and it neutered the banks' control over FOA. Crucially, it prevented them from firing Ecclestone or diluting his power by appointing additional directors. It also gave him his own shares to show that he had taken steps to represent himself after the judge had ruled that he had been nominated by the trust.

It may have seemed like a perfect Christmas present for the man who has everything, but it ended up adding to Ecclestone's problems. This was clear from the festive cartoon that he commissioned for his annual Christmas card. The hand-drawn scenes on them usually give an insight into his sharp wit and the 2004 edition was no exception. It showed him juggling balls while the bosses of the car makers surrounded him. The message inside read, 'Let's hope there are not so many balls in the air in 2005.' No sooner had he written this than another ball landed in his lap.

The share issue led to the banks filing a new lawsuit in January 2005 against Ecclestone and Bambino to void the transaction and regain control of FOA. The law firm Lovells advised the trust that it would be risky to issue the share but it did so anyway to stall the banks and keep Ecclestone in the driving seat, as he was still negotiating with the renegade manufacturers.

As Mullens explained, 'If by doing this it was possible to stall the banks for six to nine months then it was worth it for us.'

Ecclestone had his work cut out for him.

13

THE PAY-OFF

On 4 December 2003, Geneva's posh Hotel du Rhône was bristling with bodyguards when senior executives from the car manufacturers' GPWC group met Ecclestone, Mullens and the banks. After a few hours, they shook hands on a deal intended to avert a breakaway and two weeks later the handshake was turned into signatures on a confidential Memorandum of Understanding (MOU).

Its term sheet stated that the teams would receive 50 per cent of F1's total profits, that a trust for the teams would hold up to 6.6 per cent of SLEC's shares, that GPWC would have a 'special share' in SLEC and three directors on its board. It meant there would be more people than ever before looking over Ecclestone's shoulder, so it's perhaps no surprise that the MOU hit the skids in April 2004, after just four months.

Some observers believed Ecclestone was deliberately obstructing progress, and his own comments later added fuel to that fire. 'I see myself as something of a firefighter and I never get tired of it,' he said, adding that 'if there are no fires, we light a few of our own'. The more unstable F1 became, the more the teams relied on Ecclestone to safeguard their investments, the more power he thereby gained and the more entrenched his position became.

The banks blew a hole in this carefully concocted system, and the controversial share issued to Ecclestone was barely a sticking plaster solution as Bambino had no hope of winning in the upcoming court case for control of FOA. It was a minority shareholder that had seized majority control so it was on a road to nowhere. What's more, just days after the court ruled that Bambino had no right to control FOH it had used its dominance over the company's subsidiary to wrest further power away from the banks.

While F1's shareholders had been squabbling GPWC had upped its game. In autumn 2004 it announced that it had appointed International

Sports and Entertainment AG (iSe) to run the rival series at the start of 2008 when the Concorde expired. A subsidiary of marketing giant Dentsu, iSe had been involved with the World Cup and the Olympic Games, so it came with a strong pedigree. Ecclestone – as always – had a trick up his sleeve.

Few teams had ever had such a grand homecoming as Ferrari did at the 2004 Italian Grand Prix at Monza. At the previous race in Belgium, Michael Schumacher had secured his record seventh world championship with almost a quarter of the season still to run. At the race prior to that, Ferrari had secured its sixth consecutive constructors' championship – again a record. The *tifosi* – Ferrari's passionate fans – turned out in force at Monza to cheer the scarlet cars home to a decisive one–two.

There has been much debate over whether F1 needs Ferrari more than Ferrari needs F1. In the history of the sport, neither side has had the nerve to find out. So when Ecclestone looked for a way to break the GPWC, Ferrari was his focus.

With the house of cards looking like it could fall down at any moment, Ecclestone went to di Montezemolo and offered Ferrari an estimated $100m to commit to race in F1 under a new Concorde Agreement from 2007 until 2012. With Ferrari getting exactly what it wanted, di Montezemolo abandoned the other car manufacturers and accepted the offer. The agreement was announced in January 2005 to the shock of the other GPWC members, DaimlerChrysler, Renault and BMW, which knew nothing about it until they received the press release. Ecclestone, under intense pressure, had pulled off one of the greatest deals of his career, putting F1 back on top in the battle with the car manufacturers and showing the banks just how much they needed him.

The Minardi team owner, Australian businessman Paul Stoddart, told *Reuters*, 'I don't think it's the end of the GPWC but it is the end of them starting a separate championship.' The car manufacturers had other ideas. Down to three members, due to Ferrari's defection and Ford's exit, by the end of the month the GPWC had persuaded the two Japanese manufacturers, Honda and Toyota, to publicly offer their support, although they stopped short of becoming full members.

It was unlikely to worry Ferrari. As an added sweetener, the FIA formally granted the team a veto over changes to F1's sporting and technical regulations, which had been the stuff of F1 legend for decades, dating back to the 1980s when Ferrari was powered by a V12 engine despite the majority of its rivals using a V10. Ferrari founder Enzo Ferrari asked for a right to block changes to prevent its engine from being banned and the rest is history. As former Ferrari team boss Jean Todt later explained, Enzo Ferrari 'was very isolated in Maranello compared to all the British teams. He was alone and you will remember, in the 1980s, Ferrari was the only full car manufacturer of engine and chassis. And he was facing private teams, like Williams, Lotus, McLaren and Brabham that were all using the same engine. If I remember it was a Ford Cosworth engine. So he got that [veto] in his discussions to implement.' This was finally formalised 20 years later in a letter from the FIA dated 17 January 2005.

Eight years later it was written into the Concorde Agreement itself, giving Ferrari a right of veto in respect of the introduction or modification of any F1 technical or sporting regulations (except for safety requirements). It stressed that Ferrari could only exercise its veto if it reasonably considered that the new regulations were likely to have a substantial impact on its legitimate interest and if doing so was not prejudicial to the traditional values of the F1 Championship and/or the image of the FIA.

The foundation for this was laid when Ferrari's veto was formalised in the letter in 2005. Combined with the financial windfall, Ferrari had what it wanted from F1. This significantly dented the chances of any rival series as it was hard to imagine it succeeding without F1's most famous name.

Although Ecclestone's strategy of divide and conquer wasn't enough to tempt all of the teams, it had an additional benefit. Doing the deal with Ferrari at a time when Ecclestone's control of FOA was in question had shown the banks who was really in charge. Making such a large payment to a single team also threw the gauntlet down to the banks to oppose it. If they had attempted to overturn the payment it would have driven Ferrari further away from F1, so Ecclestone could have justifiably blamed the banks for the sport's likely collapse. In turn, it would have made it even easier for the trust to buy the shares on the cheap and both Ecclestone and Ferrari would have probably supported this. It was far from theoretical; BayernLB had sounded out Bambino about buying its shares for $700m in October 2004. Mullens responded, 'You must be joking,' and threw the gauntlet back with a $275m offer for the bank's shares, which in turn was firmly rejected.

Less than a week after the Ferrari deal was done, a judge at London's High Court set a date for the FOA trial in May and required Ecclestone to attend in person. It was suddenly only a matter of time before the chicanery was laid bare for all to see.

Driving up the pressure, in early 2005 the banks' lawyers, White & Case, requested a meeting with Sacha Woodward Hill, who attended alone without a legal advisor. She later said the banks had initially told her that the meeting would be 'about the events at the FOA management board meeting of 20 December 2004. In fact this was just a pretext, since in the course of this three-hour conversation [I] was only asked a few questions about this. Most of the time was rather dedicated to what I knew about the structure of the trust and Mr Ecclestone's influence on this trust. That showed me that there was a plan to put Mr Ecclestone under pressure using dirty tactics.'

As the court case loomed, the pressure was building on Ecclestone. The compromising cache of information about him now came into its own, as BayernLB's Alexandra Irrgang later explained. 'Our lawyers at White & Case always said that they were absolutely sure that Bernie Ecclestone would never appear personally in court in these second proceedings but rather would try to reach an out of court settlement. Bernie Ecclestone would certainly be asked by the court about this connection with Bambino and he clearly wanted to avoid that.' HMRC was paying close attention to the proceedings.

With his back firmly against the wall, Ecclestone tried to calm matters. On 23 March 2005, he and the trust agreed to settle with the banks and invalidate the disputed share that had given him 50 per cent of the voting power on the board of FOA, the company that operated F1. Ecclestone settled through gritted teeth and, even though he had no choice but to hand over the share, he still didn't let it go willingly, such was his worry about what the banks would do next.

On 25 May, Ecclestone and Woodward Hill met two BayernLB executives – Michael Krowarz and Harald Glöckl – in London and, according to their minutes of the meeting, 'Ecclestone let us know that he felt specifically threatened that he would be dismissed.' He also said that he 'didn't want someone looking over his shoulder every half an hour but wanted largely to retain his traditional way of working'.

Given Ecclestone's age, the banks were keen to appoint someone to the company who could eventually take over his job. Ecclestone told them he 'was only able and willing to work with an addition who had been accepted by him. His network was non-transferable.' Nevertheless, Ecclestone recognised that the banks needed a succession plan for corporate govern-ance reasons and proposed former Ferrari team boss Marco Piccinini, who until 2001 had been a director of FOA when he had agreed to step in as chief executive if ever Ecclestone wasn't able to continue.

The litigation between the shareholders finally reached the end of the road in a settlement agreement dated 25 August 2005. It entitled Ecclestone to remain CEO of all F1 operating companies and also protected his position. As long as Bambino owned at least 5 per cent of SLEC, it had the power to block his removal 'for any reason other than a failure to comply with a lawful direction of the board of a company of which he is Chief Executive Officer which is likely to have a material effect on the business or becoming of unsound mind'.

It was just what Ecclestone was looking for, and the day after the settlement agreement had been signed, the controversial company share was finally declared invalid by consent order. By then, Ecclestone had been handed another convenient opportunity to demonstrate his impor-tance to F1.

Formula One in the United States has a chequered history. By 2005, Grands Prix had been held at nine different venues in the US but none of them stuck around. Ecclestone had made a big push to break into the market after the signing of the first Concorde Agreement and in 1982 there were three different races in the States. But his flagship Grand Prix in Las Vegas took place against the uninspiring backdrop of the Caesars Palace car park, folding after two events, and a New York Grand Prix never took off. Just 20,000 people turned up for the Grand Prix in Phoenix in 1991, leading to a nine-year absence for the United States Grand Prix.

Ecclestone didn't stop trying and, rather than trying to break into glamorous new markets, he theorised that F1 would have better success in motorsport's US heartland. He signed a deal with Indianapolis Motor Speedway boss Tony George to bring F1 to a circuit on the infield of the historic racing oval and for the first race in 2000 an estimated 200,000 people turned up. It looked like Ecclestone had finally cracked the US, but it was all about to go farcically wrong.

The 2005 race got off to an ignominious start when several tyre fail-ures before the race caused major accidents for Ralf Schumacher's Toyota during Friday practice and then for his stand-in Ricardo Zonta later in the day. Both were using Michelin tyres, which caused the French manufacturer to investigate the cause of the blowouts. Although it had provided stable tyres for the race since 2001, it discovered that they were no longer suitable at Indianapolis as the track had been repaved during the previous year. In contrast, the six cars that were using Bridgestone tyres had no problem with the new surface as they were made differently to the ones from Michelin.

Come race day on 19 June the 14 cars with Michelin tyres only completed the formation lap before retiring to the pit lane ahead of the start of the race. The remaining six cars of Jordan, Minardi and Ferrari toured around for close to two hours, with the latter finishing in an inevitable one-two. Jordan's Tiago Monteiro took the third podium place and scored his first F1 points along with the other three competitors, emphasising the loss of big names from the race. It infuriated fans and made F1 the laughing stock of world sport. Remarkably, it could have been prevented.

Michelin had proposed installing a temporary chicane to slow down the cars and cool down their tyres. However, Mosley refused to go along with this and later explained that 'Had we altered the track and had an accident, the US legal system would have been very tough on us. Lawyers and judges would have said, "Why didn't you go through your standard procedures?" What would I be supposed to say to that?' The embarrassing spectacle was broadcast to tens of millions of viewers around the world, but the bigger problem was at the circuit. Michelin eventually had to refund the fans their ticket prices, but it was the beginning of the end for F1 at Indianapolis. It lasted two more years before it dropped F1.

The embarrassment made F1 a less appealing acquisition target and put more importance on Ecclestone's shoulders, as he had to steer the sport through the aftermath of the scandal. The event also demonstrated the immense power that Mosley held to control events, so having someone like Ecclestone onboard who had a chance of countering his authoritarian approach appeared to be essential. In light of this, it made sense for the banks to give Bambino a right of veto in the settlement agreement regarding replacing Ecclestone as F1's CEO. Nevertheless, he didn't get his tough-guy reputation by settling court cases, so this showed that for the first time in his career he was vulnerable.

And Gribkowsky was still a loose cannon.

The livery that started it all: Graham Hill drives the newly Gold Leaf–branded
Lotus to victory at the 1968 Spanish Grand Prix.

Jochen Rindt and Colin Chapman discuss tactics at the 1970 Austrian Grand Prix
while Jochen's wife Nina prepares the timing sheets.

The two most powerful
people in the history of
F1 – Bernie Ecclestone and
Max Mosley – talk business
at Brands Hatch in 1978.

Max Mosley and
Jean-Marie Balestre
have a dispute
in the pit lane at
Hockenheim in 1981.

Brazilian legend Ayrton
Senna prepares for his
final race at Imola in 1994.

Jos Verstappen's Benetton is engulfed in flames during a pit stop at the 1994 German Grand Prix at Hockenheim.

Benetton team boss, Flavio Briatore, celebrates with Michael Schumacher on the podium at the 1995 Pacific Grand Prix at Aida, Japan.

Paddock Club hospitality boss, Paddy McNally, shows the Duchess of York round the paddock at Silverstone in 1997.

Frank Williams and Ron Dennis deep in discussion at the 2000 Spanish Grand Prix at the Circuit de Catalunya.

Gerhard Gribkowsky and Bernie Ecclestone accompany CVC's Donald Mackenzie at the private equity firm's first race as owner of F1, the 2006 Bahrain Grand Prix.

Ferrari's Luca di Montezemolo and Renault's Flavio Briatore face the media at the height of the GPMA struggles in Monaco in 2009.

Bernie Ecclestone and FIA president Jean Todt sign off the framework for a new Concorde Agreement at the Hungaroring in 2013.

Lewis Hamilton and Toto Wolff celebrate Mercedes' first constructors' championship at the inaugural Russian Grand Prix at Sochi in 2014.

Red Bull Racing boss, Christian Horner, with Bernie and Fabiana Ecclestone in 2015.

F1 CEO Chase Carey walks past the sport's old-style logo at Silverstone in 2017. A few months later he would replace it with a new design.

Max Mosley and Bernie Ecclestone in 2015, more than four decades after they first teamed up to transform F1.

Charles Leclerc and Max Verstappen battle for the lead at the
2023 Las Vegas Grand Prix.

Following the FOA litigation settlement, the banker took a closer interest in the races and in 2005 he was spotted at glamorous Grands Prix in China, Italy and Turkey. It reminded Ecclestone of the risk he posed, as HMRC was still scrutinising him and the trust. If Gribkowsky gave HMRC the impression that Ecclestone treated the trust as his own property, it could have led to it forcing him to pay 40 per cent capital gains tax on the $3.3bn that it had raised from F1.

Ecclestone laid bare the risk that Gribkowsky posed when he said that 'had he have written to the Revenue they would have had to investigate. And, at that time, I was told that whatever I gave my wife that's settled in the trust would have to come back, I would pay 40 per cent tax on, which would probably be something close to 2 billion.' Gribkowsky made it clear what it would take to keep his mouth shut.

As Bambino director Frédérique Flournoy, put it, 'Gribkowsky was making insinuations for a very, very long period of time without seemingly wanting anything in exchange. And then, at some point, he simply said that he was going to be a consultant and he wanted to start up his consultancy and he would need some help; and he would very much want to be a consultant for Bambino.' He got what he wanted and Bambino and Ecclestone took desperate steps to pull it off.

Just a couple of months after the settlement with the banks, Gribkowsky met Ecclestone at F1's headquarters in London. Fresh off the banks' court victory, Gribkowsky later said that he thought 'he had won and everything was fine for him'. However, Ecclestone started by setting some ground rules and, according to Gribkowsky, he said, 'I'll tell you how the world works and what you really control, not a thing.'

According to Gribkowsky, Ecclestone nevertheless added, 'I will take care of you,' which he took to mean a job offer with a generous fee. It was confirmed at the following year's Bahrain Grand Prix in March 2006 when Gribkowsky met Ecclestone for lunch in his hospitality suite. According to Gribkowsky, Ecclestone . . .

. . . asked me about my further plans for the future. I took this to be a hint and reference to our agreement back in April/May 2005, and I told him that I could imagine working as a consultant in Formula One and that I had already spoken to Mr Mullens about it.

Mr Ecclestone commented [on] this latter phrase with the words, 'Forget Stephen' and challenged me to 'tell me a number', whereupon

I told him 50. To me it was clear that that meant USD 50 million. The conversation ended with Mr Ecclestone saying that he would think about it. On the Sunday before leaving for the airport, I handed over to Mr Ecclestone in an envelope the draft contract which I had drawn up and taken with me.

The precise amount wasn't finalised until 10 May 2006, when Ecclestone and Mullens met Gribkowsky for dinner in the Rib Room restaurant at the plush Carlton Tower hotel just minutes from F1's headquarters. According to filings, 'Ecclestone had told Mr Mullens of the likely need to make a substantial payment to Gribkowsky from the Bambino Settlement' (which referred to the trust itself).

At the dinner, Ecclestone and Mullens agreed to give Gribkowsky $45m, as the banker later explained. 'Part of this meeting was spent discussing the issue of Formula One and part the prospective payments to be made to me by Mr Ecclestone. Mr Ecclestone said that I would receive 45 million. He meant US dollars, as was usual with Formula One. Mr Mullens was apparently going to take care of everything else, i.e. the contractual agreements and the processing of these. In this discussion, we also established that the Advisory Agreement between myself and Mr Ecclestone would begin on 1 June 2006.'

However, the payments from Ecclestone didn't start for more than 16 months after that. The first payments were from Bambino and they began on 26 July 2006, just one month after Gribkowsky claimed his agreement with Ecclestone began. When HMRC eventually found out about this it lit the blue touchpaper.

The day after the Rib Room meeting, Mullens wrote to Emmanuele Argand saying that Bambino shouldn't be named on a contract with Gribkowsky. 'I do not believe that there is any merit in such a contract and would not advise your client to enter into such an arrangement,' he wrote. There was good reason for this as there was little public evidence of what Gribkowsky had done to deserve the money.

To swerve around this hurdle, the money was disguised as compensation for consultancy agreements with an Austrian company and foundation that Gribkowsky had set up. The former was Salzburg-based GG Consulting, which was wholly owned by Gribkowsky. Between July and September 2006 it received $21.2m from Bambino through a company called First Bridge Holding in Mauritius.

Remarkably, Bambino accidentally paid $1.2m more than was stated on the agreement with Gribkowsky and, according to Bambino director Frédérique Flournoy, 'When we realised our mistake we briefly considered whether it would be worth trying to recover the money from Gribkowsky but we quickly came to the decision that there would be no chance of us getting the overpayment back, we would run the risk of creating further tension.' Instead, to explain the additional payment, First Bridge sent GG Consulting a letter saying that the consultancy arrangement between them should be extended by two months. Gribkowsky couldn't believe his luck – but it soon balanced out.

He then turned his attention to Ecclestone's share of the payment, which took longer to arrange. Following the advice of Austrian tax consultant and lawyer Professor Gerald Toifl, Gribkowsky set up a new company structure to receive the money. He founded Sonnenschein Privatstiftung, an Austrian private foundation that owned an Austrian company called GREP – short for 'Gribkowsky Real Estate and Participation' in a sign of what the banker did with the money.

In the middle of 2007, GREP entered into a written agreement with Lewington Invest, a British Virgin Islands company, which had been acquired on Ecclestone's behalf by Swiss tax advisor Jean-André Favre of the Geneva-based firm JAF Conseil. According to Favre, Ecclestone approached him early in 2007 about money that he said he owed to Gribkowsky and explained that he 'did not want his name to appear in any circumstances'.

Ecclestone himself only covered $5m of the money that was transferred to Favre and then paid to GREP via Lewington. Flavio Briatore paid a further $17.8m, as Ecclestone explained. 'Gribkowsky told me that he did not want a direct payment coming from me to him or for money to come to him from the UK. For this reason, I asked Flavio Briatore, a friend and business associate who held funds outside the UK and who owed me some money at the time, to pay some money on my behalf to Gribkowsky. I also recall that I had some contact with Andre Favre, a contact of mine in Switzerland, and that he assisted in arranging the payments.'

It brought the total to $22.8m, which was $2.2m less than the $25m stated in the consultancy agreement, so Toifl sent Ecclestone and Favre a letter asking for immediate payment. In response, Ecclestone telephoned Toifl and gave him short shrift. According to Gribkowsky, 'Dr Toifl explained to me that Mr Ecclestone had called him and asked if he could hear this noise. In the background the noise of a paper shredding machine could be heard and Mr Ecclestone said that he was currently shredding the demand from us. Subsequently we decided not to pursue the outstanding remaining amount any further.'

It was perhaps a coincidence that Ecclestone underpaid Gribkowsky by a similar sum to the amount that Bambino overpaid him. However, it wouldn't go down well with HMRC. In an interview with us, Ecclestone himself even claimed that he was behind both rounds of payments to Gribkowsky and although that could have been a slip of the tongue, he explained that there was a good reason for it.

'I paid him to not do something. What did I actually get from him? Nothing, because I could have paid the bastard and he could have still said something to the tax authorities. That's why I paid him one lot and then another lot in a year's time to make sure.'

The $22.8m from Lewington and the $21.2m from First Bridge gave Gribkowsky a total of $44m. The money was declared and taxed in Austria but Gribkowsky kept it a secret from BayernLB. The payments were so large that Austrian authorities launched an investigation into them in 2006, but put the brakes on it the following year. Receiving payments of that size from tax havens would have raised suspicions of money laundering, as the ultimate source would be uncertain. Gribkowsky managed to convince the authorities that the money came from F1 consultancy contracts but their suspicions had been raised and a time bomb started ticking.

Dealing with Gribkowsky didn't give Ecclestone time to relax. He still had the renegade car manufacturers of the GPWC to deal with, and some of the teams were easier to bring onside than others.

When Ford quit F1 after scoring only two podiums in five seasons, it was so desperate to get out that it sold the Jaguar team for just $1. The buyer was Austrian energy drinks titan Red Bull, and in time it would become one of the most successful teams in the sport.

The new Red Bull Racing impressed immediately, scoring more points in 2005 than Jaguar had done in the past two seasons. Although it was the first time it had its name on a team, it had a long history in the sport, sponsoring Austrian driver Gerhard Berger in the 1980s before becoming a sponsor and then partial owner of Sauber. In 2001,

Sauber and Red Bull parted ways, reportedly because Peter Sauber insisted on putting young inexperienced Kimi Räikkönen in the car ahead of Red Bull-sponsored Brazilian, Enrique Bernoldi. If this was the case then failing to recognise future champion Räikkönen's potential was a rare error of judgement for Red Bull owner Dietrich Mateschitz, who gained a reputation for making all the right decisions with his own team.

Shortly after buying the team he hired Christian Horner who, aged 32, became one of F1's youngest-ever team bosses when he stepped into the driving seat. Red Bull wasn't just banking on his youth but also his experience, as he had already founded the championship-winning Arden team in F1 junior series Formula 3000. By the following year, Horner would bring on board Adrian Newey, one of F1's most successful designers, who was attracted to Red Bull Racing by an annual salary estimated at $10.2m.

Billionaire Mateschitz was a good friend of Ecclestone and at the end of January 2005 Red Bull Racing and Jordan announced that they were joining Ferrari in agreeing to extend the Concorde Agreement. Three teams wasn't enough for a credible series, but it was enough to concern the car manufacturers, particularly as Ferrari and Jaguar had been in its own camp just a few months before. However, Ecclestone still needed more teams, so he next turned his attention to Williams.

Given their spats it was perhaps a surprising choice, but times had changed. Although Ron Dennis never forgave Ecclestone for taking over the F1 rights, Frank Williams still had time for him as he had often helped his team keep its wheels turning in the early days. What's more, Williams now needed help again. BMW's decision to drop the team in order to buy Sauber was reportedly a factor in sponsor Hewlett-Packard abandoning the team. In 2004, Frank Williams had sold his private jet – which was more than just a luxury for the paraplegic team boss – in order to pay for a new wind tunnel. The infrastructure upgrade was sorely needed as the once world-beating team hadn't won a title since 1997.

In November 2005, in need of financial stimulus, Williams became the fourth team to agree to extend the Concorde Agreement. Ecclestone now had two of the most successful teams in the history of F1 on his side, but with ten teams on the grid he was still in a minority. It was Mateschitz who came to his rescue in an unconventional way.

It came at the Belgian Grand Prix in September 2005 when Red Bull announced that it was acquiring F1 minnow Minardi from Paul Stoddart. The team changed its name to Scuderia Toro Rosso ('Team Red Bull' in Italian) and ran alongside the drinks company's flagship Red Bull Racing. It was music to Ecclestone's ears, as Stoddart had been one of Mosley's fiercest critics. In contrast, Mateschitz was loyal to Ecclestone and his allies and wasn't ashamed to admit that he had bought Minardi to influence the outcome of the dispute between the teams. Red Bull's acquisition announcement said that one reason it had bought Minardi was to get 'a second vote in any matters raised regarding the future of Formula One'.

It was the first time in the modern era of F1 that an individual or company had majority owned two teams and it sent sparks flying. One F1 insider asked, 'How can any fair and equitable decisions be taken when one party – namely Red Bull GmbH, which is the registered owner of both teams – controls double the votes of others?' It opened the door to accusations that the two teams could rig their results, but anyone who thought the FIA would oppose the acquisition was sorely disappointed. 'There is a provision in the Concorde Agreement dealing with the ownership of two teams and voting rights,' explained Mosley. Other sports, however, aren't as tolerant: UEFA and World Rugby both restrict an individual from owning a major share of two clubs in the same tournament. Indeed, in 1999 the UK investment firm ENIC complained to the Court of Arbitration for Sport (CAS) after its clubs Slavia Prague and Vicenza were prevented from playing each other in UEFA competitions.

Gaining a second Red Bull squad gave Ecclestone signatures from half of the ten teams. However, the rest of them dug their heels in. Honda and Toyota officially joined Mercedes, BMW and Renault in the car manufacturers' group, which changed its name from GPWC to the Grand Prix Manufacturers Association (GPMA). It shared its predecessor's aim of increasing its members' take from F1 or launching a rival series if this wasn't possible.

There was another fly in the ointment. On 1 November 2005, Super Aguri, a new team owned by former F1 driver Aguri Suzuki, registered to join the sport in 2006. The fledgling Japanese outfit would be powered by Honda and raised the number of teams to 11. Despite his hard work, Ecclestone would soon be in the minority again.

★ ★ ★

The payments had dealt with the threat from Gribkowsky but, being the majority shareholder, the banks were still in control of the business. That soon started to change. In August 2005 Ecclestone was introduced to private equity firm CVC Capital Partners by Eric Hersman, an American investment banker whose company Churchill Capital secured financing for the expansion of Wynn Resorts, which was run by Ecclestone's friend Steve Wynn. Hersman invited Ecclestone and CVC's Scottish co-founder Donald Mackenzie to his villa in St Tropez because he could see the synergy. One of CVC's most successful investments was MotoGP rights holder Dorna, which Ecclestone was well acquainted with as he had sold it the rights to the series just over a decade earlier.

CVC was founded by Leeds-born Michael Smith and Donald Mackenzie, who both worked at American bank Citicorp. In 1981 they launched its venture capital department, which invested in promising start-ups and companies with potential for substantial, rapid growth. Called Citicorp Venture Capital, the bankers spun it out of Citicorp in 1993 to form an independent private equity firm, CVC Capital Partners.

A giant in the world of private equity, CVC works on essentially simple principles. The company buys businesses using its investment funds, which are fuelled with money from wealthy individuals and institutions. The idea is that the companies it buys will generate a high return on investment (ROI) when they are sold, floated or raise money that is paid to their owners. CVC has a knack of betting on winners.

Over the past 30 years, CVC's funds have raised around $140bn, including €26.8bn in July 2023, which created the largest buyout fund in history. Along the way, CVC has acquired corporate titans such as Samsonite, watch-maker Breitling and the AA in the UK. It has also made a name for itself in sports through owning stakes in the Spanish football league La Liga, Six Nations Rugby and the women's professional tennis organisation, the WTA.

When CVC raced onto Ecclestone's radar it was on a roll. Its first fund in 1996 raised just $840m but its Fund IV, finalised in 2005, was Europe's largest ever private equity fund at the time with $7.2bn to spend. CVC wanted to make a splash by buying a trophy asset but didn't let its heart rule its head.

The battles between F1's shareholders and teams had depressed the value of the group but it was still firing on all cylinders financially thanks to thrilling on-track action, which saw Renault's Fernando Alonso dethrone Michael Schumacher as the champion in 2005 after five years of Ferrari dominance.

In 2005 FOA generated $463.5m of underlying profit while APM and Allsport made $125m, giving the combined entity earnings of $588.5m on revenue of $1,071.6m and a profit margin of 54.9 per cent. Remarkably, F1's profit in 2005 was just 25.6 per cent lower than in 2024. There is good reason for this.

F1's biggest single cost is the share of its profits that is paid to the teams as prize money. Their take today comes to around 63 per cent of the sport's total profits, but back in 2005 they only received 47 per cent of the TV rights revenue. It kept FOA's costs down and helped it to make turbocharged profits. The company also has a clever trick under its bonnet to boost its bottom line: the majority of F1's race, TV and sponsorship contracts contain escalator clauses that increase the fee by up to 10 per cent annually.

However, tantalisingly, between 1999 and 2005 F1's owners couldn't pocket any of its riches and the reason for this was buried in the terms of the prospectus for the $1.4bn bond it took out in 1999 after its float was thwarted. Those terms prevented FOA from paying a dividend to shareholders to ensure that its profits would be stored up in its reserves to pay bondholders if the company fell on hard times.

Thanks to Ecclestone's wheeling and dealing, FOA went from strength to strength and by late 2005 it had a balance of just $144.7m left to pay on the bond. It meant that by the end of the year F1 was only months away from being almost debt-free once again, so the predators began circling, and not just because they wanted a piece of the high-octane profits that could soon be paid out.

The other reason that F1 was an attractive acquisition target related to a seemingly innocuous line on page 35 of the bond prospectus. It said that 'the company will, subject to certain limited exceptions set out in the loan agreement, undertake not to dispose of or to create any security interest over any of its assets'. In short, until the bond was paid off, FOA couldn't take out another loan but when the balance was almost clear it could do this and give its owners another payout. This wasn't lost on CVC.

Private equity firms are famous for using loans to get deals across the finish line. Known as leveraged buyouts, they involve the private equity firms partly financing an acquisition with a loan that will be secured on the company they plan to buy.

Banks usually require the private equity firms to use a good deal of their own money too and, once the fortunes of the acquisition improve, the bank typically gives the private equity firm an even bigger loan, which is again secured on the company. The bigger loan is used to repay the original one, which means that the private equity firm gets its money back and the bank can seize the company if it fails to repay.

Any instability or risk to the company can cause the banks to shy away and this is exactly what happened when CVC began to consider purchasing F1 in August 2005. Mackenzie's first meeting was with Ecclestone and the two hit it off. After the false starts with the flotation, Ecclestone had become averse to money men in suits but Mackenzie was cut from a different cloth. He was a self-made man who shared Ecclestone's love of racing. Buying F1 was a dream opportunity as his childhood hero was fellow Scot Jim Clark, who won the F1 championship twice in the 1960s.

Nevertheless, Mackenzie hadn't yet had a chance to analyse F1's financials so when the subject of money came up he suggested buying the business for $1bn just to get the wheels of discussion turning. 'The $1 billion was not a serious offer by me but instead served as a test. I wanted to trigger the conversation.' He added that 'it's what I would call an opening shot . . . I had done back-of-the-envelope work at my office on it.'

The offer was rejected but Mackenzie wasn't deterred and next met Gribkowsky at London's Four Seasons hotel on Park Lane on 31 August 2005. Then, after doing more due diligence, he came back for round two. 'I visited Ecclestone in his office and told him that we had sufficient information for a first non-binding offer. I asked him to recommend a price at which the shareholders would sell. I insisted that he state a figure. He wrote on a piece of paper and slid it across the desk. It said, "USD 2 billion".' Mackenzie said that the price was prohibitive but in typical Ecclestone fashion he was told that if he couldn't afford it he shouldn't bother wasting his time. Mackenzie knew right then that it was going to be an uphill struggle.

CVC's internal investment committee was nervous about the risk of buying F1 given the infighting with the teams and even its own share-holders. Mackenzie added that 'another reason why we and the banks were nervous was the reputation of Mr Ecclestone. He was very powerful and difficult to control. On the other hand, he also played a very important role for the company . . . Without him, however, the business was more or less worthless. CVC was normally used to having greater influence over the managers of a company than was possible with Mr Ecclestone. Mr Ecclestone was important for the business but also an additional risk factor.'

For all these reasons, it was difficult for CVC to raise the debt it needed to finance the deal. It usually turned to Barclays or the Royal Bank of Scotland (RBS) but the banks declined to back the F1 acquisition. 'Both banks had said that they were only willing to lend against the next two years' cashflow because of the problems with the Concorde,' explained Mackenzie, adding that Barclays completely walked away 'because of the disputes that had been going on between the shareholders and the litigation, among other things'.

Mackenzie met Ecclestone again in his office and told him that CVC could only raise $1bn on its own. Most business managers would have seen that as the end of the road, but it was merely a challenge to Ecclestone. 'He asked me who I was talking to . . . I mentioned RBS; and he said, "I know RBS. I will call the chief executive now," and he called up Fred Goodwin. Goodwin was tracked down by his PA and Bernie basically said, "I have somebody in the room who would like to borrow some money from you," and he handed the phone over to me . . . it is quite unusual to have a chief executive call a chief executive of a bank, but that sort of reflects Bernie's influence in the world.'

Goodwin was at the height of his power as the boss of RBS and Ecclestone had a direct line to him, as the bank advertised at a number of races and sponsored the Williams team. This was three years before Goodwin abruptly left his post when RBS hit the wall in the midst of the financial crisis, leaving UK taxpayers to bail it out to the tune of £45bn. Its problems ultimately stemmed from the £49bn record-breaking takeover of Dutch bank ABN Amro in 2007, which caused some RBS shareholders to accuse Goodwin of megalomania. No doubt dealing with a celebrity CEO like Ecclestone contributed to that.

'I told him exactly what was going on,' said Ecclestone. 'I said, "Fred, these people need some help to buy the company." And he said, "How much?" I said, "Well, I really don't know." At the time I said, "I think it is well over 500 million." I said, "Why don't you speak to the people who want to borrow the money, to Donald?" And he called Donald or Donald called him.'

Mackenzie adds that 'after some negotiation RBS promised us a loan of around $600m to $650m . . . We found that we were very lucky that Ecclestone was friends with the CEO whose bank was a sponsor in Formula One and that the CEO enjoyed going to motor races so much. Without RBS there would have been no deal.'

It enabled CVC to send a preliminary offer letter to the directors of BayernLB and Bambino on 9 September 2005. The offer implied an enterprise value for SLEC of $2bn, with $1.7bn going to its shareholders and $313.6m being used to pay off the loan that funded its purchase of the 100-year rights to F1. The offer was conditional on F1 having no net debt at completion, on Ecclestone continuing as CEO, and on Bambino reinvesting $100m in return for a 10 per cent stake in the company, which it was given at a discount to tempt it to collaborate.

The letter added that CVC 'would wish to support [Ecclestone's] plans for developing the business' and that it endorsed proposals to buy Paddy McNally's trackside advertising and hospitality businesses as well. It also stated that CVC wanted Gribkowsky to remain a director of F1's parent company 'to enable a period of continuity of management and to enable us to benefit from his knowledge and understanding of the Formula One companies'. It ended up coming to an abrupt end.

14

A FRIEND IN NEED

When CVC's offer letter landed on the desks of BayernLB's directors they could hardly believe their luck. The private equity firm's proposed price gave the bank $828.9m for its 46.7 per cent SLEC stake and, although this was less than the $987.5m that it had loaned Kirch, it was still much more than it expected to get, as over the past few years the uncertainty over F1's future had gradually driven down the value of BayernLB's investment in F1.

In comparison, Robin Saunders made a $600m offer through her new investment firm Clearbrook Capital. Likewise, the F1 teams were given another chance to take over the driving seat of the sport through what was known as the Team Trust Proposal. This was developed by Ecclestone's ally Brian Powers and involved the teams buying all of F1's shares for about $1bn plus deferred payments amounting to another $300m – but, ultimately, the teams' prime concern was competing in, not running or owning the sport.

Another opportunity presented itself to BayernLB when Lord Jacob Rothschild from J Rothschild Capital Management Limited emailed Gribkowsky saying, 'Let me confirm my group's interest.' It wasn't pursued, and the same goes for an offer from Bluewaters Communications, an American investment firm run by John Gregg, the co-founder of Virgin Net and former chief financial officer of Virgin Media. On 15 November 2005 Bluewaters wrote to BayernLB, JP Morgan and Lehman Brothers offering them $1bn for their 75 per cent F1 stake, which was far lower than the price proposed by CVC. However, Bluewaters also sent a cover letter to Gribkowsky saying that it 'is prepared to pay 10 percent more in cash consideration . . . above any genuine bona-fide offer put forward by any other accredited buyer'. That too was ignored, and it would come back to bite both Ecclestone and Gribkowsky.

The banker found his buyer when CVC's offer arrived and between September and November 2005, the private equity firm and its advisors, Freshfields and Ernst & Young, carried out further due diligence on F1. It involved Mackenzie having some stern words with Ecclestone: 'We made it clear to him, when we were buying the business, that we would not make the same mistakes that the bank had . . . We made it clear to him right at the beginning that if we were buying it we'd want 100 per cent control. We'd want his shares, if he had any; Bambino's shares; and the banks' shares, so that we would have a clear majority in every circumstance; and that CVC would have absolute control of the business and all subsidiaries.'

CVC devised an ingenious mechanism to ensure this. This involved changing the Articles of Association of F1's key companies to designate CVC's directors as what were known as 'I Directors', which meant they could outvote any number of other board members. It was designed to stop them losing control like the banks had, but time would prove that this was far from the only potential threat to their investment.

Despite a number of the potential bidders leaking to the media, CVC's name had somehow managed to stay a complete secret, so when its $2bn acquisition was announced on 25 November 2005 it stunned the F1 community. That included the GPMA because even the car manufacturers' group hadn't been briefed about the sale in advance.

In order to buy the shares owned by all of the shareholders, CVC set up a new company ('newco') named Alpha Prema in a nod to the codename of 'Project Alpha' that it had given to the F1 acquisition. Alpha Prema signed a contract employing Ecclestone as F1's CEO for an initial period of three years in return for an annual salary of £2.5m and agreement to cover the costs associated with his private plane.

Under the terms of the contract, Alpha Prema was entitled to terminate Ecclestone's employment immediately if, for example, he failed to comply with a lawful direction of the board that was likely to have a material effect on the business of an F1 group company. Despite this loss of power, Ecclestone was happy with the acquisition. Not only was BayernLB out of the picture, but he respected Mackenzie and it was likely that any purchaser would have requested similar – or harsher – restrictions on his role. He couldn't have got off to a much better start.

Thanks to Ecclestone's help, CVC financed the acquisition with two loans – one of $1.1bn from RBS and another of around $965.6m from

CVC's own investment Fund IV. It came to 13.9 per cent of the total amount available in Fund IV, making it one of its largest investments and a tremendous gamble. One of the next-biggest at the time was Dutch chemical distributor Univar, but that only represented 8 per cent of the fund's total commitment.

While the $828.9m from CVC gave BayernLB an unexpected windfall, it left EM.TV short-changed. The German media company had an agreement with BayernLB that it would receive a cut if the bank's F1 stake sold for more than $1.057bn. So although the amount that BayernLB was paid far exceeded its expectations, it meant that EM.TV didn't get a penny. It didn't let it lie.

After all the litigation and threats of breakaways, BayernLB couldn't wait to exit F1. It booked a valuation yield (the difference between the valuation and the amount paid) of £272m (€328m) in its 2006 results and stated that the sale of the F1 shares 'decisively contributed to the positive result'. It could have got even more if it had waited.

Pitpass got hold of a letter sent by CVC to BayernLB on 19 September 2005 offering the bank the opportunity to 'invest $100 million at completion in newco for a 10% stake'. The bank was so eager to exit F1 that it firmly rebuffed the offer. It was a costly decision: it would have made a 360 per cent return on investment if it had reinvested and waited for CVC to sell F1 to current owner Liberty Media just 12 years later. This is exactly what Lehman Brothers did. In December 2005 Alpha Prema also bought JP Morgan's F1 shares for $210m, with Lehman Brothers getting $209.3m for its stake, which was less than the loan it had provided to Kirch but still a good sum given the uncertain future of F1.[2]

CVC was in the driving seat; the two banks owned minority stakes so they were passengers in the business. CVC didn't need to buy the banking duo's shares to get control, so it bought them for around 16 per cent less than the price it paid the other shareholders. Remarkably, BayernLB and Bambino hit the jackpot twice as they had an agreement that if Alpha Prema managed to acquire JP Morgan's and Lehman's shares at a discount, the company would pay them 25 per cent of the saving. It fuelled a payment of around $8.6m to Bambino, with BayernLB getting a similar sum.

But in order to get the green light to buy F1, CVC still had to pass a number of checkpoints. The European Commission had to give its approval and to reduce the risk of anti-competition it forced CVC to sell

MotoGP operator Dorna, which it had owned since 1998. It was bought for a reported €500m by rival private equity firm Bridgepoint.

CVC also requested a warranty that F1 was in good health, with accounts in good order. BayernLB refused to provide this, as it hadn't been responsible for the operation of the business, so Ecclestone stepped in and, yet again, put his money where his mouth was. Ecclestone provided a $100m indemnity and was paid a commission equal to 5 per cent of the sale price, giving him $41.4m from BayernLB and $22.25m from Bambino. He later explained that BayernLB and the trust 'would not have been able to sell their shares to CVC without my support, because the FIA needed to approve any change of control. If I was going to leave or be removed as the representative, or if I had not thought that the new owner was suitable for Formula One, the FIA would have been very concerned and would be likely to refuse its approval.' BayernLB gladly signed off the commission, thankful that Ecclestone had facilitated the sale rather than being a roadblock in its way.

Mullens drew up the agreement between Ecclestone, Bambino and BayernLB. Dotting the I's and crossing the t's, he said it was even described as a consultancy agreement for VAT reasons. On 15 November 2005 all three parties signed, but Ecclestone made a single significant error. He failed to disclose the commission to CVC even though its purchase contract required him, the trust and BayernLB to disclose all arrangements between themselves that may affect F1. Another time bomb started ticking.

Blissfully unaware of the payments, CVC retained Ecclestone as F1's boss and worked closely with him for more than a decade. CVC even structured its deal to suit Ecclestone by giving him a single share in F1's new parent company to ensure that HMRC could see he was representing himself and not the trust. Even though this mirrored the previous arrangement, when Ecclestone had awarded himself shares, this time it was entirely above board, as it was done with the owner's consent.

CVC paid Bambino $445m and it reinvested $100m, giving it a 9.4 per cent stake. Again, the UK taxman didn't see a penny of it, despite F1 being based in London. Tax on a total of $3.8bn had slipped through its fingers as a result of the bond and the sale of the trust's stakes in F1. It was thanks to Mullens, as he revealed in a letter to Emmanuele Argand:

> As you know I left my law firm in 1999 in order to devote all my time to the Formula One Group and the family trusts. Our primary

objective at that time was to achieve an IPO based on the foundations of a successful bond structure. In the event this was not possible, but nevertheless we will at the conclusion of Project Alpha have realised $3800 [million] without incurring the usual 40% charge to capital gains tax. This has been achieved through my structure and our joint endeavours to preserve the rights we had under the various shareholder agreements.

Ecclestone had not wanted the banks to sell to an investor who professed to want to work with him but then attempted to frustrate his every move. He made it clear how he would have reacted if he had disagreed with a new owner when he said, 'If anyone ever tries to grab Formula One I'll do a scorched earth. I'll make sure there's nothing left after I've gone.' With CVC in pole position, Ecclestone didn't have to worry about losing his grip on the wheel.

PART 4

INSTITUTIONALISATION

15

ALL CHANGE

The 2006 Bahrain Grand Prix was the start of a new era for F1. It was the first race held since CVC announced it would buy the sport and was the first time that one of the non-traditional markets had hosted the prestigious season opener. The stunning venue in the desert had cost nearly $200m to build for its debut in 2004. The wealth was on display for all to see thanks to a lavish circular spectator tower at the heart of a circuit that even features the name of the country painted next to one of the run-off areas.

The influx of new races meant that 2006 would be Imola's last year on the calendar for almost two decades, while in Japan Honda-owned Suzuka was being forced out in favour of Toyota-owned Fuji Speedway, which had undergone an expensive renovation. The season also marked the end of Germany holding two Grands Prix a year, with Hockenheim and the Nürburgring alternating from 2007. There was good reason for the country's waning interest.

Michael Schumacher started the season on pole, but it was the first time in five years that he did so without the number one of the reigning world champion on his car. Having lost the crown to Spain's Fernando Alonso, who became the youngest F1 champion in history, the German superstar would retire at the end of the year, replaced at Ferrari by Finnish hotshot Kimi Räikkönen. The fastest lap of the Bahrain Grand Prix was set by a rookie – Nico Rosberg – who was the first champion to graduate from the new GP2 junior series that had launched the previous year. He would be followed in 2007 by Lewis Hamilton. Between them the four youngsters – Alonso, Räikkönen, Rosberg and Hamilton – would go on to win 11 championships.

Following the Indianapolis fiasco, Michelin was also on the way out, but it wasn't the only change on a technical front. The FIA had mandated an engine freeze from the Japanese Grand Prix until the end of 2008 in one of the first major attempts by the regulator to curb spiralling spending by the manufacturers. It was not enough to help Cosworth, which dropped out at the end of the season for the first time since the 1960s, having failed to match the manufacturers' performance on its smaller budget.

One of the biggest changes was a highly visible one. The introduction of a European Union ban on tobacco advertising brought an end to an era of sponsorship that had dominated the sport. It was a major blow for the teams, many of which still relied on cigarette money for a large part of their budgets. In 1999, the tobacco brands had spent an estimated $285m on F1, a record for any single year, and by 2004 they still comprised 21 per cent of all sponsorship by value. With the ban looming, West and Gallaher quit the sport at the end of 2005 while Mild Seven limped on to the end of the following year. BAT had sold British American Racing to Honda, but still displayed its logos where it could. Due to a regulatory loophole, Ferrari sponsor Philip Morris International stayed on after the ban, but the last time an actual cigarette logo would be seen on an F1 car would be when Räikkönen took victory at the 2007 Chinese Grand Prix in his Marlboro-branded car.

Despite predictions of doom, F1 did not implode due to the ban but it meant that the teams were more reliant than ever on the car manufacturers and the blue-chip sponsors, such as tech and financial services companies, that wanted to associate with them for business reasons. Williams' head of marketing, Jim Wright, told the *International Herald Tribune*, 'Tobacco companies can only contribute cash. Technology companies can contribute cash and technology.'

The rise of the manufacturers was bad news for the struggling independent teams. Jordan had been sold to Canadian businessman Alex Shnaider the previous year and would change ownership twice more before becoming Force India in 2008. Sauber had become BMW and Minardi had become Toro Rosso, meaning that Williams and newcomer Super Aguri were the only teams not owned by a billionaire or a car company. They would finish a lowly eighth and eleventh in the championship respectively. But despite this dominance and Ecclestone's coup in poaching Ferrari, the GPMA teams were still threatening to go it alone.

In the run-up to the start of the season, the manufacturers' mood had got progressively worse, and this time it wasn't the fault of Ecclestone. Max

Mosley had suggested an increasingly radical catalogue of changes to the regulations that seemed designed to infuriate the car makers by negating one of their biggest advantages – budget.

The FIA president had previously attempted to curb ever-higher spending through the technical regulations, such as the FIA's 2001 ban on beryllium. The exotic but carcinogenic metal was used in F1 engines and at the time was more expensive than gold. The FIA banned it on safety grounds, but it upset some of the manufacturer teams. Ron Dennis complained that 'there was no reason why we should not have been able to continue using what was a very good technical advantage coming out of months and months of research and a great amount of funding'. The ban failed to deliver, however, as the manufacturers switched to a boralyn and aluminium alloy that cost even more. But Mosley did not give up.

In April 2005, the FIA commissioned TNS Sport to conduct a survey of 93,018 F1 fans worldwide about the current state of the sport. On the face of it, the survey seemed to support the manufacturers as it found that 83 per cent of fans thought that showcasing the best technology was an essential part of F1. However, only 40 per cent felt that technological innovations had led to competitive racing and just 38 per cent thought technology was the most exciting aspect of F1. Almost all fans wanted more overtaking, something that was being obstructed by advances in aerodynamics that created 'dirty air' in an F1 car's wake. Interestingly, more than half of fans thought intrigue was an essential part of the sport.

In September 2005, the FIA announced that the 2008 regulations would 'eliminate unnecessary expenditure'. A statement declared, 'The duty of the FIA is clear – it must ensure that Formula One continues with a mixture of independent teams and manufacturers, all competing on an equal footing in the traditional way.' Mosley next suggested that in order to make the sport more financially fair, manufacturer teams could be denied prize money. The GPMA claimed it was surprised by the move and that the European Commission would be unhappy to find the FIA interfering in the commercial side of the sport.

It didn't stop Mosley and in May 2008 the FIA took drastic steps to try and stop F1 teams from collapsing due to the increasingly unstable global financial climate. The FIA's technical consultant Tony Purnell wrote to all of them outlining the governing body's intention to introduce a budget cap, which started at €175m in 2009 and reduced to €140m the following year then €110m the year after. All of the teams, especially

F1's biggest spenders, strongly opposed the cap, arguing that it was too sudden a reduction.

Although it might seem logical that the manufacturers would be glad of an opportunity to save money, that was not the case. They spent hundreds of millions of dollars each year not only to gain an advantage over their competitors, but also to use F1 as a test bed for potential road-car technologies. Mosley's plans would bring an end to that. The days when a clever independent could take on the big guys were slipping away and in 2006 the six manufacturers occupied the top six places in the championship. Even so, it did not mean that money alone could buy a championship. Toyota was the biggest spender but had never won a race and finished last of the six that year.

Yasuhiro Wada, the head of Honda's racing arm, claimed that a financial deal with Ecclestone was now within reach, but that the manufacturers were not sure they could reach a regulatory consensus with the FIA. 'The reason we race is for technical things,' he said. 'We are not racing for commercial reasons, so money allocation and so forth we can compromise on – that is not our priority. If the regulations go with the 2008 proposals there is not much to work with. Where is the technology?'

It was time for F1's new owner to take action.

CVC was F1's first shareholder in a long time that actually invested in the sport. Until 2006 the teams' only share of the spoils had been 47 per cent of the income from TV rights as prize money. However, in March 2006, CVC paid $385m to buy Allsport and the APM business, bringing all of F1's key revenue streams under the same roof for the first time in history. It boosted the fortunes of Paddy McNally, who was already a rich man with homes in the Swiss ski resort of Verbier, the Côte d'Azur and Wiltshire, where he owns Warneford Place, the former residence of Ian Fleming. The acquisition was funded by $285m of debt from RBS and $99m of loans from the shareholders. It wasn't long before they got their money back.

Once the deal was done, Ecclestone offered the teams a 50 per cent share of all of F1's profits from the following year, which would double their prize money. They jumped at the chance and quickly repaid the favour. At the Spanish Grand Prix on 14 May 2006 the GPMA teams signed a new Memorandum of Understanding (MOU) to continue racing in F1 after the Concorde expired at the end of 2007. It gave CVC

– and Mosley – time to negotiate the full details of a new Concorde Agreement to run until 2012; although it wasn't guaranteed to get to the finish line, the outlook was rosier than it had been for years.

The MOU led to the teams putting the brakes on their plans for a rival series for the time being and, although it was not legally binding like the Concorde, Ecclestone had his own carrot to entice them to put pen to paper on the contract. He offered teams that signed the next Concorde a windfall payment representing the difference between the prize money they received from 2004 to 2006 and the amount they would have received over that period at the new higher 50 per cent rate. Since the difference came to around 25 per cent of F1's profits, it was a pretty big carrot.

Then, to appease the manufacturers, CVC began to institutionalise F1 through the creation of an audit committee as well as two other boards that had a say over Ecclestone's successor. This gave F1 a more corporate structure, which appealed to the car manufacturers, investors in CVC's funds and the banks that loaned CVC money. The icing on the cake was that CVC offered the manufacturers board seats on F1's new ultimate holding company, Delta Topco, and in November 2006 also appointed two respected non-executive directors.

As we revealed in the *FT*, advertising boss Sir Martin Sorrell and former Nestlé chief executive Peter Brabeck-Letmathe took up the seats, with the latter becoming F1's non-executive chairman. They were each handed a 0.3 per cent stake in Delta Topco and, more importantly, had oversight roles. However, although it helped to win over the manufacturers, it made life tougher for Ecclestone. With more people than ever before looking over his shoulder, it was only a matter of time before they came to blows.

The first explosion came a few years after the duo was appointed. Following his seemingly inbuilt divide and rule sensor, Ecclestone gravitated towards just one of them – the elderly Austrian executive Brabeck-Letmathe. 'Peter is super. He is a different type of person to Martin Sorrell,' Ecclestone told us. Sorrell, on the other hand – the multimillionaire Jewish boss of advertising and marketing firm WPP – advised that Ecclestone not travel to the German Grand Prix following the F1 boss's depiction of Hitler in *The Times* in July 2009 as a man who 'got things done'. Ecclestone ignored his advice. Sorrell didn't hide his feelings for Ecclestone: 'I am appalled by what he said about Hitler. His comments were disgusting . . . Any other CEO in any other business would be gone.'

Ecclestone's comments necessitated a follow-up piece where he attempted to clarify what he meant. 'During the 1930s Germany was facing an economic crisis but Hitler was able to rebuild the economy, building the autobahns and German industry,' he said. 'That was all I meant when I referred to him getting things done. I'm an admirer of good leadership, of politicians who stand by their convictions and tell the voters the truth. I'm not an admirer of dictators, who rule by terror.' He subsequently issued a rare apology.

Meanwhile, even though he was the subject of an HMRC investigation, the company he ran was busy pulling off one of the most audacious tax manoeuvres in UK corporate history.

The tax move wasn't driven by Ecclestone but by F1's go-getting chief financial officer Duncan Llowarch. Unlike Ecclestone, the then 39-year-old chartered accountant is a company man who originally worked for FOM's auditor Ernst & Young before he joined F1 in March 2002 under Kirch. No sooner had CVC taken over the wheel than Llowarch began to make a name for himself. Eager to please his new paymasters, he gave the green light to a shrewd, and perfectly legal, scheme that left F1 with one of the lowest tax bills of any major company in the UK.

The wheels began turning in 2008 and spun behind the scenes for several years until a description of the scheme was buried in F1 company filings. When we broke the news about it in the *Independent* in 2013 the paper was so astonished by the revelation that it made it the cover story rather than the birth of Prince George on the same day. There was good reason for this.

We revealed that, thanks to the financial trickery under F1's bonnet, in 2011 it paid just $1.5m of tax on profits of $474.4m even though the standard rate of corporation tax in the UK came to 26 per cent.

Step one of the scheme began shortly after CVC acquired F1, when it set up a web of companies in the UK and offshore jurisdictions including Jersey and Luxembourg. This structure served a financial purpose as it enabled F1 to shift profits from its UK headquarters to offshore subsidiaries where little to no tax is due. It is a practice known as transfer pricing, which is usually only open to multinational companies and is perfectly legal. In fact, HMRC actually endorsed it.

FI's key revenue generating company, Formula One World Championship Ltd, is located in the UK and in 2011 the country was also home to another 13 of the 30 companies in the group. They received the lion's share of FI's $1.5bn revenue but their tax bill was minimised by a series of loans they received from their offshore counterparts in the FI Group. In 2011 FI had $3.9bn of intra-group loans and HMRC allowed the interest on them to be tax deductible. The interest came to a staggering $601.8m and payment of it is counted as a cost on a UK company's financial statements, so it pushed them into a paper loss. In turn, this dramatically reduced their tax bill, which is calculated as a percentage of a company's profit. The loss was only on paper as the interest simply moved from one hand to the other. This is because both the British and offshore companies had the same controlling shareholder – CVC.

In summary, the profit of FI's key UK companies was essentially wiped out by the interest payments to their offshore counterparts that provided the loans. This money ultimately ended up in the hands of FI's parent company Delta Topco, where it was paid to shareholders as a dividend. The filings revealed that no tax was deducted on that either. That was because Delta Topco is based in Jersey and is 'subject to Jersey corporation tax since it is a Jersey incorporated company. However, the current corporation tax rate in Jersey that is applicable to the company is zero.' Ultimately, any of FI's investors who were also based offshore received the dividend with no tax lost in the entire process.

The avoidance scheme came with HMRC's tacit blessing as it had to approve the amount of interest that was tax-deductible.

The agreement lasted until the end of 2017 and was all that was needed as CVC ended up selling FI to Liberty Media by then. The tax scheme was one of the driving forces behind the deal and it made Llowarch a rich man.

In 2008 Delta Topco issued new shares so that it could throw its weight behind FI's management. Llowarch was rewarded with around 1 per cent of Delta Topco, with a similar stake handed to Woodward Hill and McNally. The biggest beneficiary was Ecclestone whose stake accelerated to 5.3 per cent, while Bambino's share reversed by almost a percentage point to 8.5 per cent. The tax scheme wasn't the only reason they were given a pat on the back.

With FI on a firmer footing CVC was able to get an even bigger loan. As we revealed in the *Sunday Express*, in November 2006 FI was lent a massive $2.9bn by RBS and Lehman Brothers, two banks that would soon get into significant difficulty in the 2008 financial crisis. The money enabled F1 to pay back the original $1.1bn loan and CVC's share of the purchase price as well as the $99m of shareholder loans that were used to buy APM and Allsport.

So, not only did CVC get its money back just eight months after it bought F1, it left the sport on the hook for repaying the loan that it had used to buy it. Mackenzie was astonished when the banks loaned the money: 'The banks were at the height of a banking boom. They didn't read the MOU properly. They didn't quite work out that it wasn't a Concorde and they lent money against something that turned out to be very flimsy.'

In November 2006, as part of the paperwork for the loan F1 engaged top accountancy firm Ernst & Young to provide an independent view on its value. It concluded that the business was worth $5.914bn. However, Mackenzie later disputed Ernst & Young's valuation and said, 'I don't think we ever valued it around 5 billion until probably 2010/2011.'

The $5.9bn 'was a value that the banks provided themselves to Ernst & Young', said Mackenzie. 'I think they put it in because, well, the client asked them to and because they could make the numbers work. They made all sorts of ridiculous assumptions in that document. That the Concorde Agreement would stay in place forever. That earnings would go up endlessly forever. And the risk of the whole business was as low as you could imagine. So they got it wrong.' He added that 'we hadn't even signed the Concorde from 2008 to 2012. So it was a very pie in the sky valuation, in my opinion.'

Mackenzie said, 'I laughed when I heard about that valuation. I laughed out loud as we all did in the office. It just seemed ridiculous that they had done it.' He added, 'I thought it was certainly an inaccurate value of the company as it stood that day . . . It was not based on the reality that we were in at that time it was written, not anything close to it.'

The loan went ahead and, although it made a lot of money for CVC, the private equity firm's financial success put it on a collision course with the teams, which were constantly in need of more money thanks to a business model that sees them spending all their revenue in a bid to win on track, leaving them with little profit or reserves to deal with bumps in the road. In 2009, one team boss told *The Times* that 'we don't like how CVC uses this sport as a short-term cash cow with no thought or care about promoting it and investing in its future'.

Ironically, CVC had already invested more than most of the previous owners. As well as buying Allsport and the APM business, in 2007 it bought the GP2 junior series and brought that into the F1 Group too. However, CVC's motives weren't altruistic. It was investing in F1 in order to increase its value, as its ultimate objective was to exit and make a profit.

But the roadblock here was the WMSC's power to block a sale of F1 if it didn't approve of the new owner. Private equity firms are used to selling to the highest bidder, not having their hands tied, so CVC tried to strip the FIA of its right to approve the buyer of its F1 stake.

Mosley hinted at this in his autobiography when he mentioned that 'CVC initiated discussions with us to try to change the hundred-year agreement. They wanted to loosen or remove some of the FIA's retained rights, to make their investment more marketable and therefore, presumably, more valuable.'

The precise details of what CVC asked for were disclosed in an internal FIA memo sent by Mosley in May 2008. He wrote that as part of the renegotiation of the Concorde Agreement, F1 (in effect CVC) had asked the FIA for 'the right to sell the business to anyone – in effect to take over Formula One completely. I do not believe the FIA should agree to this.' Mosley refused to budge. The FIA therefore retained its right to approve a change of control for the moment, although CVC would manage to find a way around it five years later. It didn't have an easy ride in the meantime.

With the expiry of the current Concorde Agreement approaching at the end of 2008, there was still no replacement in sight. Mackenzie admits that even CVC underestimated how hard it would be to sign a new contract, as it needed agreement from the FIA as well as the teams. 'We took it for granted that they would agree and they didn't. And, in fact, the negotiations with them turned out to be extremely difficult and nearly led to the break-up of this company.' It was no exaggeration. The dispute almost led to the end of Formula One as we know it because the teams were on the verge of leaving the sport and starting their own championship. The hard-won peace was set to be short-lived.

16

TOO BIG TO FAIL

Formula One has always been a cut-throat business, but as the 2008 season got underway few could have predicted how few of the sport's power brokers would still be in situ 18 months later. A colossal war of attrition was about to begin.

The first blow was struck on 30 March 2008. In a move that shocked almost everyone in F1, the Rupert Murdoch-owned tabloid newspaper the *News of the World* splashed secretly filmed photos of Max Mosley on its cover, engaging with five prostitutes in a five-hour sadomasochistic (S&M) sex romp featuring concentration-camp role-play in an underground 'torture chamber' in Chelsea.

It was particularly eye-opening as Mosley was reserved to the point of seeming prudish. He initially thought the revelation would boost his image and make him seem more racy in the eyes of the public, but his family background put paid to that as the newspaper claimed that the marathon episode had a Nazi theme. Mosley admitted an interest in S&M, but strongly objected that it had anything to do with Nazism. He also suggested that his sexual preferences should not preclude him from remaining as the FIA president. He argued that his right to privacy was paramount.

It didn't wash with the stuffy F1 community, especially as many of them were already looking for a reason to get rid of the autocratic president. Within a matter of days of the exposé Toyota, Honda, BMW and Mercedes issued statements calling his position into question, using words such as 'disgraceful' and 'disappointed'. Even Mosley's most staunch ally turned on him.

'Since the story broke I have been under enormous pressure from the people who invest in Formula One, sponsors and manufacturers, over this issue,' Bernie Ecclestone told the *Daily Telegraph*. 'They point out that as a chief executive or chief operating officer of a major company they would have gone either immediately or within 24 hours, in the same circumstances. They cannot understand why Max has not done the same.'

In a hammer blow to his friend, Ecclestone added that Mosley 'should stand down out of responsibility for the institution he represents, including F1'. It was an astonishing outburst given how close the two had been and how much money Mosley had made for Ecclestone's family. It wasn't long before Ecclestone regretted it.

'I wouldn't change a single thing we've done over the years, except for my failure to support Max that one time,' said Ecclestone in an interview for the 2013 *Formula 1 Opus* book. 'I didn't support Max over the *News of the World* business and I should have done. I let a friend down and I apologised to him. As for what Max actually got up to, I phoned him and said: "Max, in all the years we've worked together I've been to every single meeting you've ever suggested, every single meeting except this one, and I'm a little pissed off I wasn't invited."'

With even Ecclestone against him, Mosley was forced to write to all FIA clubs and bodies to apologise for any embarrassment caused by the revelations. He proceeded to spend nine weeks lobbying them and eventually convinced two-thirds of voting members that the revelations were insufficient reason to remove him from office. It won him a vote of confidence in his presidency in June, but his greatest victory came the following month when he won £60,000 in damages from the *News of the World* over its false claim that his romp had been Nazi-themed.

It didn't calm tensions with the teams, which were still red raw, especially as Mosley declared that he thought the *News of the World* had been tipped off by one of his enemies from F1. He revealed that he had been engaging in this kind of activity in his private life since his early twenties, which raised the question of why it had leaked at this time. 'There's never been the slightest hint of that coming out,' he said, adding that he thought the source of the exposé was 'not from my private life. It's most likely something to do with motor racing.'

This tallies with comments to *The Times* in June 2008 from Dean Attew, an intelligence consultant who formerly worked for Ecclestone. He revealed that in the months leading up to the exposé, he had been contacted by an intermediary representing someone who wanted Mosley removed from office. Attew said he discussed this with Ecclestone, who then warned Mosley of the plot. However, he said that, surprisingly, 'It was clear that Max disregarded the advice and failed to realise his vulnerability.'

Attew said he 'asked Bernie if there was anything anyone was going to find out about Max and he said, "You're not going to find anything because there's nothing there, he's Mr Boring in that sense." Mosley had kept this a good secret.'

Testimony to this, Attew added, 'When we saw what was in the *News of the World*, Bernie was as flabbergasted as I was.' The shock would have been enough to finish off Mosley's old adversary Balestre, but the Frenchman narrowly missed the ignominious episode as he passed away, aged 86, just three days before the exposé.

The manufacturers were smarting from their failed attempt to force Mosley's resignation over the scandal and stepped up their pressure. The GPMA was replaced with the Formula One Teams Association (FOTA), the new name emphasising that it was formed by the teams, rather than the car manufacturers that owned many of them. The battle between it and the FIA would become known as the FIA–FOTA war.

Unlike the GPMA, FOTA was unified; Ferrari wasn't just a member of the group, it was a leading light. In fact, in an attempt to show that Ferrari meant business, FOTA was even launched at its headquarters in Maranello in July 2008. However, it had the same core objective as the GPMA, which was to get a bigger share of F1's spoils.

Some of the teams were getting desperate. In September 2008, the eyes of the world were on F1 for the inaugural Singapore Grand Prix, the series' first ever night race in a country that was paying a record $40m for the privilege. Even the floodlights didn't come cheap at a cost of $14m, and the hospitality tents were full of some of the region's most powerful executives. The pressure was not only on F1, but also the teams, to put on a good show.

Nearly two years after last winning the championship with Fernando Alonso, Renault was in trouble. The team hadn't won a race since the middle of 2006 and had scored only one podium so far in 2008. There were persistent rumours that the car manufacturer was poised to quit the sport. The team's engineering director Pat Symonds allegedly devised a daring strategy with team boss Flavio Briatore to put the brakes on this threat and help the team win the Singapore race.

Symond's plan involved one of the team's drivers deliberately crashing on the twisting street track so that all of the other teams headed to the pits to refuel while the debris was being cleared. Renault would ensure that its other driver had already made an early pit stop, so he wouldn't need to do so again and would therefore be in the lead when the racing resumed. Nelson Piquet Jr, son of the three-time F1 champion, drew the short straw and didn't have much choice about the matter as he was managed by Briatore. On lap 14 of the race, he crashed into a wall while Alonso cruised on to victory in an incident that would later be dubbed 'Crashgate'. It didn't take long for the rumours to start.

'There were a few conspiracy theories after the race, but nothing of any great substance,' said Charlie Whiting, the FIA's race director, in an interview for the documentary *Mosley: It's Complicated*, which was released in 2021. However, Whiting added that things changed at the season-ending Brazilian Grand Prix in November 2008.

By then Alonso had won another race, calling Piquet's seat into question as the Brazilian was languishing 12th in the championship. Bearing this in mind, Piquet Sr blew the lid on the incident to Whiting, who had been his mechanic in his days driving for Brabham. 'The essence of what he was saying was that: "Flavio made my boy crash,"' Whiting explained. 'I said, "Wow, this is pretty serious stuff." I don't know who else he had told but he just said, "Keep it to yourself." In doing that, he would have known that I would tell Max.'

This version of events was endorsed by Piquet Sr, who later confirmed that he first informed Whiting at the Brazilian Grand Prix. 'I got him and I said, "Look, what could happen to Nelson if I bring this up?" And I was afraid to screw up the career of Nelson.' With his father's pedigree and his seat at a championship-winning team, Piquet was seen as a rising star and he didn't want to risk it all by telling on his team boss and manager.

The FIA steered clear of launching a formal investigation at the time because, according to Mosley, there was no concrete proof Piquet had been told to crash deliberately. 'This [Piquet's chat to Whiting] confirmed what I suspected and it also confirmed what a lot of other people suspected,' Mosley told the film makers. 'But of course, I said nothing to anyone. There was no evidence.' As Piquet was still under contract to Renault he couldn't easily testify against the team.

Accordingly, the incident didn't go any further at that moment, which had immense significance for the future direction of the sport. Not only did it spare big-spending Singapore from embarrassment, but if the result of the race had been annulled, Brazilian Ferrari driver Felipe Massa would have been crowned F1 champion rather than McLaren's Lewis Hamilton, who at the end of the year became the first black driver to win a major motorsport championship.

The Briton's victory was no bad thing for Ecclestone. Just as Michael Schumacher's success led to money pouring in from Germany, Hamilton's reign fuelled the signing of one of F1's biggest ever contracts. It came in 2012 when British broadcaster BSkyB became one of the sport's first major pay-TV broadcasters, paying an annual fee estimated at $73m. Sky initially shared the live rights, first with the BBC and then Channel 4, but in March 2016 was awarded the exclusive rights from 2019. It marked the first time in the UK that the vast majority of races were only available to pay-TV subscribers and Sky paid for the privilege. The blockbuster deal was estimated to be worth a staggering $225m annually.

By then Hamilton had three F1 championships to his name, but his string of success was all kick-started by the win in 2008. It wasn't the only consequence of the FIA's decision not to investigate Crashgate. Keeping the Singapore incident under wraps also ensured that Renault and all of its sponsors stayed in the sport. This too suited Ecclestone to a tee as the team's title partner was Dutch bank ING, which was also F1's biggest trackside advertiser, paying an estimated $24m annually.

However, Mosley and the Piquets did not forget about the incident and it would not be long before it came back to bite those involved.

As the drama of the 2008 Singapore Grand Prix unfolded, Crashgate wasn't the only crisis bubbling under the surface. A different kind of crash was poised to throw the sport into chaos.

Less than two weeks before the race, following months of turmoil on the financial markets, F1 minority shareholder Lehman Brothers filed for Chapter 11 bankruptcy. It was the largest bankruptcy filing in US history and sent shockwaves around the world. By the end of the day, the Dow Jones stock market index had fallen by 4.4 per cent – its biggest drop since 9/11. CVC was quick to offer reassurance that Lehman's F1 stake was in safe hands. By the following summer, Lehman had secured the right to keep its F1 shares. It was the indirect effects of its bankruptcy, however, that were set to have the greatest impact on F1.

The financial crisis was an unwelcome obstacle for all of the teams but one in particular had more on its plate than the others. Since Honda took full control of the British American Racing team in 2005 it had poured almost £900m into it, but had won only one race. By 2008, the team's annual spending had accelerated to £166.5m, a record for a UK-based F1 squad at the time, and it didn't even include the investment in engine development, which was handled by a separate division.

Despite the worsening economic climate, the team's desperate push for success led to it taking on 50 additional staff, giving it a total of 717, over a hundred more than any of the other UK-based teams. One of those new hires proved to be far more crucial than the rest. In late 2007, Honda announced that Ross Brawn would take over as team principal the following year, with a blockbuster salary estimated at £6m.

Signing Brawn was a last-ditch attempt by Honda to save its entire F1 enterprise. He had risen to almost legendary status at Ferrari, as he was seen as the architect of Schumacher's five consecutive world championships. The driving force behind Honda's poor performance was its engine, which was reportedly underpowered, but the team was also struggling to get used to its new high-tech wind tunnel and chassis design had suffered as a result. F1 cars are designed the year before they race, so Honda's 2008 contender had largely already been developed by the time that Brawn took the wheel. It soon became clear to him that the car wouldn't be competitive, so he diverted financial resources into developing the 2009 car instead.

The 2008 season was predictably a disaster. The team scored a single podium place and finished the year just ninth in the championship. With the financial crisis forcing Honda to look at ways to cut costs, the manufacturer pulled the plug on the team at the end of 2008. At the time the teams were still racing under the MOU, rather than the legally binding Concorde Agreement that had expired at the end of 2007, so it was easy for Honda to pull out.

It was a disaster for FOTA. The manufacturers' support was crucial in maintaining the credibility of a breakaway as the teams on their own did not have the resources to fund a championship to rival F1. Honda's exit demonstrated the vulnerability of the manufacturers and backed up Ecclestone's assertions that they could not be relied upon to stick around. It made the teams nervous and more likely to consider a pay-off from Ecclestone if they were uncertain about the commitment of their own backers. It also threatened to bring the number of competitors down to nine, as Super Aguri had gone bust mid-season and finding a buyer for Honda in the prevailing economic climate would be extremely difficult.

Although Honda put the team on the market, only one credible bidder came forward. On 5 March 2009, just 24 days before the first race of the season, Honda sold the team in a management buyout. It was led by Brawn himself, who renamed the team Brawn GP. The group paid a symbolic £1 for it and committed to retaining the bulk of the staff on the understanding that Honda would hand over the money that it would have spent on redundancies if it had closed the team. It ensured that the proud Japanese company did not lose face by making over 700 people redundant, but it came at a hefty cost. Brawn GP's accounts showed that Honda paid it £92.6m to keep the operation going.

Brawn put the money to good use. He replaced the underwhelming Honda engines with ones made by Mercedes for an estimated annual fee of £7m. The Mercedes engines were the same ones that had powered Hamilton to his first world championship the previous year with McLaren and were generally accepted to be the best in the sport. But these Honda-funded Mercedes units were just the start of the irony.

Not only did Brawn GP win the 2009 championship, it scored more points in its first race than Honda did in the entire 2008 season and ended the year with eight victories to its name. Brawn GP's championship was the first ever won by a team in its debut season and the first in more than a decade won by a team not owned by a car manufacturer. It may sound like it was down to incredible management, but there was actually a technical formula to this success.

In addition to the car's lengthy gestation period and the technical expertise of its boss, Brawn was involved with writing the new regulations. He was head of F1's Technical Working Group, which decided upon the sport's technical rules and any potential changes to them. This, as one might expect, gave him and his team a huge working advantage, as Ecclestone pointed out when he said Brawn 'probably knows what's going to happen before other people, or is in a position to guide things'.

Brawn didn't waste this opportunity. With his in-depth knowledge of the regulations, he decided to employ an aerodynamic device known as a double diffuser from the first Grand Prix in 2009. It meant that Brawn's car was by far the quickest on track for the early races of the season. Indeed, by the time other teams implemented it, the championship was more or less done and dusted, with Brawn's Jenson Button having won six of the first seven races.

Despite all this, the team decided to tighten its belt. Its accounts reveal that its total costs reversed by 18.8 per cent to £135.1m in 2009, with £7.5m of the fall coming from slashed staff costs. During 2009, it made 184 employees redundant, with the bulk dropped from the design, manufacturing and engineering departments. Contrary to popular belief, it was far from one of F1's poorest teams. As we revealed in the *London Evening Standard*, the funding from Honda drove the team's total revenue to a staggering £234.5m in 2009. A team having annual revenue of almost a quarter of a billion pounds was unheard of in F1 and it was the highest reported tally for any team in F1 history. Indeed, it was more than the combined total made by Williams, Force India and Toro Rosso. It clearly demonstrated why Mosley thought that a budget cap was necessary.

The lack of a Concorde Agreement opened the door to more teams pulling out of F1 if they didn't get what they wanted, although it would have led to them losing the retrospective uplift to their prize money that Ecclestone promised them for signing the Concorde – a sum that came to around 25 per cent of F1's profits, so not to be sniffed at. However, the teams were so incensed that the FIA was pushing forward with its plan to introduce a budget cap that they were prepared to turn their backs on the money.

As is often the case with FIA proposals, the details of the spending limit changed as time passed. By June 2009 the governing body had settled on a limit of £40m, which would be introduced in 2010 and, crucially, would offer technical freedom to teams racing under it. Teams that refused to restrict their spending would have to build cars to rigid rules, effectively creating a two-tier system. It fuelled even more anger from F1's biggest spenders but the WMSC approved the regulations regardless and, throwing down the gauntlet, set a tight deadline for the teams to sign up to them. It didn't bank on the twists and turns to come.

FOTA hit breaking point. On 19 June, the Friday of the British Grand Prix, it issued a press release announcing plans for a rival series featuring 'the major drivers, stars, brands, sponsors, promoters and companies historically associated with the highest level of motorsport'. There was no doubt about the reason for this as it said that 'the teams cannot continue to compromise on the fundamental values of the sport and have declined to alter their original conditional entries to the 2010 world championship'.

Within 24 hours of the breakaway announcement, the FIA had threatened to sue FOTA, with reports suggesting it could claim as much as £1bn in damages. The FIA had long asserted that it had binding agreements with Ferrari, Red Bull and Toro Rosso, so much so that it put these teams on the 2010 entry list without them filing unconditional entry forms, and this seemed to be the basis of its legal threat. It accused the teams of 'serious violations of law, including wilful interference with contractual relations'. However, the most astonishing manoeuvre was yet to come.

The FIA is not known for backing down on its threats but this is precisely what happened next. Just two days later it mysteriously dropped the lawsuit. Media reports suggested that the FIA backed down due to pressure from CVC and Ecclestone, but didn't say what pressure was applied. Evidence of what was going on behind the scenes was tucked away in trademark filings made by an obscure offshoot in the F1 empire. When we revealed the grand plan in the *Sunday Express* it was clear that it had Ecclestone's fingerprints all over it.

Just one day after FOTA announced it would set up a rival series a stunning set of trademark filings were made by Epsilon Limited. To even the most seasoned of F1 observers the company had little meaning, but we knew its significance. Epsilon was owned by Jersey-based Omega Group Holdings, which in turn was owned by Alpha Topco, the F1 holding company sitting below F1's ultimate parent, the CVC-owned Delta Topco.

Epsilon's function was ownership of intellectual property and the previous year we had revealed in London's *Evening Standard* what it related to. We broke the news that Ecclestone was planning to launch a series called GP3, which would be a low-cost entry point for drivers and would take place during F1 race weekends. Significantly, unlike F1, GP3's rights were wholly owned by CVC as it didn't carry the FIA name. Accordingly, Epsilon was a fine place for intellectual property that the FIA had no claim on. Enter GP1.

Ecclestone's personal company, Formula One Promotions and Administration (FOPA), had held the trademark rights to the word 'GP1' since 2005 and it had long puzzled observers. They wondered why CVC allowed Ecclestone to own trademarks to words that could clearly be used as the name of a rival series to the one he ran for the private equity firm. Ecclestone himself didn't do anything to quell such speculation when we asked him what the trademarks were for and he replied, 'We will see.' We suggested that they could be for a rainy day and he replied with a smile, 'Who knows?'

That rainy day came on 19 June 2009 – the same day that FOTA announced its breakaway series – when Epsilon, which was ultimately owned by CVC, made new trademark applications for logos that it had designed for GP1 and 'GP1 Series'.

The applications covered categories crucial to hosting races and protected the logos in the areas of broadcasting, clothing, printed matter, including programmes, and importantly, sporting and cultural activities. On the same day that Epsilon lodged the applications for the logos, it also applied to trademark the words 'Formula Grand Prix' and 'Formula GP', which could be used as brands for races themselves.

Protecting logos and words in this way is an important step in the preparation of a new sports series and it showed that plans were at a developed stage. If CVC had just applied to protect the word 'GP1 Series' it could have been said that it was done just to stop FOTA from using it, but CVC didn't stop there. Designing its own logo gave CVC protection over that specific image, so it clearly didn't create it for nothing. With GP3 and GP2 already in CVC's arsenal it didn't require much imagination to work out what GP1 was designed for.

It looked like Mosley's authoritarian approach at the FIA had finally gone too far and F1's owner, CVC, could no longer support it. Moving the existing F1 teams and circuits to a new GP1 Series would have left the FIA with nothing, whereas Ecclestone and CVC would have had the grand prize. Not only did the FIA drop its lawsuit but it apparently caved in completely.

On 24 June 2009, just five days after FOTA announced it would launch a rival series, the plan went up in smoke. The world was told that FOTA had got its way – the 2009 regulations would remain in force, with no budget cap, and Mosley would not put himself up for re-election as FIA president in October. In return, FOTA agreed to race in F1 until 2012 and committed to reduce costs in other ways.

At the press conference a stony-faced Mosley certainly looked like a man who had been browbeaten into agreement. Effectively, with that, one of the most powerful figures in the history of motorsport had gone. From his role in realising the first Concorde Agreement, to forcing out Balestre and re-merging FISA and the FIA, to his push for safety and cost controls and his decision to hand Ecclestone F1's commercial rights, Mosley's influence had been almost unparalleled. His exit brought the chequered flag down on an 18-year career. Instead of spending his time governing motorsport he concentrated on campaigning against Rupert Murdoch's media empire and, under pressure from Mosley and others, the *News of the World* closed in 2011.

All that remained was the matter of who would replace him, but Mosley had a natural successor. When the exposé about him was published in 2008, Ferrari's Jean Todt had been one of the few manufacturer team bosses who had refused to speak out against him, despite the encouragement of CVC. Todt was duly rewarded when Mosley endorsed him as his replacement and he became FIA president the following year. Unlike the more reserved yet confrontational Mosley, Todt liked to be seen and enjoyed the high life with his celebrity partner, the future Oscar-winning actress Michelle Yeoh. Ecclestone described his work at the FIA to us as 'travelling around the world doing what Max didn't do too much – kissing the babies and shaking the hands'.

Todt would become president in October 2009, but in the meantime Mosley wasn't quite finished with the teams.

In August 2009, after not scoring a point so far that season, Nelson Piquet Jr was dropped by Renault. With nothing to lose, he gave the FIA a formal statement on Crashgate, claiming that 'Mr Symonds, in the presence of Mr Briatore, asked me if I would be willing to sacrifice my race for the team by "causing a safety car".' He added, 'I agreed to this proposal and caused my car to hit a wall and crash.'

When Piquet Jr's statement was leaked to the press in September 2009 we were at lunch with Ecclestone, whose Brabham team had powered the young driver's father to two F1 championships in the 1980s. During our lunch Ecclestone took a call from Briatore about Piquet Jr's claims. 'There's no evidence. It's just what he said,' said Ecclestone on the phone. 'I honestly think it's [come from] his father . . . See if you can find out who did the investigation and then I'll find out.'

Wheels soon began turning at the FIA in response to Piquet Jr's claims. Mosley first launched an investigation and then called a hearing of the FIA's decision-making body, the WMSC, later in September. Pat Symonds was handed a five-year ban from motorsport while Briatore was excluded for life. The WMSC instructed 'all officials present at FIA-sanctioned events not to permit Mr. Briatore access to any areas under the FIA's jurisdiction'.

In early January 2010, a French court ruled that the WMSC's decision to ban Briatore and Symonds was flawed because, unlike drivers, team personnel didn't carry licences issued by the FIA so it had no authority to ban them. Shockingly, not a single member of the WMSC had raised this gaping flaw in the process, despite some of them being trained lawyers.

The straw that broke the FIA's back was that by launching the investigation into the race-fixing allegations against Briatore, and then presiding over his ban from the sport in his role as chairman of the WMSC, Mosley was effectively acting as judge, jury and executioner. It was ironic, as Briatore benefited from that very structure in 1994 when Mosley advised Benetton's barrister what to say in a bar the night before a WMSC hearing.

That matter didn't end up in front of an actual court but the 2009 ban did. The court ruled that 'the decision of the World Council was presided over by the FIA president . . . with Mr Mosley having played a leading role in launching the enquiry . . . in violation of the principle of separation of the power of the bodies.'

Briatore's lead lawyer Philippe Ouakrat explained to *Gazzetta dello Sport* that 'it is against French and international laws for an organism to be jury, procedural body and investigating body at the same time, with the president of an institution that decides who to investigate, that controls investigators, and that presides over the judging organ.' On 5 January 2010, the court overturned the WMSC's decision, but it was already too late to save Briatore and Symonds.

The WMSC verdict resulted in Briatore resigning from his role as team principal and drove the team's title sponsor ING out of F1 almost immediately. Renault itself followed suit at the end of 2009 when control of the team was sold to Genii Capital, a private equity firm run by another of Ecclestone's friends, Gerard Lopez, an early investor in Skype.

In April 2010, now under Todt, the FIA announced that it had reached a settlement with Briatore and Symonds and agreed not to appeal the French court's verdict. The statement said that Briatore and Symonds had recognised their 'share of responsibility for the deliberate crash', expressed regrets and apologised. They also agreed not to take on any operational role in F1 until 2013.

Ironically, both Briatore and Symonds later worked for F1 and were hired by the sport's ultra-corporate current owners Liberty Media. Briatore became an ambassador for F1 in 2022, while Symonds was appointed its chief technical officer in March 2017. Briatore even eventually returned to the team that was formerly Renault when he became Alpine's executive advisor in June 2024. Liberty's overtures supported the theory that Mosley had been particularly harsh on Briatore because he wanted to get back at Ecclestone and had a strained relationship with Briatore as a result of his work for FOTA.

Two months after the FIA dropped the plan to introduce the budget cap, the teams signed a new Concorde that ran until the end of 2012. It was a big payday for them as they pocketed windfall payments representing the difference between the prize money they were paid from 2004 to 2006 and the amount they would have received over that period at the higher 50 per cent rate.

The contract was signed a staggering four years after Ferrari had received a $100m bonus for being the first team to commit to staying in the sport for the same period.

Ferrari is the only team that has competed in F1 every year since it began in 1950 and has won more titles than any of its rivals. To this day, it is also the only car manufacturer involved with F1 that directly signs the Concorde Agreement rather than using a subsidiary to do so. This gives F1 the recourse to make a claim from the parent company if the contract is breached, whereas a subsidiary can easily be shut down.

For all these reasons, Ferrari gets preferential treatment and from 2008 it was granted a 2.5 per cent cut of F1's underlying profits in addition to its share of the 50 per cent split between all of the teams as prize money. This bumper haul set a high barrier to beat in the negotiations for the next Concorde, but Ferrari soon proved that it was up to the task.

The groundwork began a matter of months after Ferrari's rivals signed the 2009 Concorde. That only ran until the end of 2012, so Ferrari chairman Luca di Montezemolo already had his eye on the next agreement. As early as January 2010 he suggested that a rival series could still get off the ground if the amount paid to the teams did not increase. 'Theoretically speaking, we can have one of three alternatives,' he said, explaining that 'one is that we renew with CVC, but only with better financial conditions. For how many years, we have to discuss, but I am in favour of many years because I don't want to be back every three or four years. So, assume five-to-eight years . . . The next option is that we find a different [rights promotion] company and start discussions. Third, we can establish our own company.'

Ecclestone's response to the threat was brutal: 'It's all nonsense,' he said, adding that 'they're not going to break away. They've tried it all before. Luca's a lovely guy but he likes to say these things and then he forgets what he is saying.'

There was good reason why Ecclestone was snappy. Between September and October 2009 he had lost his two closest allies with the departure of Briatore and Mosley. However, he still had access to F1's war chest and this proved to be his biggest asset in the contract negotiations with the teams. Surprisingly, the money wasn't enough for all of them.

At the end of 2009 the financial crisis drove Toyota out of F1. It had invested an estimated $2.1bn in its F1 team but never won a single race over its eight years in the series and shut its team completely without trying to find a buyer. BMW also quit, with a single victory to its name, but handed its team back to its former owner, Peter Sauber. With the departure of Honda and Renault, it left Mercedes and Ferrari as the only manufacturers remaining in the sport. Ironically, it seemed that Mosley's controversial hard stance against the manufacturers had actually saved F1. Had they got more control over the series, leading to the smaller teams being priced out, there might not have been much of F1 left to fight over when they quit.

Despite Toyota's departure, there were a total of 12 teams on the grid the following year when Hispania Racing, Lotus Racing and Virgin Racing signed up. They had been lured in on Mosley's promise of the £40m budget cap, which was due to be combined with a minimum level of prize money to give the teams guaranteed profits and level the playing field.

The lack of a budget cap had the opposite effect, and all three teams ended up at the back of the grid, even Virgin Racing, which was backed by Richard Branson. As Virgin Racing's sporting director John Booth explained to *Grandprix.com* in 2011, 'There was going to be £30 million TV money, that was going to be the cost of the season and it all sounded like a great idea.'

Within seven years of joining F1, all three outfits had pulled out of the sport with the loss of more than 400 jobs in the UK alone.

The final change to the line-up of teams was the most significant. On 16 November 2009 Mercedes stunned the F1 world when it announced that it would invest in Brawn GP and sell its 40 per cent stake in McLaren to its co-shareholders – Dennis, Saudi tycoon Mansour Ojjeh and Bahrain's Mumtalakat sovereign wealth fund. Just over a month later Mercedes' parent company, Daimler UK, bought 45.1 per cent of Brawn GP for £76,987,000 and renamed the team Mercedes Grand Prix.

Ross Brawn and the other owners had already reaped rewards after the team's pre-tax profit accelerated from £1.3m in 2008 (when it was still known as Honda) to a staggering £98.7m in 2009. It gave the team one of the highest profits in the history of F1 and allowed the management to share a £20m dividend. Ross Brawn himself owned 54 per cent of the team, which gave him £10.8m from the dividend.

By the end of 2012, Daimler had acquired the whole team. The total price it paid came to £137.3m, which gave Brawn GP's owners a turbo-charged return given that they had only paid £1 for the team less than 12 months earlier. Following the acquisition, Brawn remained in the team's driving seat but its performance reversed. In 2010 Mercedes finished fourth in the standings and remained in the same spot the following year before slipping to fifth in 2012. The following year Mercedes began to turn this around.

Step one involved hiring three-time F1 champion Niki Lauda as non-executive chairman. The straight-talking Austrian bought a 10 per cent stake in the team for £10m and made an immediate impact by recommending that Mercedes should hire Lewis Hamilton, who had been hampered by underperforming equipment since winning the title five years earlier. By the time he joined Mercedes in 2013 the team had only won one race, but it added three more to its tally that year. It was helped by having an extra hand on the wheel.

In 2013 Mercedes head-hunted Austrian entrepreneur Toto Wolff, who was a non-executive director of Williams. Brawn retired to spend his windfall and the tall Austrian took the wheel from him. As Wolff explained to us when he took over, he told Mercedes he 'wouldn't do it without being a co-shareholder because I'm an entrepreneur. That's how I function. I need to be able to develop the value of the company.' Wolff got what he wanted; his company Motorsports Invest bought a 30 per cent stake in Mercedes' team for £30m.

Wolff was not just an experienced businessman but also a former driver, which made him ideally placed to liaise with the three key divisions that drive an F1 team – commercial, sporting and engineering. As a teenager, he convinced his mother to pay for lessons at a racing school in exchange for his next ten birthday and Christmas presents, but at 6 feet 2 inches he knew his height would be a hindrance so he turned to business instead. Eventually he founded his own venture capital firm, Marchfifteen, which focused on technology, software and internet investments.

It made a string of high-profile deals, including an investment in Austrian content delivery software provider UCP, co-financed by T-Mobile, which was eventually sold to American group Amdocs in 2006 at a value of $275m. Marchfifteen grew to have offices in Vienna, Berlin, Zürich, Warsaw and Tel Aviv. In 2004 Wolff set up a successor called Marchsixteen, an investment company with a similar focus to its predecessor but mainly focusing on more mature Austrian public companies in the internet and technology space.

By then he was already so wealthy that his network of companies stretched from the UK to the British Virgin Islands, where he owned shares in sports management company Ducker Trading.

In 2006 his passions for business and motorsport crossed paths when Marchsixteen bought 49 per cent of HWA, which develops components for Mercedes race cars. He considered investing in an F1 team but concluded that an independent outfit couldn't compete with manufacturers like Honda, Toyota and BMW. However, at the same time as all three of them pulled out, a door opened for Wolff to come in. Another of his companies, Nextmarch, paid an estimated £15m for a 15 per cent stake in Williams in 2009. This gave Wolff a seat at the team's table as he became a non-executive director.

In spite of its spluttering performance, Wolff helped Williams to become the first listed F1 team when it floated 24 per cent of its shares on Frankfurt's junior exchange in 2011, valuing it at around €250m. It put him on Mercedes' radar and when he jumped ship he sold most of his 15 per cent stake in Williams to American healthcare entrepreneur Brad Hollinger to avoid a conflict of interest.

Having a single decision-maker at the wheel of the team was a key part of the formula for its success. It gave Mercedes a streamlined reporting structure that has allowed it to operate like a speedboat in the world of FI, where success is down to quick decision-making. In contrast, the teams owned by rival manufacturers like BMW, Toyota and Honda had been structured more like committees. Testimony to this, Mercedes won its first FI title of the modern era in 2014 with Lewis Hamilton at the wheel, the year after Wolff joined.

'In any business, you need a clear-sighted analysis of what makes you successful,' Wolff told us. 'In Formula One, there are a number of key factors: the drivers, the chassis, the power unit, the right technology, the necessary budget and the best people. You need to make the right decisions in these areas and make sure they are all aligned. But there is one factor that money cannot buy: time. Our key stakeholders have given us the time for the building blocks to come together and gel. That has been a vital factor in our success.'

It paid off as Mercedes won a record eight consecutive constructors' titles under Wolff, bringing the team a long way from struggling to make the podium in its days as Honda. It has proved it has staying power, unlike its rival manufacturers: after making so much noise, they disappeared from the sport shortly after they finally got what they had been campaigning for. The efforts of manufacturers such as Toyota and BMW had, ironically, paved the way for the success of their rival Mercedes, which reaped the rewards due to its dedication to staying in the sport for the long term and issuing in a new silver-coated era of FI.

<h1 style="text-align:center">17</h1>

THE BEGINNING OF THE END

The FIA–FOTA war wasn't the only dispute reaching resolution. In April 2008, Ecclestone's wife Slavica paid HMRC £10m to finally put the brakes on the tax investigation into her and her husband. The settlement covered the 2008/09 tax year and stretched right back to April 1994, when their family trust's subsidiary Valper Holdings was founded in the British Virgin Islands. No assessment was made by HMRC against Ecclestone and he was not required to make any payment.

The outcome was the culmination of years of Mullens liaising with Bambino and HMRC, both on the phone and at meetings in Luxembourg and Switzerland. It paid off.

On 19 May 2008 Mullens received a payment of $19.5m from Slavica to his Swiss bank account; this proved to be a poisoned chalice. It was one of a total of £37.9m of payments from Ecclestone's family that Mullens didn't declare on his tax return as he claimed they were gifts. HMRC eventually found out and in 2021 forced Mullens to pay more than £20m tax on the payments. At the time it was one of the largest ever findings against an individual, but by then HMRC had its eyes on an even bigger haul.

The tax settlement was the start of a new era in Ecclestone's personal life, but not in the way that he expected. In November 2008, tired of asking her 78-year-old husband to retire, Slavica filed for divorce on the grounds of Ecclestone's 'unreasonable behaviour'. As he explained in the *Lucky* documentary series, 'Slavica was fed up of my travelling and I think, in fairness to her, I had promised her so many times that this is going to be the last year. I'm going to step down. I think she knew it wasn't true, it wasn't going to happen.'

To this day most media reports about the break-up claim that it was one of Britain's biggest divorces because Ecclestone had to pay Slavica. In fact that couldn't have been much further from the truth. As we reported in a cover story for the *Daily Telegraph*, as Ecclestone had transferred his most valuable assets to Slavica in the late 1990s, she actually paid *him* when they got divorced, not the reverse. It made him an even richer man, as he received around $100m per year under the terms of the divorce.

Despite his advanced years, Ecclestone was an eligible man and it was no secret that he was single. Photos of him wandering the aisles of a Waitrose store in west London, alone with a shopping basket in his hand, were soon splashed over the papers. It didn't last for long. In 2009 he began dating Fabiana Flosi, vice president of marketing for the Brazilian Grand Prix 46 years his junior. They married in 2012.

With the threatened breakaway finally put to bed, CVC too was set on a new direction. Mosley's rejection of its request to strip the FIA of its right to approve a change of control of F1 had put CVC's plans to cash out through a sale in the lap of the gods, as the FIA would have to approve it. Instead, CVC announced that it planned to float F1 on the Singapore stock exchange. The flotation swerved around the need to get the FIA's approval as, unlike a sale, it was excluded under its agreements with F1.

One of the reasons for selecting Singapore rather than the more conventional choices of London or New York was that it is more common for listed companies there to have older management. In other words, it was a show of support for Ecclestone. However, it was unclear if he was as eager as CVC, and the F1 boss now seemed to be tiring of the restraints put on him by financial institutions. As he told us a few years earlier, 'There's no way I would sit in front of a load of shareholders. It wouldn't float under me.'

By the time of the planned flotation, CVC had established layers of bureaucracy, with audit, ethics and remuneration committees causing Ecclestone to tell us that 'Formula One has been run to the standard of a public company for years.' However, the thorough planning was all about to come to nought through events outside the private equity firm's control.

The bomb that had been ticking since Ecclestone's dispute with the banks was finally about to go off. In April 2008, the sport's former shareholder BayernLB had reported €4.3bn in write-downs driven by the financial crisis and a disastrous investment in Austrian bank Hypo Group

Alpe Adria. It had bought just over 50 per cent of Alpe Adria for €1.6bn in 2007, but its fortunes plummeted during the economic downturn and BayernLB was forced to sell it to the Austrian government for just €1 in 2009.

The outcome heaped embarrassment on BayernLB and in a bid to control the damage it fired a number of its management, including Gerhard Gribkowsky. It was one of the biggest business stories of the year in Germany and caused the media to carry out their own investigation into what had happened. Reporters from the *Süddeutsche Zeitung* newspaper dug deep into the business interests of the BayernLB board and found out about Gribkowsky's Austrian foundation due to the property portfolio of its subsidiary GREP.

They discovered that Gribkowsky had a collection of expensive watches and a €6m villa in Munich with a cellar containing 900 bottles of vintage wine. The initial concern was that the money he had received might have been connected to Alpe Adria as an explanation of why BayernLB had seemingly overpaid for the bank.

In December 2010 Gribkowsky was interviewed in Munich for four hours by public prosecutor Hildegard Bäumler-Hösl and, to extract himself from the Alpe Adria rumours, he told her that he had received $44m from Ecclestone and the trust as commission for helping with the sale and purchase of companies. According to the minutes of the meeting, Gribkowsky claimed he 'acted as middle man for Bambino's investment in the [German medical firm] Schön Group. This was normal business.' He added that he also 'proposed a commercial property deal in Frankfurt. He knew his way around the property industry because of his career as a banker.'

Tellingly, the minutes also state that Gribkowsky said he 'received the money because he had accumulated so much knowledge of the [F1] company structures etc through his job and therefore was the only one who could consult'. As Gribkowsky put it, Ecclestone paid him because 'it's better to have him inside the company pissing out than outside the company pissing in'.

It didn't wash with the authorities. The sums were extremely large for the services that had been rendered and they suspected that Gribkowsky had actually been bribed by Ecclestone to sell F1 to CVC, as it had agreed to retain him as the boss of the sport. Initially, they even believed that Gribkowsky had improperly arranged for BayernLB to pay Ecclestone's commission so that he wouldn't have to fund a bribe himself.

Ecclestone hadn't needed to pay someone to stop F1 from being sold to a company that would subsequently fire him. At the time there were more than enough measures in place to ensure he wouldn't need to do that, not least the fact that any sale would need to be approved by the WMSC.

The authorities carried on regardless and on 5 January 2011 arrested Gribkowsky on charges of corruption, breach of trust to BayernLB and tax fraud. He was held in Munich's Stadelheim prison, where Adolf Hitler was once incarcerated, and faced a grim outlook.

Gribkowsky is German and lived in Munich, but prosecutors said that he didn't declare the $44m as income in Germany. If he had done so, he would have had to pay 40 per cent in tax, whereas the Austrian authorities only took 25 per cent.

Ecclestone was well aware of this and was keeping it in his arsenal in case Gribkowsky couldn't keep his mouth shut. 'I knew that he had got the money paid in a way he shouldn't have done because he was a resident of Germany. Now let's assume that I found out that he had spoken to the English [Inland] Revenue, I would have spoken to the German Revenue and I would have said to him, "You know I paid you not to speak to the Revenue and you know you did, now you had better pay me my money back because I am going to speak to the Germans."'

But the German authorities had discovered it without Ecclestone's help. The authorities there knew that Gribkowsky had no defence to tax fraud so this was their fallback charge against him. However, it was the corruption charge that worried Ecclestone the most. Gribkowsky pleaded innocent and Ecclestone sprung into action by telling the German media in January 2011, 'I have got nothing to do with these payments to Gribkowsky.' He added, 'I never made any consultancy contracts with Gribkowsky or his firm.'

CVC acted quickly and called a board meeting of Delta Topco, which voted to remove Gribkowsky as a director. It also engaged the law firm Freshfields and the fraud investigations team of its accountants Ernst & Young to search through the bank account and cashbook records for every company in the F1 Group from early 2005 to the end of 2010 to make sure there was nothing in them that might implicate the company.

It was extremely onerous, as F1 was trying to put its final budgets in place for the year at the same time, but it was worth it in the end as the investigation gave F1 and CVC a clean bill of health.

All the while, CVC pushed on with its plan to float F1 in Singapore. After Ecclestone's attempt to list the business hit the buffers in the late 1990s because the group of rebel teams refused to sign the Concorde, he knew what needed to be done first this time.

The Concorde in force at the time only ran until the end of 2012 and Ecclestone knew that it would take too long to get everyone to agree on the terms of a new contract. So instead he proposed the solution of sign-ing separate team agreements with each squad. They ran for eight years from 2013 to 2020, which gave F1 breathing room to negotiate a longer-term Concorde Agreement with the FIA during that time.

To stop the teams from creating a roadblock to the float again Ecclestone turned his attention to the remaining troublemakers from the first attempted float in late 1990s first. To keep them happy he devised a new prize money structure that would reward Ferrari, Williams and McLaren – the three survivors from the previous dispute. In order to give them guaranteed payments, Ecclestone divided the prize fund into three different components and based the eligibility on a team's longev-ity, heritage and results.

The first component was a general prize fund that enabled all of the teams to share 47.5 per cent of F1's operating profits. This sum was divided into two, with half going to the top ten teams equally and the other half split between them depending on their position in the standings.

In addition, Ferrari, McLaren and Red Bull Racing shared a dedi-cated annual prize fund of at least $100m. This was known as the Constructors' Championship Bonus (CCB) fund and was awarded to the top three teams based on the number of races won in the four seasons prior to 2012. Red Bull Racing was the leader of the CCB pack thanks to its string of four championships from 2010. This gave it a minimum of $37m annually from the CCB fund, with McLaren getting at least $33m for being ranked second and $30m going to Ferrari.

In recognition of its unrivalled heritage, Ferrari's annual share of F1's underlying profits was doubled from 2.5 per cent to 5 per cent, giving it a minimum of $62.2m every year. Combined with the CCB fund, this gave Ferrari guaranteed payments from F1 of at least $100m annually and that's before it was even paid from the general prize fund. The $100m one-off bonus it received for committing to the previous contract suddenly seemed small in comparison.

In 2014 we revealed in the *Daily Telegraph* that Ferrari had also received options on a 0.25 per cent stake in Delta Topco, which had a high-octane value. In an interview for the *Guardian*, a source close to CVC revealed that the value of the listed company 'could shoot for $12bn'. He added that 'sport businesses and content businesses are in significant demand and F1 is one of the very best'.

Ferrari's chairman Luca di Montezemolo was appointed to Delta Topco's board as a non-executive director and McLaren was made the same offer. Although Williams didn't get a director on the board of Delta Topco in the 2013 agreements, it wasn't left out as it received payments from a smaller fund in recognition of its heritage.

Overall, at the expense of CVC and F1's other shareholders, the new structure gave the teams 63 per cent of F1's profits from 2013, but there was a huge gulf between the top and the bottom of the grid. The top three teams shared around half of the entire prize fund, with Ferrari alone getting as much from the CCB fund and its dedicated prize pot as the total annual revenue generated by F1 minnow Marussia, formerly Virgin Racing. It was one of three teams that pulled out of F1 between 2012 and 2016, with its counterpart Caterham (the former Lotus Racing) resorting to crowdfunding in a failed bid to keep its wheels turning.

As always, Ecclestone had a pragmatic take on the matter: 'It is 100 per cent not fair that the top teams get so much but lots of things are not fair in this world. Everyone signs up and they know what they are signing up to.'

Now watching from the sidelines, Mosley had a different view. 'I think the money should probably be distributed more fairly,' he told us. 'The FIA would only be justified in getting involved if the competition itself were being distorted. Obviously, the FIA should intervene if one team were running a bigger engine than the others and that is covered by the regulations. However, the effect of having vastly more money is exactly the same as having a bigger engine.' Nevertheless, all the teams signed up, with eight of the 12 putting pen to paper on the new deal in 2012 before the previous Concorde expired. There was a good reason for this.

It was buried on page 176 of the flotation prospectus, which revealed that F1 had made signing payments to the teams totalling $180m. With such significant financial incentives, the bigger teams had finally got what they were looking for and threats of a breakaway subsided, paving the way for the float. The sport seemed to be on course for the stock market, but as every day passed it became increasingly clear that it would have to navigate the bribery allegations against Ecclestone in Germany before it could get to the finish line.

18

TAKING IT TO THE BANKER

As pressure mounted on Ecclestone's shoulders, he couldn't continue to keep up the pretence in public that he hadn't paid Gribkowsky. So he did a U-turn and dropped a bombshell by revealing to us in an article for *The Daily Telegraph's* website that not only had he paid Gribkowsky but he did so because the banker threatened to tell HMRC that he was in control of the trust.

It came completely out of the blue to the wider F1 community, and some struggled to believe it. Even the *Times'* motor racing correspondent at the time wrote, 'It seems that Ecclestone volunteered the story about Gribkowsky threatening to drag him into a tax case with the Inland Revenue to a tame website journalist. It all seems a little odd.' We initially sent it to the deputy companies editor at the *FT* and it was such an unexpected bombshell that the paper sent the entire article in advance of publication to Ecclestone to check that it was true. The *FT's* approach didn't instil confidence in us so we took the news to the *Telegraph* instead.

Ecclestone had realised that everything could come out in court so, in February 2011, he told Donald Mackenzie about the payment to Gribkowsky and the commission he received from BayernLB for facilitating the sale to CVC. Mackenzie later revealed that Ecclestone 'said he was embarrassed at having forgotten them. And it wasn't until Bruno Michel, one of his colleagues at the Formula One group, had reminded him that he remembered them.'

Mackenzie was furious and admitted that Ecclestone 'could see I was very, very angry with him. He told me he'd never lied to me. And I must say I said I had trouble believing that you could forget a payment of $40 million.' Mackenzie added:

I told him I was extremely unhappy about the fact that that [the commission] had been withheld from me because it was a clear breach of our purchase contract, which required him, the trust and BLB to disclose all arrangements between themselves that may affect Formula One. And that was never disclosed to us.

I asked him why it hadn't been disclosed and he said it was the business of, how did he put it, he said it was to do with the shareholders at that time and nothing to do with me.

Uncomfortable with hearing this privately, Mackenzie told Ecclestone 'to go forward to the prosecutor in Germany and tell them what he knew and what he had told me. And he said he would do that.' Mackenzie wasn't the only one who saw red mist.

Ecclestone's revelation came to the attention of his old sparring partner Dieter Hahn, Kirch's former deputy chairman. In 2007, five years after the German media giant had hit the wall, the eponymous media mogul's family and Hahn pulled off a corporate manoeuvre that ultimately changed the face of F1. They became shareholders in another German media company,

Constantin Medien, which was actually the successor to EM.TV, the former F1 owner that had to be bailed out by Kirch when its share price plunged. Kirch had bought EM.TV's SLEC shares in stages and ended up going bust before it had acquired all of them. This led to Kirch owning 58.3 per cent of F1, with 16.7 per cent left in EM.TV's hands. Kirch funded the acquisition with $1.6bn of borrowings and ironically this contributed to the company's collapse.

Hahn wanted to bolster the Kirch family's coffers, which Leo Kirch himself couldn't do as he passed away in 2011. Constantin was the key to this.

After the banks seized Kirch's F1 shares as security for their loan in 2002, BayernLB acquired EM.TV's remaining 16.7 per cent SLEC stake for the bargain-basement price of €8.5m. EM.TV gave the green light to the sale on condition that if the bank eventually sold its combined F1 stake for more than $1.057bn, it would get a cut of the proceeds. EM.TV missed out on this because CVC paid the banks $828.9m, and Hahn smelled a rat when he heard Ecclestone's comments about his secret deal with Gribkowsky.

In July 2011 Constantin filed a civil lawsuit against Ecclestone, Mullens, Bambino and Gribkowsky in London's High Court claiming that the banks' 47.2 per cent F1 stake was undervalued when it was sold to CVC in 2006. The lawsuit alleged that Ecclestone and Bambino paid a $44m bribe to Gribkowsky to ensure that he sold the stake to CVC as it had agreed to retain him as F1's chief executive.

Constantin claimed that CVC made the highest offer to BayernLB but the stake would have sold for even more if a bribe had not been paid. It alleged that other buyers would have bought the stake for a higher price but Gribkowsky did not explore them as he had an incentive to sell to CVC. The media company claimed for $140.4m in damages.

It came completely out of the blue for Ecclestone, who said that he 'did not have any knowledge that EM.TV or any successor to it had any such rights'.

The money it wanted wasn't his biggest worry. Although it was a civil claim, it could have had criminal implications for him. The worst-case scenario was for the court to conclude that Constantin's stake was undervalued because Ecclestone had bribed Gribkowsky to sell to CVC. This was the catalyst that the German authorities needed to bring a criminal bribery case against Ecclestone, so he knew his defence would be put to the test; in turn this drove him into a tight spot. The more Ecclestone stressed that he didn't bribe Gribkowsky to sell to CVC – he'd paid him, of course, only to stop the German contacting HMRC – the more it looked like he had something to hide from the tax authority. So he also needed to demonstrate that Gribkowsky's claims were unfounded as he didn't actually exert any control over the trust.

By this point, Ecclestone's admission about why he paid Gribkowsky had also come to the attention of HMRC. Understandably, it was curious as to why Ecclestone had paid so much money to stop Gribkowsky from tipping them off if the German had no concrete evidence that Ecclestone had a hand in steering how the trust's money was spent. Accordingly, in March 2012 HMRC informed Ecclestone that it was investigating his tax affairs, focusing primarily on his direct and indirect connections to offshore trusts.

The investigation began amicably enough and proceeded in accordance with what is known as Code of Practice 8, which is applied in cases where there is no suspicion of tax evasion and the purpose of the investigation is simply to identify if there are any amounts of underpaid tax. The following year Ecclestone gave HMRC what it was looking for when he told the tax authority that he hadn't been entirely truthful about the interest he still owned in Brabham's Chessington factory all those years later.

However, instead of backing off now that it had an admission, HMRC doubled down on its pursuit of Ecclestone. He knew HMRC was serious but so too was Hahn. So on the one hand he had to demonstrate to the High Court that he didn't bribe Gribkowsky to sell F1 to CVC, he paid him to stop him telling HMRC that he controlled the trust. However, on the other hand he had to demonstrate to HMRC that the trust was outside his control. It was an incredibly tight corner and it was about to get even tighter.

One of the other entities that had shown an interest in buying the banks' stake in F1 was American investment firm Bluewaters Communications Holdings, and it too smelled money. Bluewaters claimed that it offered to pay more than CVC for F1 but was rejected by Gribkowsky because he had a personal incentive to sell to CVC. It filed a lawsuit in New York against Ecclestone, Bambino, CVC and Gribkowsky claiming $650m in damages. Bluewaters claimed that CVC's profits from F1 'rightfully belong to Bluewaters and its financial backers'.

The case was thrown out by Eileen Bransten, Justice of the New York Supreme Court, who said that 'the "critical events" underlying the claims in this lawsuit took place in Germany, England and elsewhere in Europe'. Although Bluewaters itself was based in New York when it lodged the lawsuit, at the time of its offer for F1 it was located in Jersey. Crucially, Bransten added that Bluewaters' offer stated that it was 'governed by the laws of England, and that all claims and matters arising out of it would exclusively [be heard] in English courts'.

Bluewaters then took its fight to the UK courts and eventually reached a confidential settlement with Ecclestone and BayernLB in 2018. It wasn't so easy to shake off Hahn.

'If Gribkowsky is found to have received a bribe then Hahn has got leverage,' Ecclestone told us at the time. It soon became clear what he meant.

Gribkowsky had been incarcerated since his arrest in January 2011 and ten months later he finally had his day in court. The case against him took place in Munich and was Germany's biggest post-war corruption trial. Gribkowsky denied the charges against him but refused to speak for months, causing the court to hear more than 40 witnesses – including

Ecclestone, who testified in return for immunity from prosecution unless new evidence was unearthed during the case. Ecclestone said he had done nothing illegal and repeated that he paid Gribkowsky to keep him quiet. He added that a tax probe would have tied him up for years and was 'something I didn't need'.

The trial was drawn out as Gribkowsky's lawyers claimed that their client was suffering from stress. It was still in full swing by June 2012 when the judge Peter Noll tried to put the brakes on it. It was clear Gribkowsky was fighting a losing battle so Noll said that 'a fully comprehensive confession encompassing all the allegations, would impose a cumulative custodial sentence of between 7 years and 10 months and 9 years'.

Gribkowsky finally cracked on 20 June 2012 when he did a U-turn and admitted that the allegations of bribery were 'essentially true'. He explained: 'I allowed myself to be bribed' after Ecclestone told him at a meeting in May 2005 that 'the practice in Formula One is that you scratch my back and I scratch yours'. Giving more detail, Gribkowsky claimed that Ecclestone told him, 'If you help me to sell Formula One, I will employ you as a consultant.' The banker said he wanted $50m, even though he knew that '$10 million would be more normal'. He got what he wanted as Ecclestone and the trust paid nearly the full amount.

Attempting to explain why he had originally pleaded innocent, Gribkowsky said, 'It has taken me a long time to come to terms with what I did and to admit even to myself – yes, it was bribery, and yes, I should have paid tax. Even today I have troubles accepting this as reality. With hindsight, I know now that I should have said no to [Ecclestone's] demands.'

Although his explanation may sound contrived, it was actually perfectly logical. Even though Ecclestone did not pay Gribkowsky to steer the sale of F1 to CVC, the banker was in charge of finding buyers. It would have been natural for him to go along with Ecclestone's wishes having received so much money from him and the trust. At the very least, this may have been subliminal, which was why it took time for Gribkowsky to describe it as bribery.

Naturally, Gribkowsky's about-turn fuelled Ecclestone's ire. 'I suppose he would say that so maybe he gets seven years instead of 14 years,' he said. 'The poor guy has been banged up for 18 months. He would have said anything to save himself. He was going to be locked up whatever happens.'

Precisely one week after his confession, Gribkowsky was jailed for eight years and six months, which was in the middle of the range that Noll gave him but was still a severe sentence for a white-collar crime. For the sake of comparison, Andrew Fastow, the former chief financial officer of Enron, was only jailed for six years even though he was one of the key architects of one of the biggest corporate frauds in US history, which left the company bankrupt with debts of \$31.8bn.

Ominously for F1's boss, in his concluding statement Noll said that 'in this process we assume the driving force was Mr Ecclestone'.

Now that the recipient of the alleged bribe had been locked up, it was only a matter of time before the German authorities prosecuted the person they believed had paid it.

19

PLAYING AN ACE

Even for a master multitasker, 2012 was a tough year for Ecclestone. Not only did he have to prepare for the inevitable charges from the German authorities at the same time as running F1, but he also had to plan his defence in the Constantin case. Assuming it actually went ahead.

Gribkowsky's confession gave Hahn's claim an almighty boost because if Ecclestone was found guilty of paying a bribe to steer the sale of F1 to CVC it would show that higher bidders could have lost out. At the time, Ecclestone told us that Hahn seized the moment and tried to negotiate a settlement to 'get this all out of the way'.

In an interview with us for the *Independent*, Ecclestone said that CVC paid 'a very good price. They didn't buy the shares under value, it was the opposite. There could have been a big bust-up with the teams. It was so close that it was easy to happen.' This is the very reason why BayernLB reduced the value of its F1 shares to around $400m and it wasn't lost on Ecclestone. 'The price I got them for their bloody shares was double what they were in the books at,' he boomed.

It is little wonder that Ecclestone was angry. Gribkowsky's confession constituted new evidence that was uncovered during the trial and this enabled the prosecutors to press charges against Ecclestone. A few days before the German Grand Prix at Hockenheim in July 2012, the *Süddeutsche Zeitung* reported that public prosecutors in Munich were investigating 'with high pressure' the possibility of charging Ecclestone with bribery. It didn't seem to bother CVC as it pressed on with its plan to float F1 in Singapore.

Throughout 2012 CVC sold minority stakes in F1 to so-called cornerstone investors in order to put an early value on the business in advance of a flotation. This was a crucial step because there are few comparable floated businesses that could be used to gauge the value of

F1. Its closest competition is the World Cup and the Olympic Games but even they only take place every four years and neither is run by a listed company.

CVC got the year off to a flying start when money manager Waddell & Reed paid $1.1bn in January 2012 for a 13.9 per cent stake in Delta Topco. There was more good news in May 2012 when Delta Topco paid out an $850m dividend. More share sales came later in May when asset management firm BlackRock paid $196m for a 2.94 per cent stake in Delta Topco, followed by the sale of 4.5 per cent for $300m to Norges, the investment division of Norway's central bank. In June 2012 CVC announced that Waddell & Reed had invested a further $500m, which took its stake to 20.9 per cent.

Then, capping off a bumper year for F1's owners, in December 2012 Delta Topco paid out another dividend that this time came to $1.2bn and was fuelled with income from another debt refinancing. A $796m dividend was paid out two years later followed by $197m in 2015. It brought the turbocharged total that had been raised from share sales and dividends in two years to a staggering $5.1bn. The biggest beneficiary was CVC, which had reduced its stake in Delta Topco to 38.1 per cent but still controlled the company through its I Directors, which had the power to outvote the rest of the board.

However, everything was thrown up in the air in summer 2013. The moment Ecclestone had been dreading came on 17 July when German prosecutors charged him with paying a $44m bribe. It effectively put the brakes on the flotation of F1, as it would be hard to imagine listing a company with a CEO who was facing the possibility of jail time due to criminal charges for bribery. Ecclestone himself admitted this when he told *Bloomberg* that 'it would be silly to go into the market, you don't want any single question' hanging over the sport. It sent CVC into a spin.

The private equity firm had to take urgent action to get the business back on track and its first manoeuvre came just a few hours after the prosecutors contacted Ecclestone. CVC issued an unexpectedly candid press release noting that 'Ecclestone has 6 weeks to provide a response to this bill of indictment, prior to a decision being made by the Court on opening proceedings.' This bought the firm some time and it made the most of it. With its plans for a flotation up in smoke, it was left with the option of selling its 38.1 per cent F1 stake to exit and boost its return on investment. However, in order for CVC to sell F1, the FIA had to vote on whether to approve the buyer.

As Mosley had explained to us, 'In practice, this is almost a complete veto because if there were a dispute as to whether the FIA were being reasonable or not, it would have had to go to arbitration. This would have meant a delay of 12 to 18 months with no certainty of outcome.' He added that in real terms, if a purchaser had been faced with this it 'would almost certainly have walked away'.

In short, CVC faced the prospect of finding a buyer for F1 only for the sale to end up stuck at the lights if the FIA did not approve of them. Just five days after Ecclestone was charged, CVC swerved around this hurdle in dramatic fashion by signing perhaps the most controversial contract in F1 history. It gave the FIA a $69.5m incentive to approve the buyer of CVC's F1 stake even though it had no idea who it would be.

With the Concorde coming up for expiry at the end of 2012, CVC seized the opportunity to sign a new agreement that had an even longer term than its predecessors. This was initially designed to make F1 seem more secure so that investors would buy shares in it if it floated but it also made CVC's stake look more attractive to buyers.

Negotiations for the agreement had been less fraught than for its predecessors. The teams had signed up to separate agreements committing them to race from 2013 to the end of 2020 but CVC wanted to go one better in F1's contract with the FIA. It proposed entering into the Concorde Implementation Agreement, which involved signing a contract until the end of 2020 as well as committing to renew it on substantially the same terms until 2030.

Although CVC had been negotiating with the FIA over the content of the contract for around a year, the discussions hit top gear after Ecclestone was charged. CVC wanted to get the contract across the line as soon as possible so that it maximised the value of the business when it was talking to buyers.

The FIA was in pole position to make the most of CVC's desperation, and not just because it had to approve the buyer. Todt had a more collaborative approach than Mosley and on 22 July 2013 the FIA's French and Swiss divisions signed the agreement with CVC, FOWC, SLEC, Delta Topco and Formula One Asset Management, the company that controls the mechanism for the F1 rights to revert to the FIA after 2110.

Although the FIA issued multiple press releases announcing the new contract, not one of them revealed the biggest benefit that it had received. Like all previous instalments of the contract, the Concorde Implementation Agreement was confidential but, over time, sources close to the signatories circulated copies of the executive summary, which revealed that the agreement granted the FIA the right to buy a 1 per cent stake in Delta Topco for the bargain-basement price of $458,197.34, even though it was worth 'approximately $70m' at the time. Crucially, the terms of the share purchase stated that the 1 per cent could 'only be monetised on a pro rata basis in the event of a sale by CVC'. Put simply, this meant that the only way for the FIA to cash in its stake was to sell it when CVC sold its shares – and this required the FIA's approval. In other words, it revealed that the FIA was in a conflict of interest.

Filings reveal CVC's involvement with the transaction as the FIA acquired the 1 per cent stake from Delta Topco, which was controlled by the private equity firm so it had to give its approval. There is a good reason why CVC did this. It had the most to gain from Delta Topco being sold as it was the biggest single shareholder in it with its 38.1 per cent stake valued at $2.7bn in 2013.

The 1 per cent wasn't the only bonus that the FIA received under the agreement. The annual regulatory fee paid by F1 to the FIA accelerated from $11.5m to $25m, with $1m paid for every additional race if there were more than 20 on the calendar. In addition, the F1 Group increased the amount of freight it transported to long-haul races for the FIA at no cost from 12,500kg to 16,000kg. It also gave it 10 economy class and 10 business class air tickets to each long-haul Grand Prix compared to 20 economy tickets previously.

By the end of 2020, when the Concorde Implementation Agreement's initial term came to an end, the increased fees and sale of the 1 per cent stake had boosted the FIA's coffers by more than $200m compared to what it would have received under the previous arrangement. It was a major boost for its coffers, but the benefits weren't only financial.

Under the 2013 contract, the FIA also committed to new sporting governance arrangements, including the creation of an organisation known as the Strategy Group, which became the sole body in charge of making proposals for changes to the F1 regulations.

Prior to 2013, changes were proposed by a body called the F1 Commission, which included the FIA president and F1's CEO as well as representatives from all of the 12 teams, eight of the tracks, two of the sponsors, one tyre supplier and one engine supplier. Each party had one vote, with decisions carried when 18 of the 26 were in favour.

In contrast, the new Strategy Group had 18 votes, with decisions carried by a simple majority. The votes were evenly split three ways between the FIA, the F1 Group and the six top-ranking teams based on their results at the time – Ferrari, McLaren, Mercedes, Red Bull Racing, Williams and Force India. This meant that the voting power of the FIA and the F1 Group increased from 3.8 per cent each under the previous structure to 33 per cent through the Strategy Group. It put F1 in a position of significant power as it only needed the support of either the FIA or the teams to get new regulations passed to the WMSC.

In turn, that made F1 more valuable, which benefited its shareholders, including CVC. The FIA also benefited, not only financially but also because of the increased power the Strategy Group brought it, while the bigger teams had their role in the decision-making cemented in place. It might look like everyone had something to be happy about, but one major party lost out.

The lowest-ranking teams lost their votes, contributing to the demise of two of them, Caterham and Marussia.

The Strategy Group cemented the dominance of the front-runners, as they were able to block significant proposals such as another budget cap, set at $200m, which was mooted to be introduced to F1 in 2015 and would have helped the backmarkers.

Caterham and Marussia had originally been tempted into F1 by the promise of the FIA's £40m budget cap that never happened and were then driven out partly by being stripped of their voting rights when the FIA introduced the Strategy Group.

According to Ecclestone, there was a good reason why the FIA went ahead with it. 'They sold the rights. The Strategy Group that we have got,' he told a group of journalists in 2014. 'They sold the rights to have this new group set up in the way we thought it should be set up.' Giving further detail, he added, 'We were really helping out the FIA because it was in deficit and looking to get some money somehow.'

It reflects comments from Ecclestone in 2012 before the contract with the FIA was signed. He told us that 'the FIA want more money from anybody. Who pays them depends on what they have got to offer . . . We will have a look and see whether we pay them more money. If they really need the money we probably will help. They are going to try and get more money from everybody . . . I think they want to have a more impressive building and establishment . . . If you look at the IOC, if you look at FIFA, they have all got nice big offices.'

The financial boost wasn't enough, as the FIA's accounts show that its operating loss came to €12.8m in 2019, €22.1m in 2020 and €24m in 2021. Impressively, Jean Todt's successor, Mohammed Ben Sulayem, managed to reduce it to €7.7m in 2022 and then €0.8m in 2023, finally making a profit of €2.2m in 2024. He revealed that he was shocked by the state of the FIA's finances when he arrived in December 2021. 'There was a financial issue that we didn't know about,' he said a few months after taking over. 'We had a deficit, even before the pandemic, but I'm pleased to have cleared that.'

Ben Sulayem made a great impact on the FIA even before he became president. A 14-time Middle East rally champion, he has a strong track record in racing and in June 2013 was appointed as the chairman of the new Motor Sport Development Task Force set up by the FIA to build a ten-year plan for the sport's global development. He is also the former head of the United Arab Emirates motorsport authority, which gave him industry experience at the highest level before he was elected FIA president. Crucially, he is a straight talker who says what he thinks, which has put him on a collision course with F1's teams on a number of occasions.

The FIA deficits that Ben Sulayem reduced came about despite the financial boost in 2013, which also included a lump-sum one-off payment of $5m from F1 to the FIA for signing the agreement. The FIA claimed that it received the money 'to balance the service costs FIA has to pay to ensure its regulatory role in the long term'. Giving further detail, it added that it got the $5m 'to ensure that the FIA be properly remuner- ated for its regulatory role'.

Both of these reasons explain why the FIA needed the money, but not why it thought it was acceptable to take it in return for signing an agree- ment that saw the smallest teams stripped of their voting rights, espe- cially given that its own statutes compel it to act in a way that promotes 'the fair and equitable running of motorsport competitions'.

It wasn't lost on Anneliese Dodds, an MEP who represented the south-east of England where Caterham and Marussia were based. On 20

November 2014 she wrote to the EC's Competition Commissioner Margrethe Vestager to say that the collapse of the teams has had 'a resulting loss of jobs in a highly skilled sector of the UK manufacturing industry. The failure of these businesses has occurred amid concerns that smaller teams have been treated unfairly while also being excluded from the F1's rule-making process.'

Dodds added, 'It is therefore disturbing that the FIA now seems to be powerless to act to ensure that all F1 teams are treated fairly. In fact, it appears that last year the FIA accepted a dilution of its regulatory authority in a new agreement with the promoters of F1.'

While interested in the case, Vestager was unable to act unless a formal complaint was made.

This came in September 2015 when Force India and Sauber lodged an official complaint to the Competition Commission regarding F1's governance and payment structure. The midfield teams accused CVC of bias towards the five biggest teams – Ferrari, Red Bull, Mercedes, McLaren and Williams. A statement from Force India said that it 'is one of two teams to have registered a complaint with the European Union questioning the governance of Formula One and showing that the system of dividing revenues and determining how Formula One rules are set is both unfair and unlawful'.

Mosley, one of the leading experts on F1 regulations, told us he thought there was good reason why the FIA was paid $5m to sign up to the Concorde. 'I think perhaps there was a need to give the FIA an incentive to enter into the agreement (as I understand it) in that (i) the Strategy Group increased Formula One Management's power and meant that together, the FIA and FOM could outvote the teams, and (ii) the new Concorde included the very unfair financial arrangements for the teams which, given the need for sporting fairness, the FIA should arguably not have agreed to.'

The FIA put the money to good use as it spent the increased income on establishing a Sport Grant Programme to award its member clubs up to €50,000 each per year for spending on grass-roots motorsport projects.

No matter how altruistic this may have been, it didn't change how the FIA came by the money. In summary, according to its then-CEO, F1 bought the right to increased voting power from its regulator, at the expense of the smallest teams, thereby increasing the value of the company, which was subsequently sold for $8bn.

The financial incentives granted to the FIA stayed largely under the radar for the next four years. The first step towards them coming under the spotlight occurred in September 2013, when Liberty Media made an initial approach to CVC about a sale. The following month Liberty acquired financial data produced by our Formula Money consultancy company about all key aspects of the F1 industry. Discussions about the deal then revved up at meetings between Liberty and CVC in New York and London in late 2014. By then F1 had been through yet more twists and turns.

In October 2013, the long-awaited trial to determine the outcome of Constantin's claim against Ecclestone, Mullens, Bambino and Gribkowsky got underway. It wasn't music to CVC's ears. The court case thrust the famously secretive private equity firm into the spotlight. Looking uncomfortable in court, CVC's co-founder Donald Mackenzie testified that Ecclestone had not told him about the payments to Gribkowsky until they came to light in the media. Not used to such scrutiny, he described F1 as being 'a successful investment apart from the adverse publicity'. He added emphatically that CVC has 'always taken the position that if it's proven that Mr Ecclestone has done anything that's criminal or wrong, we will fire him. But until that happens we will give him the benefit of the doubt provided it is not seriously damaging the business of Formula One. And if that was to happen we would also remove him from office.'

Ecclestone took it in his stride and testified that he didn't need to pay a bribe to remain F1's CEO, because 'I am in the fortunate position that I don't need a job and I could have gone. I'm happy doing what I do as long as I can do what I do; and when I can't, I leave. And that goes for today.'

After little more than six weeks, the judge, Mr Justice Newey, ruled against Constantin as he said there had been 'no loss' to it. Quite simply, there was insufficient evidence that another bidder would have actually paid more than CVC. However, he added he believed 'that the payments represented a bribe' under which Gribkowsky was rewarded for selling BayernLB's F1 shares 'to a buyer acceptable to Mr Ecclestone'.

It was not a criminal case about the alleged corruption so the judge's view was not binding, but it nevertheless had consequences. Most immediately, Ecclestone was told he must bear around half of the reported £8m-plus costs he incurred while successfully defending the lawsuit.

Justice Newey ruled the cost order should reflect his conclusion that the payments to Gribkowsky were a bribe, so Constantin should only pay 41 per cent of Ecclestone's costs rather than 100 per cent as would usually be the case for the losing party.

But that wasn't the biggest consequence for Ecclestone. After the judge in London ruled that he'd paid a bribe, the Munich court had little choice but to put him on trial.

On 16 January 2014 the Munich court announced that the trial would go ahead in the spring and it had an immediate and seismic impact. On the same day CVC released a statement saying that at a Delta Topco board meeting:

> Ecclestone has proposed, and the board has agreed, that until the case has been concluded he will step down as a director with immediate effect, thereby relinquishing his board duties and responsibilities until the case has been resolved . . . The board believes that it is in the best interests of both the F1 business and the sport that Mr Ecclestone should continue to run the business on a day-to-day basis but subject to increased monitoring and control by the board. Mr Ecclestone has agreed to these arrangements. The approval and signing of significant contracts and other material business arrangements shall now be the responsibility of the chairman, Peter Brabeck-Letmathe, and deputy chairman, Donald Mackenzie.

It was the first time that an owner of F1 had clipped Ecclestone's wings, and he came out swinging. 'If people want to shake someone's hand [on a deal], whose hand do they shake? It will still be my hand,' he told the *Daily Mail*. In a rare admission of error, Ecclestone told *Pitpass*, 'I regret paying [Gribkowsky]. I should have let him write the letter to the Revenue and let the Revenue try to prove what he said. It's a wonderful thing, hindsight.'

In contrast to Ecclestone's attitude in the aftermath of the tabloid sting on him, Mosley was first to rally behind the embattled F1 boss. Getting to the core of the flaw in the case against Ecclestone, Mosley said, 'What guarantee would he have had that CVC (who, like all private equity groups are quite ruthless) would not anyway fire him at the first opportunity?'

Equally, if Gribkowsky hadn't sold to the highest bidder it would have disadvantaged not only BayernLB but also Bambino, as it owned 25 per cent of F1. It would have made no sense for Ecclestone to engineer a situation where his family's trust paid around $20m so that it could lose out on the sale. It puzzled Ecclestone too as he asked us, 'What advantage was there for me paying him money to sell the shares for cheap?'

D-Day came on 24 April 2014 when Ecclestone's trial began in Munich. Everything was on the line for Ecclestone. Not just his job but also his freedom, as he faced up to ten years in jail if he was found guilty. Before the trial began we revealed an exit route in the *Mail on Sunday*; Sven Thomas, Ecclestone's lead German lawyer, explained that once the trial begins, a settlement could put the brakes on it.

Worryingly for Ecclestone, however, the judge presiding over the trial was Peter Noll, the man who'd convicted Gribkowsky and had said that he believed the F1 boss was the 'driving force' behind the alleged bribe. Ecclestone needed to prove that the banker was blackmailing him and the document from Ecclestone's old adversary Wolfgang Eisele was the smoking gun, as it fuelled Gribkowsky's threats to report Ecclestone to HMRC. There was just one problem: the document was nowhere to be found.

The German authorities searched Eisele's house in Heidelberg but couldn't find it and he denied that he had it. That was no surprise, as he had handed it over to Gribkowsky's colleague Alexandra Irrgang in the presence of the GPWC and GPMA spokesperson Xander Heijnen. Thanks to his role with the car manufacturers' groups, Heijnen was often at loggerheads with Ecclestone, but he ended up being an unlikely ally when he took to the stand as a witness after around three months of hearings. His testimony in the Munich courtroom was the turning point in the proceedings but has never before been reported. Until now.

'I think I got Bernie off the hook,' says Heijnen, adding that he had met the public prosecutor when Gribkowsky was under arrest and had been concerned by the conclusions she was drawing. 'I told her, "I think you're wrong. I don't think that Gribkowsky was bribed for selling the sport below its value because the car makers were not willing to pay what CVC offered."' He recalled the document that Eisele had shared with Irrgang and raised his doubts with the prosecutor.

'What if Gribkowsky was not bribed by Bernie to sell the sport under its value but he was blackmailing Bernie with a document proving he was actually controlling the trust even though he didn't have the right to do so?'

He says that the prosecutor, however, seemed to be focused on proving the bribery allegations and was dismissive of his theory. 'She said something along the lines of "that is stupid",' explains Heijnen. 'I didn't even have an attorney with me and I couldn't care. She did not put this in my witness statement. She left it out because she thought it was such nonsense.'

When appearing as a witness at Gribkowsky's trial, Heijnen was advised by his lawyer to only answer questions and not to share any other knowledge about the case. He was never asked about Eisele and, as a result, his information did not come out then. It was a different story when Ecclestone was on trial.

'He was always either angry with me or he ignored me completely as if I wasn't there,' says Heijnen about his dealings with Ecclestone at F1 races. However, when the F1 boss saw him in the witness box during his trial, that all changed. 'For the first time ever he was friendly. I will never forget it,' says Heijnen.

'Bernie is very smart,' he adds.

His lawyer said, 'Ask Xander about a meeting in Heidelberg with Eisele.' Then I said, 'Yes, there was a meeting, yes, Irrgang was present, I don't know what was on the document but I had the impression that it was very important . . .' Then the judge said, 'Mr Heijnen, you are under oath. Please be aware that you are making a very important statement here. Can you please remind me what you are saying.' And I said it again. And he said, 'If that is the case, Mr Heijnen, why did you never tell the prosecutor before?' And I said, 'I told the prosecutor three days after Mr Gribkowsky was in jail and she said it was nonsense.' You could hear the gasps of breath in the courtroom because there was huge embarrassment. I think if she had written this in the statement years earlier, Gribkowsky would have been in jail for something else.

Heijnen's testimony bolstered Ecclestone's defence and opened cracks in the case against him. Soon afterwards the world of sport was rocked when Ecclestone settled the case on 5 August 2014 and avoided jail by paying $100m, with $99m going to the German treasury and $1m to a German children's hospice charity. In a world exclusive, we broke the news about the staggering size of the settlement on the cover of the *Independent* sports section and revealed that Ecclestone did not initiate the discussion about it. 'The prosecutors said, "Do we want to have a chat about it?"'

We can now reveal that, even faced with the threat of a jail sentence, Ecclestone couldn't resist haggling and, as he told us, 'They wanted €150m. I offered $100 million [around €75m]. That's what I agreed with them.'

Ecclestone preserved his innocence and his criminal record remained clear, as in the eyes of the law someone is innocent until proven guilty. What's more, in his concluding remarks, Noll said that 'the charges could not, in important areas, be substantiated'. In a statement, the court added that 'prosecution of the accused due to bribery is not probable as things stand'. It claimed that after hearing the evidence so far, 'the court did not consider a conviction overwhelmingly likely from the present point of view'.

It was a staggering about–turn, as Noll had previously ruled that Gribkowsky had received a bribe from Ecclestone. And given that the judge admitted it wasn't likely that Ecclestone would be convicted, it raised the question of why the prosecutors demanded $100m from him to settle.

'The prosecutors didn't know the judge was going to come up with that [conclusion],' Ecclestone explained. The judge's comments were made after the $100m had been agreed, so Ecclestone had been driven into a corner. He later declared that he was 'a bit of an idiot' for paying the settlement and it clearly preyed on his mind. His 2014 Christmas card showed a snowy street scene in Munich with a highwayman atop a horse pointing a gun at a cartoon version of Ecclestone. The billion-aire is seen reluctantly handing over a swag bag with '$100 million' written on it while the bandit declares, 'This is not a robbery. I am collecting for the Bavarian state.'

Despite shelling out a staggering sum, the savvy CEO still didn't end up paying cash from his pocket. The $100m was more than covered by the proceeds Ecclestone received from selling some of his Delta Topco shares, going from just over 5 per cent to 3.3 per cent by 2016. With the shadow of Gribkowsky finally lifted, it was time for him to focus all his attentions on F1 again. The bitter irony was that, having demonstrated in court that he hadn't bribed Gribkowsky to sell to CVC in order to remain F1's boss, his downfall would come from CVC selling to a company that would show him the door.

20

EXIT STRATEGIES

Aside from the Gribkowsky affair, CVC's decade in control of F1 had been a resounding success. By 2015 the sport's revenues totalled $1,697m, a 58.5 per cent increase on the $1,071m generated in 2006, the private equity firm's first year in charge.

Freed from the constraints placed upon him by the banks, Ecclestone had done a sterling job. He gave the biggest boost to race hosting fees, which accelerated from a total of just $296.5m in 2006 to a record $599.1m in 2015, overtaking broadcast rights as F1's biggest revenue stream. Over the previous two seasons, Ecclestone had added races in Russia, Austria and Mexico, while Azerbaijan was set to debut in 2016. The US had returned to the calendar in 2012 with a brand-new venue in Texas called Circuit of the Americas. Its inaugural race-day crowd hit 117,429, showing that the Indianapolis fiasco was finally in F1's rear-view mirror. This success had come at the cost of some traditional venues: France lost its race in 2008 and Germany was off the calendar for 2015.

Sponsorship was another area of growth and, since CVC took over the business from APM, Ecclestone had transformed the landscape. A decade prior, most of the championship's sponsorships had been straight-forward trackside advertising or race title deals. These are agreements to sponsor a specific race, with branding and hospitality at the track being the biggest benefits. However, F1 also has global partners that receive trackside and race title packages at multiple races as well as other benefits, including the right to use the F1 name and logo in their advertising and product placement such as supplying champagne or the safety car.

In 2006, 23 individual race sponsors contributed an estimated 75 per cent of F1's $190m sponsorship revenues, with just five global partners generating the rest. By 2015 that had reversed with only 11 single-race sponsors, mostly race title partners, contributing just over a quarter of the sport's sponsorship revenues. The majority of the $244.4m sponsorship haul came from the ten global partners, which included the likes of Rolex, Emirates and UBS. As the global partners get trackside advertising and race title sponsorship packages in their deals, it leaves little room for one-off advertisers.

There had also been a change to the broadcast rights model driven by the dawn of the digital age. A report from Accenture found that world-wide sports viewership on TV dropped 10 per cent between 2014 and 2015 as audiences moved to newer media. The decline meant that free-to-air coverage was no longer as important to F1, as it could no longer deliver the same big audience numbers, so Ecclestone was happy to sacrifice existing broadcast partners in favour of pay-TV broadcasters, such as Sky Sports, which had even fewer viewers but bigger budgets. It meant that broadcast revenues were on the up ($546.5m in 2015 compared to $395m in 2006), even though audiences were down. In 2016, F1 recorded a global TV audience of 390 million unique viewers, a drop of more than a third from its high of 600 million in 2008.

Ecclestone, however, was doing little to engage the online audience, perhaps still burned by his digital TV failure. F1's digital media offering was vastly underdeveloped compared to other major sports; in 2015, a company it set up to handle this had revenue of just $5.6m. Only 13 per cent of users of the F1.com website were under 25.

This was symptomatic of Ecclestone's strategy, which was focused on attracting high-earning older fans who appealed to the sport's biggest-spending sponsors. In late 2014, he even claimed that youngsters were of no value to F1. 'I'm not interested in tweeting, Facebook and whatever this nonsense is,' said Ecclestone in an explosive interview with *Campaign Asia-Pacific*. 'I tried to find out but in any case I'm too old-fashioned. I couldn't see any value in it. And, I don't know what the so-called "young generation" of today really wants. What is it?' Asked why he thought there was no value in attracting a young audience, Ecclestone said, 'Young kids will see the Rolex brand, but are they going to go and buy one? They can't afford it. Or our other sponsor, UBS – these kids don't care about banking. They haven't got enough money to put in the bloody banks anyway.'

Not everyone was happy with the strategy. The teams' pitches to sponsors heavily depended on large TV audiences to attract brands. While F1's global partners were looking to access a smaller group of high-net-worth enthusiasts, many team sponsors simply wanted to get their logos in front of as many people as possible. Between 2006 and 2015, external team sponsorship fell from an estimated $984m to only $795m, while sponsorship from team owners plummeted from $1.5bn to $479m. Teams now shared in the growth of the sport's revenues through their prize money, which came to around 63 per cent of F1's underlying profits, but a rise from $185.7m to $903.8m over the same period was not enough to cover the deficit.

Zak Brown, then the boss of leading sponsorship agency JMI, told *Reuters* in 2015 that the sponsorship economy 'is very much down in Formula One. That's a fact – just look at the cars . . . Attendance is down, TV ratings are down, car count is struggling.' He laid some of the blame on the mix of races: 'Some of the new markets, Mexico, are fantastic. Some of the other markets that are new, less so . . . There is speculation of a third race in the Middle East. How can you have three races there and none in Germany? I think the two they have are outstanding and contribute a lot to the sport but a third? I don't think the market can support that.'

The wider societal trend may not have been the only reason for dwindling TV audiences. Between 2010 and 2013, Red Bull Racing's Sebastian Vettel had taken four consecutive championships and the team won more than half of all races. New technical regulations in 2014 introduced a greener engine and other features that were intended to shake up the order, but they were only partly successful. Red Bull's reign finally came to an end, but competition was actually reduced as Mercedes won a huge 84 per cent of the races in 2014 and 2015.

Against this backdrop, F1's revenues fell in 2015 for the first time since CVC had bought the sport. Whether it was caused by Ecclestone's attention being sapped by the court case, companies being cautious to deal with the controversial boss, or the tumbling audiences, it was a warning sign. Although the drop was tiny in percentage terms at less than $5m, it indicated that it might be time for CVC to sell up.

Ecclestone still had some issues closer to home to deal with. Just when he thought that his problems were behind him he received a letter from HMRC on 17 December 2014 with a demand for payment that was large, even by his standards. Despite all his efforts at keeping Gribkowsky's claims from the attention of the taxman, it had heard chapter and verse about them in court and issued a demand for a cool £1bn, comprising

£674m of tax and £349m of interest, with the possibility of penalty charges on top.

It was calculated on 15 years of income earned by the trust stretching back to the tax year ending 5 April 1995 when Valper Holdings, the first offshore ultimate parent company of F1's rights holder, was founded.

HMRC told Ecclestone that it had torn up its 2008 settlement agreement, arguing that it had been 'misled and relied on representations that were false'. This was reflected in a letter sent to Slavica the day before, which added that HMRC was 'misled into entering the settlement agreement and that it was induced to do so by misleading express and implied statements made by you and Mr Ecclestone'. HMRC believed that Ecclestone steered the payments from Bambino to Gribkowsky, so he should have paid tax on the money.

It is easy to see where HMRC was coming from. Filings show that 'Ecclestone had told Mr Mullens of the likely need to make a substantial payment to Gribkowsky from the Bambino Settlement'. Furthermore, when Ecclestone's share of the money reached Gribkowsky in 2007, he underpaid the banker by a similar sum to the amount that Bambino overpaid him.

On the other hand, it was harder to understand HMRC's other claims. It suggested that the commission Ecclestone received from Bambino on the sale to CVC was also evidence that he could influence or benefit from the trust. However, Ecclestone also received a commission from BayernLB, so HMRC's argument would mean that he also had some kind of hold over the bank, which was clearly absurd.

Ecclestone strongly disputed HMRC's claims and on 22 April 2015 began legal proceedings against it, saying that the 2008 settlement agreement was binding. 'We are effectively suing them for breach of contract,' he told us in an interview for the *Independent*. Little did he know then that it would not be resolved until December 2023.

Ecclestone wasn't the only F1 luminary who was facing a troubled time.

After Mercedes bought Brawn GP it parted ways with McLaren, which signed a disastrous engine deal with Honda. The Japanese manufacturer had returned to the sport as a supplier but failed to master the change in F1's engine regulations in 2014 that involved switching the previous 2.4-litre V8s for 1.6-litre V6 turbos. It led to McLaren slipping to an all-time low of ninth in the championship in 2015 and hampered the team's efforts to find a title sponsor after the exit of telecoms firm Vodafone at the end of 2013, which left a $75m hole in its budget.

Ron Dennis was still in the driving seat as the chairman and CEO of McLaren Group, but he was on borrowed time given the team's performance. Dennis owned 25 per cent of McLaren but reportedly wanted to take control with Chinese investors. In response, his co-shareholders, Mansour Ojjeh and Bahrain's Mumtalakat wealth fund, suspended him pending the expiration of his contract in January 2017. Dennis failed in an attempt to block the suspension, so he exited in November 2016 after 36 years in F1. McLaren also ditched Honda engines from 2018; ironically, they would go on to power Max Verstappen's Red Bull to successive championships from 2021.

Dennis's departure left Ecclestone and Frank Williams as the last remaining signatories to the original Concorde Agreement in 1981. Williams, knighted in 1999 for services to the motorsport industry, was one of the world's longest-living quadriplegics following an accident on the roads of southern France in 1986. He had announced in 2012 he would step down from the board of his eponymous F1 team, though he remained team principal in name with his daughter Claire taking a hands-on role as his deputy. She stayed in the job until the squad was sold to Dorilton Capital in 2020 as the coronavirus pandemic gathered pace.

Luca di Montezemolo was also out, having been replaced as president and chairman of Ferrari in 2014, though he remained on the F1 board as a non-executive director until 2017. It was clear that a new era of F1 was approaching, but the biggest change was yet to come.

The start of the 2016 season did little to rev up F1's lagging audience. Nico Rosberg's Mercedes won the first four races and a new elimination-style qualifying format designed to shake up the order was dropped after just two rounds following widespread criticism. The Chinese Grand Prix was the second time in nine races that all cars finished the race – a result that had previously been so rare it had only happened on four occasions in the history of F1 until then.

The lack of action didn't deter Liberty Media, which was still chasing a deal with the sport. In late May, Liberty sent a delegation to the Monaco Grand Prix, headed by media executive Chase Carey, where they met Ecclestone for dinner in a bid to get a firmer grasp of how F1 operates.

Liberty wasn't the only company in the running. Other bids reportedly came from Sky, Qatar Sports Investments – the majority shareholder in football club Paris Saint-Germain – and the private equity group Silver Lake in partnership with US talent agency WME-IMG. However, the companies that didn't make it to the starting grid were far more interesting.

According to the *FT*, among the approaches rejected was one from Jim Durkin, former CEO of Cenkos Securities, a UK-based brokerage that was attempting to build a consortium from interested parties in the City of London. Also involved was Ecclestone's former private investigator Dean Attew, who said that the plan was to create a 'British bid with British money'. It was not to be. The newspaper claimed that 'after the consortium insisted that Mr Ecclestone would play a continuing management role, CVC did not entertain further discussions'. It was not an isolated occurrence.

In June 2015 *Reuters* reported that CVC received another offer from RSE Ventures, the investment vehicle of Miami Dolphins NFL team owner Stephen Ross. Ecclestone reportedly met Ross in London and said, 'I like him, he is one of us. He can help us and I would be happy to have him [as F1's owner].' Crucially, a source revealed to *Reuters* that if RSE acquired F1, 'Ecclestone would stay on to lead the racing side of the business.'

Initially it didn't appear that this bid would skid off track like the one driven by Durkin, as the *FT* reported that Ross and CVC had 'shaken hands', according to two people close to the negotiations. 'We are well along the way,' said one member of Ross's consortium. However, in the end, just like Durkin's deal, it too didn't get off the starting grid as CVC dropped the bombshell on 7 September 2016 that it had agreed to sell F1 to Liberty.

The sale gave F1 an enterprise value of $8bn, which was calculated by deducting the company's $624.4m of cash from its $4.1bn of bank borrowings and adding it to the company's equity value of $4.6bn. The latter was the amount that Liberty actually paid to buy F1. It was bad news for Ecclestone. It is unknown why CVC would have walked away from a deal with a buyer that wanted to retain Ecclestone, as the *FT* claimed. The private equity firm had stood by him through thick and thin so an about-turn could suggest that it was payback for the F1 boss keeping shtum about his side deals with BayernLB and Gribkowsky that led to the private equity firm being dragged into court. However, there is no evidence for that and such a strategy could have ended up in the pits.

If Ross did indeed shake hands with CVC, as the *FT* claimed, then he could have pursued the private equity firm through the courts to get it to stand by its word. The verdict of the litigation between Twitter and Elon Musk shows that courts can force even the richest business magnates to honour their commitments.

Accordingly, Ross could have driven Liberty's deal off the road, but instead he has become one of its most valuable partners. No sooner had Liberty taken the wheel of F1 than it proposed partnering with him on a Grand Prix in Miami and doggedly pursued the plan despite fierce local opposition. Indeed, such was Liberty's support for Ross that the race debuted in 2022 on a specially created course through the parking area and perimeter roads of the Hard Rock Stadium – home to his beloved Miami Dolphins.

Keeping Ross sweet suited CVC down to the ground. The private equity firm got an estimated $2.1bn from Liberty, giving it a total of $6.4bn from F1 – a staggering 563 per cent return on investment, as CVC only put in $965.6m when it bought F1 in a leveraged buyout in 2006.

Perhaps the luckiest man in the deal was Chase Carey, the moustachioed media executive whose first taste of F1 had been from the luxurious viewing point of a yacht in the Monaco harbour. He replaced Ecclestone's friend Peter Brabeck-Letmathe as chairman of Delta Topco. Liberty's Irish-American billionaire chairman John Malone chose Carey because of his two decades of experience on the board of Rupert Murdoch's News Corporation, but it is likely this would have been a roadblock for him had Mosley still been at the helm of the FIA.

During Carey's time at News Corp he was the driving force behind the emergence of the Fox News Channel and he remained a director of its parent company Fox Corporation even after he joined F1. Carey was also involved in the successful launch of Fox Sports in 1994 and helped to broker a $1.6bn deal between the network and the NFL. However, he had never even been to an F1 race before Monaco and Liberty's only major involvement with sports was through its ownership of the Atlanta Braves baseball team. Its most well-known investments were travel booking website Tripadvisor, event organiser Live Nation and radio station SiriusXM.

Carey's first F1 race as chairman was just two weeks after his appointment, when he visited the Singapore Grand Prix and was candid about his inexperience. He told Mercedes team boss Toto Wolff that 'I will be asking more questions at the beginning.' Likewise, Liberty's CEO Greg Maffei said in a conference call, 'I have got to know the business better. I certainly didn't know it at all when we started this process.' There could be good reason why he was thrust into this in a whirlwind. According to the *FT*, one of the bidders for F1 was Chinese e-commerce group Alibaba, but it walked away when it was told that it would have had to buy the business effectively blindfolded. The *FT* explained that 'from the outset, all bidders were told by CVC that access to the "black box" – the data containing F1's broadcast contracts and monetary awards for the racing teams – would only be shared at the very end of the sale process.' Allegedly, CVC feared that the information could be used to set up a rival racing series, even though there had been no successful precedent for this.

A source close to the sale process told the newspaper that this restriction 'made the sale extraordinary', because 'people were buying a trophy asset with very little information'. The *FT* revealed that not only did Liberty only get access to F1's key information right at the end of the process but, remarkably, it had just one day to review it and was told that another buyer – Hellman & Friedman – was ready to step in if it walked away.

If the *FT* was right about this then Liberty was essentially against the clock even though it had been in contact with CVC about buying F1 for three years. 'I don't think they really know what they have bought,' Ecclestone told the *FT*. 'Only because nobody would let them know.'

That said, Liberty structured the F1 takeover in such a way that its outlay couldn't have been much lower. The \$4.6bn was offered to F1's owners in three components. They were: cash; shares in Liberty's Nasdaq-listed 'FWONK' stock, which tracks the performance of F1; and loan notes that could be exchanged for shares in the tracking stock.

Trackers are an unusual type of stock that enable a company to float on a stock exchange without the owners actually selling any of their shares. In F1's case, the stocks track the performance of F1, but Liberty itself is not floated. Crucially, the tracking stock is not a separate legal entity and, although this may sound like a technicality from the pages of business management course books, it is far from it. It means that owners of the F1 shares have no direct claim to its assets. So although they may think they are getting a piece of F1 itself this is not the case. In fact, they aren't even getting shares in a company at all, and they have no direct claim on F1's commercial rights, its logos or any other intangible assets. Likewise, any of Delta Topco's tangible assets, such as its high-tech broadcasting equipment and the company jet, are all far beyond the grasp of the tracking stock owners, no matter how many of the shares they own.

The scheme must surely have made Ecclestone envious. If he had thought of using it he could have floated F1 without losing control of the company.

Liberty's purchase of Delta Topco took place in two stages. First, on 7 September 2016, when Liberty announced the deal, it paid $746m in cash for an 18.7 per cent stake in Delta Topco and agreed to buy a further 0.4 per cent the following month. The second step came on 23 January 2017 when Liberty issued the tracking shares and loan notes and paid the remaining cash to the sellers of Delta Topco, giving it 100 per cent of the company. It was mostly what is known as other people's money.

For the first stage, Liberty raised $445m by offering debentures that could be converted into Time Warner shares that it owned. Essentially it used its Time Warner shares to borrow $445m, meaning that when the debentures are exchanged, the holder gets stock, cash or a mixture of both and, in the meantime, interest accrues. The remaining $301m came from Liberty's cash in the bank. It didn't have to put its hands in its pockets again.

After paying F1's owners $746m, Liberty still had to raise around $3.8bn to give them the $4.6bn that it had promised. Liberty issued 137 million shares to offer F1's owners at the pre-takeover announcement price of $21.26 each. That came to $2.9bn and Liberty also offered F1's owners a further $351m of loan notes that could be exchanged for shares in the tracking stock. This gave a total of $3.25bn and the remainder was covered by one of Liberty's subsidiaries. It had up to $500m available having borrowed the money using its 34 per cent stake in Live Nation as collateral.

However, after F1's sellers received the $746m they decided that they wanted more cash rather than shares. Accordingly, Liberty sold 62 million of the shares to seven investment funds, thereby raising $1.5bn as they were bought at a price of $25.

In order to further boost the sellers' cash haul, on 20 January 2017 Liberty announced that it would pay them $400m in order to buy 19 million of the FWONK shares it had initially offered them. Liberty took out yet more debt to fund this purchase and put the 19 million shares into its treasury before attempting to recoup its investment by offering them to F1's ten teams. It was a steal, as the teams were offered the shares at the pre-takeover announcement price of $21.26 each, even though the stock was trading at around $30 when Liberty announced that it would buy it.

Nevertheless, the teams gave it the red light. If Liberty had read the F1 history books it would have known that the teams have no interest in owning the sport, regardless of how much they say they do or how much money it would make them. If the teams had bought the shares from Liberty and sold them at the start of 2025 they would have made a $1.3bn profit. Instead, the shares slipped through their fingers and Liberty retired the 19 million shares in July 2017.

The first stage and the subsequent transactions left the sellers of Delta Topco with $2.65bn of cash and 56 million shares in FWONK, worth $1.2bn at the September price of $21.26 a share. The sellers still needed around $700m to hit the $4.6bn purchase price, so on 20 January 2017 Liberty's subsidiary drew $350m from the loan secured on its Live Nation stake. That left $351m, which came from the loan notes that could be exchanged for shares in the tracking stock.

So, to summarise, in order to buy Delta Topco, Liberty borrowed $445m using its Time Warner shares, $350m using its Live Nation shares and it got a further $400m of debt. In addition, the seven funds paid the sellers of Delta Topco $1.55bn for 62 million shares, leaving them with 56 million shares, which were worth $1.2bn when the F1 takeover was announced. Liberty also offered the sellers $351m in loan notes exchangeable for cash or FWONK shares. That gives $4.3bn, and then comes the $301m in cash paid by Liberty to bring the total to $4.6bn. This is exactly what was needed as it was Delta Topco's equity value.

When Liberty took the wheel of F1 it signalled its intention to keep Ecclestone on for at least the remaining three years of his contract. However, Chase Carey quickly came to the realisation that his seat-of-the-pants approach wasn't in line with the slick corporate future that Liberty had in mind for F1.

Push finally came to shove on the morning of 23 January 2017 when Carey invited Ecclestone to a meeting and told him that he wanted his job. As Ecclestone explained on the *Lucky* docuseries, 'I said, "Well, you've bought the car, you might as well drive it." And then a lawyer that had been with me for years appeared with a bit of paper and they said, "This is saying you're going to leave."'

With Liberty and Carey in the driving seat, Ecclestone had run out of options. He simply grabbed a pen to sign the document and that was that. He was given the honorary title of 'chairman emeritus', but he had no more say in the running of the sport that he had built up for almost four decades.

He went quietly, but his actions gave away his true feelings. Like the other Delta Topco shareholders, Ecclestone was handed tracking stock and cash in return for his shares. However, despite being a dyed-in-the-wool trader, Ecclestone sold around half of his shares at the end of January, just days after he got them, and offloaded more in the next few months. Had he held on to them until the start of 2025 he would have made three times as much money.

For someone who knew so much about F1 you might have expected Ecclestone to sell his shares on a high, but it looks like he wanted to wash his hands of them in a show of disgust at the way he had been treated by Liberty. Perhaps surprisingly, Sorrell too sold around half of his shares at the same time, suggesting that, despite all their spats, he believed that F1 would not thrive without Ecclestone at the wheel.

In an interview with the *Daily Telegraph* in March 2023 Ecclestone acknowledged for the first time that he felt disrespected by the way Carey dropped him. 'I like things to be done fairly. What was wrong was the way it was presented. It would have been nice for him to have sat down and said, "Bernie, are you happy continuing, because this is the sort of thing I'd like to do." These guys wanted me to leave. They thought, "We Americans, for sure we can do a better job than he has."' He said that his new title 'was all about how they could justify getting me out'.

The F1 world was waiting for him to retaliate but the fightback never came. In the wake of the sale we were astonished by how guarded Ecclestone was about Liberty. He even went as far as to avoid events where he knew media would be present so that he didn't have to comment on the new owners of the company he founded back in 1981.

For someone who, figuratively speaking, knew where all the bodies were buried, Ecclestone's silence seemed extraordinary. Liberty had to pay a pretty penny as a penalty for breaking Ecclestone's contract, and it wouldn't be a surprise if this put them in the driving seat. That is because it is customary for these kind of agreements to contain a non-disparagement clause, preventing the signatory from criticising the company they are leaving.

After decades of sparring over F1's regulations, there was no love lost between Ecclestone and Liberty's new motorsport boss Ross Brawn, who had been the architect of eight titles for Benetton, Ferrari and his eponymous team. He was well aware that Ecclestone knew all the ins and outs of the business and he was in pole position to advise Liberty that an agreement with the former F1 boss had to be watertight.

The last major deal that Ecclestone signed for F1 was on 5 December 2016 when he arranged a five-year contract for the return of the French Grand Prix, ironically at the trust's Paul Ricard circuit. The annual fee came to an estimated $20m, although none of this came from the trust; the circuit was merely a hired venue for the promoter, which was funded by the local government.

Ecclestone would not be in the driving seat to see the fruits of either that or of his biggest ever deal, the record-breaking contract with Sky Sports for the UK TV rights that he had signed in March 2016. At a reported $225m a year it came to more than $1.3bn over the course of the entire contract, but it would be Liberty that reaped the benefits. In 2019 when the contract began, F1's TV rights revenues leapt by 26 per cent to $762.8m.

The full extent of Ecclestone's impact on F1 is shown through the deals he did, signing contracts worth more than $27bn during his time at the wheel of the series. It is believed to be more than any other individual has raised in the history of professional sport.

Most global sports series have senior managers who are each responsible for securing and signing new deals in sectors such as sponsorship, television and corporate hospitality. F1 under Ecclestone was the exception as he was directly in charge of bringing in new business across all of its major revenue streams. Until Liberty came along, the series had no chief marketing officer or even a press officer.

Most of what he achieved would not have been possible if not for the first Concorde Agreement signed in 1981. Second in importance was

Mosley's decision to award the F1 rights directly to Ecclestone's companies from 1997, which led to the 100-year rights agreement in 2001. It changed the power dynamics of the sport, but angered the teams as a result. Through making the sport saleable to shareholders who were beyond his control, however, it ultimately brought about Ecclestone's downfall.

The manoeuvres left his family more than $4.6bn richer, but when he exited in January 2017 many observers thought he might have been happier if he was still at the wheel.

PART 5
THE ENTERTAINMENT ERA

21

TAKING LIBERTIES

The 2017 United States Grand Prix was the sixth to be held at the Circuit of the Americas in Texas, but it was the first under F1's new American owners.

Determined to make an impact on their coveted home market, Liberty invited former president Bill Clinton to hand out the winner's trophy. But perhaps the most Americanised element of the race was the inclusion of Michael Buffer, the legendary boxing announcer who coined the phrase 'Let's get ready to rumble', to introduce the drivers during the pre-race build-up.

'Ladies and gentlemen, it's time to unleash the greatest racing spectacle on the planet,' began Buffer. The drivers emerged from a smoky doorway onto a red carpet, surrounded by cheerleaders, while Buffer bigged up their achievements and gave them nicknames, such as 'Ricky Rocket' Daniel Ricciardo and 'The Heartbreaker' Lance Stroll.

Some of the drivers, including reigning champion Lewis Hamilton, were smitten. 'That is the best start to a Grand Prix that I have seen,' he enthused. 'It was kind of cool coming out with the smoke and everything and I didn't know where I was going. There were hot ladies on the walkway, so that was exciting, and there was a mixture of sports excitement, sex appeal there. That is what has been missing for a long time really.' Ricciardo was emphatic: 'I love it.'

Others weren't so sure. Former champion Jenson Button tweeted a blushing emoji, while Fernando Alonso described the display as a 'bad joke'. Reaction among fans was equally divided. Red Bull team boss Christian Horner summed up the feelings of many when he said, 'It's America, isn't it? We're under new ownership now and we have to be prepared to try new things.' However, he added, 'I can't see that working well at Silverstone.'

265

The main issue was that the pizazz of the intros did little to disguise a bigger problem – the lack of competition on track. Mercedes wrapped up its fourth constructors' championship in a row in Texas, four races before the end of the season, despite a start to the year that indicated Ferrari might pull off a miracle. Liberty had a steep incline to climb if it was going to make F1 appeal to American fans, but the potential for expansion into new markets certainly wasn't the only thing that had attracted it to the sport.

Investigative journalists usually have to go to great lengths to get company bosses to make controversial comments on the record. Undercover filming is often the order of the day, but none of that was needed to expose Liberty's intentions.

Within a matter of days of buying the sport, executives from the investment firm began publicly praising the way that F1 avoids paying money that would otherwise fund critical services in the UK. It was an astonishing admission for a company that prides itself on its squeaky-clean corporate image. The approbation revved up in September 2016 on the same day that Liberty announced the takeover. Its then chief tax officer Albert Rosenthaler told analysts that 'from a tax standpoint, F1 has done a wonderful job in terms of creating a structure that is extremely tax efficient. We will be stepping into that structure.'

Two months later, in an earnings call with analysts, Liberty's chief executive Greg Maffei stressed that F1 has 'an attractive low tax rate structure. He hammered the point home two days later, at Liberty's 2016 Investor Day Presentation, saying that F1 has 'a very tax-efficient structure'. This time he wasn't a lone voice. 'It's a great structure. It's a great tax arrangement,' said Liberty's billionaire chairman John Malone. He even eulogised about the tax scheme in an interview with the TV channel CNBC when he said that on being informed about the F1 acquisition he exclaimed, 'Eureka! And even the tax structure is brilliant.' There was good reason for his elation.

In November 2016 we laid bare in a report for ITV News how little tax F1 pays. Analysis of more than a hundred sets of company accounts showed that between 2006 and 2015 its annual corporation-tax rate came to an average of approximately 2 per cent despite the standard rate being around 25.8 per cent. During the period, F1 paid just $122.9m of tax on $5bn of profits. In 2015 alone its parent company Delta Topco made a

$463.6m profit on $1.7bn of revenue, with the vast majority of this received by its subsidiaries in the UK. However, it only paid $6.5m of tax thanks to what is known as an Advance Thin Capitalisation Agreement (ATCA) with HMRC, as we had revealed on the cover of the *Independent* years earlier.

The ATCA allowed F1 to use the interest on internal loans to generate losses on paper and reduce its tax bill. To recap, the UK-based companies, which generate the lion's share of F1's profit, borrowed billions from their offshore counterparts and the interest on these loans forced them into loss, meaning that they didn't need to pay tax. Their profit was essentially switched for the interest payments, which ended up in F1's offshore companies where they could be paid out with no tax deducted.

If F1 had been charged at the standard rate it would have had to pay at least $500m more in corporation tax over the decade to 2015, so it is little wonder that Liberty thought this was a winning formula.

As CVC, and the majority of F1's other shareholders, were based offshore, HMRC received little in capital gains tax from the proceeds of the blockbuster sale to Liberty.

'Cases like these leave taxpayers baffled as people struggle to make sense of our insanely complicated tax system,' said John O'Connell, chief executive of the TaxPayers' Alliance. 'Politicians talk the talk but have completely failed to address the problems that arise from a complex tax code, including the loss of people's faith in the system.'

The UK's Labour Party seized on the opportunity to say it was looking out for the man on the street and referred to F1 in its 2017 manifesto as an example of corporate greed. Labour claimed that the UK government could raise between £0.5bn and £1bn in revenue from 'an investigation of ATCAs and clampdown on their use'. It added that 'Formula One had generated significant losses by making huge loans between different groups, charged at exceptional (10 per cent) rates of interest, and which were allowed as a loss under an existing ATCA with HMRC. Had the tax been levied at the more usual level, Formula One would have been liable for a further £400 million [$517 million].' Labour's criticism didn't fall on deaf ears.

In April 2017, seven months after Liberty agreed to buy F1, the UK government introduced a cap on the amount of interest on intra-group loans that could be used to offset tax. The limit was set at 30 per cent of taxable profits, which was far lower than the 90.1 per cent F1 was utilising at the time and a long way off its 127 per cent peak. F1 company documents had a bleak outlook and stated that 'the new rules could reduce significantly the amount of Formula 1's interest expense that qualifies as tax deductible. These changes could adversely affect Formula 1's financial results and position.'

Liberty was left with little choice but to restructure the tangled web of F1 companies.

This involved running Delta Topco and other offshore companies in the F1 group from the UK, which was met with approval from the taxman. However, despite the changes to the law, F1 still paid an extremely low rate of tax in 2017. According to Liberty's chief financial officer Mark Carleton, it was approximately 2 per cent due to what he referred to as 'one-time items and charges'. One dominated them all.

Documents released by Liberty showed that in 2017 it received a staggering $253m in settlements with tax authorities, which it described as a 'net tax benefit for a settlement reached by Formula 1 with the U.K. tax authorities'. This coincided with the end of F1's ATCA, though it wasn't the end of its tax manoeuvres. Analysis of the latest accounts of F1's key UK-based companies shows that they are still paying interest on loans from their offshore counterparts, with one of the biggest bills borne by SLEC's indirect owner Delta 3 (UK). In 2023 it paid $109.9m in interest on $2.4bn of loans to Luxembourg-based Delta 2, a direct subsidiary of Delta Topco which had a tax bill of just $2,187 on more than $450m of profit.

There is nothing illegal with this structure, as companies are allowed to use interest on intra-group loans to offset up to 30 per cent of their taxable profits and Liberty made the most of this. Indeed, it was one of the reasons F1 was an attractive investment. In many cases the companies also have what are known as tax losses carried forward from when they made a loss in previous years, which can be used to lower their profits in future and thereby reduce their tax bills. However, that's just the start.

In late 2016 Rosenthaler had made the stunning admission that Liberty had purchased F1 'in a way that will permit an efficient repatriation of money back to the US without incremental tax for many, many years'. Company documents show that Liberty itself did not directly acquire Delta Topco. Instead it was bought by a Cayman Islands-based indirect subsidiary that doesn't file publicly available accounts, so it isn't possible to confirm where its funding came from. However, if it received a loan from Liberty the interest on it would need to be repaid. This could be the missing piece of the puzzle, as Liberty is based in the US state of Delaware, where no corporation tax is charged on interest received by companies.

In summary, the profits of some of F1's UK companies are partly wiped out by interest on loans from their offshore counterparts. If this interest is channelled to the Cayman Islands, no tax will be deducted on it as it is a tax haven. From there it could be paid to Liberty in Delaware, where no tax is charged on interest, and all that too would be perfectly legal. Liberty found the perfect partner in Llowarch, the architect of the tax structure that saved CVC more than $500m. That made Llowarch a rich man, as Liberty's acquisition put an estimated $46m equity value on the 1 per cent stake in Delta Topco that he received in 2008.

Liberty was hailed as a breath of fresh air with an almost altruistic approach that some said would save everything, from teams to tracks. However, eulogising about F1's tax avoidance scheme suggested that its driving force was actually no different to F1's previous owners – profit.

Once Liberty had structured the deal in a way that minimised tax and didn't require much of its cash, it went full speed ahead to buy F1 regardless of the roadblocks in its way. Instead of drawing a line under the previous escapades in the sport, Liberty embraced it by paying the FIA $51.6m as a result of approving its takeover of F1.

The money was due under the Concorde Implementation Agreement, which in 2012 had awarded the FIA a 1 per cent stake in Delta Topco for the bargain basement price of just $458,197.34. The contract created the structure for the FIA to receive a huge financial incentive as a result of approving the sale of F1, but CVC didn't pay the money. Liberty did.

Based on the purchase price of $4.6bn, the FIA estimated that its 1 per cent would give it $46,617,547. However, as Liberty paid partly with shares that went up in value, the FIA ended up getting more than this. In 2018 it revealed that it received $26.5m in cash, shares worth $21.6m and convertible bonds that were exchangeable into loan notes and were worth $3.5m. It came to a total of $51.6m, leaving the FIA with a profit of $51.1m after deducting the cost of buying the stake.

Liberty knew that it was paying the regulator of the company it was buying as a direct consequence of it giving the green light to the deal, but it didn't disclose this to its shareholders. However, it didn't hide the fact that the FIA had to approve its takeover. In fact, its initial press release announcing the deal stated that it was subject to the FIA's approval.

In contrast, despite being a public company, Liberty did not reveal in any of its filings that it paid the FIA. When Liberty itemised the Delta Topco shareholders that it would be paying, the FIA wasn't one of them. Its 1 per cent stake fell below the 2.8 per cent cut-off used in Liberty's filings.

There is no suggestion that Liberty breached any obligations by failing to disclose that it was paying the FIA. However, one would expect that a company that professes to be transparent would have wanted to voluntarily disclose such a controversial transaction. Payments to sports regulators came under intense scrutiny in the wake of the FIFA scandal and, although this wasn't the same type of transaction, it still put Liberty in a position where it gave money to a regulator as a result of it approving its purchase of a company. Liberty was well aware of this but chose not to disclose it.

Liberty did, however, disclose that it thought the FIA would give the green light to its purchase, though it didn't say why. On 8 November 2016, Liberty's then-CEO Greg Maffei told analysts that 'Chase Carey and I have met with the FIA, in particular, Jean Todt, the head of the FIA, several times and had good conversations with him. We're proceeding forward with the necessary processes they have for change of control, and I have every reason to believe we'll have a favourable outcome.' Indeed they did.

When the WMSC voted on whether to approve the sale to Liberty on 18 January 2017, it seemed like the odds were stacked against the investment firm. The FIA stood to gain tens of millions of dollars as a direct result of approving the acquisition, which thereby gave it a significant financial interest in the outcome of its own vote.

What's more, just over two weeks before the vote, the FIA had introduced a Code of Ethics, which stated that its representatives 'may not perform their duties in situations involving an existing or potential conflict of interest'. It defined a conflict of interest as a situation where the FIA or its representatives 'has, or appears to have, financial or personal interests that may detract from his ability to perform his duties with integrity and in an independent and diligent manner'. So the FIA did not actually have to be influenced by the money it would make from approving the sale in order for there to be a conflict of interest; it was sufficient if it *appeared* that the FIA may have been influenced by it, and that was clearly the case.

In the words of British sports lawyer Charles Braithwaite, as a result of the FIA owning a stake in F1 that could only be cashed in when it approved the sale of CVC's shares:

> People may question whether the approval was driven by the desire to get the multi-million sale proceeds from the sale of its share; despite the fact that the FIA is the governing body and regulator of Formula One and so one would expect it to be independent and to act in the interests of the sport rather than its own interests. Hence the potential conflict of interest; despite the FIA's own Code of Ethics requiring all FIA Parties (which includes the FIA itself) to endeavour to avoid any conflict of interest.

Despite the hurdles it faced, the FIA didn't let anything get in its way.

The copies of the Concorde Implementation Agreement in circulation revealed that the FIA could only sell its 1 per cent stake if CVC also sold its shares, and this required the FIA's approval. When we discovered this we wrote to WMSC members to ask them several questions: Had they raised this matter with the FIA and, if so, what feedback had they received? Additionally, did they think the member clubs should injunct the FIA's decision on approving the sale of F1 until there was no doubt that there was no conflict of interest?

Instead of responding to the questions, some of the WMSC members asked the FIA what to do. This came to light when a WMSC member at the time forwarded us a letter sent by Jean-Louis Valentin, the FIA's then Secretary General for Sport. On 11 January 2017, Valentin wrote to all WMSC members saying that he was not doing this 'because I believe that there is a risk in members acting against the best interests of the FIA, but because I have been asked by some members what is the correct course of action that should be adopted'.

Rather than leaving it up to the members to decide how to respond to our questions, Valentin advised them what to say. He said, 'As per all WMSC meetings, we will issue a press release at the conclusion of the meeting containing the relevant information and details of all the decisions (as required). I would suggest that this should be the essence of any response.' He added that if the WMSC members received further questions from us they should 'refuse to comment further'.

Stressing this point, Valentin's letter said, 'As is the case with all matters before the World Motor Sport Council, I would expect that no members would make any public comment regarding decisions of this body – this is especially important regarding decisions that have not yet even been brought before the WMSC.' The members did exactly what they were told, as we did not receive any responses to our questions.

In a final note of warning, Valentin's letter said, 'It would be hugely unfortunate if the FIA was to be placed in a difficult situation because of information being circulated "out of turn".' It was highly ironic as although the members heeded this advice, the FIA still found itself in a difficult situation.

Remarkably, the letter was sent just 40 days after the FIA changed its regulations following a report from the consultancy firm Deloitte, which advised it to improve its monitoring processes to ensure that it is free from conflicts of interest.

Jean Todt gave further insight into this in the introduction to the FIA's 2016 Activity Report. 'The FIA requested Deloitte to carry out a compliance analysis to evaluate our organisation with regard to the fight against bribery and corruption,' he explained.

A summary of Deloitte's findings is buried deep in the Activity Report and reveals that although the threat of corruption reversed after the FIA improved its compliance policy, 'residual risks remain'. Deloitte made a number of recommendations to deal with them and the summary states that one was 'the improvement in the monitoring of the independence of certain FIA bodies and of the absence of conflicts of interest'.

The Activity Report said that 'the World Councils and the FIA General Assembly adopted these recommendations in December 2016.' This was confirmed by a spokesperson who said the FIA was 'implementing recommendations made by Deloitte following its compliance analysis that was carried out in 2016, at the request of the FIA, to assist it in reaching its compliance goals. This also included the appointment of a new compliance officer to lead oversight.'

The Deloitte report certainly wasn't directly connected to the vote on the sale of F1, as that took place the year after Deloitte carried out its analysis. The FIA didn't leave anything to chance with it. The first time its 1 per cent stake was mentioned in its public filings was on 18 January

2017, which was after Liberty's stockholders and the WMSC had approved the takeover. The WMSC voted unanimously in its favour, giving the FIA a profit of $51.1m.

The vote sent sparks flying.

Talking to *Pitpass*, Tim Owen QC, a public and criminal lawyer at London's Matrix Chambers, said that 'no regulator exercising quasi-judicial powers can have a financial interest in the very subject matter it is supposed to be regulating as an independent, unbiased body'. Giving further explanation, Owen said, 'Since a case in 1852 about a canal company where it emerged that the Lord Chancellor, Lord Cottenham, had presided over a case despite owning shares in the company, it has been a basic principle of English law that no Judge can sit in a case in which he has a direct financial interest in the outcome. Once a financial or proprietary interest is established, the risk of bias is presumed.' Owen added that the underlying legal principle transcends geographic boundaries and industries. So although judges in a court of law were the subject of his example, it is clear that others in a decision-making position could be at risk of bias if they have vested interests in the subjects they are deciding on. The thrust of Owen's point is that if a regulator has a financial interest in the outcome of a decision it makes it can create the possibility of bias and expose it to accusations of bias even if it has actually acted entirely independently. Not only is this a breach of the law but also the FIA's Code of Ethics.

Owen says there is a presumption of bias rather than giving the benefit of doubt and, testimony to this, after the WMSC vote, former F1 champion turned television pundit Damon Hill tweeted, 'maybe I missed something but if the Liberty deal was not approved, they would not get money?'

The FIA reacted strongly to the criticism. In December 2017 Todt insisted to French newspaper *Le Monde* that 'the payment of the 1 per cent stake did not constitute a conflict of interest, but a way for FOM [Formula One Management] to pay the FIA without dipping into its cash'. The FIA's lawyer, Jean-Pierre Martel, echoed this and said, 'Ecclestone told us: "I have no money, but I will give you 1 per cent of the company."'

The explanation that the stake was a way to reward the FIA without needing cash would be understandable if the 1 per cent had not come with the caveat that it could only be sold when CVC offloaded its stake. This meant that the only way for the FIA to cash it in was to approve the sale of CVC's shares, and that fuelled the conflict of interest.

Ecclestone denied that he was behind the controversial transaction and told *Le Monde*, 'I was not involved in the negotiations on the 1 per cent. It was managed by Donald Mackenzie.' CVC declined to comment, while Liberty claimed that it had been 'transparent and always ready to collaborate fully with the authorities'.

The FIA seemed to think that Liberty's credibility was a defence to the charge of conflict of interest when, in fact, it was nothing of the sort. Todt told *Le Monde* that Liberty 'is a perfectly respectable group and we had no way, even if we wanted to, of blocking the sale'. Not according to Mosley, who, of course, oversaw the introduction of the FIA's approval right and described it as 'almost a complete veto'.

Indeed, Todt's own description of the limits of the FIA's power seems to be at odds with the way he described it six years earlier. In a 2011 interview with *Autosport* magazine he said, 'If one day CVC is deciding that they want to sell the rights they have for the commercial organisation of F1 . . . I need to speak with my people in the FIA to give an agreement about whether they are happy with the people who take over or whether we are not happy.' That sounds very different to his claim in 2017 that the FIA 'had no way, even if we wanted to, of blocking the sale'. The FIA conveniently ignored this in the wake of Liberty announcing its takeover of F1's commercial rights holder (CRH). It reiterated that there was 'no conflict of interest on the part of the FIA' and added that 'The FIA could only have withheld its consent in the event that the change of control would materially alter the ability of the CRH to fulfil its obligations; it is obvious that the taking of control of the Formula One Group by Liberty does not create such a risk.'

Even if this argument stood up to scrutiny it is hard to see how it could be valid because Liberty had not yet approached CVC when the FIA was given the blockbuster incentive for approving the sale in the form of a 1 per cent stake in F1. The FIA had no idea who would buy F1 at the time, but it knew it would get tens of millions of dollars for approving the sale.

In summary, the FIA claimed it was obvious that Liberty deserved to be approved so it would not matter if it had a $51.1m incentive to approve it. There are two fundamental flaws with this.

Firstly, who says it was 'obvious' that Liberty deserved to be approved? The answer is the organisation that stood to gain $51.1m from approving it, and that is at the heart of the conflict of interest. As Owen explained, 'It's no defence to a charge of apparent bias to say, "Oh, don't worry, you can trust me to be fair and independent".'

Secondly, and crucially, the very presence of the financial incentive is what created the risk of bias and that is completely independent of the calibre of the subject of the vote.

'The whole point of the modern law of bias and automatic disqualification from a regulatory or quasi-judicial role is that the relevant body or person must be free of any influence which could prevent the bringing of an objective judgment to bear or which could distort the exercise of judgment,' said Owen. 'A direct – and in this case huge – financial stake in the outcome of a takeover is, on the face of it, the clearest possible evidence of an interest that is fundamentally incompatible with discharging a regulatory function.'

So the FIA's ownership of the stake presented an obstacle to the approval of the sale to Liberty regardless of whether it was actually biased in its favour. That's because the FIA's Code of Ethics prevents even the potential for bias, as it states that the governing body should not perform its duties 'in situations involving an existing or potential conflict of interest'.

Liberty should surely have examined the FIA's Code of Ethics as part of its due diligence process, so it should have known that it stood in the way of the takeover.

In short, Liberty paid more than $50m to the regulator of F1 as a result of it waving through its purchase of the business. Faced with the need to pay the regulator, Liberty could have backed out of the purchase. Instead it embraced the situation and had no explanation for it. On 24 January, the day after the takeover closed, Carey was quizzed about the conflict of interest by Joel Hills, business editor of ITV News. When asked whether he felt uncomfortable with the idea that the FIA stood to make millions from approving the sale, Carey responded, 'No. They owned a percentage. They got a fair value for what they owned.' ITV followed it up by reiterating that the FIA 'were the regulator. They are meant to be at arm's length from the sport and they stand to gain from approving the deal. Isn't that a conflict of interest?' Carey replied, 'No. I think they have regulated the sport from what I have seen. My experience with them is a handful of months. They regulate the sport in a fair and even-handed way.' Carey's response failed to explain why Liberty wasn't concerned about paying the FIA, and it wasn't lost on higher authorities.

One was Anneliese Dodds, who was still seething following the collapse of the teams in her constituency. 'My concerns in relation to Formula One's regulator, the FIA, are purely focused on the conflicts of interest that can arise when the regulator of a particular industry also has a financial stake in that same industry,' she said in a statement, which continued:

> In that situation, the prospect of the regulator making a profit from developments within an industry that it is supposed to be regulating is something which requires close attention. As I see it, there are two key instances where such a conflict of interest could have arisen. The first is the $5m 'signing bonus' that the FIA received from Formula One during the establishment of the sport's 'Strategy Group'. The second and more concerning instance, relates to the FIA's purchase of a 1 per cent stake in Formula One for a cut-price deal of $458,197.34.

She added that 'if I saw the Financial Conduct Authority take a 1 per cent stake in Barclays, I would be incredibly alarmed. Any decision that the FCA took that could have even an indirect impact on Barclays would affect its share price and therefore any current or future financial gain from that stake . . . I would welcome a more detailed outline of the reasoning behind its acceptance of these payments.' Dodds got some of what she was looking for.

The FIA failed to justify the catches attached to its bargain-basement 1 per cent stake in F1 and it was equally unsuccessful at explaining the $5m signing bonus. It was a tough task, as the FIA had taken money from F1 in return for signing a contract that disadvantaged small teams, contributing to several of them going bust.

Referring to these financial benefits, Ecclestone said, 'This is what they wanted in order for them to go along with it. A lot of things happen in business that if you look at it you can't understand why it is allowed to happen.'

The FIA took a different view and said there was no reason why it shouldn't have been allowed. It claimed that one of the purposes of the Concorde Implementation Agreement had been:

. . . to ensure that the FIA be properly remunerated for its regulatory role. Within this agreement, a lump sum payment of $5m was made to the FIA as part of the global consideration received in connection with the renegotiation of the terms of the agreements between the commercial rights holder and the FIA, and of the Concorde Agreement, at that time. Following its approval, the Concorde Implementation Agreement came into force and this sum was paid to the FIA and properly accounted for. No individual received any payment out of this sum.

CVC added that 'the agreement does not breach the bribery act, and any suggestion to the contrary can only be based on a misunderstanding of the facts and is false. We have recently confirmed this with our outside legal advisors. Any suggestion that CVC or Mackenzie was involved in bribery, whether through these arrangements between F1 and the FIA or otherwise, would be baseless and wrong.'

That wasn't the end of the story.

In April 2017 we revealed in a report for ITV News that the UK's Serious Fraud Office (SFO) had begun looking into the Concorde Implementation Agreement after a tip-off from Damian Collins, then-chairman of Parliament's powerful Culture Media and Sport Committee. Collins said he had closely examined the Concorde Implementation Agreement and could find 'no logical explanation' for the deal agreed with the FIA. The SFO's then director David Green replied to him saying that it would 'conduct a thorough examination of the facts in order to determine whether or not there are suspected offences that on reasonable grounds involve serious or complex fraud'.

According to the *New York Times*, this spurred the SFO's counterparts in France to look into the case, but the enquiries ground to a halt.

In order to prove that the WMSC's decision was not independent, investigators were looking for proof that the people who actually approved the sale were aware of the financial benefit it would bring to the FIA. If the FIA had put it to an independent panel that had no knowledge that it stood to make a financial gain from approving the deal, the decision might not have been tainted. It depended on the information given to the WMSC members and that was under lock and key.

The vote was the culmination of five years of twists and turns for CVC. When Ecclestone was charged with bribery in 2013 it had to drop its plans to exit F1 through a float and was left with the option of selling up, which required the FIA's approval. A few days later it signed the Concorde Implementation Agreement, giving the FIA a 1 per cent stake in F1 that could only be cashed in when CVC sold its shares.

CVC didn't leave anything to chance and offered the FIA $5m for signing the contract, which also boosted the F1 group's voting rights while stripping them from the smallest teams. The signing of the contract increased F1's value and the FIA too became ever richer. The contract more than doubled the FIA's annual fees from F1 to $25m and it used the money to create a sport grant programme for the benefit of its member clubs. In 2017 it voted in favour of the sale of F1 to Liberty, giving the FIA a $51.1m profit while CVC banked $2.1bn.

The FIA used the proceeds of the sale of its stake in F1 to create an innovation fund which supports sports, safety and mobility projects including a motorcycle helmet safety rating system and a black box for reporting accident data in junior racing series. The innovation fund came into its own in 2020 when it was used to top up the sport grant programme in order to give member clubs more money to help restart their activities after the pandemic. Thanks to a twist of fate, we found out about the remarkable lengths the FIA went to in order to ensure that the sport grant money reaches its members.

22

CHARITY BEGINS AT HOME

When most people think of a charity, cash-strapped organisations rattling collection boxes come to mind. Not in F1.

Launched in 2001, the FIA Foundation was founded with the $300m that the FIA received for the 100-year rights to F1. The UK-registered road safety charity is independent from F1 and even the FIA itself and is instead controlled by 15 trustees, many of whom are multi-millionaires.

At the time of the sale of F1 to Liberty, the Foundation was run by Lord Robertson, a former secretary general of NATO and secretary of state for defence in the Tony Blair government. Todt sat alongside him on the board of the Foundation and in 2018 the Frenchman was joined by his partner (now wife) Michelle Yeoh. She was also one of several ambassadors of the Foundation and shared in a €150,000 grant covering international travel and participation in advocacy activities. Likewise, the Foundation also provided €750,000 per year to cover the cost of Todt's office in his role as the United Nations Special Envoy for Road Safety.

The donations made by the Foundation aren't to animal homes or orphaned children. Instead, it grants money to causes that promote sustainability as well as motoring and motorsport safety. Although it is entirely separate to the FIA, the two organisations do have some connections.

In 2001, Mosley issued a mandate that the Foundation would cover the cost of FIA projects that are in line with the Foundation's objectives. This link deepened in 2011 when the Foundation began providing an annual grant to the FIA's mobility department so that it could fund a road safety programme, which was also in line with its objectives. Likewise, the FIA's sport grant programme was funded with €1m from the Foundation and €2.75m from its internal funds, which had been boosted by the Concorde Implementation Agreement.

Naturally, when the Foundation handed over its money to the FIA it assumed it would ensure that it would follow its instructions, but this didn't always happen. The Foundation's accounts confirm that in 2019 a technical coding error on its website 'resulted in private board and other administrative papers housed in a private and password-only section of the website being searchable via Google'.

This led to the public being able to access thousands of pages of previously confidential documents, including the mobile numbers, addresses and signatures of all of the trustees; precise details of hundreds of payments to and from the Foundation; extensive correspondence with lawyers and authorities such as the UN; and full minutes of Foundation board meetings.

We found them through a simple Google search and couldn't believe our eyes. The bombshells in the documents included defamatory comments about F1 journalists and allegations that an FIA contractor had stolen from the federation. The documents also revealed that the FIA had used the Foundation's money to pay grants even though it could not assess the effectiveness of the projects they funded.

In March 2015 the Foundation wrote to Ortrud Birk, then head of the FIA's motoring programme, to demand that its 'grant funding is not used to support programmes in either [Syria or Iran]. Further, in the case of Syria, we do not believe that it is possible to organise an effective road safety programme in a country which is in the midst of a civil war.'

It didn't stop the FIA and between 2015 and 2017 €145,965 of the grants it paid to the Syrian Automobile Club (SAC) came from the Foundation's money. This funded motoring initiatives like courses teaching children how to use seatbelts and the organisation of a road safety training course in Beirut for 26 Syrian participants. It was also spent on motorsport projects such as buying timing equipment, helmets and overalls, and training officials. There is no suggestion that sanctions were broken or that the projects which received the funding were illegitimate. Nevertheless, this wasn't the outcome that the Foundation wanted.

At the time, an FIA spokesperson told us that it paid the money to the SAC against the Foundation's wishes as a 'result of miscommunication. The concerns of the FIA Foundation secretariat in relation to grants to sport and mobility organisations in Syria were not addressed to FIA senior management prior to 2017.'

The small matter of a civil war didn't even prevent the FIA from getting the money to its member club. In September 2017 the FIA sent a letter to the Foundation's executive director Saul Billingsley revealing that 'the policies of our regular banking partners' prevented it from paying the money to Syria directly, so it had to send the funds through its member clubs in Saudi Arabia and Kuwait instead.

Minutes of Foundation meetings state that 'the FIA benchmarked its activities against those of similar organisations and had to take a non-political stance. The FIA felt therefore that it could not refuse to fund sport projects in countries like Iran, Syria or Yemen.'

However, the letter from the FIA to Billingsley admitted that 'in the case of Syria, there is the added complication that significant areas of the country remain in an active state of conflict and it is unsafe for travel. Under current conditions the FIA could not contemplate sending its personnel or contractors into the country, making it impossible for us to assess the effectiveness of any project undertaken within the domestic borders of this country.'

The FIA spokesperson claimed that 'all grants made by the FIA were disclosed to the FIA Foundation on an annual basis'. However, the Foundation claimed to have been unaware that its money had ended up in a war zone, as its documents revealed that its grant monitoring procedures 'had failed to pick up the Syrian road safety grants'. Likewise, it did not 'pick up, through our project monitoring, that our grant funding was being used in Syria in conjunction with FIA-financed sport grants'.

The Foundation ultimately put this down to miscommunication within the FIA so did not penalise it. A Foundation spokesperson stressed that it gave the FIA 'written instruction to not make grants from our funds in Syria while the country is undergoing its tragic war. While it was unfortunate that this instruction was not followed, it is clear this was the result of internal miscommunication within the FIA rather than a deliberate action.'

The spokesperson added that when the Foundation discovered what had happened, it halted any further funding to Syria and 'since that issue, we have taken steps, together with the FIA and all of our other grant partners, to improve monitoring, reporting and compliance, and have implemented strict reporting requirements'.

This was highly logical as the Foundation's website leak revealed that it only discovered that its money had been paid into Syria when it carried out an internal review in anticipation of a television report we produced on the payments for ITV News in September 2017. We revealed that money from F1 had ultimately funded the projects in Syria, but it has never come to light that the Foundation was involved. Until now.

Our report spurred the Foundation to look into the source of the payments to Syria and this led to it discovering that the motorsport grants to the SAC had indeed been paid with its money, specifically the Motorsport Safety Grant it gave to the FIA. On 30 November 2017 Billingsley explained in a letter to the Charity Commission, the Foundation's regulator, that 'between 2015 and 2017, the FIA disbursed payments totalling €97,390 to the Kuwait International Automobile Club, such payments being from the proceeds of the Motorsport Safety Grant. The Kuwait IAC then transferred these disbursements to the Syrian AC.' Similarly, over the same period, the FIA paid €48,575 from the Foundation's Mobility Grant to the Saudi Automobile Federation and in turn it too transferred the money to the SAC.

The Foundation's 2017 accounts state that 'the Charity Commission was satisfied that the grants in question met our charitable objectives and did not breach any international sanctions in force against Syrian entities or individuals'. The accounts add that 'changes have been made to grant processes; sanctions compliance has been toughened; and a new member of staff has been appointed, on a consultancy basis, to provide enhanced oversight of motorsport safety projects. The Foundation will not make, or allow partners to make, grants in Syria for the foreseeable future.'

Covering all bases, the FIA carried out a review of its grants. This was done in 2016 by Deloitte, which recommended 'the improvement in the monitoring of the independence of certain FIA bodies and of the absence of conflicts of interest.' Deloitte also suggested 'strengthening of the monitoring of the use of grants awarded by the FIA'. As a belt-and-braces measure, the FIA launched a grants audit process in 2018, four years after its grant programme began. In the wake of our report, the FIA's website also stopped allowing pesky journalists to find out the recipients of recent sport grants. It was followed by a surprise change behind the scenes too. In 2021 the FIA's deputy president for sport, Graham Stoker, ran for the top job after getting endorsement from incumbent president Jean Todt. Historically that has given candidates a fast lane to the top job, but this time Stoker suffered a shock defeat to Ben Sulayem.

After Todt had supported Liberty's takeover, Ecclestone threw his weight behind Ben Sulayem, who subsequently appointed Bernie's wife Fabiana to the FIA as vice president for sport in South America.

For the first time in his career, Ecclestone was in the back seat. He has even remained largely muted about Liberty since his title of chairman emeritus expired in 2020. That year his priorities changed when his son Ace was born; almost one year later, he announced that he had commissioned doctor turned film maker Manish Pandey to make *Lucky*, the eight-part streaming series about his life story.

Pandey is a favourite of the FI media thanks to a film he made about Ayrton Senna, so even outlets that had been highly critical of Ecclestone gushed about *Lucky*. Former colleagues of Ecclestone said that leaving a 'legacy' had become the driving force for the man who once said that when he passes away he 'will disappear and be forgotten within a few months like most people'. He even began planning for a time he won't be around any more. In March 2025, Ecclestone announced that he had sold his beloved collection of classic cars to Dietrich Mateschitz's son Mark. The collection is thought to be the biggest in the world and had a reported record price tag of £500m. It wasn't because he needed the money but because he didn't want his wife Fabiana to be lumbered with the job of finding a home for them when he was no longer around.

In his early nineties he had become perhaps the world's least likely family man. He has made the most of it. Coming full circle, he took Ace to MotoGP and FI races in 2023. The photo on the young boy's pass to the MotoGP race showed him wearing a crash helmet, while he proudly wore a T-shirt with the 'Lucky' logo on it to the Brazilian Grand Prix. It seemed that Ecclestone had finally put his years of drama behind him in favour of a quiet retirement . . . but HMRC would soon have other ideas.

23

THE AMERICAN WAY

Chase Carey never seemed at home in F1 and when he became CEO in 2017 aged 63 it was clear he wasn't going to be at the wheel for as long as his predecessor. He had never run a sports team, let alone a sports series, and it showed. No sooner had he got his feet under the desk than he started eradicating traces of Ecclestone to shape F1 into something new.

Ecclestone was followed out the door by a string of his hand-picked lieutenants with decades of experience in F1 under their belts. Paddock boss Pasquale Lattuneddu, statistics chief David Gillett, logistics director Alan Woollard, sponsorship go-getter Alex Wooff and hospitality head honcho Kate Beavan all left within five years of Liberty taking over.

The few old guard who remained included Sacha Woodward Hill, Duncan Llowarch and F1's media rights director Ian Holmes, though by 2024 Woodward Hill had also departed. They were joined by a suite of new staff filling a roster of newly created roles. F1 got its first chief marketing officer, a global research director and a strategy director. Many of the new hirings had little motorsport experience, so Liberty, Carey and co were no longer the odd ones out. Unsurprisingly it led to a revolving door in some roles, with F1 having no fewer than four commercial directors in the seven years after Liberty took over.

Safe in the knowledge that he was not retaliating, Liberty almost made it a sport to bad-mouth Ecclestone. Referring to the sky-high hosting fees that F1 receives from race organisers, Liberty's CEO Greg Maffei said, 'Bernie's attitude was: how much can I extract from them, how much up front? I heard him call them the victims.' The irony was clearly lost on Maffei that were it not for these high-octane fees, F1 would not have even been on Liberty's radar and he wouldn't have been in a position to criticise Ecclestone.

F1's first commercial chief, Sean Bratches, stepped the rhetoric up a gear by saying that when Liberty bought the company 'there was no business'. He explained that there was 'no digital structure, no market research, nothing. There was no strategy, only Bernie Ecclestone.' It was one heck of an exaggeration given that the year before Liberty bought F1 it had 363 staff on its books.

Carey increased the headcount and quickly outgrew the office underneath Ecclestone's penthouse in London's Knightsbridge district. He moved his new crew into a plush new office in St James's and opened another one in New York amid rumours that he planned to relocate there.

He wanted a new sign to hang over the door and this showed how determined he was to mould F1 into his own image. F1's logo at the time cleverly created the silhouette of a number one between a slanted letter 'F' and the speed lines opposite it. Carey ostensibly wanted to change it because it wasn't easy to stitch onto clothing, but it also happened to be Ecclestone's pride and joy. So much so that the former F1 supremo proudly displayed it on the collar of the crisp white shirt he wore to the races.

Carey turned to Bratches, who was previously the marketing director for ESPN. The sports channel had worked with Wieden+Kennedy, the advertising agency behind Nike's famous 'Just Do It' slogan, and Bratches appointed it to rebrand F1. Wieden+Kennedy was new to F1 and made a schoolboy error. Among the options it produced for Liberty, one resembled Ferrari's iconic lettering while another looked just like the logo for a brand of therapeutic clothing produced by Post-it note maker 3M. Carey couldn't resist it. The logo is formed from a curved stripe with a white line running through the middle followed by a straight line representing the number one. When 3M opposed the trademark application for it F1 had to restrict its use to settle the dispute. Carey was so determined to steer F1 away from the Ecclestone era that he even brushed off criticism of the logo from the drivers. 'I don't think the new one is as iconic,' said Hamilton, while his then Ferrari rival Sebastian Vettel added, 'I liked the old one better.' Fans described it as 'hideous', 'horrible' and being changed 'for the sake of it'.

Contrary to Ecclestone's desire to appeal to an older audience who wanted to purchase Rolex watches and bank with UBS, in a bid to make F1 appeal to a younger audience Carey signed a string of sexy deals, including F1's first ever music playlist, a perfume partner and even an official theme tune written by Brian Tyler, composer of the scores for

Marvel Studios blockbusters *Iron Man 3* and *Thor: The Dark World*. It didn't escape the attention of the teams.

The following month, Ferrari's chairman Sergio Marchionne warned that it would pull out of F1 when the team agreements expired at the end of 2020 if Liberty 'change the sandbox to the point where it becomes an unrecognisable sandbox'. Maffei took it on the chin and made his position clear by saying that F1 'is about selling glamour and parties'. It set the scene for yet another battle between F1 and the teams but, just like before, money could be used to pick them off.

Liberty made it clear from early on that it had four goals for F1's teams. On a sporting level it tasked Ross Brawn with devising new regulations to generate more overtaking opportunities after years of dominance from Mercedes.

It also planned to introduce a $200m fee that any new team would have to pay to join the sport. This would be shared among the existing ten entrants, because a new team could kick one of them out of the running for the core prize fund. No new teams were on the horizon but the fee essentially put a minimum $200m value on the existing squads, which meant that if they went bust in future they wouldn't be worthless or be sold for £1 like so many of their predecessors.

The remaining two goals were designed to stop the teams from getting into that kind of a precarious financial position. The first involved introducing that old chestnut of a budget cap, and the second proposed balancing out the prize money payments by redistributing the bonuses paid to the top three teams. It was music to the ears of Force India and Sauber, which withdrew their complaint to the EC's Competition Commission in January 2018. A joint statement from the two teams stated that Liberty's approach had 'brought a new culture of transparency to the sport and illustrate[d] willingness to debate fundamental issues such as the distribution of the prize fund monies'. It took time to bear fruit.

In 2017 F1's prize money fell by 4.9 per cent to $919m, followed by a $6m drop the following year. After years of complaining about Ecclestone's approach, the teams suddenly realised that his strategy of putting profit first was essential for them, as their prize money is a share of the spoils.

During Liberty's first two years at the wheel, F1 burned up combined operating losses of $51m. This was driven by accelerating costs and largely flat revenue, which fell in 2017 before nudging up by just 2.4 per cent to $1.8bn in 2018 due to limited growth across its four key revenue streams: race hosting fees, broadcast rights, sponsorship and hospitality. The day after Liberty's acquisition got the green light, Carey had been asked by CNBC which stream had the greatest growth potential. In response, he forecast that 'the one that grows the fastest is probably sponsorships. Realistically today, we have a one-man sponsorship operation. There are many categories we're not even selling into. Putting an organisation in place that enables us to execute on that probably is the most immediate impact.' Carey did just that, but it wasn't the quick fix he predicted.

In an interview with the *FT* in November 2018 he admitted that 'the perception was just there are sponsors waiting . . . They were lined up out there and as soon as we had somebody to go call on them, they were just going to sign up. The world's not that simple.'

Between 2016, the year before Liberty's takeover, and 2018, F1's sponsorship revenue only increased by 1.7 per cent to $266.4m; the following year it was just $34.7m higher. Revenue was boosted by Liberty's first major partner deal, signed with Amazon's AWS cloud computing service. Big names such as Saudi oil giant Aramco, Crypto.com and Qatar Airways would follow over the next few years but it was still a far cry from Liberty's sponsorship projections. A source revealed to us that he was told by one of Liberty's F1 appointees at the outset that 'we are going to double the numbers Bernie did within two years'.

Backtracking in 2018, Carey explained that 'the challenge in the sponsorship world is probably tougher than it was a few years ago. For anybody who is not Google or Facebook, the broader advertising world is more challenging . . . I think it is fair to say that the sponsorship world has probably been more challenging than we would have expected it to be a couple of years ago.'

It was a similar story after Liberty launched its F1 TV Pro streaming service in 2018. This was a tremendous gamble because it competed with the broadcasters that generated F1's second-biggest source of revenue. It was positioned as a game-changer, but it was beset with so many technical glitches that Liberty was forced to refund subscribers and decided to re-launch it in 2019.

This time Maffei was more realistic and said that, as F1 only has little more than 20 events a year, its streaming service 'is probably never going

to be as big as some people who have much more tonnage and differenti-
ated unique content'. F1's then US broadcaster NBC Sports dropped F1
months later, reportedly because it didn't want to compete with F1 TV
Pro.

It led to Liberty signing a deal with ESPN for no fee on the condition
that it would show some races on ABC, the closest equivalent to BBC in
the US. The free contract stood in stark contrast to Ecclestone's deal-
making but the continued criticism was all too familiar.

Just a few months after Liberty took the wheel of F1, Maffei said that it
had inherited a business 'with races in places like Baku in Azerbaijan
where they paid us a big race fee but it does nothing to build the long-
term brand and health of the business. Our job is to find partners that
pay us well but also help us to build the product.'

His comments sent shockwaves through the field of F1 race organisers, which pay an average of $33.5m annually for the privilege of hosting
events that attract as few as 40,000 spectators on race day. Arif Rahimov,
the then-organiser of the Azerbaijan Grand Prix, took strong exception
to the opprobrium and told *Reuters* that 'it does upset us, obviously. Mr
Maffei has been involved in F1 for less than half a year.' He added, 'We've
been working on this project for three years now so we have more experience with F1 than them. I think saying something like this is
ignorant.'

Likewise, in 2020, British Grand Prix boss Stuart Pringle complained
to fellow race organisers that the fees from his race were funding F1's
bloated ranks. 'I see that despite the challenging times, the headcount at
F1 continues to grow. I really do struggle with quite what they all do,' he
said in an email, continuing:

They now have as many people delivering 'events' for the marketing
department (I am not quite sure what they are in this context) as we
have in our entire Events Department at Silverstone who deliver 40+
public events per annum including four world championships, three
national championships and the largest historic festival in the world!
This simply reinforces my view that if I am going to drive my people
hard and manage the overhead of our business with a rod of iron, I
have very little enthusiasm for paying for the cost of their inefficient
operation.

Again, Carey stayed the course and gushed about how he envisaged turning each race into the equivalent of the NFL's Super Bowl. He also made no secret of his desire to hold new races in so-called 'destination cities' like Las Vegas, Miami and New York. Miami helped to appease spurned bidder Stephen Ross. Not only did the race end up in the grounds of his Miami Dolphins NFL team stadium, but sources suggest that Ross gets one of the best deals in the business with advertising, hospitality and race hosting rights for less than the latter alone usually cost.

Unlike events under Ecclestone, the race wasn't designed to be a cash cow for Liberty but a marketing vehicle for F1 in the US. It ticked that box, as the inaugural race in 2022 attracted celebrities such as Venus and Serena Williams, Michelle Obama, Paris Hilton, Michael Jordan and David Beckham. Sure, F1 had had big names at races in the past. George Clooney and Brad Pitt promoted *Ocean's Twelve* at the race in Monaco in 2004, Prince Harry was the star guest at the British Grand Prix in 2011 and Taylor Swift played a concert at the US Grand Prix five years later. But few races in F1's history have been hyped as much as Miami in 2022, and it paid off. It was watched by an average of 2.6 million viewers in the US, the country's largest ever live audience for an F1 race. (Ironically, before Miami, the first new race that Liberty signed was in Hanoi, just the kind of far-flung location that Maffei had complained about. That race didn't even get the green light due to political upheaval.)

Soon after Carey took over he set the wheels in motion of a plan to court the US audience. It started with street demonstrations of F1 cars in locations like Chicago and Hollywood. He also loosened the broadcasting rights deals to allow more race footage to be reproduced on social media – another step that Ecclestone wouldn't have sanctioned.

In the end, however, the catalyst for F1 gaining traction in the US was completely outside Liberty's control. It is widely attributed to the launch in 2019 of the Netflix *Drive To Survive* docuseries, which was another deal Ecclestone would likely have scoffed at as it competed with big-spending broadcasters. Ferrari and Mercedes refused to participate in the first season of the show and, contrary to popular belief, it failed to set the world on fire from the start. In fact, by the end of 2019, the wheels appeared to be coming off F1 following six straight years of dominance by Mercedes.

Noted motoring commentator Jeremy Clarkson said he would 'far rather watch [flowers] grow than watch a Formula One race, and I love F1 racing'. He added that he wanted to watch drivers going 'wheel-to-wheel on the last lap of the French Grand Prix and if Ferrari don't like that they can fuck off. In fact, Mercedes can fuck off. They can all fuck off. Let's turn it into a proper sport again and not some health and safety exercise.' He was far from a lone voice.

'I think a lot of the excitement is draining from Formula One,' said Eddie Jordan, the former F1 team owner turned pundit, in November 2019. 'The younger people, the teenagers, 90 per cent of them are looking at their phones all the time. The world has changed.' In fact, the situation was so bleak that there was even talk of Liberty selling up at a discount, with Ecclestone believed to be in the frame.

Anger among the top teams was also revving up at the thought of a budget cap being introduced when the team agreements expired at the end of 2020. Liberty got lucky in 2018 when their chief critic, Ferrari's Sergio Marchionne, unexpectedly passed away, but Mercedes boss Toto Wolff took over the mantle. As the dominant team with one of the biggest budgets, Mercedes had the most to lose from a cap. Wolff steadfastly refused to sign a new Concorde Agreement, arguing that the team had spent so long at the top of F1 that the loss of the bonus payments would hurt it more than most of its rivals. Then came the pandemic.

24

DRIVING TO SURVIVE

On the face of it the coronavirus outbreak should have sent Formula One into the wall. The pandemic put the brakes on mass gatherings and made it tougher for fans and personnel to travel around the world, both of which are essential to the smooth running of F1. However, it emerged from the turmoil firing on all cylinders.

In F1's 75-year history, few seasons have got off to a worse start than 2020. Its ten teams were on their way to Australia for the season-opening Grand Prix just as Covid began to sweep around the world. Ferrari's staff only just made it out of Italy before lockdown set in, but it was in vain. The event was given the red light minutes before the action was due to begin, which put the eyes of the world on the sport. A series of race cancellations quickly followed, with no end in sight.

The pandemic looked like the end of the road for F1. No races meant no revenue from broadcasters, sponsors or organisers, which in turn jeopardised the teams' prize money, putting their futures in question. Worse still, with the team agreements coming up for expiry they all had an option to leave.

F1 itself was saddled with $2.9bn of debt, partly dating back to Liberty's acquisition in 2017, and if it defaulted on repayments it could have ended up in the hands of its lenders, just as had happened when Kirch got into trouble and the banks took over.

It was far from unimaginable and F1's management even began discussing the consequences. 'If the sport collapses there's thousands and thousands of people out of work,' said Brawn in April 2020. In the end the pandemic actually ended up having a silver lining and Liberty benefited from it perhaps more than any other sports operator. Fittingly for Liberty owner John Malone, he had the luck of the Irish.

★　　★　　★

Acting with F1's trademark speed, the FIA insisted that teams would use their existing cars in 2021 to put the brakes on development costs during 2020. It also delayed by a year new regulations designed to improve overtaking, which were due to be introduced in 2021. The teams were banned from working on the new regulations in 2020 in order to cut costs.

F1 had firmly become a battle between the biggest spenders. The top teams had budgets of around $500m whereas the backmarkers spent less than a third of that, giving them little chance of catching up. The more the teams invest in their cars, the faster they go and the more prize money they get when they win. That allows them to attract the best drivers, which further cements their lead. This vicious circle was compounded by the bonuses awarded to the best performers, meaning that the top three received around half of the $1bn prize money handed out in 2019.

For decades the top teams had resisted the introduction of a budget cap as it would stop them spending their way to victory. However, Covid called their existence into question and the FIA seized on it. First it did the unthinkable by pushing through a budget cap that started at $145m in 2021 and gradually reduced to $135m in 2024, with slight flexibility for inflation and additional races.

It also used the impending expiry of the Concorde to scrap most of the bonuses from 2021 onwards and distribute the prize money more evenly. As late as July 2020 Toto Wolff told us that he was 'open to racing without an extension because in the auto world things change pretty quickly and if we were not signed up for five years that would give us flexibility'. But the pressure of the pandemic soon became too great even for him.

With the teams on the ropes, they ended up signing the new Concorde Agreement four months before it expired. It was somewhat of a record and all the more surprising given that just before the pandemic several of the teams said they would hold out until the eleventh hour. Signing up made a big difference.

Frederic Vasseur, then-team boss for Alfa Romeo, told *Motorsport. com* that his squad had no choice but to agree to the changes. 'We were in such a tough situation that we had to,' he said. 'Thankfully that did happen, because I'm not sure that we would have been able to survive.'

The new Concorde was signed on 20 August 2020, began the following year and expires at the end of 2025. As Liberty promised, the new agreement redistributed the bonuses previously paid to the top performers, though Ferrari still gets a premium, albeit a smaller one. Likewise, the new contract finally did away with the controversial Strategy Group that had concentrated the power to vote on regulations with the biggest teams. The $200m joining fee was also given the green light, which came in handy as it put a minimum value on the existing squads and several of them were sold to keep their wheels turning during the pandemic. Even grandee McLaren needed new investment to keep its wheels turning as Zak Brown, CEO of its racing operation, revealed during a media roundtable in late 2024. 'We were definitely on the brink,' he said adding that 'we were in a situation where if we didn't have a cash injection, we would have been a risk at [not] starting the year.' His team also got a helping hand from the government. That's because McLaren, like most of the teams, is based in the UK which offered companies generous furlough scheme.

Liberty also made moves to steady its own finances. To give it breathing room it amended the terms of F1's debt, which state that its profits usually have to remain at a certain level to avoid default. This was deferred by several years and F1 also raised $1.4bn by selling its shares in event organiser Live Nation to another Liberty offshoot, the online radio network SiriusXM, which was booming in the pandemic as more people turned to the internet during lockdown.

F1 itself shared in this glow.

All over the world people were stuck indoors craving new content online, and they came across *Drive To Survive*. Its popularity was fuelled by expletive-ridden tirades from Guenther Steiner, team boss of plucky American underdogs Haas. Clips of them went viral and fuelled a fascination with F1 in the US in particular.

It led to races being broadcast on ABC more regularly, along with exposure on leading breakfast show *Good Morning America*. Even minor crashes were shown in videos on its YouTube account, drivers were guests on Ellen DeGeneres's hit talk show, celebrities regularly talked about their love of F1, race results were covered in the *Washington Post* and drivers were interviewed in *Vanity Fair*. It has even led to F1 hitting the silver screen in a 2025 movie starring Brad Pitt made by Joseph Kosinski, director of *Top Gun: Maverick*. These developments boosted the hype about F1 to new highs. It finally cracked America and, although it was thanks to Americans, they weren't Liberty. Haas can take the credit for that along with the pandemic.

'That was really the turning moment of our success,' said F1's current CEO Stefano Domenicali in an interview with *Speedcafe.com*. 'As always, when there is a problem, there is a big opportunity.' He added that 'we were able to create the protocol and the procedure to go around the world. We kept the system alive in the worst moment ever.'

Each of the measures F1 implemented to combat Covid alone wouldn't have had an impact but together they packed a punch. The FIA introduced strict Covid protocols and although several F1 drivers had to sit out races, entire events weren't cancelled by an outbreak after racing resumed in July 2020. Before the pandemic F1 planned to hold 22 races in 2020 and in the end 17 took place. F1 made the brave move not only to hold races without spectators but to slash the hosting fees of some of them and even to pay some circuits for hosting others. It led to fan-favourite but cash-strapped tracks returning to the calendar, and one has even stayed the course. Despite being on a cut-price deal, the calendar still features the Emilia Romagna Grand Prix at Imola, where Domenicali, born just minutes away from the track, did work experience in his youth.

The Italian's greatest claim to fame is that, to this day, he is the last team boss to steer Ferrari to an F1 title when Kimi Räikkönen and Felipe Massa brought home the constructors' title in 2008. He stayed at Ferrari until 2014, when he was hired by Audi, fuelling rumours that the German brand could head to F1, a move which won't happen until 2026 when it takes control of Sauber.

In March 2016 Domenicali was appointed CEO of Ferrari's arch-rival Automobili Lamborghini and such was his gravitas he was soon credited for the successful launch of the Urus SUV, introduced the following year, even though the project was actually driven by his predecessor Stephan Winkelmann. Domenicali's experience at Lamborghini gave him the credibility that F1 investors needed, while Carey became the link between him and Liberty.

It wasn't meant to be that way.

Liberty originally wanted Toto Wolff to take over from Carey, but soon hit a roadblock. One of Ferrari's benefits for being F1's oldest team was that it had the right to sit on F1's audit and ethics and nomination committees and, according to company filings, this meant that F1 had to get Ferrari's written consent to appoint a CEO who in the past five years had been a senior executive at or owned more than 5 per cent of a rival team or engine supplier.

Ferrari exercised its right of veto. A source close to the situation told us that Ferrari 'said, "We would be against Toto because we don't think that anybody who is involved with a team should run Formula One."'

Wolff could have taken them to task according to the source, who added that 'there is no board of a public company in the world that would ever be able to accept one of the stakeholders, be it a client or a supplier, saying, "We do not allow the choice of CEO." I mean, this is almost the perfect case of discrimination or anti-competition.'

Ferrari had no qualms with its former team boss Domenicali taking the wheel, however, and he joined in January 2021 just as F1 was hitting full stride thanks to a titanic tussle between Max Verstappen and Lewis Hamilton.

It hit top gear by July when Hamilton won the British Grand Prix after a controversial collision with his arch-rival and championship leader Verstappen, who ended up slamming his Red Bull Racing car into a wall. Asked if Hamilton's move could have killed his driver, Red Bull Racing boss Christian Horner said, 'Of course. His actions have put in jeopardy another driver's safety and for me that is unacceptable.'

The incident fuelled a torrent of racist abuse towards Hamilton. Toto Wolff told Sky Sports that Horner's comments triggered 'an avalanche of comments in the social media, a lot of controversy, added to further polarisation and I think we as a sport should do the contrary. We should de-escalate.'

Carey wasn't perhaps the best person to calm tensions. Prior to climbing into F1's driving seat he had spent two decades working for Rupert Murdoch, where he was the driving force behind the emergence of the Fox News Channel. Fox News is known for its ultra-right-wing position and has been the target of protests from anti-racism groups. 'I actually think its news coverage is fair and balanced,' said Carey in 2013, adding, 'I very much endorse Fox News.'

★　　★　　★

Once again, the stars had aligned for Liberty. The development freeze and budget cap led to several mid-grid teams winning races during 2021 and, after years of Mercedes dominance, the team was finally facing a serious challenger in the form of Red Bull Racing. The season ended with one of the most thrilling finales in F1's history.

The tumultuous turn of events was triggered by Williams driver Nicholas Latifi hitting the barriers on lap 50 of the Abu Dhabi Grand Prix, leading to the safety car coming out. F1's race director Michael Masi allowed some cars to unlap themselves but not others. This saw Red Bull's title challenger Max Verstappen move up right behind race leader Lewis Hamilton just as the safety car was being brought in, closing an 11-second gap. Verstappen, who was on fresher tyres after pitting behind the safety car, overtook Hamilton on the last lap to seal the title.

It was far from the most radical sporting decision the FIA has ever made. That accolade surely goes to Mosley refusing to approve the chicane at the 2005 US Grand Prix, which prevented 70 per cent of the participants from starting the race. Had a championship not been at stake it would have likely blown over fairly quickly. However, the finale of the 2021 Abu Dhabi Grand Prix was easily the biggest test Masi had faced since he took over as F1's race director in 2019 following Charlie Whiting's untimely death.

Making tough decisions goes with the territory in the FIA, as we found out from Tony Purnell, the architect of the £40m budget cap plans that nearly caused the teams to leave F1 in 2009. 'One of the first things Max said to me is: "Have you ever seen a football match where the crowd liked the referee or cheered for the referee?" It's not going to happen,' said Purnell.

Masi found that out the hard way. With the Netflix crew trained on Toto Wolff's pained expression he showed his frustration, and millions of Mercedes fans vented their anger at Masi on social media in the wake of the race. 'I felt like I was the most hated man in the world. I got death threats. People saying, they were going to come after me and my family,' he revealed.

Masi was widely castigated for his call and Mercedes fanned the flames, with Wolff heard shouting demands at the Australian over the radio: 'You need to reinstate that lap before, that's not right.' Although Wolff subsequently admitted that he 'overstepped' the mark in his own criticism of Masi, he didn't let up. In 2022 he said, 'You hear from the drivers and how the drivers' briefings were conducted [by Masi] and some of the guys said it was almost disrespectful how he treated some of them.' He added that Masi 'was a liability for the sport'. The following year he still couldn't let bygones be bygones and described Masi as 'an idiot who made the wrong decision'.

Even in 2024 Wolff was quoted describing Masi as 'really a total, pathological egomaniac.' Then at the end of the year he went further on the actor Dax Shepard's *Armchair Expert* podcast saying that 'it was so clear that the referee decided to do something that was not in the rule book. But it was in the madness of it.' His stance seemed incredibly surprising and ironic given the abuse that his star driver Hamilton had experienced and the fact that Mercedes had taken such a strong public position against hate speech.

Understandably, the online abuse took its toll and Masi stepped down in 2022 to be replaced with a rotating series of race directors. The engineered drama of Netflix and Liberty's open-doors approach to social media had a human impact amplified by one of the teams. Marchionne's worst fears had come true: the F1 sandbox was no longer recognisable and the need for drama now reigned supreme.

The dramatic finale to the season would have a big impact for Liberty regardless. Once again, it reaped the rewards of developments beyond its control. TV audiences in the UK and the Netherlands soared, boosted by interest in home heroes Hamilton and Verstappen. Sky in the UK recorded its highest ever F1 audience for the race at 3 million viewers, while Ziggo Sport, the broadcaster in the Netherlands, set a record with 5.3 million. Sky extended its contract to 2029 with a deal estimated at more than $200m a year, but Ziggo had already become the victim of its own success as it was replaced from 2022 by Viaplay, which at a reported $39m per annum had outbid it by three times.

Audiences also set records in France, Australia, Austria and Canada, while Spain saw its biggest audience since 2017. Though perhaps most satisfying for Liberty was the US audience. Viewing figures there were up 41 per cent on 2019 and in October 2022 ESPN fought off Amazon for the rights to show F1 from 2023 to 2025, paying an estimated $75m a year. It was a big turnaround for a country that had paid nothing just a few years before.

Interest was also booming online. Liberty claimed F1 was the fastest-growing major sports league in the world in 2021 in terms of social media followers, with a rise of 40 per cent compared to 2020, while total engagement was up 74 per cent. Around 63 per cent more users visited F1.com.

It seemed that Liberty had finally struck gold, but it had reckoned without the crushing dominance of Red Bull and Max Verstappen.

25

VIVA LAS VEGAS

Just three months after the dramatic finale in Abu Dhabi, Liberty unveiled the most high-profile deal of its first five years at the wheel of F1. At a red-carpet announcement poolside at the Cosmopolitan hotel, Greg Maffei and Stefano Domenicali proudly revealed that they had signed a deal to bring F1 to Las Vegas from November 2023.

Once again, and fittingly given the race's location, Liberty's luck had played a role. When the casinos in Vegas shut down during the pandemic the authorities in the city realised it would need to make a splash when they reopened. F1 was the new sensation thanks to *Drive To Survive*, though the city still wasn't prepared to pay the average $33.5m annual race hosting fee. It did, however, pave the way for the famous Strip to be closed so that F1 could race on it. The casinos lining the Strip gave their consent to the closure on the grounds that the race would give them a vital boost of business and promotion.

Liberty could barely have engineered a better dig at Ecclestone, whose persistent efforts to make F1 a fixture in Vegas had resulted only in two races around Caesars Palace's car park in the early 1980s. F1 had never before hosted races on the Strip, so this made all the difference. It was far from a racing certainty that it would be a financial success but Liberty was so excited that it became the promoter of the race. It turned F1's typical business model on its head.

Hosting fees are Liberty's biggest source of revenue from F1 races but, instead of signing a contract with a government paying guaranteed fees every year, Liberty relied on the fickle tastes of fans and took the ticket sales that go to the event organisers.

Increasing the gamble, it spent around $435m on building permanent facilities, which are usually temporary at street circuits. For the first time in F1 history, it also held the race on a Saturday night rather than the usual Sunday. This was done so that it could be broadcast on

Sunday morning, rather than the middle of the night, in the sport's heartland of Europe.

There was also the question of whether Sin City suited F1's new corporate image, with one motorsport broadcasting personality describing it to us several years ago as 'false, vapid, and living off the glories of the 1960s? Yep, Vegas is a perfect fit for F1.'

Liberty showed its inexperience by picking a street race as the first Grand Prix it organised and there are a number of reasons for this.

Converting city streets to a temporary race track and building temporary facilities causes tremendous disruption for residents. However, if the government is paying a high-octane fee for the event, it has the reason (and the power) to pacify locals and make it a success. In contrast, a private promoter is left to shoulder the blame itself, which generates bad will and dents ticket sales.

More importantly, unlike permanent circuits, which have to be located out of town due to the space they take up, street circuits are usually home to public places where people can see the on-track action for free, which reduces the potential for ticket sales. Likewise, local resorts and restaurants compete with F1's corporate hospitality, which has high margins due to its turbocharged ticket prices.

City streets also lack the space to build the gargantuan grandstands that surround permanent circuits. Testimony to this, the British Grand Prix at Silverstone has a capacity for 480,000 spectators over race weekend, whereas only 315,000 could fit into Liberty's facilities in Vegas. When the Grand Prix was announced, little did Liberty know that the F1 landscape was set for a seismic shift that would make it even harder for the race to be a success.

The 2022 season had all the potential to be a thriller after the finale of the previous year but in practice it was far from it. Again, Liberty showed that it still hadn't got to grips with F1. The introduction of its much-vaunted new regulations didn't improve overtaking but instead made the races more predictable than ever before.

The processional nature of F1 races isn't the drivers' fault but is actually down to physics. The cars are designed to cut through the air and this leaves waves of turbulence behind them, which makes it harder to overtake. Essentially, F1 cars are designed like upside-down plane wings so that they stick to the track at high speed. However, turbulent air reduces this downforce as it doesn't flow as smoothly over the cars' sleek shells.

The regulations introduced in 2022 were designed to ensure that F1 cars retain more downforce when they are in turbulent air. In order to write the new regulations Liberty created a research and development division that spent around £13m and clocked up 16.5 million core hours of computing working on more than 10,000 computational fluid dynamics simulations spanning half a million gigabytes. In comparison, the capacity of a DVD is less than five gigabytes.

Red Bull Racing's chief technical officer Adrian Newey described the new rules as 'the biggest single regulation change' in F1 since the 1980s. Tips on the edges of the new rear wings were designed to deflect much of the wake over the top of the following car. They were coupled with new tunnels down the side of the cars that stick them to the track using the aerodynamic phenomenon of ground-effect. It returned to F1 after a 40-year ban, hence Newey's reference to the 1980s. He wrote his university thesis on ground-effect, so it is perhaps no surprise that Red Bull Racing got to grips with the new regulations better than any of its rivals and Verstappen ran away with the 2022 title.

The new rules coupled with the budget cap have been a perfect storm. When the spending limit was announced, we revealed in *Forbes* that it actually appeared to be little more than window dressing designed to make F1 look attractive to potential team owners and thereby increase the hype about the sport. Our research showed that a staggering $1.8bn of the teams' annual spending would still be unlimited due to gaping holes in the cap. In financial terms, the biggest exemption is the development and production of the cutting-edge 1.6-litre V6 turbo engines. The high-octane salaries paid to F1's drivers are also exempt, along with the three highest-paid employees, bonuses up to $10m, marketing costs, property costs, legal and finance costs and even flight and hotel costs for racing or testing.

However, remarkably, that was not the biggest flaw with the cap.

It appears Liberty assumed that spending was all it took to put the teams on a level playing field, when actually this didn't address the biggest discrepancy between them. Before Red Bull Racing's controversial victory in 2021, it had won four F1 championships, not just because it had a blockbuster budget but because Newey designed its cars. Red Bull paid him around $20m annually and he had access to the most advanced facilities in the sport, which were all accrued during F1's years of unchained spending.

These facilities enabled Newey to amass his encyclopedic knowledge of aerodynamics and the ways to find loopholes in the regulations. This knowledge didn't suddenly disappear when the budget cap was introduced because it was sitting on Red Bull's servers and in Newey's head. The real value in any business is in its people, so it was no surprise at all that a financial cap failed to make a major difference.

Of course, the staff at Ferrari and Mercedes also retained all their knowledge. Those teams remained at the sharp end of the grid (even though they rarely won races) because they too were big spenders before the cap was introduced. In other words, the budget cap failed to have the impact that Liberty expected as Mercedes' dominance was simply swapped for Red Bull Racing. In fact, the cap cemented the team's dominance in a way that wasn't previously possible.

In 2023 Aston Martin surged up the standings and, although it has billionaire owners, the budget cap prevented them from pouring extra money into the team to capitalise on its advantage and challenge Red Bull for the championship. Likewise, after years of dominance, Mercedes lost its edge, but if it wasn't for the budget cap it could have tried to spend its way out of its hole.

In short, the budget cap prevented competition because it reduced the chances of Red Bull Racing being challenged. There were plenty of seasons of dominance by certain teams before them but there was no cap to stop their rivals from catching up.

As a result of this, Verstappen didn't just win the title again in 2023, he had the most podiums in a season, the most consecutive wins and scored the most points in a season. Red Bull Racing itself also won the record for the most number of wins in an F1 season, taking victory at 21 out of 22 races. Indeed, Red Bull Racing's contender was ticking over so nicely that it was able to begin development of the 2024 car while most teams were still improving their 2023 cars during the season. That gave it a head start for 2024 and, despite a strong challenge from McLaren resulting in a more exciting season, Verstappen claimed his fourth title. It wasn't only thanks to his driving, but also due to the regulations being locked in until 2026 and the budget cap preventing Red Bull Racing's rivals from boosting their spending to compete. The problem was so severe that in 2023 Hamilton called for F1 to impose a ban on teams starting development early in the season, though nothing was done about it.

Toeing the party line, Wolff claimed that actually the new regulations had worked because – if you ignored Verstappen's performance – the racing had been close and exciting. However, F1 had close and exciting racing down its ranks long before the budget cap and the new regulations were introduced, so they were redundant if that was all they achieved. More importantly, fans of any sport rarely care who finishes second or third, so it isn't realistic to ask them to ignore the most dominant team and driver, much as Liberty might want them to.

As Verstappen and Red Bull enjoyed the limelight of world champions, Mercedes licked its wounds having lost its first drivers' title since 2013. The team was left reeling from that decision in Abu Dhabi in December 2021 and it took a year for it to win another race.

The week after the 2021 Abu Dhabi Grand Prix, INEOS, the chemicals giant founded by billionaire Jim Ratcliffe, announced it would buy a 33 per cent stake in the team. The precise price came to light in February 2023 when accounts for INEOS Industries Holdings revealed that 'on 25 January 2022, the company purchased one-third of the share capital of Mercedes-Benz Grand Prix Limited for consideration of £208.4 million.' However, just one year later, the sale of stakes in Alpine and Aston Martin valued the teams at $908m and $1.2bn respectively, despite their weaker track records. Indeed, in November 2023, Maffei boasted that 'Liberty has been involved with F1 for about seven years now and literally when we started the bottom team got sold for one pound. Now, the bottom teams are worth close to a billion dollars, maybe $750 million, and the top teams are probably worth $3 billion.' Although INEOS didn't spend that much, the price of its stake was nearly five times more than the amount Mercedes initially spent, so the car manufacturer wasn't left out of pocket. Likewise, given its low purchase price, it's perhaps no surprise that INEOS couldn't be happier and in February 2025, Wolff told Sky Sports that 'Jim Ratcliffe is one of us three amigos – Mercedes, Jim and I. We are never going to part ways.'

However, the team's lack of success since the 2021 Abu Dhabi Grand Prix still came at quite a cost and it contributed to Hamilton's shock decision in February 2024 to switch to Ferrari from 2025, where he is expected to close out his F1 career.

Meanwhile, it appeared that the budget cap was not having quite the effect that Liberty had intended, which might explain why the teams had finally agreed to it being implemented. Fuelled by the long list of exclusions from the cap, costs actually rose in 2021 at three of the eight teams that file publicly available accounts when compared to 2019 (Red Bull Racing, Aston Martin and Williams). At the other five teams, the biggest reduction was unsurprisingly at Mercedes, the highest-spending team. It lopped £34.1m off its spending, but at less than 10 per cent of its overall costs it was not the drastic shift that had been predicted.

By 2022, on paper it looked like the budget cap had never happened. Seven of the eight teams that file accounts posted record costs for that season, with only Haas spending less than it had before the cap was introduced. The average costs per team ballooned to £256.5m, an increase of almost 25 per cent on 2019. The increase in costs wasn't entirely supported by growth in revenue and three of the teams made a loss, including McLaren and Aston Martin, which each saw deficits of over £50m.

There was also growing discontent among some of the teams. Adrian Newey admitted to *Motor Sport* in June 2024 that 'since the cost cap has been introduced the competitive order hasn't really changed so in that sense you question how much it has really brought. I do think trying to contain an arms race is a good thing to do. But I'm not convinced the way it's done is right.' He added that:

> . . . the cost cap has a lot of shortfalls, some of them not immediately obvious when it was introduced. For instance, because it is a cost cap and not a people cap we as an industry can't keep up with inflation. So F1 has gone from being the best-paid engineering industry in the world to most definitely not any more. A lot of start-up electric car companies, tech companies and other racing series are now actually better paid as an industry than F1. At Red Bull we aren't alone in losing people – not to other teams, but other industries.

It seemed that spending had simply shifted away from areas delineated by the cap. It was true that for the first time in F1 history, the smaller teams no longer had an axe constantly looming over them, but this was less due to the budget cap than the surge in commercial revenues generated by the *Drive To Survive* effect, which was a far less reliable saviour.

★　　★　　★

At a time when the racing was more predictable than ever, a promotional programme like *Drive To Survive* that lured in new viewers with sensationalist storytelling was only going to emphasise the lack of action on the track. *Drive To Survive* has been accused of the 'Hollywood-isation' of F1. Sound effects are added to the footage, famously creating the anomalous screeching of tyres as cars bump over gravel traps, and some of the commentary is post-recorded to reflect the focus of the producers. Often small disagreements between mid-grid drivers are blown up into major ongoing conflicts. Verstappen refused to take part in Season 4, depicting his dramatic victory in the 2021 championship, claiming that 'because the series is all about excitement . . . they position you and whatever fits the episode.' Even when he was persuaded to return for Season 6, his record-breaking 2023 season barely featured as Netflix focused on more exciting conflicts lower down the pecking order.

The Netflix show made it seem like there was drama around every corner but when its viewers tuned in to the races they found the same team winning every Grand Prix. It explained why F1's TV audience started reversing even though hype about the sport accelerated.

Every year since Liberty took over F1 it had distributed a press release around the start of the season about the previous year's TV audience. This was mysteriously absent in 2023. Instead, Liberty's filings referred to global 'cumulative TV viewers of 1.54 billion in 2022'. This stood out like a sore thumb as it was one of the few results that wasn't listed as being up or down on the previous year.

It was another big change from the days of Ecclestone, who despite being known for his secrecy had produced a detailed Global Media Report about F1's TV audience for every year from 2005 to 2016, even at times when audiences had fallen. The move was spearheaded by industry expert Michael Payne, who was previously responsible for the overall marketing strategy and the full commercial operations for the Olympic Games during a 20-year tenure at the International Olympic Committee. He explained that the transparency would make F1 more attractive to sponsors, saying that 'what marketers want and need to know is how many people actually watched the whole event'. Liberty seemed to disagree.

Deeper research into F1's filings revealed that the sport's audience fell by 0.7 per cent in 2022, so its popularity wasn't heading in the right direction despite appearances. Looking further back revealed an even more alarming trend. Remarkably, F1's global TV audience in 2022 was a staggering 19.9 per cent down on the pre-pandemic total of 1.922 billion in 2019. Many sports surged in popularity on TV during the pandemic but F1 crashed and hasn't recovered since then. In early 2025 Liberty announced that a cumulative 1.6 billion people watched F1 races in 2024, nearly 17 per cent down on the 2019 total despite the boost the sport supposedly got from *Drive To Survive*. Although the figure was a small increase on 2023's 1.5 billion viewers, this change was driven by a longer calendar and the average audience per race actually dropped from 68.2 million viewers to 66.7 million.

In 2021 Liberty attempted to boost the excitement further by introducing a short sprint race to determine the grid at a handful of races instead of the more mundane and traditional qualifying format. Held on a Saturday afternoon, the 100km sprint format has been through several iterations since then and from 2023 became a standalone session, rather than a qualifying round, in order to encourage drivers to take more risks and produce more exciting racing. It awards a small number of points to the top finishers, who don't get a podium celebration as that is reserved for the winners of the main event. The number of sprint races was doubled in 2023, which ended up backfiring when Verstappen won the title by finishing second in one of them in Qatar, so didn't even get to celebrate his championship on the podium. Many viewers tuned in to Sunday's Grand Prix to find out that the Dutchman had already secured the title.

Liberty has been quick to challenge reports that suggest F1's social media audience is also dwindling. A September 2023 report from monitoring agency Buzz Radar entitled 'Have we reached Peak F1?' painted a bleak picture, claiming that social media mentions had declined 70.7 per cent in the first five months of the year, while new followers were down 49.2 per cent. F1 countered the report by providing media outlets with data that showed an increase in follower growth across its official channels that was eight times what Buzz Radar had claimed.

Even *Drive To Survive* was no longer the promotional powerhouse that it was made out to be. Despite the hype, when Netflix started releasing audience data in 2022 figures showed that, although moderately popular worldwide, none of seasons four to six made it into the top ten weekly TV programmes in the US. The fifth season, which was released in 2023, was watched by a grand total of 569,884 viewers in the

States in its first week, according to Nielsen. In contrast, the sixth season of *The Crown* was watched by 2.8 million people on its first week in the smaller market of the UK alone.

If anything, *Drive To Survive* was most popular in countries where Liberty Media was doing little to capitalise on interest. It featured repeatedly in the Netflix Top 10 in Norway, Morocco, India, South Africa and Kenya – none of which have a race. One Kenyan social media influencer told the BBC, 'When you're scrolling on Netflix and then you see *Drive To Survive*, you end up watching and then you get interested in the sport.' However, she had to fly more than 2,000 miles to Abu Dhabi to see F1 live. Arguably, Liberty's focus on the United States has meant that it has left money on the table in other markets, something it could come to regret if F1's popularity in the States turns out to be a fad.

Liberty also faced an uphill battle to convert its American *Drive To Survive* audience into fully fledged F1 fans. A report by market researchers Nielsen admitted that the series 'inspired US audiences to start watching Formula 1 races', but it also demonstrated that many viewers of *Drive To Survive* did not also watch F1 races on TV. Only 41 per cent of *Drive To Survive*'s US viewers also watched the first three weeks of the new F1 season in 2022. It made F1 heavily dependent on the show over its own programming.

Liberty's race attendance data was initially even more impenetrable than its TV figures. In 2017 it showed an annual percentage increase in attendance at certain races that was higher than the actual difference in the number of spectators. For example, F1 claimed that attendance at the 2017 Azerbaijan Grand Prix accelerated by 138.2 per cent on the previous year, contradicting a statement from the promoter that referred to 'a 30 per cent increase in ticket sales'. We broke this news in a report for the BBC and a spokesperson for F1 was forced to reveal that 'there was a systematic error in the percentage calculation'.

In light of this, F1 updated its attendance data, but as a result several races showed a higher attendance than the race promoters reported. This time we blew the lid on it in *Forbes*, so F1 went into damage limitation mode the following year. Its 2018 data came with the caveat that F1 had made 'adjustments . . . to certain 2017 attendance figures subsequent to the release of last year's attendance results'.

In short, as F1 was on the ropes it had no choice but to retrospectively reduce the 2017 attendance data so that it did not clash with the year-on-year percentage increase. However, this again meant that F1's data conflicted with the figures from at least one of the race promoters, which understandably refused to comment for fear of biting the hand that feeds it.

Fortunately for F1, as the company itself is not directly floated it was not subject to any penalties from regulators, even though it issued inaccurate data that could have affected shareholders' decisions about whether to purchase the tracking stock.

F1 benefits from waves of hype through its social media channels and this has helped to pump up its stock price, which has increased more than fourfold since the takeover. Liberty itself talks a good fight and even manages to make obvious weaknesses seem like strengths.

Drive To Survive has been applauded for attracting new fans to F1 but it has also made it incredibly unstable. In March 2023 Maffei boasted that 'one in three fans globally started following F1 in the last four years'. Most sports trumpet the exact opposite of this and instead say how loyal their fans are and how long they have been followers. There is good reason for this.

There is no guarantee that new fans will stick around and they could leave as quickly as they joined. In contrast, fans who have been following F1 for years are far less likely to stop watching it; they have stayed through bad patches before, so are likely to do so again. This means that 33 per cent of F1's audience is at risk, and if Max Verstappen continues to win every year it could turn them off, especially as this predictability is far from the drama of *Drive To Survive* that attracted them to the sport in the first place. Bearing this in mind, it is perhaps no surprise that the TV audience of the Miami Grand Prix fell by 24.6 per cent in the US in 2023. It rebounded to record levels in 2024, but the sharp fluctuations demonstrate the volatility of an audience drawn by on-track drama.

Ironically, two areas where F1 has definitely surpassed expectations are race attendance and team sponsorship. Moving past its earlier glitches, race attendance soared in the post-pandemic economy, with several tracks reporting record crowds. Meanwhile, total team sponsorship, which had slumped to an estimated $791m in 2017 when Liberty took over, soared to almost $1.2bn in 2021 with the addition of big deals such as Oracle's $100m title sponsorship of Red Bull Racing. However, F1 does not usually benefit directly from either of these revenue sources as the money goes to the promoters and the teams. This may explain why Liberty was so keen to get involved in the promotion of Vegas.

Given how much Liberty had on the line, it's remarkable that it picked the end of the calendar for its inaugural Vegas race, as it knew there was a good chance that Verstappen would have sewn up the title long before then, which is exactly what happened. It meant there was nothing significant at stake in the race, making the scheduling looked like a foolhardy decision. Liberty learned its lesson the hard way.

Automotive channel *Oversteer48* compared the nightly prices that the top 22 hotels on the Strip were charging during the Grand Prix a year before the race and then a week before the race. This revealed that their rates were on average 58 per cent cheaper a week before the race, with the biggest reductions at the Circus Circus hotel, which dropped its prices by 83 per cent. According to the research, some fans who booked early managed to secure compensation or rebook at the drastically lower prices, while others with non-refundable bookings were left counting the cost of the price drop.

It was a similar story with the ticket prices. Ticketing platform TickPick showed that in the month running up to the race, the price of the cheapest tickets crashed by 58 per cent to $162 for Thursday, 62 per cent to $312 for Friday and 34 per cent to $1,087 for Saturday. The day before the race, grandstand tickets were still available, seemingly dashing forecasts from Liberty's chief legal officer Renee Wilm that the race would be a sell-out. And fans weren't just put off by the poor quality of the racing.

The majority of spectators at street races usually come from the local area because of the high density of the on-site population. However, in the months leading up to the Vegas race the local media was awash with negative coverage about the event due to the disruption caused by the construction work. It was so bad that just a week before the race Maffei himself was forced to issue an apology. It was far from the first backtrack by Liberty in the build-up to the race.

Liberty initially tried to charge businesses that had a view of the track $1,500 per person during the race, and then reduced it to a $50,000 flat fee due to the backlash. When that strategy failed Liberty erected barriers to block the view, but this created even more bad will as fans tore them down during the race. Remarkably, it got even worse than that.

During the practice for the race on Thursday evening a loose manhole cover severely damaged Carlos Sainz's Ferrari, causing the session to be stopped for hours. It only resumed at 2.30am but one hour before that, all of the spectators, including hospitality guests who had paid tens of thousands of dollars, were ejected from the circuit due to the security shift ending. It led to a class-action lawsuit against Liberty which was still rumbling on by the end of 2024. This was no surprise.

The justification for a negligence claim was that as Liberty is F1's owner it should have known that manholes can come loose, especially on new circuits, and it was not the first time this had happened. Even if the track itself had caused no problems, there could have been a major accident on it or torrential rain that caused the session to be delayed into the night, so Liberty should have had contingency measures in place. Paying customers expect sports events to run like clockwork, especially if they are promoted by the owner of the sport. It wasn't even the first time that something like this had happened under Liberty's watch. That came in 2021 when the Belgian Grand Prix was cancelled after just two laps behind the safety car due to torrential rain, something hardly uncommon in the region. As Liberty was the promoter of the race in Vegas it had even less of an excuse.

'Let's not get into how the locals were blinded to see any parts of the race for free and how multiple businesses were axed off if they didn't pay up some F1 Liberty Media dividends and of course, the lateness really killed the whole beauty of the event,' said Max Bitton, executive director of Canadian motorsport store FANABOX.

Oliver Kent, managing director of ticket agency ZK Sports & Entertainment, echoed this. 'Speaking to many other agencies and part-ners, there were some that witnessed huge losses and others that felt it took too much of their time for the output.'

Even some of the drivers weren't impressed with the spectacle, which included an opening ceremony where they were introduced on towering platforms. 'An F1 car does not come alive on a street circuit. It is not that exciting. It is about proper race tracks. And when you go to Monza and Spa, these kinds of places have a lot of emotion and passion, and for me seeing the fans there is incredible,' said Verstappen in Vegas.

People come here, but they become a fan of what? They want to see maybe their favourite artist and have a few drinks with their mates, and then go out and have a crazy night. As a little kid, I grew up wanting to become a world champion. More time should be invested into the actual sport, and what we are trying to achieve. The sport should explain what the team has done throughout the season, and what they are working for. That's way more important than having these random shows all over the place.

Most worryingly for Liberty, the authorities in Las Vegas were underwhelmed by the event. 'I think that we have to get much better than we were last year,' said Clark County commissioner, Marilyn Kirkpatrick, adding that 'the jury's still out for me'. It put the future of the event at risk. 'The commission has been very clear,' she said. 'You will do it a certain way, or there won't be a third time.'

Even if F1 can keep Vegas on the calendar, the disruption and predictability of the racing could make it even tougher for Liberty to attract spectators in years to come, especially as the race won't be new to the calendar then. In turn, it is far from certain that it will turn a profit in the absence of a hosting fee.

In contrast, a decade ago, long before all the hoopla of *Drive To Survive*, motorsport entrepreneur Tavo Hellmund managed to convince the state of Texas to put up $25m in annual funding in order to get a green light for the US Grand Prix there.

That doesn't mean the Las Vegas Grand Prix was a complete bust. Holding it on a Saturday tested the waters of midweek racing, which may be exactly what Liberty needs to convince investors that the business has growth potential.

Races are the engine behind the growth of F1's revenues thanks to their blockbuster hosting fees as well as revenue from trackside advertising, race title sponsorship and hospitality. If a new race is in a key market it can even enable Liberty to boost its broadcasting fees. A second race in Italy might not move the needle much in terms of the fee paid by Sky Italia but if, for example, the much-mooted South African Grand Prix returned to the calendar it could significantly drive up the amount that a local broadcaster pays.

The teams are the roadblock in the way of adding more races to the calendar, as the Concorde states that the consent of 70 per cent of them is required if there are more than 24 in a season, which was the record total on the calendar in 2024.

The majority of the teams are based in the UK, so the more races that take place in far-flung destinations, the greater their travel costs become and the more time they spend away from home. So how does holding races on a Saturday help matters? Well, if Saturday was viable, then why not Friday? And if that went ahead then how about Thursday or even Wednesday?

Unsurprisingly, F1 is under increasing pressure from the green lobby and not just because its participants are 20 gas-guzzlers. When F1 released its first ever sustainability report in 2019, emissions from the cars themselves represented only 0.7 per cent of the total environmental impact of the sport. The report found that in 2018 F1's total carbon footprint came to 256,551 tonnes of carbon dioxide, but even this wasn't the full picture as it didn't include the impact from spectators or suppliers. Crucially, the biggest component of the impact was logistics, followed by business travel, which together came to 72.7 per cent of the total.

Ironically, until recently F1 global partner DHL frequently produced infographics and press releases promoting the large amounts of freight it shipped to each Grand Prix and the high number of kilometres travelled. Since F1 announced its sustainability strategy, these declarations have been less prominent and there has been more of a focus on reducing environmental impact in DHL's communications. According to DHL, in 2022, F1 travelled more than 120,000km, with up to 1,400 tonnes of equipment needing to be delivered to each race. As many as 120 sea freight containers, 30 trucks and eight planes were used to transport the equipment.

F1 has set a 2030 target of cutting 50 per cent of its absolute carbon emissions compared to its 2018 baseline. In order to do this it needs to find a way to reorganise the growing calendar, which is one of its biggest revenue generators. This led to an overhaul of the calendar for 2024, which involved moving the Japanese Grand Prix at Suzuka to the early part of the year for the first time and slotting Azerbaijan in before Singapore in order to minimise distances flown by freight. However, to significantly reduce its environmental impact, F1 may need a more radical solution.

Even under the revised calendar, the sport travels from one part of the world to another and back again later in the year on multiple occasions. If instead of visiting the US at three different times of the year it held the three races there in one week, it would be a lot more environmentally friendly.

It wouldn't just tick that box, it would also save on travel costs. What's more, there wouldn't be time for practice, so the races would be more unpredictable too. But the biggest benefit is that it would mean F1 could fit more races into a shorter space of time. The greater the number of races it holds, the more revenue it generates. If it took the midweek racing approach in every market F1 could significantly boost the number of races on the calendar while reducing the time spent on the road away from home. That sounds like a win-win and the sport seems to be heading in precisely this direction.

Vegas tested the water, but the first two races of 2024 – in Bahrain and Saudi Arabia – also took place on Saturday evening to avoid the Ramadan festival. Both countries are between two and three hours ahead of F1's heartland in the UK and Europe, so the races were on primetime TV. The same can't be said of Vegas.

The race was held on Saturday night to put it on TV on Sunday morning in Europe, but that plan backfired. Vegas is eight hours behind the UK and nine behind mainland Europe, so it was still too early in the morning to attract a significant audience. Meanwhile, Vegas is three hours behind the east coast of America, which put the race on TV in the middle of the night there. It was on at primetime in Asia, but F1's top TV markets aren't located there. This explains why, despite all the fanfare, the Las Vegas Grand Prix attracted an average of just 1.3 million viewers on ESPN in the US, half the number who tuned in to the inaugural Miami Grand Prix. In 2024, the audience for the race dropped to just 905,000, despite the more dramatic on-track action during the season.

Overall, F1's average TV audience in the US fell by 8.3 per cent to just 1.1 million per race in 2023 as Verstappen's dominance drove viewers away from the sport. Remarkably, the closer championship in 2024 had little effect on the average audience, which stayed at 1.1 million. The total was lower than the audience of F1's US based rival NASCAR, even though the stock car series only races in North America. It also represents around half the number of viewers that F1 has in Germany, a market with no races, something former Mercedes motorsport boss Norbert Haug described as 'a tragedy that every motorsport enthusiast can only be ashamed of'.

Each Grand Prix has around 66.7 million viewers on average worldwide, so Liberty had added two races in the US, and all the associated razzmatazz, to pander to a country with an audience that represents just 1.5 per cent of the global total. Courting the States was an expensive strategy and not a consistent one.

In January 2024 Liberty turned down an opportunity to boost US interest in F1. After the FIA launched a tender for new teams it approved American squad Andretti, which was run by former F1 driver Michael Andretti and backed by Cadillac. F1's ten teams were opposed to Andretti joining because it could kick one of them out of the running for prize money, which is divided among the top ten, and the entry was rejected by F1, despite the FIA's backing.

F1 justified Andretti's rejection on the grounds it did 'not believe that the applicant would be a competitive participant'. This seemed unlikely given the credibility of its backers and the fact that if it wasn't likely to be competitive the existing teams would surely have welcomed it as it wouldn't pose a threat. F1 initially considered raising the entry fee from $200m to $600m to mitigate this risk but did not address the simplest solution, which would have been to insist that the team waived its right to earn prize money for the duration of the next Concorde Agreement. With hindsight, Andretti appeared to have been a pawn in the battle between the teams and Liberty on one side and the FIA on the other.

Andretti didn't take it lying down. In May 2024 Michael's father Mario, the 1978 world champion, went to the US Congress, where a bi-partisan group of senators launched an enquiry on the grounds that rejecting Andretti's entry may violate anti-trust law as it prevented competition with the existing teams. Crucially, they asked the Biden administration to launch a formal anti-trust investigation, raising the prospect of regulators raking F1 over the coals yet again.

It become a bitterly personal battle with Mario claiming in May 2024 that Maffei had said to him 'I want to tell you that I will do everything in my power to see that Michael never enters Formula One.' However, just five months later Michael stepped down from the day-to-day running of the prospective Andretti Racing team and, sensationally, one month later, Maffei followed him out of the door. He was replaced with Derek Chang, a former boss of the NBA in China, while Chase Carey returned to Liberty's board.

Just under two weeks after Maffei departed, F1 announced that it had approved Cadillac's entry, putting the team on track to enter F1 from

2026. Andretti Racing changed its name to Cadillac Formula Racing and appointed former Virgin Racing CEO, Graeme Lowdon, as team principal. The car maker will join Audi, which is taking over Sauber, as a first-time entry on the 2026 grid, heralding a new era of manufacturer participation.

Although that battle came to an abrupt halt, another was still simmering. This followed a frosty exchange in 2023 when Ben Sulayem reacted to reports that investors from Saudi Arabia were considering buying F1 for $20bn. In a statement on social media he said:

> As the custodians of motorsport, the FIA, as a non-profit organisation, is cautious about alleged inflated price tags of 20bn being put on F1. Any potential buyer is advised to apply common sense, consider the greater good of the sport and come with a clear, sustainable plan – not just a lot of money. It is our duty to consider what the future impact will be for promoters in terms of increased hosting fees and other commercial costs, and any adverse impact that it could have on fans.

The mere hint of the FIA's right of approval of a sale of F1 appeared to light the touchpaper with Liberty, especially as Ben Sulayem was suggesting that it is far from a rubber-stamping exercise. In response, Renee Wilm and Sacha Woodward Hill wrote to all of the grid's major players saying 'The FIA has given unequivocal undertakings that it will not do anything to prejudice the ownership, management and/or exploitation of [F1's commercial] rights. We consider that those comments, made from the FIA president's official social media account, interfere with those rights in an unacceptable manner.' It is unclear what the justification is for this as Ben Sulayem's comments did not denigrate F1; on the contrary, they outlined the high standards that surely Liberty would want a buyer to meet. Wilm and Woodward Hill also claimed it is wrong to say that 'any potential purchaser of the Formula One business is required to consult with the FIA'. It was a surprising claim given the hoops Liberty had to jump through at the FIA in order to get its acquisition of F1 across the finish line. Indeed, Ben Sulayem's view was not too dissimilar to Jean Todt's comment in 2011 that if a company wanted to buy F1 he would 'need to speak with my people in the FIA to give an agreement about whether they are happy with the people who take over or whether we are not happy.'

That didn't elicit opprobrium from F1 so it is unclear why Ben Sulayem experienced this. Wilm and Woodward Hill claimed that his comments had 'overstep[ped] the bounds of the FIA's remit', but that too does not seem to make sense, as he said that a buyer should 'come with a clear, sustainable plan', which seems entirely reasonable. Their final remarks warned that 'any individual or organisation commenting on the value of a listed entity or its subsidiaries, especially claiming or implying possession of inside knowledge while doing so, risks causing substantial damage to the shareholders and investors of that entity, not to mention potential exposure to serious regulatory consequences.' They concluded, 'To the degree that these comments damage the value of Liberty Media Corporation, the FIA may be liable as a result.'

Ben Sulayem did not claim to have inside knowledge or even suggest that he has it, so the ferocity of the criticism of him fuelled questions about what was driving it. While that is unknown, there is no doubt it touched a raw nerve and the FIA's right of approval might not have been the only reason for this.

The $20bn price point highlighted how high the barrier is for Liberty to make the same return from F1 as its predecessor. CVC bought the business for $2bn and sold it for $8bn, so for Liberty to get a similar return it would need to sell at approximately $32bn which is much more than the Saudi Arabian investors reportedly offered and more than the $23bn market value of the F1 tracking stock as of February 2025.

Hype and excitement have been key to Liberty's formula for making F1 seem like it is firing on all cylinders, so it seems likely it will head even further in this direction. In F1's early days it was purely a sport. Then Ecclestone and Mosley made it a billion-dollar business, and now Liberty wants to turn it into a form of entertainment. It may have to perform some drastic manoeuvres to do this.

It is an open secret in F1 that the way to ensure every race is exciting is to introduce what are known as reverse grids. They would see the cars starting a race in the reverse order that they finished the previous one in. This would mean the top drivers would have to carve their way through the field, and whenever this has happened in previous races it has made for electrifying racing, such as Michael Schumacher's first victory for Ferrari at the rain-soaked Spanish Grand Prix in 1996 or Verstappen powering to first from 17th on the grid in Brazil in 2024.

FI purists strongly object to reverse grids because it artificially creates excitement and doesn't reward the best driving. However, purists are no longer FI's target audience, *Drive To Survive* viewers are, and many of them don't like what they see when they watch the races. It caused Chase Carey to think the unthinkable, and in 2020 he revealed that talks about reverse-grid sprint races were underway with the teams. However, fierce opposition ultimately led to them not getting the green light.

'Most sports, when they have talked about changes, the hardcore fans resist change,' said Carey on FI's *Beyond the Grid* podcast.

> Major League Baseball, when they had a designated hitter, everybody didn't like it. The NBA put in a three-point line, the hardcores didn't like it . . . Really, in most of those cases – not all but most – those changes have ended up being viewed as positive, bringing fresh energy, bringing a fresh perspective.
>
> I think you have to be careful you don't gimmick-up the sport, that you're recognising the importance of history and the importance of what has made this sport special, but not let that become a straitjacket that doesn't enable you to consider changes that may truly enhance the sport for fans.

Carey acknowledged that reverse grids would cause an uproar with FI supporters but added that this shouldn't be a roadblock to implementing them. 'Not every fan will like it, you'll never get 100 per cent, and that's why we have to make the judgement of whether it's something we think, on balance, will improve the sport.

'Without making it sound like we're just throwing ideas against a wall, we should always be trying to push ourselves to look at other ways to make the sport more interesting and exciting for fans.'

It will take a lot more than a few discussions to get reverse grids across the line, but that appears to be the direction FI is heading in.

Indeed, the beginnings of this seismic change were introduced in 2021 when FI adopted rules that grant the winning team the least amount of time in the wind tunnel to design its car for the following year. The rules operate on a sliding scale, with the first-placed team getting the least and the last-placed team getting the most time to test their car the following year.

Focusing on making the sport entertaining still doesn't mean that Liberty will have an easy ride selling F1. Quite apart from the need for FIA approval, there is also the question of who would buy it.

The valuation of a business is based on a multiple of its income with media companies usually valued at around 20 times their underlying profit. Liberty arrived at its $8bn purchase price for F1 by multiplying the sport's 2016 underlying profit of $439m by 18.3. By 2024, F1's underlying profit had increased to $791m, which is 80.2 per cent higher than it was eight years earlier. This puts a value of around $14.5bn on F1, far less than the $20bn that the Saudi consortium was reportedly asked to pay.

As F1 is privately owned by Liberty it can charge whatever it wants. However, buyers usually only pay more than a business is valued at if they have a personal emotional connection to it or if it can benefit them in a way that isn't factored into the valuation. F1 has the power to do the latter as its races could give a broadcaster exclusive content. It is particularly pertinent because several of the world's biggest media companies, including Amazon, Apple and Netflix, already have links to F1, which puts them in pole position to make a bid for the business. However, it isn't actually as simple as that.

During Constantin Medien's 2013 trial against Ecclestone, he revealed that F1 had recently rebuffed a takeover approach from Rupert Murdoch's News Corporation because the sport's contracts prevented it from being controlled by a broadcaster or media group. He explained that this was 'recently raised when Murdoch tried to buy into the company because the FIA wouldn't be very happy with it and could, at any time, withdraw our licence'. This severely restricts who Liberty can sell to and puts the keys to F1's future firmly in the FIA's hands.

Liberty isn't taking it lying down, as shown by its robust response to Ben Sulayem's comments. Liberty probably also realises that its run of good luck has to come to an end at some stage. So far, Liberty has been one of the luckiest owners in the history of F1. It managed to get Stephen Ross on its side, its critic-in-chief Sergio Marchionne passed away, the Serious Fraud Office investigation skidded off track and the pandemic enabled it to sign a new Concorde, introduce the budget cap and level out the prize money as well, of course, as being the driving force behind the success of *Drive To Survive*.

In contrast, during Ecclestone's time in the driving seat he had to navigate hostile takeovers, shareholder coups, lawsuits from his partners, blackmail attempts, on-track fatalities, breakaway threats, team bank-ruptcies and the deaths of his friends and allies.

Perhaps inevitably, Ecclestone's retirement had also been full of drama. Although he hadn't been at the wheel of F1 since early 2017, he had been dealing with the consequences of his 40-year career in the sport ever since he stepped down.

26

A TAXING PROBLEM

Following the sale to Liberty, Ecclestone finally made the jump and permanently moved offshore to Switzerland. However, it was too late to shake HMRC off his tail. It revved up its claim for £1bn after rescinding its settlement agreement with him in 2014 on the grounds that his court testimony showed he had the power to influence or benefit from his family trust. Ecclestone had counter-sued HMRC, claiming that it had no right to tear up the 2008 settlement agreement, and it initially looked like he was in pole position to get what he wanted.

In May 2015 Ecclestone's tax advisor David Pert told HMRC that the F1 boss had said it would be best 'if he sat down with HMRC and answered any questions they had' in order to resolve the investigation once and for all, because he was tired of having to 'pay huge bills for advice'.

The meeting took place two months later and little did Ecclestone know it would be one of the costliest of his career. Towards the end of the talk, HMRC asked him if he had set up or benefited from any trusts since it entered into the settlement with him in 2008. Ecclestone replied 'no' and HMRC didn't forget it.

After a year had passed HMRC hadn't made a great deal of progress with its investigation and it feared it didn't have much left in the tank. Ecclestone seized the moment in May 2016 and made an offer of around £70m to put an end to the dispute into three of the tax years on the understanding that the 2008 settlement remained in place. HMRC still wanted £1bn from him but in June 2016 reluctantly put the wheels in motion to accept his offer. Then, at the eleventh hour, it made a break-through from the most unlikely of places.

After Ecclestone was charged with bribery in 2013, Swiss private bank Julius Baer kept an eye on an account he had access to in its Singapore branch. The account contained £416m and wasn't held by

Ecclestone but by a company called Regent Capital Services, which was part of a structure involving two trusts – the Kinan Trust and the Nanki Trust.

Regent specialises in buying and selling foreign currency and the transactions through its Julius Baer account in Singapore generated gains and losses running into the tens of millions of dollars every year, so it was clearly in the hands of a master trader. The bank knew that Ecclestone had used the account to conduct foreign currency transactions and had met with its relationship manager. Once he had been charged with bribery in 2013 it required all of his transactions to be flagged for scrutiny and approval but, apart from that, he carried on using it as usual.

The turning point came in 2017 when Switzerland's financial markets watchdog, Finma, appointed an agent to investigate Julius Baer after its accounts were involved with alleged cases of corruption connected to FIFA and Venezuelan oil company PDVSA. This caused the Monetary Authority of Singapore (MAS) to inspect Julius Baer's local branch to assess its controls for mitigating money laundering and terrorist financing risks.

While doing this it came across the account that Ecclestone had access to. According to Singapore's minister for finance Lawrence Wong, the MAS 'specifically reviewed the bank's handling of its relationship with Mr Ecclestone. While MAS found that there was room for improvement in the bank's anti-money laundering processes, it did not find gaps or weaknesses that were systemic in nature.' He added that 'Singapore proactively shared relevant information with our UK counterparts, which helped them develop their case.' HMRC couldn't believe its luck.

The tip-off was manna from heaven for HMRC, most importantly because Ecclestone hadn't declared the account in Singapore. HMRC also remembered what Ecclestone had told them at the meeting in 2015. He claimed he was not a beneficiary of any trusts HMRC didn't know about; but the information from MAS linked him to two that he hadn't disclosed already. HMRC made the most of this.

Interestingly, although Ecclestone had access to the bank account and used it, there is no evidence that he actually withdrew money from it or even that he was ultimately its sole owner. He certainly wasn't the direct owner of the account as that was Regent Capital Services, and the secret of who was the ultimate owner of that was safe in the Kinan and Nanki trusts.

In 2010 £416m was transferred into the account from a bank in Switzerland where Ecclestone does indeed have an account. However, that still doesn't mean to say the account in Singapore was his as he stressed to us in London in 2012 that 'I have only got two bank accounts, a local bank here and one in Switzerland where I put money there 25 years ago when we had all the trouble in England where you could only take out so much. I thought I will move what I have got just in case they lock it down.'

If Ecclestone wasn't the owner of the Singapore bank account, it raised the question of who was. Likewise, why was Ecclestone making money for them by trading currency and what did he gain from doing this? Presumably Ecclestone was well aware who the ultimate owner of the account was and why he used it. HMRC knew these kind of details would come out in court and it also knew Ecclestone could avoid this happening by settling with them before it went to trial. However, this was only part of its strategy.

Crucially, regardless of whether Ecclestone ultimately controlled the Singapore account or paid himself from it, there was no doubt that he had access to it. In financial parlance that gave him the power to 'enjoy' the money, so he should have declared it to HMRC, especially when it questioned him.

Ecclestone had told HMRC he was not the beneficiary of any trusts it didn't know about, but the Singapore account was owned by two that he hadn't disclosed, meaning he gave false details to the tax authority. HMRC claimed that Ecclestone was liable to pay tax on the money and had concealed it from them, which is fraud. This carries a prison sentence and HMRC knew that in order to avoid it Ecclestone would have to show he had made amends by paying the money it had asked for and dropping his counter-claim.

Ecclestone hadn't declared that he had access to £400m in an account which was part of a structure involving two trusts, so he was hardly in a position to start claiming that he didn't actually influence them or bene-fit from them. HMRC had used his own tactics against him and had him over a barrel.

It turned the screws by formally withdrawing its acceptance of his £70m offer and questioned him about the Singapore account on 21 August 2017 in London's Bishopsgate police station. When asked if he had heard of the Kinan Trust he replied, 'Recently, yes. But very recently.' That didn't matter, as he was linked to the trust so shouldn't have said he wasn't.

HMRC's next step was to double down by drawing in other members of his family, as Ecclestone revealed to us in an interview for the *Daily Telegraph*. 'I went to the police station to answer some questions under oath to do with tax,' he said, adding that 'the children as well had to do the same thing. They had to go into the nick because when you are giving a statement under oath you have to do it at the police station.' It raised the prospect of HMRC pursuing Ecclestone's children if he didn't manage to put the brakes on the matter.

It stepped up a gear in 2022 when, after four years of intense investigations, the Crown Prosecution Service authorised criminal charges against Ecclestone. Andrew Penhale, Chief Crown Prosecutor, said that he had been charged with 'fraud by false representation in respect of his failure to declare to HMRC the existence of assets held overseas believed to be worth in excess of £400m'.

Ecclestone came out fighting and pleaded innocent. He said that not only did he not know about the trusts when HMRC asked him, he assumed that the arrangements had been set up in such a way as to avoid any UK tax liability. HMRC didn't buy it.

At the age of 92, his freedom was in danger and – perhaps equally alarming for the billionaire – so was his family's fortune. As a source told the *Daily Mail*, 'Bernie once played cards with Lord Lucan, and in this case he was a shrewd enough operator to realise that he'd ended up in a poker game where he held a terrible hand, and needed to escape without losing everything.'

He must certainly have been feeling his age. After the deaths of Niki Lauda and Charlie Whiting in 2019, his old friends were disappearing fast. Over a 17-month period in 2021 and 2022, Max Mosley, Frank Williams and Dietrich Mateschitz also passed away. Ecclestone was the oldest of all of them and was increasingly looking like an isolated icon of a bygone age, the last survivor of the Heathrow airport meeting in 1971 that had set him on the road that ultimately led to the courtroom in London.

In a dramatic about-turn, he changed his plea to guilty and admitted tax fraud in October 2023. HMRC's plan had worked a treat.

The judge, Mr Justice Bryan, said that Ecclestone 'dishonestly lied' when he denied he was involved with other trusts. However, his lawyer,

Clare Montgomery KC, claimed that it was never his intention to avoid paying tax and he 'did not know the true position' of his affairs at the time. 'He simply didn't know the answer to HMRC's question and he should have said, "I don't know" instead of "no".' She added that his answer was an 'impulsive lapse of judgement'.

Ecclestone's advanced years played into his hands when the judge was considering whether to hand down a jail sentence. However, the most decisive factor was the £652.6m that he agreed to pay HMRC to settle the investigation into his tax affairs dating all the way back to 1994. It covered the period right up to April 2022, giving Ecclestone some comfort that he had at least finally shaken the tax authority off his tail.

Precisely as HMRC expected, he had to pay up to stay out of prison. The judge said that one of the factors 'that reduce seriousness' was that he engaged with HMRC and 'reached a settlement agreement'. Bearing this in mind, he was handed a 17-month prison sentence, suspended for two years.

His £652.6m payment was believed to be the largest personal tax settlement in UK history, and the Crown Prosecution Service stressed that part of it was a 'penalty for offshore non-compliance charged at the maximum rate of 200 per cent'. However, Ecclestone still had the last laugh as the sum was a staggering £347.4m less than what HMRC originally asked for in December 2014 – and that was before it found out about the £400m in Singapore.

It brought the chequered flag down on nearly 25 years of investigations by HMRC and, in a sense, the tax authority only had itself to blame. Ecclestone gave his shares in F1's operating company to his wife, who put them in an offshore trust that HMRC said he should not influence or benefit from as he was a UK taxpayer. However, HMRC allowed him to continue running F1's operating company, which was the trust's key asset. If instead HMRC had insisted back in the late 1990s that he had to stand down or that F1 too had to move offshore then this could all have been avoided, although it would not have walked away with £650m 25 years later. HMRC presented it as a big win and, surprisingly, Ecclestone went along with it.

Just a few hours after the judge spared him jail he was seen in London's historic Borough Market queuing up to buy doughnuts. Ecclestone didn't seem fazed about his unprecedented penalty and told a passing journalist that his 'bloody lawyers' told him not to comment. It was a very different story a few months later when *The Times* let him know that he was second on their list of Britain's biggest taxpayers. 'I have always paid tax in the UK,' Ecclestone told the paper. 'The issue was about the tax I earned overseas that the [UK] taxman thought I should pay UK tax on. When I went and saw them they asked me if I was a beneficiary to a trust and I said "no". I did that because I thought at the time I wasn't.'

Perhaps giving insight into his motivation for the interview, Ecclestone said, 'I feel as fit as I've ever felt – a three-and-a-half-year-old son keeps you young.' Legacy was now Ecclestone's driving force and he stressed that his denial to the taxman 'was an honest mistake and I think everyone knew that'. The latter seemed like an attempt to re-write history, as the headlines of his sentencing were harsh. 'Bernie Ecclestone given suspended sentence after pleading guilty to fraud', wrote the *Guardian*, while *Reuters* said, 'Ex-F1 boss Bernie Ecclestone spared jail after admitting tax fraud' and the *FT* added, 'Bernie Ecclestone pleads guilty to £400mn tax fraud'.

The irony is that it may well indeed have been a mistake. It appears Ecclestone was at least a part owner of the infamous Singapore bank account, as he told *The Times* that he 'didn't know someone acting on my behalf had in fact set up a trust'. However, if he didn't have ultimate control of the account it would explain why he didn't think of declaring it, especially as it wasn't in his name. Likewise, if he genuinely didn't know there was a trust in the ownership structure then it's no surprise he didn't mention it to HMRC in 2015.

What's more, the blockbuster payment to HMRC was the very thing Ecclestone was trying to avoid by paying the $44m to Gribkowsky. It is evidence that the $44m was indeed paid to stop Gribkowsky reporting him to HMRC rather than a bribe to steer the sale of F1 to CVC. Ecclestone paid $100m to settle the bribery charge against him, which makes it seem all the more pointless. As he said after the trial, he was 'a bit of an idiot' for paying it and it would have done more good if he had paid it all to charity. Contrary to popular belief, Ecclestone is one of the UK's biggest donors and, according to research by *The Times* in 2008, he gave £50m to charity annually.

The relevance of the verdict in Ecclestone's tax case was lost on much of the media, even *Sky Sports*' Craig Slater, probably the most perceptive

F1 broadcaster. When asked whether it had any link to the sport of F1 he replied, 'It doesn't. This all relates to Mr Ecclestone's personal finances.' Of course, Slater was talking with his hat on as a sports reporter and indeed there was no connection between the court ruling and events unfolding on track. However, the court ruling couldn't have been much more closely connected to events in the F1 industry.

Ecclestone's record-breaking penalty was paid to settle HMRC's investigation into the influence he had over his offshore family trust, which raised around $4.6bn of tax-free money from shares in F1's operating company that he transferred to his wife Slavica in 1996.

The company was able to raise such a significant sum due to Ecclestone's efforts to transform F1 from an amateur sport into a professional business. This began when he became a team principal in 1971 and it resulted in the signing of the first Concorde Agreement a decade later. The agreement defined the structure of the sport and appointed Ecclestone to manage its commercial rights on behalf of the teams, which he did to great success. However, in 1995 Ecclestone's closest ally, FIA president Max Mosley, chose to award the rights to Ecclestone directly, cutting out the teams and making his company saleable to investors. It was a decision that would cause strife in the sport for years to come, in terms of Ecclestone's relationship with both the teams and the subsequent owners of F1.

Fast-forward to 2002 and a majority stake that the trust sold in the company ended up in the hands of a trio of creditor banks that had never intended to become owners of the sport. They were looking to sell up but the trust put roadblocks in their way, so the lead banker Gerhard Gribkowsky started looking into its links to Ecclestone and put him under pressure. Ecclestone gave Gribkowsky $44m to keep him quiet, paving the way for peace between two of the most powerful figures in F1. Together they helped to steer the sport into the hands of private equity investors who were by nature investors rather than racers and their goal was profits not points, unlike the teams, which would spend every last penny chasing victory on track.

Threats of breakaways frequently arose as the teams tried to wrest back control and get a bigger share of the spoils. As F1's owners sought to increase profits while paying out an ever-greater share to the teams, race hosting fees soared, driving out some of F1's more traditional markets, and broadcast contracts switched to pay–TV, much to the chagrin of fans, who were left with the choice of shelling out or not being able to watch their beloved sport.

Ecclestone's decision to transfer his company to the trust ultimately led to Liberty Media's ownership of F1 and the changes it has made to attract younger fans in new markets such as the United States.

So, his fine wasn't just connected to F1, it was inextricably tangled with the deals that built the sport.

Ecclestone is now the sole remaining founding father of F1 following the loss of Williams and Mosley, whose favourite expression was one often used by Charles de Gaulle – 'graveyards are full of indispensable men'. As ever, Mosley was right.

So too when asked by ITV in 2017 to sum up the impact Ecclestone has had on F1. 'Formula One is his legacy,' he said, and although the people at the wheel have changed, the same business engine he began tuning more than five decades ago is still under the bonnet.

POSTSCRIPT

For as long as we can remember we have been fascinated by Formula One. This fascination was initially driven by the speed of the cutting-edge cars, the colourful characters who drive them and the exotic locations where they race.

As 1996 world champion Damon Hill eloquently explained to us, in his era, F1 drivers embodied the spirit of the Marlboro man, the rugged, risk-taking cowboy who first appeared in adverts for the iconic tobacco brand in the 1950s. Like the adventurers from the Wild West, F1 drivers are daring and dynamic heroes who travel from city to city to do battle.

This intoxicating mix tempted us into the sport but the closer we followed it, the more we realised the events on track are nowhere near as fascinating as the machinations behind the scenes that keep the wheels turning.

Accusations of spying and rule-breaking are common in F1 and every year rumours abound of teams planning to poach rival drivers and personnel. The higher the stakes, the more intriguing it gets. Stories of suitcases stuffed with hundreds of thousands of pounds, bogus companies in the British Virgin Islands and tens of millions of pounds in hush-money payments all play a part in the battle for control of the sport.

At times it reads like a script for a James Bond film but it's far from fantasy, as we soon discovered when we began reporting on the F1 industry in 2002. We have done it all in F1 media since then. We are the only journalists who have ever specialised in writing about the business of F1 for national media and we have contributed to more publications than any other journalist who covers the sport.

To name a few of these titles, we have appeared on the BBC, Bloomberg, CNN, CNBC, Channel 4 and ITV, and have written for *The Times*, the *Daily Telegraph*, the *Independent*, the *Daily Mail*, the *Daily*

Express and the *Guardian*, as well as business and trade titles including the *Financial Times*, *Forbes*, the *Wall Street Journal*, *SportBusiness*, *ESPN*, *Autosport*, *Autoweek* and *Motor Sport*.

Many of these reports have been cover stories of the magazines and appeared on the front pages of the newspapers. Likewise, interviews with us have been shown on sports programmes as well as nightly news broadcasts such as ITV's *News at Ten*, CNN's *Quest Means Business*, BBC's *Newsnight* and the *Six O'Clock News*. In 2007 we became research consultants for the BBC's eight-part series *Formula for Success* and the previous year we wrote our first book on the F1 industry.

Over the following years we visited the majority of the races on the F1 calendar; however, unlike many sports writers, we didn't become journalists to get closer to the racing. We wanted to find out what really drives the business, and the more we analysed it, the more we found that it lives up to its Bond-like billing.

Over the years, disgruntled parties, from competitors to management, have attempted to discredit us or get the upper hand. A former senior motorsport administrator once falsely claimed we were employed by F1's chief executive, while his counterpart instructed his associates not to talk to us after we discovered a severe conflict of interest at the heart of his organisation.

Others have asked us to covertly record meetings, intercepted our mail, offered us work in return for giving evidence in court, sent emails threatening to disseminate false information about us, threatened to assault us, attempted to blackmail us and warned they would bring defamation proceedings against us (which weren't followed through because they eventually admitted that our reporting was actually accurate).

Navigating these hurdles has required a firm grip on the wheel and access to some of the best lawyers in the business. We warned that the attempted blackmail and illegal threats to disseminate false information about us would be met with litigation. We shrugged off the threat of assault. The requests to give legal evidence and tape the meeting were declined.

Undeterred, we founded Formula Money, the only business information service dedicated to F1, and moved to the Middle East in the pandemic to set up a new office of the company there.

Formula Money produces data about all aspects of the industry and operates the world's largest search engine of F1 sponsorship values.

Around a third of the Grand Prix race organisers have acquired our data or commissioned us to produce economic impact reports that have been covered by the BBC, Bloomberg, CNN, the *Financial Times* and *Reuters*.

Our clients span the entire spectrum of F1 from existing and potential teams, race organisers, broadcasters and sponsors to investors, analysts, debt holders and governments. We worked with OC&C Strategy Consultants when it advised CVC on its acquisition of F1 in 2005 and then supplied data to the private equity firm when it was planning to float the sport in 2012. Our work with F1's shareholders didn't stop when CVC sold F1, as its new owner Liberty Media bought data from Formula Money; we have also supplied data to many of the ten largest funds that invest in it. We even introduced our contacts at Disney to Liberty's new team, leading to the creation of a life-size garage based on the hit animated film *Cars*, which was installed at the 2017 British Grand Prix to promote the latest instalment in the movie series.

Our work with Formula Money has given us an inside track on the biggest deals in the industry over the past two decades. Back in 2007 we broke the news that F1 had acquired the GP2 junior series and then revealed that GP3 would be launched as a feeder to it.

Our news has even uncovered the reasons behind the shape of the current landscape in F1. In 2013 we revealed that Ferrari has a veto not just over F1's regulations but also its chief executive, and in 2020 it used it to put the brakes on plans to replace then-boss Chase Carey with Toto Wolff, the head of its arch-rival Mercedes. Instead, the job went to former Ferrari boss Stefano Domenicali, who remains in the role to this day.

Likewise, in 2016 we broke the news on the BBC that F1 was considering a bid to host a race in Las Vegas, which finally revved onto the calendar in 2023. Reporting from the less glitzy surroundings of central England, we revealed in 2020 that Aston Martin had been given an option to invest £200m in its F1 team. This led to its three new factory buildings, the first of which opened in style in July 2023 when Lance Stroll drove his F1 car along the 160m-long main corridor on the ground floor. The third building became fully operational in the first quarter of 2025 and tempted design genius Adrian Newey to join the team.

He is one of many F1 powerbrokers we have come into contact with over almost 25 years of involvement with the sport. *Fast Money* is the fruit of hundreds of interviews with F1's key players spanning more than a thousand hours, including around a hundred with former F1 boss Bernie Ecclestone alone.

Memorable meetings include trips to Sir Jackie Stewart's country estate, cerebral discussions with Damon Hill in Pret a Manger and lunches in London's Armani Caffe with Ecclestone and his closest confidant Flavio Briatore. Equally illuminating meetings were held with former F1 governing body boss Max Mosley, who spent tens of hours talking to us about the inner workings of the industry at his office in Monaco, his London mews home in posh Knightsbridge and over the phone. He disclosed everything from the precise split of prize money that each team receives to objections he raised with the governing body after he stepped down in 2009. Mosley and Ecclestone opened up as they knew we are the only national media journalists who have ever specialised in covering the F1 industry.

It wasn't the only way we came into contact with the power players. Long before Liberty introduced a centralised marketing department for the sport and hosted its first-ever group launch at London's O2 arena in 2025, we developed one of F1's first marketing initiatives involving all of the teams, team bosses and drivers.

After around a decade working in F1, we became tired of seeing the drivers giving signed photos of themselves to fans and VIPs. We realised they would prefer to receive photos taken by the drivers, as it would show more of their personality, so in 2012 we launched a company to arrange this. Over the majority of the following decade all of the F1 drivers and team bosses took a photo every year exclusively for our company so they could be published in an annual book, with a share of the sales going to charity. One copy of every photo was signed by the drivers and team bosses before being sold in live auctions, with all of the proceeds going to good causes too.

We named the project ZOOM in a play on the speed of F1 and a camera lens. We soon found that F1's biggest stars are a dab hand with it, as the spectacular photos they took include Max Verstappen's view from the window of his plane on the way back home from a race, Fernando Alonso's shot looking down 44th Street in New York City and Lewis Hamilton's photo of his beloved bulldog in front of the Colosseum in Rome.

Other pictures showcased everything from the view from the drivers' bedrooms to behind-the-scenes photos at the races. It gave fans a glimpse into the lives of F1's biggest stars long before *Drive To Survive* was even a glimmer in Netflix's eye. There is a story behind all of them and the photos are accompanied by descriptions written by the drivers and team bosses. In total, we have received more than 250 photos, with 47 taken by world champions, including every driver who has won the F1 title over the past 20 years.

Since ZOOM was launched in 2012 we have sold almost 75,000 copies of the book and raised more than $250,000 for charity. It is the only organisation that gathers personal photos taken by sports stars and this unique format has been so successful in F1 that in 2022 we began expanding it to other sports, starting with the Aramco Team Series golf tournament. In addition to publishing more than a dozen editions of the book, ZOOM has produced artwork for many of F1's biggest names, including Mercedes, the United States Grand Prix and the Mexican Grand Prix, as well as the management of former F1 champions Michael Schumacher and Nigel Mansell.

The artwork is a twist on the Art Deco posters from F1's heydays as it features modern cars against period backgrounds. It too has been a hit, so we expanded it beyond posters. In 2022 the boss of the US Grand Prix commissioned ZOOM to produce artwork for hand-made guitars that were signed by F1's drivers before being given to the management of the sport at the race. Then in 2024 we signed a partnership with the world's leading puzzle manufacturer, Ravensburger, which now sells jigsaws of our artwork.

As the artwork also bears the ZOOM brand, it too benefits charity and has been displayed at our live auctions that we held in London before the pandemic. Coming full circle, those events led to this book coming to life.

The events attracted an array of celebrities including TV chef James Martin, presenter Charley Boorman, reality-TV star Stephanie Pratt, Iron Maiden guitarist Adrian Smith, former Spice Girl Geri Horner and *Game of Thrones* actor Liam Cunningham.

Joining them were drivers like Damon Hill, Jolyon Palmer and Karun Chandhok, team bosses and managers such as Mosley, Anthony Hamilton, Claire Williams, Ecclestone, Christian Horner and his star designer Adrian Newey, who came along with his wife Amanda. Following one of the events she kindly introduced us to agent Jack Fogg, who published her husband's book, and he subsequently began to represent us.

Jack's deal-making skills are almost up there with those of Ecclestone himself. He brought eight of the world's biggest book publishers to the table to bid for *Fast Money* and worked tirelessly with the renowned Hodder & Stoughton, which won the rights to tell this fascinating story. It has taken more than three years to bring it to life and it is the product of nearly a quarter of a century of analysing the F1 industry. As F1 celebrates its 75th anniversary in 2025, this book explains what it took to reach that momentous milestone.

Picture Acknowledgements

Page 1 top: © Bernard Cahier/Getty Images
Page 1 bottom: © Rainer Schlegelmilch/Getty Images
Page 2 – all three: © Rainer Schlegelmilch/Getty Images
Page 3 top: © dpa picture alliance/Alamy Stock Photo
Page 3 bottom: © Paul-Henri Cahier/Getty Images
Page 4 top and bottom: © Sutton Images/Getty Images
Page 4 middle: © Andreas Rentz/Bongarts/Getty Images
Page 5 top: © Pascal Guyot/AFP via Getty Images
Page 5 bottom: © Sutton Images/Getty Images
Page 6 top: © Martini/Sutton Images/Getty Images
Page 6 bottom: © Mark Sutton/Sutton Images for ZOOM
Page 7 top: © Dan Mullan/Getty Images
Page 7 bottom: © Patrick Lundin for ZOOM
Page 8: © Jared C. Tilton/Getty Images

Notes

1 In full, the arrangement was much more complicated. In 1997, Stephen Mullens helped Slavica Ecclestone settle multiple trusts in Vaduz, the capital of Liechtenstein. One was settled in June 1997 and was called the SLEC Trust after Slavica's initials. In November 1997, the SLEC Trust became the owner of a company called Valper Trading, which had been founded in the British Virgin Islands in April 1994 by de Pfyffer, the Swiss law firm where Luc Argand was a partner. He was one of the first directors of Valper Trading, which was originally owned by the Lion Trust, a trust settled by Slavica to benefit her children and their descendants.

In June 1997 Valper Trading changed its name to Valper Holdings after it bought Petara from Slavica. In return for this, Slavica was handed $1,000 and shares in Valper Holdings. The manoeuvre made Valper Holdings the ultimate owner of F.O.C.A. Administration, F1's rights holder. Five months later Slavica transferred her shares in Valper Holdings to the trustee of the SLEC Trust. This made the SLEC Trust the owner of Valper Holdings, which, in turn, owned Petara and its subsidiary F.O.C.A. Administration – F1's rights holder. It didn't stay that way for long.

Two other trusts had to enter the fray before F1's company structure reached the finish line. The Slavica Ecclestone Revocable Trust was settled by Ecclestone's then-wife in May 1997 and owned Jersey company SLEC Holdings, which bought Petara from Valper Holdings between November 1997 and March 1998. Petara still owned F1's rights holder F.O.C.A. Administration so the ultimate owner of the sport was The Slavica Ecclestone Revocable Trust through its company SLEC Holdings. There was one more move to come.

In October 1997 Mullens helped Slavica set up another trust – this one was called the Bambino Trust (or Bambino Settlement) in another nod to the two young children. As with the other trusts, its trustee is a Liechtenstein-based company called Corfiducia Anstalt, which is run by professional trustee Cornelia Konrad. Likewise, Tamara and Petra are the beneficiaries of all the trusts along with their descendants and Slavica herself.

On behalf of its beneficiaries, the Bambino Trust owns Bambino Holdings, another company based in Jersey. In October 1998 the trustee transferred

337

SLEC Holdings from The Slavica Ecclestone Revocable Trust to Bambino Holdings for $1. Accordingly, after all of these twists and turns, F1's commercial rights holder, F.O.C.A. Administration, was owned by Petara and, in turn, that was owned by SLEC Holdings, which was a subsidiary of Bambino Holdings, a company controlled by the Bambino Trust. Bernie Ecclestone is forbidden from being one of the Bambino Trust's beneficiaries, who include his now ex-wife Slavica as well as their daughters Tamara and Petra and their descendants.

Similar transactions took place with two other companies owned by Ecclestone and trusts that benefit his wife and children. One of the companies proved to be insignificant but the other – International Sportsworld Communicators (ISC) – later played a pivotal role on Ecclestone's road to riches.

Ecclestone gifted his shares in ISC to Microner Investments, a Jersey-based company owned by Slavica, and eventually they became owned by a British Virgin Islands company called Cormack Corporation. In turn, Cormack was owned by the trustees of the Petara Trust in Liechtenstein, which was settled by Slavica, who was one of the beneficiaries along with her brother, her children and their descendants.

Likewise, Corfiducia is also the trustee of the SE Property Trust in Liechtenstein, which benefits Slavica and her two children. As its name suggests, it has invested in property whereas Bambino's most famous investment by far has been F1.

2 Lehman's loss was only on paper as it made the smart decision to reinvest much of its money. Its F1 shareholding settled at 15.3 per cent by 2008, while JP Morgan had around 3 per cent as it only reinvested $42m. Lehman itself famously went into Chapter 11 bankruptcy in September that year and moved its F1 stake from its bankrupt arm, Lehman Commercial Paper, into LBI Group, a newly formed holding company containing the valuable assets in its portfolio.

LBI's purpose is to generate cash from its assets, which is then used to pay Lehman's creditors. CVC's sale to Liberty in 2017 gave Lehman a turbocharged payout and brought the total it has made from F1 to around $1.5bn from an initial $300m loan.

Bibliography

In addition to our own interviews and research, we have consulted a trove of company filings, court transcripts, regulations, reports, press releases and other official documents in the process of writing *Fast Money*, as well as decades of media about Formula One. A list of the major books, articles and broadcasts referenced in the text is included below.

TV, FILM & PODCASTS

9 Days in Summer, Ford Film Unit, 1967

Armchair Expert with Dax Shepherd: Toto Wolff, Armchair Expert, 4 December 2024

Beyond the Grid: Official F1 Podcast, 'As Bernie Ecclestone celebrates his 90th birthday, listen to his episode of Beyond the Grid', Formula 1, 4 December 2019

Beyond the Grid: Official F1 Podcast, 'Listen to Chase Carey discuss his role in shaping F1's future and guiding the sport through a global pandemic', Formula 1, 14 October 2020

DriveTribe short video, DT Digital, 20 July 2019

The Exclusive Bernie Ecclestone Interview, Tom Hartley Jnr Ltd, YouTube, 4 December 2024

Formula for Success, Sunset + Vine, 2007

Formula for Success Podcast, 'Teammates, taking the money & when Faldo met Schumacher', Whisper, 16 March 2023

Liberty Media Chairman John Malone on Donald Trump, AT&T-Time Warner, Media (Full Exclusive), CNBC, 12 November 2016

Lucky! Jiva Maya, 2022

Mosley: It's Complicated, Flat-Out Films, 2021

Panorama: The Ringmaster, BBC, 16 November 1998

Squawk Box, CNBC, 24 January 2017

BOOKS

Tom Bower, *No Angel: The Secret Life of Bernie Ecclestone*, Faber & Faber, 2011

Timothy Collings and Stuart Sykes, *Jackie Stewart: A Restless Life*, Virgin Publishing, 2003

Luc Domenjoz, *Michael Schumacher: The Rise of a Genius*, Chronosports, 1997

Dave Friedman, *Indianapolis Racing Memories 61–69*, Motorbooks, 1997

Maurice Hamilton, *Niki Lauda: The Biography*, Simon & Schuster, 2020

Niki Lauda, *To Hell and Back: An Autobiography*, Stanley Paul, 1986

Mike Lawrence, *Colin Chapman: Wayward Genius*, Brooklands Books, 2002

Terry Lovell, *Bernie's Game: Inside the Formula One World of Bernie Ecclestone*, Metro Publishing, 2003

Ted Macauley, *Grand Prix Men*, Carlton, 1998

Max Mosley, *Formula One and Beyond: The Autobiography*, Simon & Schuster, 2015

The Official Formula 1 Opus, Opus, 2013

Joshua Robinson and Jonathan Clegg, *The Formula: How Rogues, Geniuses, and Speed Freaks Reengineered F1 into the World's Fastest-Growing Sport*, Monoray, 2024

Christian Sylt and Caroline Reid, *The Business of Formula One*, SportBusiness, 2006

Murray Walker, *Unless I'm Very Much Mistaken: My Autobiography*, Harper NonFiction, 2002

Professor Sid Watkins, *Life at the Limit: Triumph and Tragedy in Formula One*, Macmillan, 1996

Susan Watkins, *Bernie: The Biography of Bernie Ecclestone*, Haynes, 2011

Richard Williams, *The Death of Ayrton Senna*, Viking, 1995

ARTICLES

Guy Adams, 'Why Bernie Ecclestone Being Forced to Pay £653 Million to the Taxman Could Be a VICTORY for the Wheeler-dealer as He Avoids Jail', *Daily Mail*, 12 October 2023

Tim Adams, 'Retirement Would Kill Me', the *Observer*, 12 December 2004

Murad Ahmed, 'New Formula One Owners Need to Attract Larger Audience', *Financial Times*, 15 December 2017

Murad Ahmed and Jim Allen, 'Liberty Adopts a Stop-go Strategy', *Financial Times*, 22 November 2018

Derick Allsop, 'FIA Rejects Benetton Claim over Missing Fuel Filter: Championship leaders could be banned from Formula One as manufacturer backs governing body in fireball controversy', the *Independent*, 11 August 1994

Gloria Aradi, 'Africa's New F1 Fans Who Want a Race on the Continent', *BBC.co.uk*, 30 May 2024

Simon Arron, 'How F1 Picked up the Habit', *Motor Sport*, July 2015

Autosport, 'FISA/FOCA War over F1', 26 May 1980

Autosport.com, 'Ecclestone Ups the Pressure', 21 April 2003

Alan Baldwin, 'Ecclestone Dismisses Talk of Rival F1 Series', *Reuters*, 17 December 2010

Alan Baldwin, 'F1 Must Cut Costs to Bring Back the Buzz – Brown', *Reuters*, 1 May 2015

Alan Baldwin, 'Ferrari Abandon F1 Rival Series Plan', *Reuters*, 20 January 2005

Alan Baldwin, 'Stewart Hails Clark, 50 Years on from Fatal Crash', *Reuters*, 6 April 2018

BBC.co.uk, 'Honda Attack Mosley's F1 Plans', 25 January 2006

BBC.co.uk, 'On This Day 7 April 1968: Jim Clark Killed in Car Smash', Undated

Claire Bloomfield, 'Baku Promoter Hits Back at Liberty Media', *Reuters*, 15 March 2017

Tom Bower, 'Pay Us £28m in Two Days or Your Mother's Head Will Be Sent Home in a Shopping Bag', the *Sunday Times*, 7 August 2016

Oliver Brown, 'Bernie Ecclestone Interview: "People Don't Go to F1 for a Lecture from the Drivers"', *Daily Telegraph*, 3 March 2023

Anas Bukhash: '#ABtalks x Red Bull with Max Verstappen', *Bukhash Brothers: YouTube*, 18 February 2020

BusinessAge, 'Bernie Ecclestone and Max Mosley: Why Europe Has to Accept Sport's New Order', January 1999

Tom Cary, 'Attention Turns to Bernie Ecclestone after German Banker Is Jailed in Formula One Corruption Case', *Daily Telegraph*, 28 June 2012

Filip Cleeren and Alex Kalinauckas, 'F1's Cost Freeze Helped Alfa Romeo Survive, Says Vasseur', *Motorsport.com*, 6 January 2021

Mat Coch, 'Domenicali: F1 Growth Due to More than *Drive to Survive*', *Speedcafe.com*, 6 April 2023

Keith Collantine, 'Only One Thing Mattered in the Ecclestone Era', *Racefans*, 25 January 2017

Adam Cooper, 'The Day Bernie Took Control of F1 . . . by Accident', *Autosport*, 28 August 2014

Carlos Costa and Isa Fernandes, 'Volverá Masi a la F1? "Un Imbécil Que Se Equivocó", Dice Toto Wolff', *Motorsport.com*, 2 December 2023

Andreas Cremer, 'Probed German Banker Admits to Secret Ecclestone Deal', *Reuters*, 21 June 2012

James Croft and Emma Agyemang, 'Bernie Ecclestone Pleads Guilty to £400mn Tax Fraud', *Financial Times*, 12 October 2023

Ronald Van Dam, 'Schumacher Had Hulpmiddelen', *Nusport*, 7 December 2011

Joe Davies, 'Max Mosley Tells ITV News: Liberty Media Should Have Kept Bernie Ecclestone on as Formula 1 Boss', *ITV News*, 4 February 2017

Bernd Debusmann Jr, 'Winning Formula: F1 CEO Chase Carey', *Arabian Business*, 23 November 2019

Alex Duff, 'Ecclestone Says He Rejected King as Formula 1 Executive', *Bloomberg*, 31 May 2013

Phil Duncan, 'Toto Wolff Questions New Race Boss as Lewis Hamilton Defies Jewellery Ban', *PA Media*, 11 April 2022

Kevin Eason, 'Bernie Ecclestone Insists He Has "Nothing to Hide" after Bribe Accusations', *The Times*, 23 July 2011

Kevin Eason, 'Ecclestone Shrugs Off Court Defeat with $500m Offer', *The Times*, 7 December 2004

The Economist, 'Grand Prix, Grand Prizes', 13 July 2000

ESPN.com, 'F1 CEO Compares Women to "Domestic Appliances"', 18 June 2005

Evening Standard, 'Bernie Ecclestone: If There Are No Fires to Fight Then I'm Happy to Start One', 14 April 2012

Paul Fearnley, 'When F1 Had Its First Tobacco Spat', *Motor Sport*, 7 March 2019

Alexandra Felts, 'Sir Stirling Moss: The Danger Brought out the Spirit of the Driver', *Classic Driver*, 17 July 2015

James Fontanella-Khan, Murad Ahmed and David Bond, 'Leaving the Bernie Model Behind', *Financial Times*, 2 March 2017

James Galloway, 'Mercedes Boss Toto Wolff Says Red Bull's Lewis Hamilton Collision Criticism Went "Step Too Far"', *Sky Sports*, 31 July 2021

Alex Gassman, 'Las Vegas F1 Ticket Prices Plummet as Major Issue Leaves Thousands Unsold', *Oversteer48*, 10 November 2023

Audrey Gillan, 'Grand Prix Teams Tell Mosley He Is a Disgrace and Put Pressure on Him to Quit after Sex Video', the *Guardian*, 4 April 2008

Mark Glendenning and Jonathan Noble, 'Montezemolo: Ecclestone Presence Vital', *Autosport.com*, 17 December 2010

Edward Gorman, 'Max Mosley Was "Warned of Plot Against Him"', *The Times*, 27 June 2008

Grandprix.com, 'Virgin Racing: Shooting at a Moving Target', 22 January 2011

John Griffiths, 'The Case That Will Decide Formula One's Future', *Financial Times*, 21 November 2004

The *Guardian*, 'Bernie Ecclestone Says Hitler Was a Man Who Got Things Done', 4 July 2009

The *Guardian*, 'Cheats Will Be Excluded', 25 February 1994

Sebastian Hamilton, 'Ecclestone Leads Drive to Float Formula One', *Sunday Times*, 9 March 1997

Patrick Harverson and John Griffiths, 'Racing Demon with All the Cards', *Financial Times*, 16 November 1998

Cliff Hayes, 'Dirty Tricks Robbed Me of Schuey', *News of the World*, 11 July 2004

Alan Henry, 'Ecclestone Urges Owners to Quit Split', the *Guardian*, 19 April 2003

Joel Hills, 'MPs Raise "Severe Conflict of Interest" at Heart of F1 Takeover', *ITV News*, 24 January 2017

Vanessa Houlder, 'Bernie Ecclestone Battles with HMRC over £1bn Tax Bill', *Financial Times*, 21 May 2015

John Huck, 'Clark County Commissioner on "Do-or-Die" Year for Formula 1 Las Vegas Grand Prix', *FOX5*, 20 June 2024

Mark Hughes, 'Max Mosley: F1 Teams Are Loonies', the *Sunday Times*, 21 June 2009

Mark Hughes, 'Renault Blew It! The Pioneering F1 Turbo That Failed Prost in Title Bid', *Motor Sport*, January 2001

Siba Jackson, 'Bernie Ecclestone Says He Would "Take a Bullet" for "First Class" Vladimir Putin as He Defends War in Ukraine', *Sky News*, 30 June 2022

François Janin, 'Anglo-Saxon Manufacturers Create a Second International Federation', *Le Monde*, 3 November 1980

François Janin, 'The Crisis in Formula 1', *Le Monde*, 10 October 1980

Denis Jenkinson, 'Continental Notes', *Motor Sport*, January 1968

Denis Jenkinson, 'Cosworth GP Engines – the Fifth Season', *Motor Sport*, March 1971

Denis Jenkinson, 'Formula One – Teams for 1978', *Motor Sport*, January 1978

Denis Jenkinson, 'Reflections in a Sandstorm', *Motor Sport*, July 1980

Denis Jenkinson, 'Reflections on the Italian Grand Prix', *Motor Sport*, October 1965

Jasper Jolly, 'Bernie Ecclestone Given Suspended Sentence after Pleading Guilty to Fraud', the *Guardian*, 12 October 2023

Sahil Kapur, 'Mario Andretti: Formula 1 Owner Personally Threatened to Shut out Team Andretti', *NBC News*, 23 May 2024

Amit Katwala, 'Lewis Hamilton Opens up about Activism and Life Beyond F1', *Wired*, 1 April 2021

Mike Lawrence, 'FOCA's Former Legal Adviser Looks at Formula One', *Motor Sport*, May 1986

Joshua Levine, 'Ringmeister', *Forbes*, 9 July 2001

Jarret Liotta, 'News Corp.'s Carey Told New Canaan Audience: "Local, Local, Local"', *New Canaan Advertiser*, 9 May 2013

Matt Majendie, 'If There Are No Fires Then I'm Happy to Start One', *Evening Standard*, 21 July 2010

Jonathan McEvoy, 'Ecclestone's Boss Hits out at F1 Ringmaster after His "Disgusting" Praise for Hitler', *Daily Mail*, 15 July 2009

Jonathan McEvoy, 'I'm Still in Charge! Ecclestone Defiant Despite Stepping Down from F1 Board to Face Trial for Bribery Charge', *Daily Mail*, 16 January 2014

Jonathan McEvoy, 'Max Verstappen's Racing Genes Selected Him for Stardom, and after Sealing a Third Drivers' Championship, He Looks to Be a Potent Fighter for Years to Come', *Daily Mail*, 7 October 2023

Robert Mendick and Christian Sylt, 'F1 Boss's £60m a Year from Ex-Wife', the *Sunday Telegraph*, 27 April 2014

Lawrence Meredith, 'Scale and Pace', *Motor Sport*, October 1995

Eleanor Mills, 'She Washes, He Dries, They Clean Up', the *Sunday Times*, 19 March 2000

Malcolm Moore, Arash Massoudi, Simeon Kerr and Joseph Cotterill, 'US-Qatari Move to Take over Formula One', *Financial Times*, 23 June 2015

Motor Sport, 'American Comment', June 1968

Motor Sport, 'Pit Flashpoint', December 2004

Motor Sport, 'The Quiet Man', January 1994

Motor Sport, 'Ron Tauranac: The Pragmatist', January 2014

Motor Sport, 'Rumbles under the Roulette Wheel', November 1981

Adrian Newey, 'The Rise of the Machines in 2010s Racing', *Motor Sport*, July 2024

Jonathan Noble, 'FIA's Ben Sulayem Reveals Court Case and $20 Million Deficit Headaches', *Motorsport.com*, 6 December 2022

Jonathan Noble, 'F1 Figures Defend US GP Pre-Race Driver Entrance Presentation', *Autosport.com*, 25 October 2017

Jonathan Noble, 'FIA "Not Involved" in News Corp Talks', *Autosport.com*, 8 May 2011

Jonathan Noble, 'Formula 1 Reverses Social Media Gains amid Lack of Title Fight', *Motorsport.com*, 28 September 2023

Jonathan Noble, 'How the FIA Found out about Crashgate at Brazil 2008 F1 Finale, but Could Not Act', *Motorsport.com*, 5 April 2023

Jonathan Noble, 'Mosley: FIA Risks Losing Control of F1', *Autosport.com*, 17 May 2008

Klaus Ott, 'Was Das Gribkowsky-Urteil Für Ecclestone Bedeutet', *Süddeutsche Zeitung*, 30 June 2012

Klaus Ott and Nicolas Richter, 'Justiz Untersucht Herkunft Des Geldes – Bayernlb-Vorstand Erhielt 50 Millionen Dollar', *Süddeutsche Zeitung*, 3 January 2011

Mat Oxley, 'Mike Trimby: The Man Who Made MotoGP', *Motor Sport*, 11 September 2023

Catherine Pacary, Yann Bouchez and Eric Albert, 'Formule 1: Règlement de Comptes Dans le Paddock', *Le Monde*, 29 December 2017

Tariq Panja, 'French Investigator Seeks Information about Formula One Sale', the *New York Times*, 18 October 2017

Josh Payne and Luke O'Reilly, 'Ex-F1 Boss Bernie Ecclestone Admits Fraud after Failing to Declare £400 Million', *PA Media*, 12 October 2023

James Phelps, 'Masi Reveals What He Should've Done after Hamilton Call', *Daily Telegraph (Australia)*, 2 August 2022

Shaun Phillips, 'GP Boss Rejects Book Claim', *Herald Sun*, 8 March 2003

Pitpass, '2004 Court Case Link to Alleged Threats from German Banker', 30 October 2011

Pitpass, 'Bernie's Beautiful Game', 21 January 2009

Pitpass, 'CVC Was Prepared to Pay £255m More to Buy F1', 13 February 2013

Pitpass, 'Ecclestone Says He May Sue Gribkowsky', 21 June 2012

Pitpass, 'Exclusive: £409m Lawsuit against Ecclestone and CVC Revealed', 20 November 2012

Pitpass, 'Exclusive: F1 Gets New Owners but They Get No Control', 23 May 2012

Pitpass, 'Gribkowsky Allegations Drive CVC into the Spotlight', 25 October 2012

Pitpass, 'HMRC Adds Weight to Ecclestone's Defence', 27 January 2014

Pitpass, 'Indictment against Ecclestone Raises Big Questions', 19 August 2013

Pitpass, 'New F1 Engines to Be Scrapped Says Ecclestone', 28 September 2012

Pitpass, 'Revealed: F1's $500m Tax "Agreement" with the Government', 26 November 2016

Steve Potter, 'Bitter Split Looms for Grand Prix Racing', the *New York Times*, 15 June 1980

Steve Potter, 'Dispute over Rules and a Tire Shortage Stall Grand Prix Season', the *New York Times*, 4 January 1981

Mark Ramage, 'Obituary: Geoffrey Kent', the *Independent*, 30 September 1992

Caroline Reid, 'Ecclestone Faces New Legal Threat over Formula 1 Sale', the *Independent*, 30 August 2011

Dieter Rencken, 'F1 Is Poised to Repeat Its 1980s War', *Autosport.com*, 5 November 2015

Yvonne Ridley, 'Ecclestone Faces Probe by Taxman', *Sunday Express*, 24 September 2000

Peter Robinson, 'Classic Wheels: Ronnie Peterson F1 Death Scandal', *Wheels*, 6 October 2016

Nigel Roebuck, 'How "Primitive" Williams Won Its First F1 Championship with Alan Jones', *Motor Sport*, March 2012

Miguel Sanz, 'Former Mercedes Executive: F1 Is a Shameful Tragedy in Germany Today', *Marca*, 24 January 2023

Atifa Silk, 'Exclusive: F1 Boss Bernie Ecclestone on His Billion-Dollar Brand', *Campaign Asia-Pacific*, 14 November 2014

Skysports.com, 'Bernie Ecclestone: Former F1 Boss Given 17-Month Suspended Prison Sentence after Pleading Guilty to Fraud', 13 October 2023

Skysports.com, 'Toto Wolff: Mercedes Team Principal Rejects Sir Jim Ratcliffe-INEOS Split Talk Claims ahead of 2025 Season', 19 February 2025

Luke Smith, 'Zak Brown Reveals McLaren F1 Was "On the Brink" Financially before 2020 Investment', the *Athletic*, 7 December 2024

Brad Spurgeon, 'Ecclestone against the World', *International Herald Tribune*, 7 May 2005

Brad Spurgeon, 'Tech Firms Fill Racing-Sponsor Void', *International Herald Tribune*, 6 March 2000

Rupert Steiner, 'Court to Provide Formula for F1', *Sunday Express*, 28 November 2004

Rupert Steiner, 'Ecclestone Offers to Buy Back F1', the *Sunday Times*, 23 February 2003

Rupert Steiner, 'Ferrari in F1 Swerve', the *Sunday Times*, 23 February 2003

Ben Sutherland, 'F1 in Africa: How Team Gunston Started a Sponsorship Revolution', *BBC.co.uk*, 6 March 2023

Christian Sylt, 'The $1.8 Billion Exemptions from F1's Budget Cap', *Forbes.com*, 1 November 2019

Christian Sylt, 'The $7 Billion Legends of Entertainment', *Forbes.com*, 15 December 2015

Christian Sylt, 'The £240m Pay-Off! How Bernie Could Settle German Bribery Case', *Mail on Sunday*, 26 January 2014

Christian Sylt, 'Bernie Ecclestone Heading Straight Back to Work after $100m Court Settlement over Bribery Charges', the *Independent*, 6 August 2014

Christian Sylt, 'Ecclestone Says F1 Governors Gave Share of Power to Top Teams for $40 Million', *Forbes.com*, 11 December 2014

Christian Sylt, 'Ecclestone, the French Race Circuit and the Real Story behind That $44m "Bribe"', *Daily Telegraph*, 23 March 2013

Christian Sylt, 'European Commission Investigating F1 Anti-Competition Allegations', *Forbes.com*, 26 November 2014

Christian Sylt, 'Exclusive: Bernie Ecclestone Vows Revenge Weeks after Settling Bribery Trial for $100m', the *Independent*, 28 August 2014

Christian Sylt, 'Exclusive: Formula One Pays Just £1 Million Corporation Tax on £300 Million Profit', the *Independent*, 24 July 2013

Christian Sylt, 'F1 Boss Bernie Ecclestone Pays Staggering £60 Million out of Court Settlement to Be Cleared of Bribery Charges in Germany', the *Independent*, 5 August 2014

Christian Sylt, 'F1 Regulator Advised to Boost Its Monitoring of Conflicts of Interest', *Forbes.com*, 21 October 2017

Christian Sylt, 'Ferrari Races off with £15m Formula One Stake', *Daily Telegraph*, 14 September 2014

Christian Sylt, 'Formula 1-In Sahibi Azərbaycanı Ciddi Tənqid Edib', *BBC Azərbaycanca Üçün*, 14 March 2017

Christian Sylt, 'Formula One Race Attendance Row Revs Up', *Forbes.com*, 23 December 2017

Christian Sylt, 'Grand Prix Organizer Calls into Question F1's Attendance Data', *Forbes.com*, 6 February 2019

Christian Sylt, 'HMRC Gives Formula One £180 Million Tax Boost', *ITV News*, 5 April 2018

Christian Sylt, 'Leading Lawyer Reveals "Question" over Liberty's $8 Billion F1 Buyout', *Forbes.com*, 16 September 2016

Christian Sylt, 'Liberty Media Boasts of Formula One's "Brilliant" Tax Scheme', *Forbes.com*, 30 March 2017

Christian Sylt, 'Meet the Man Who Steers Lewis Hamilton to Victory', *Forbes.com*, 8 January 2018

Christian Sylt, 'Mercedes Races to Record $320 Million F1 Revenue', *Forbes.com*, 1 October 2016

Christian Sylt, 'Revealed: The $5m Contract That Favoured F1's Top Teams', *ITV News*, 27 April 2017

Christian Sylt, 'The Secret of My Success: Bernie Ecclestone', *GQ*, April 2013

Christian Sylt and Caroline Reid, 'Bernie Flips F1 into GP1', *Sunday Express*, 12 July 2009

Christian Sylt and Caroline Reid, 'Bernie Prepares New Grand Prix Formula', *Evening Standard*, 5 September 2008

Christian Sylt and Caroline Reid, 'Blockbuster Deal Revs Up F1', *Sunday Express*, 14 January 2007

Christian Sylt and Caroline Reid, 'Ecclestone Backtracks over F1 Flotation', *Financial Times*, 1 November 2010

Christian Sylt and Caroline Reid, 'Ecclestone Hits out at Todt', *Daily Express*, 24 March 2011

Christian Sylt and Caroline Reid, 'F1 Chief Says He Rejected Chance to Settle Case', the *Independent*, 13 November 2011

Christian Sylt and Caroline Reid, 'F1 Boss Bernie Ecclestone to Fight £1bn Tax Bill as Settlement Is Torn up', the *Independent*, 22 May 2015

Christian Sylt and Caroline Reid, 'F1 Prize Money Distribution Unfair, Says Max Mosley', *CityAM*, 24 March 2015

Christian Sylt and Caroline Reid, 'Formula One's $12bn IPO on Track', the *Guardian*, 17 May 2013

Christian Sylt and Caroline Reid, 'Mercedes F1 Boss in Favor of Extending Concorde Agreement through 2021', *Autoweek*, 11 July 2020

Christian Sylt and Caroline Reid, 'Restructuring Helps Liberty Media Reduce Tax Bill for Formula One', *Daily Telegraph*, 4 February 2018

Christian Sylt and Caroline Reid, 'Sorrell Drives F1 Shake-Up', *Financial Times*, 11 February 2009

Simon Taylor, 'Lunch with . . . Murray Walker', *Motor Sport*, April 2011

347

Simon Taylor, 'Lunch with . . . Sir Frank Williams', *Motor Sport*, May 2015

The Times, 'Schumacher Leads Fightback', 13 August 1994

Sam Tobin, 'Ex-F1 Boss Bernie Ecclestone Spared Jail after Admitting Tax Fraud', *Reuters*, 12 October 2023

David Tremayne, 'Jim Clark, the Gentleman Driver Whose Death Stunned the World', the *Sunday Times*, 24 February 2008

David Tremayne, 'Obituary: Charlie Whiting', *Formula1.com*, 14 March 2019

Helmut Uhl and Lennart Wermke, 'Meine Pläne Mit Der Formel 1', *Bild Am Sonntag*, 25 August 2018

Pablo De Villota, 'Cómo Unos Héroes Pusieron a España En El Mapa De La F1 En Pleno Franquismo', *El Confidencial*, 7 March 2022

Brian Viner, 'Bernie Ecclestone: The Goblin Driving a Hard Bargain with the Future', the *Independent*, 25 April 2005

Ferdi de Vos, 'SA Was ahead of the Curve – 50 Years of Sponsorship in F1', *News24*, 20 March 2018

Robert Watts, 'Bernie Ecclestone on His Fraud Conviction: "It Was an Honest Mistake"', the *Sunday Times*, 26 January 2024

Robert Watts, 'The Tax List 2024: The UK's 100 Biggest Taxpayers Revealed', the *Sunday Times*, 26 January 2024

Keith Weir, 'F1 Boss Ecclestone Apologizes for Hitler Comments', *Reuters*, 7 July 2009

Rob Widdows, 'Mechanics' Tales: Kerry Adams', *Motor Sport*, 3 October 2014

James Wilson and Roger Blitz, 'Banker in F1 Bribes Case Found Guilty', *Financial Times*, 27 June 2012

Yahoo Sport Australia, 'Buffer's Iconic Boxing Calls Debt in Formula One', 23 October 2017

MISCELLANEOUS

Accenture Digital Video and the Connected Consumer Report, 2015

Buzz Radar, 'Have We Reached Peak F1?', September 2023

FIA Activity Reports

FIA Global Fan Surveys

Formula 1 Global Media Report, 2004 to 2016

Formula Money Sponsorship Database, 2018 to present

Nielsen, 'Driven to Watch: How a Sports Docuseries Drove U.S. Fans to Formula 1', May 2022

The *Sunday Times* Rich List, the *Sunday Times*, 2008